PRACTICAL GUIDE TO HOME LANDSCAPING

PRACTICAL GUIDE TO HOME LANDSCAPING

The Reader's Digest Association (Canada) Ltd.
215 Redfern Avenue, Montreal, Quebec   H3Z 2V9

Acknowledgments

The editors of *Reader's Digest* wish to express
their appreciation for the creative and practical guidance they received
from the following people in the making of this book:

Gaétan Bilodeau, Chief of the Landscape Gardening Division, Montreal Botanical Garden; Pierre Bourque, Chief Horticulturist of the Montreal Botanical Garden; Dr. Yves Desmarais, former Director of the Montreal Botanical Garden; Warner S. Goshorn, Chief Landscape Architect, City of Montreal.

Douglas Baylis, Fellow of the American Society of Landscape Architects, San Francisco; Armand Benedek, American Society of Landscape Architects, White Plains, N.Y.; Thomas D. Church, Landscape Architect, San Francisco; Jerome A. Eaton, Director, Old Westbury Gardens, Westbury, N.Y.; Thomas H. Everett, Senior Horticulture Specialist, New York Botanical Garden, New York; Dr. Joseph E. Howland, Professor of Horticulture and Turfgrass Specialist, University of Nevada, Reno; Robert Malkin, American Society of Landscape Architects, New York; Theodore Osmundson, Past President and Fellow of the American Society of Landscape Architects, San Francisco; Donald H. Parker, Fellow of the American Society of Landscape Architects—Director, Department of Landscape Architecture, the Colonial Williamsburg Foundation, Williamsburg, Va.; Maurice Wrangell, American Society of Landscape Architects, New York.

Contents

Making Your Mark on the Land

Take a leisurely walk along any suburban street and you will see dozens of opportunities for more beauty, convenience and pleasure from the land around the houses. Perhaps your own plot is one that could be enhanced or transformed, with a little imaginative effort. This book will help you to recognize the potential of your own land, and will show you how best to achieve your new ambitions.

This volume is really four books in one. Its four sections on Good Ideas, Planning, Planting, and Construction lead logically from the development of ideas for your garden to the finished improvements.

First you will see landscape designs for every part of your property from the front entrance to the back fence. These wide-ranging examples include large gardens and small; new, old and remodeled gardens; and gardens in the country, suburbs and city.

To emphasize the point that landscape design includes all the land around the house, we start with plans and photographs of four complete gardens. These case studies will give you an idea of how much can be accomplished in limited space. The more specific suggestions for good ideas are organized by topics—such as the entryway, outdoor living, overhead protection and privacy-screening. Keep in mind that no matter how small an improvement you plan to make, it should be related to the whole property. Plans are often developed for an entire plot and then finished piece by piece as time and budget will allow. But remember—even when working in small areas it pays to think big.

The examples you will find in this book are the best work of outstanding landscape architects and designers. Although many of the houses shown are large and expensive, you will see how many of the ideas can apply to smaller plots and budgets! Look for details: a trellis, paving patterns, handsome combinations of materials, steps, walls, fences, mowing strips and raised beds. You will discover dozens of ideas in any well-designed landscape that can be applied to your own garden.

In the best of worlds, anyone planning to build a house or remodel a garden would consult a landscape architect from the very beginning. Most of the best gardens in the country were created this way. But there are not enough landscape architects to go around, and their skills are better used for the planning of commercial and public places that will benefit great numbers of people. Many good landscape architects, however, do find some time to do residential gardens. The best thing you could do to get more pleasure from your land would be to find one to work with. And if you do have professional help you will be a much better client for having read this book to discover the nature of the challenge and the opportunities. Landscape architects are not licensed in Canada. Nor are landscape designers and landscape gardeners, of whom some are competent and others not. So get references and see examples of a designer's work.

In the section on planting you will find carefully selected lists of the best trees, shrubs and flowers for your climate. These are not simply alphabetical listings. They are groupings of plants thoughtfully related to their use in the landscape. Also included are clear instructions for putting the plants in the ground. Whether you want to improve an old garden or make a new one, whether you need a single tree or shrub or a dozen, you will find the necessary information on these pages. Here too is advice on the best kinds of grass for your lawn and how to get it off to a good, strong start and keep it going well.

In the section on construction you will learn the essential techniques of working with each of the seven materials most used for building in the garden. And you will find detailed instructions for 100 useful projects that you can do yourself to make your landscape more useful and pleasing to the eye.

Landscaping today is more important than ever before. As highways, public parks and beaches become more crowded, beautiful places and quiet retreats where we can "get away from it all" become more essential—and they can often be right in our own backyards.

These improvements may begin at home, but they have a wider influence. When a family on the block begins to make changes, and when friends and neighbors see how much these improvements add to the quality of daily life, others will follow suit. As the appearance of just a few houses along the street is improved, the neighborhood as a whole becomes that much more attractive.

Take a walk through your own neighborhood. How does your house compare? Is the setting distinctive, attractive and inviting from the streetside? Are you satisfied with the appearance and convenience of the driveway and front entry? Do you have privacy and comfortable outdoor living where you need it? Are there inviting places to play and work in the garden? Are your shrubs, flowers and lawn a credit to the area? Even though you may answer "yes" to these questions, there are probably improvements you would like to make. Few indeed are the homes that cannot be made more comfortable and inviting by applying the principles of landscape design. And good landscaping can add dollar value to a house.

Your interest in beauty and sensible use of the land will not stop at the property line. Think about this in your own community. The people who take the greatest pride in their homes and the streets they live on are the very ones who are most concerned with the design of parks, playgrounds, schools and shopping areas. Your property is the logical place for an appreciation of landscaping to begin, but that is by no means where it ends. This book will help you to discover for yourself how much there is to gain by an appreciation and understanding of good landscape design.

SECTION

1

Good Ideas
for Your Garden

Inspiration for every aspect of the garden,
no matter where you live or how much land you have.

1

Complete Gardens In Limited Space

The property that surrounds our homes is ours to use. This is the place for the beauty of trees, shrubs and flowers. It's a place for games and hobbies, for entertaining, dining and lounging. It's a place for quiet and privacy. And with good planning all this can be had, even in crowded neighborhoods. In the backyards of Canada there's a wealth of usable space yet to be discovered.

The first step in getting more from your own landscape is to let yourself dream a little. Once you decide what you would really like to have, you may be surprised at how much can be achieved.

Consider, for example, the plan on the facing page. This is one of hundreds of similar plots in a large development. The lot is less than a quarter-acre. But because the owners knew what they wanted and were willing to invest in it, they have amenities here that are seldom found in places four times the size.

These first few pages illustrate some outstanding landscape designs that make excellent use of every foot of space. They are not all small properties but they have useful ideas adaptable to the kinds of space you'll find in your own garden.

A House Apart on Less than a Quarter-Acre

This house is much like the hundreds of others in the same development. But even from the street the landscape design sets it apart. The entry terrace, with a wide landing flush with the driveway and the easy inviting steps to the front door, shows an obvious concern for the comfort and welfare of visitors. The plantings and construction have a sense of order and pleasant proportion that is all too rare in most streetside gardens. The side yard, which can be seen from the street, is also unusual with its small "orchard" of fruit trees and espaliers.

But the real revelations come when you go past the fruit trees and through the gate to the large terrace behind the house. Here is a pleasant sequestered area with dappled shade from an overhead arbor as well as a

good-sized paved space for lounging in full sun. Sliding doors open onto this terrace from the house.

In the large raised planting bed in the corner of the terrace there's also a pool for colorful aquatic plants and a space for outdoor cooking. The terrace is large enough for comfortable dining, and the cooker is a portable pan and grill that can be easily put out of sight in the adjacent storage wall when not in use. Potted plants then go in its place until it is needed again.

The woods garden is a place of rich foliage and deep dark shade that also serves to screen out the houses on the other side of the back fence. The lath house, herb garden and vegetable plot supplement the owner's interest in horticulture.

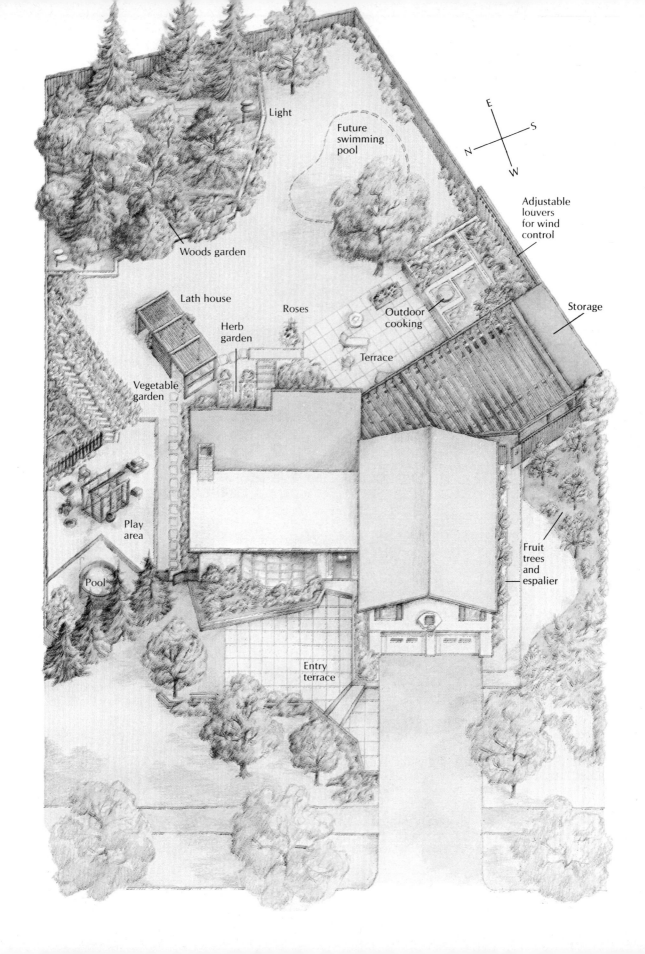

Light

Future
swimming
pool

E

S

N

W

Woods garden

Adjustable
louvers
for wind
control

Lath house

Roses

Outdoor
cooking

Storage

Herb
garden

Terrace

Vegetable
garden

Play
area

Pool

Fruit
trees
and
espalier

Entry
terrace

◀ **When they were first built,** *these suburban houses seemed much closer together than they actually were. This was because there were no outdoor "walls" of trees, shrubs and fences to set them apart. As seen here, the need for screening is twofold: To provide personal privacy for such family activities as outdoor lounging and dining and to screen the clotheslines, storage areas and other inevitable clutter from public view.*

▼ **Not long after moving in,** *the owners commissioned a landscape architect to design a garden that would give them optimum use of their land. This, of course, called for privacy. The picture below was taken about two years after planting. While not taken from the same angle as the picture at the left, it shows the neighboring houses to the rear and the need for screening. The picture at right, from the same angle, shows the result.*

▶ **Same view about 10 years later.** *The "woods garden" and other plantings have completely screened the neighbors' houses from view. This planting is a quiet shady retreat as well as an effective screen.*

This view shows the entry to the woods garden and how the plantings are arranged to provide privacy from the houses next door. The picture was taken from the site designated for a future swimming pool. A railroad-tie step serves as an edge for the lawn and to contain the wood chips carpeting the wooded area. Notice the cryptomeria (the bushy evergreen tree just left of center) which grows up and out of the picture at right.

▶ **In its maturity** the woods garden is a most effective screen and the major vertical element in the landscape. Even on the hottest days this is a cool place to sit. The feathery tree in the foreground is an Albizzia julibrissin which flowers in summer. It can be seen at the far left in the picture above. There's another entry step and an opening on the far side of this glade which encourages walking through the trees.

◀ **The lath house** is used mostly for the display of hanging baskets of fuchsias and ferns. It is also a protected place for the hardening-off of flats of seedlings and other small plants before they are set out in the adjacent vegetable plot or elsewhere in the garden.

This garden of herbs is nicely situated in a sunny spot protected from the wind and right at the foot of the steps to the kitchen. The staples here are thyme, basil, tarragon and chives. And sometimes a quick crop of radishes is grown in early spring. The raised bed is made of 2 x 12 redwood planks. The ivy in the background will soon cover the iron rail to further enclose the area. This is important because house plants are often brought out here for fresh air and rejuvenation.

The side yard, which on most suburban lots makes little if any contribution to the pleasures of life, is used here for a miniature orchard. Fortunately the orientation of the house allows enough sun for fruit trees into this area. Pears and apples are espaliered against the wall. A few more trees grown as freestanding specimens are set out in a patterned gravel-covered bed to the right of the walk. These are "dwarf" trees, which means regular fruits grafted onto dwarfing root stock. Two or three different varieties of apples can be grafted to the same tree to extend the fruiting season. The open gate leads to the covered terrace.

The vegetable garden *is somewhat screened from view by the yew hedge which is trimmed low, however, so it won't cast shade. Vegetables do best in full sun.*

Stepping stones *make it possible to pick for the table without getting shoes muddy. The concrete blocks are easily rearranged for different planting patterns.*

Play yard *in an out-of-the-way corner of the lot can be easily converted to lawn, or to vegetables when it has served its time. This is on the front corner of the lot and some of the surrounding houses can be seen in the distance. The hedge of hemlocks will soon grow up to separate this area completely from the street.*

Wall fountain
and pool

Deck

Sliding glass doors
to the house

Stepping stones
for maintenance

A Town-House Garden

The problem of how to develop every square foot of land in a city garden without overcrowding the limited space is beautifully and effectively solved in this town house. Most important are the two comfortable and inviting seating areas, a wooden deck that opens off the living room and another at the far end of the garden. These open rectangular spaces are the key to the success of the garden, which is filled with many textures, colors, levels, materials. The

decks help unify these diverse elements by framing the garden and serving as viewpoints for the outstanding display in the middle section. The separate living areas also encourage walking back and forth so the garden is enjoyed from many angles. The garden seems larger than it is because of the changing grades, curving path and choice of places to sit. The owner is an excellent gardener and wanted a landscape design that would accommodate many permanent

22

Translucent
plastic panels

Deck
above grade

Work and
storage area

plantings of choice flowers, trees and shrubs and a constant show of seasonal color. The landscape designer made this possible by developing the garden as a series of inter-related overall forms (the two decks, half-moon terrace, curved path and planting beds) in which the wide variety of plant material is neatly contained.

These forms are in scale with one another and the plants too are carefully related in height, mass and color. Beside the potpourri of flowers and shrubs on the ground there are vertical accents: the stained picket fence

at the far side of the garden, the wall fountain and the green canopy of tree branches overhead. It is because the basic proportions of this city garden are so well balanced and because it is so beautifully maintained that a great number of decorative accents can be used without creating a sense of clutter. With good proportion such a decorative concentration can be equally effective in larger gardens. More ideas on how to get the most from limited space are shown in Chapter 6. Even in gardens of good size there are places where these principles apply.

View toward the house *shows how the deck is designed as an extension of the house itself. It is built level with the ground floor rooms for a smooth transition between the indoors and outdoors (entry is through the double glass doors on the left) and its high wide walls are shingled to match the house. While the deck is obviously an outdoor living area with trees, vines and flowers, it has aspects of an indoor room. The paneled wall on the left provides privacy from the rest of the garden. The furniture is sturdy and carefully arranged. The plants and containers (note especially the bonsai and vases atop capitals on either side of the steps) are used in the same way as decorative objects are used in the house for color and interest.*

24

At the far end of the lot, the part of the garden most often in sunshine, is another wooden deck. It is built out beyond the slope (and is supported from below) to increase the amount of useful level space in the garden. Panels of translucent plastic frame the deck to provide shelter against the wind and privacy without cutting out light, color or a sense of the space beyond.

The beds on either side of the path have a basic planting of evergreens (azaleas, rhododendrons and ivy). Annuals which are bought in bloom are set into the beds to accent the greenery when needed. Seen here are tulips and daffodils set out in the fall. For a firm surface the path is covered with pea gravel. However, any fine, crushed gravel can be used.

Gentle curves of the path and planting beds help to relieve the confining borders of the long, rectangular lot and high side walls. This view taken from the deck by the house shows how these curves seem to widen the garden. (It also gives an idea of how attractive the shape of the garden is when looked down upon from the second-story windows.) The retaining walls and steps between the terrace and path, built of cobble-stones laid flat, are especially helpful to the illusion of width. They are wide enough to catch the eye and draw it away from sides and corners. Accents of color are carefully distributed in the beds. Primulas are planted in the raised bed to the left of the wooden steps as well as in the bed on the terrace below. Tulips, daffodils and rhododendron are in bloom beside the path. Plants used in the garden but not in bloom are kept on the storage platform to the right of the deck. The gnarled cotoneaster tree is an interesting shape seen against the deck, and the hawthorn, at left, is another colorful seasonal accent and sculptural form.

26

A Landscape Designed for Easy Care

Every square foot of land surrounding this custom-built suburban house is covered with low-maintenance plantings and other materials that require minimum care. Easy care is most appropriate in a garden like this that is meant for maximum enjoyment of outdoor leisure and recreation. The landscape is designed for full-time use by an active family with growing children. In the backyard are separate "carpets" of pebbled concrete to provide for outdoor living, cooking and dining and for play with space for a ping-pong table. Swimming, basketball and tennis practice are further invitations to play instead of work in the garden.

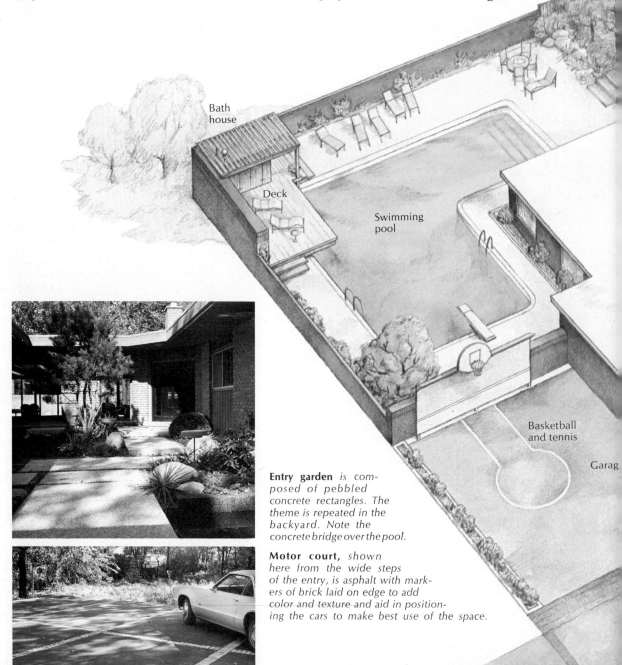

Bath house

Deck

Swimming pool

Basketball and tennis

Garag

Entry garden *is composed of pebbled concrete rectangles. The theme is repeated in the backyard. Note the concrete bridge over the pool.*

Motor court, *shown here from the wide steps of the entry, is asphalt with markers of brick laid on edge to add color and texture and aid in positioning the cars to make best use of the space.*

Entry drive

Outdoor cooking

Lounging

Table tennis

Dining area

Dog run

Rose garden

Pool

Entry garden

Motor court

Good relationship of the cooking area to outdoor dining is shown here. Dining table is adjacent to the house for convenience of table setting, clearing and serving from the kitchen. Yet it is near the barbecue for easy serving of food cooked outdoors. Heavy-duty grill slides and swivels on the steel pole for complete adjustment. The grill can also serve as a table for a hibachi or other small charcoal cooker when needed and swings to the rear so it is out of the way for bonfires.

◀ **Table tennis** has a place of its own well away from the dining table. Its pebbled concrete "carpet" can, however, be used for more tables and chairs when needed for a large party. All the spaces between the pebbled concrete slabs are filled in with river-washed stones or with saturation plantings of hardy ground covers. There are planting beds between the paved areas and some of them are raised above ground level with one or two courses of railroad ties.

The sitting area is in the back corner of the lot which is a favored microclimate here. It is protected from the evening breeze by the fence on two sides and from the heat of the day by the shade of the tall trees overhead. The fence is a "good neighbor" design which is just as attractive on one side as on the other.

Cobble stones are laid on a bed of sand at the base of two large trees as a mulch to keep down weeds, protect the sloping grade around the roots from surface erosion and to add an interesting textural pattern. This view is from the terrace end of the pool.

Night lighting is important here because this whole area is on view through the window-walls of the house. The globe lights are placed at critical points for safe footing as well as for visual effect. They have a festive quality and give a pleasant soft light.

A change of grade *between the living end of the garden and the swimming pool is bridged with this handsome wood walkway. It is of the same material as the deck over the pool and helps unify the two areas.*

The pool *is an L-shape that fits nicely around the corner of the house. The terrace, foreground, is at the shallow end and is convenient for supervising play. The deep end and diving area are around the corner.*

To get more space *for sitting in the sun, and to give a better sense of scale to the dressing-room storage-house, this deck was cantilevered out over the pool. It is high enough above the water so it does not interfere with swimming in any way. Storage is at this end of structure, door to the dressing room is just beyond the life preserver.*

32

The garden area is clearly separated from the pool but circulation between the two is inviting and easy. In building this garden the existing trees were not easy to work around and it added to the cost. But the installation was done with care and the trees were preserved. Without them the woodsy charm of the garden would be completely lost.

33

An extension of the asphalt driveway leading to the garage provided extra space for this wall for tennis and basket-ball practice. The white line is at net height. The surface is smooth and level so bounces are reasonably true. A similar space could be used for handball if the wall were extended to fit flush with the playing surface.

Raised bed of new railroad ties with clipped yew hedge and its underplanting of ivy makes an attractive green band of color that reduces the apparent height of the brick facade on the entry side of the house.

At the far end of the same retaining wall the slope of the motor court (for drainage) reduces the height to just one tie. This detail shows how neatly the steps leading back to the dog run are handled.

▶**Stepping stones** *in the entry garden parallel the wall of the garage wing and make a short cut from the house to the garage. The steps are more decorative than a straight narrow walk would be and the separate squares are in keeping with the rectangular paving patterns used all through the garden. It is often best to recognize a shortcut and make it easy to use. It probably will be whether planned or not.*

▼**Heavy slabs** *of cast concrete are used here for steps. They have the same pebbled surface as the other concrete in the garden and call for less intricate form work than steps cast in place would require. The wood bridge to the sitting garden simply rests on the top step which is heavy enough for dependably firm support. Added length of larger block also makes a platform and alcove for pots of seasonal color.*

◀**The pleasant blend** *of the materials that are used in the garden is illustrated here. The paving is pebbled concrete, the gravel ground cover is river-washed stone which is separated from the low-growing plantings with a steel edging. The rock is one of many used for accent. The raised beds of railroad ties are used only when needed to give more importance to a planting by clearly setting it apart.*

35

2

How to Make Your
Home Say Welcome

An inviting, almost arborlike entryway is divided into two parts by a Dutch door. Greenery edging the walk and hanging overhead is continued with potted plants and vines arranged informally inside the entry court.

Although the shrubs, trees and other plantings that grace the entryway and street side of a house are private property, they "belong" to the neighborhood as well, and create the image a home presents to the public. First impressions are important, and this is where they begin.

The design of the house will usually determine the character of the plantings in front. A traditional house calls for a more symmetrical arrangement of elements than a home designed in the contemporary manner. But no matter what the size and style of the house, the entryway and front garden should be planned to establish a feeling of order, warmth and graciousness.

If the entry is formal in design, it need not be so precisely symmetrical as to be forbidding. On the other hand, the plantings should not be too informal or overcrowded. A graceful classic doorway, for example, ought not to be obscured by a huge, ragged bush or an unruly growth of vines.

The height and contours of the plantings should relate in scale to the windows and doors. And here, as elsewhere in the garden, the temptation to use too many different plants should be resisted. Certain common courtesies might be considered too. For example, the walkway or driveway to the front door ought to be clearly marked and the house number easily seen, either lit at night or placed where visitors' headlights will illuminate it. In short, guests must be made to feel as welcome approaching the house as they are made to feel upon entering.

Gracefully curved walkway, *edged in sweet alyssum, is made even more interesting by laying the bricks in a basketweave pattern. The juniper in the foreground is easily trimmed to prevent its encroaching on the walk. The three trees, evenly spaced near the house, give a necessary vertical accent against the low line of the roof.*

Good use of the area *surrounding elm tree adds charm and space enough to serve as an entryway and terrace. Unless front of house has ample privacy, this arrangement works best at a side or back entrance.*

This pleasant invitation *to enter is created by smooth, cut flagstones set into a textured setting of pebbled concrete and low plantings. The sculptural fixture reflects the light downward to eliminate glare.*

Making Your Entryway Attractive

The entry walk, from the front door to the sidewalk or drive, is a visual extension of the hospitality of the house and this should be reflected in the design. Clearly define the walkway itself and be sure it is well lighted at night. Make steps an easy grade, and all surfaces skid-proof. Plan paving to be wide enough for two people to walk in comfort side by side.

Entry gardens usually include both hard surfaces and plant material, and this calls for a harmonious combination of the two. It's best that plants do not overwhelm their setting, or be too small or too few to fill their space effectively and count for what they are. Keep paved surfaces in balance with the larger "outdoor scale" of the surrounding lawns, trees and shrubs. Be sure that walkways and entrance porches are of generous scale. All too often they seem small and cramped. For unity, it is best to use one material for both walk and entryway.

Fascinating interplay *of irregularly placed brick panels with planting area gives interest to what might have been a dull, prosaic approach. There is plenty of space for planting between walk and house.*

Paving entryway *(above left) with bricks (which repeat house bricks) opens up this limited space. Fence creates sense of separation from street. Plantings lend seasonal color. Large stone planters augment greenery.*

◀**Graceful curve** *of walk dramatizes edge of lawn and leads visitors invitingly to front door. Bricks are set in running bond which accentuates sweep of walk. Mass of foliage anchors fence firmly to overall design.*

Reminiscent of an English cottage garden, this entryway creates a brilliant splash of color, but should only be undertaken by a knowledgeable and enthusiastic gardener. Such a garden, if not done with care and skill, can look messy and ragged. It also takes constant maintenance. When the season goes, many of the plantings go with it.

▶**This entryway** requires little if any maintenance. The design is not complex and yet has great style. The massive foliage (reinforcing the woodland setting of the house) provides an interesting play of color and texture against the neutral expanse of gravel. This effect would not be nearly so effective if the gravel were lawn. The walk is an open invitation to investigate as it curves gently out of sight behind the foliage and the trees.

39

Climbing roses *over the door, the random pattern of old bricks, the roughhewn stone steps—everything here perfectly complements this house. Annuals and perennials accent the permanent plantings.*

Dramatic interest *is established by the handsome tree with strong sculptural branching. Tree's foliage also softens the somewhat severe geometric lines of the house. Low-lying plantings balance height of tree.*

Rustic, woodsy effect *is achieved in this entryway by an informal arrangement of shrubs and trees. The plantings (mostly dark green) are saved from monotony by their variations in shape and texture. Color relief is provided by the azaleas pocketed in a rock formation that seems to have happened by itself. The two Japanese maples give the necessary height to what is essentially a ground-hugging composition.*

40

This lush growth of shrubs and ground cover makes an unusually interesting approach to a home and one that is very pleasant to walk through. The variety of plants used—such as Vinca minor (the ground cover), juniper and ilex—work together to form a rich juxtaposition of textures, colors and shapes that are far more eye-catching than a flat expanse of green lawn. As a bonus, the maintenance of such plantings is, of course, minimal.

41

Accommodating the Automobile

In the twentieth century the automobile has become more than a means of transportation. It is also a piece of portable sculpture in the landscape and an extension of the family home. Its accommodation (the carport or garage and off-street parking) and the facilities for moving it (driveway and turnaround) are an integral part of the landscape. The car is an element that cannot be ignored in the landscape of today.

When planning the landscape to accommodate the automobile, consider the occasional needs of guests as well as the day-to-day requirements of family transportation. The design should provide arriving guests with easy access to the house as well as a place to park their cars.

The automobile does indeed play a grand role in our daily lives, but there comes a point when the space devoted to its needs must be limited or a "tyranny of the auto" over the landscape may well be established.

While it is aesthetically important to maintain a pleasing balance between the areas of planting and the paved surfaces allocated to the automobile, the practical consideration of making daily chores as simple as possible should not be overlooked. For instance, literally tons of groceries and other household goods are carried from the car to the house every year. A properly designed driveway with a parking area built close to the service entry can make this never-ending task less of a burden.

If there is heavy rainfall in your part of the country, a protected walkway from the house to the car can be an important consideration. Where long cold winters are to be expected, the driveway should be designed to make the removal of snow as easy as possible, and the slope should be gradual so that icing does not make it dangerous.

The brick-paved area *beside this driveway clearly indicates the approach to the house. The lamp at the left of the steps ought to be of sufficient power to illuminate entire entryway from drive to front door.*

This "landing strip" *at curbside (made of brick to match walk) is designed so that visitors can exit simultaneously from both back and front doors of a car. Note decorative curb made of stones set in concrete.*

Large concrete rounds set in the lawn serve as a walkway to and from the street as well as the drive. They provide a generous amount of necessary paving without totally losing the cooling effect of green grass.

A spacious gravel court, plain in design, is nevertheless in harmony with the simple, open lines of the house. Trees and hedges at the edge provide a welcome color contrast and offer much-needed shade on the surface.

Where there is space, a turnaround is a graceful, efficient way to handle front-of-house traffic. It can be made of gravel (as above) or paved. However, any such exposed area can present an unpleasantly bare appearance. In the turnaround above, the tree planted in the center and surrounded by greenery breaks the monotony and, at the same time, offers relief from the sun's glare, always a problem with gravel or pavement.

Improving the Plantings in Front

There was a time when most houses were built on high foundations laid above ground to minimize the need of digging deeply for a basement. The result was an unsightly stretch of bare concrete that called for camouflage with trees and shrubs—and this is how "foundation plantings" came to be. They have long since outlived their day.

Almost any residential street has houses overwhelmed in front by too many trees and shrubs, all of which are obviously too large for their setting. Such decorative errors have been made in the name of foundation planting. The time has come to abandon this concept of simply pasting plants in rows against the front of the house. Instead, one ought to consider all of the front lawn as a total area to be used to best advantage.

On the following six pages are photographs of three attractive houses with problems commonly found in one form or another all across the country. Accompanying the photographs are drawings to illustrate good ways to solve these problems by the imaginative use of plants and other materials. While these solutions may not fit your particular requirements, they illustrate basic principles of landscape design which can be applied to many different situations.

Playing Down a Dominant Garage

The attached garage placed forward of the house (in the photograph below) is not an unusual design. Although it's a convenient arrangement, it does make the garage and its wide doorway the most dominant aspect of the entire façade. To help diminish the impact of the garage, a couple of basic design principles were applied in the suggestions shown at right. The visual "weight" of the garage was balanced by adding a mass of tree foliage and a coarse ground cover. The entryway was given new importance and emphasis by the addition of brick walks and the related plantings.

This typical foundation planting *has too many plants of too many sizes and shapes planted too close to the house, including the inevitable conical evergreen at the entryway. The major mistake, however, is setting all of the plants within three feet of the house instead of considering the design of the entire street-side area as a whole.*

Mass of foliage *(trees above and ground cover below) is the major element used to balance the overdominant "L" of the garage, and from some angles the trees even screen it from view. Curved line (where ground cover meets lawn) helps to interrelate the two materials and makes a less obvious division than if the line were straight. Red-leaf Japanese maples provide important color accent.*

Approach to the front door *is the dominant feature of this plan. Handsome curved walk of red brick is relieved by green lawn, trees, low-lying shrubs against the house and fence, and the semicircular flower bed that softens the projecting corner of the garage. Note the curbside brick panel for easy access to or from a car and the strong vertical accent of the well-placed entry light.*

Before landscaping, *house seemed barren and unrelated to its site. Walkway seems awkward and is too narrow.*

Relating the House to the Ground

All too often a house will loom up from its site with little or no feeling of relationship to the land on which it stands. The house seems to be on one plane, the ground on another, with nothing in between to tie the two together. One of the best ways to relate a house to the site is to plant trees in the foreground. The vertical line of a tree trunk not only tends to pull the house down, tying it to the earth and making it seem more a part of the natural setting, but the foliage of the tree softens the hard line of the roof, such as the split-level at the left. Plant the trees so that, from any angle in the street, the branches or foliage will be seen against the house. The drawings here show the difference that trees can make.

Another common problem of many new houses is that the walk from the street to the front door is too narrow in relation to the size of the house and the space around it, and, for that matter, too narrow for comfortable walking side by side. This is not an easy problem to solve inexpensively.

As in the examples shown here, fairly drastic measures were called for and, in fact, were taken. However, if you feel your budget can't embrace such elaborate changes all at once, the widening of the walk should have the first priority.

Low-maintenance front yard *is provided by free-growing ground cover (such as pachysandra, myrtle [Vinca minor], or creeping euonymus). Simulated outcropping of rock is informal in look and clearly dramatizes the entryway. Mugho pines flank walk, a Japanese black pine is against the house, and the others are white pines. Note that the new steps are closer together than on original walk.*

The front has been regraded *so that the two walks can be sloped, thereby elimi-nating a need for steps. Gentle curve of walks gives an interesting shape to the lawn and the absence of steps can be a boon in slippery weather and does away with the need for mid-lawn lighting at night. In all three projects, porch surface matches surface of walk, an attractive refinement but not necessary.*

Although original steps remain *and original width of walk is maintained, the brick-edged planting beds of dwarf day lilies create a strong center of interest on the approach to the house. Maintenance is greatly reduced by planting a bed of ivy instead of lawn in area at right of walk. Multi-trunked trees are saucer magnolias (M. soulangeana); other trees are European hornbeams.*

47

Before landscaping. *This house, with its long roof line and undersized plantings, seems bare and uninviting.*

Establishing the Entryway

In approaching the house above for the first time, a guest could easily become confused as to which of the doors is the front and which is the service entry. This is an unpleasant feeling and a homeowner owes to his guests (and delivery men) the courtesy of a plainly marked route that each should take. In all three of the improvements suggested on these pages, the main entryway, which was small and pinched to begin with, has been enlarged and clearly defined by the new walks, plantings and drives to give it an obvious dominance over the service entrance.

In addition to improving the entry, there was a need to bring more interest to the front yard and to enhance the rather plain façade of this house with trees and shrubs. The plantings in front of the house were too small and unrelated to make any kind of decorative impact on their own. A point to remember, and one valid in any situation, is to use plants in meaningful masses rather than scattering them hither and thither.

Notice in the drawings how the designer has used large groupings or rows of trees and shrubs throughout the entire area from street to house and side to side to create important pockets of visual interest. Note also how trees were placed to break the long line and weight of the roof which, when seen as a whole, tends to push down on the house.

Even minimum changes *here clearly establish the front entry and separate it from the service entrance. A nice accent is the island of barberry set in the brick walk. All of the trees are Russian olive (Elaeagnus angustifolia) and the one in the planting bed helps to break the roof line. Espaliered apple decorates empty wall space and the brick path around end of garage is a useful addition.*

For convenience of cars this front yard has been given over almost entirely to an asphalt turnaround and drive. The addition of sufficient plantings keeps it from being too austere or harsh-looking and, of course, the necessary maintenance has been reduced to a bare minimum. For exact dimensions required for a turnaround and off-street parking, see the section which begins on page 175.

Broad landing strip of brick makes an inviting entry court. Brick is used again (flush with asphalt) in the walk at the left that conveniently extends to the back of the house. These bands of brick serve both to widen the drive and help balance the design. Entry light has been lowered and moved into the planting bed by the dogwood tree. Other trees are crab apples and junipers.

49

Classic Ideas For the Traditional House

Owners of so-called traditional houses, or modern houses in the "traditional" style, will find a good source of appropriate landscaping ideas in the gardens of some of the early colonists. These gardens were developed to suit New World architectural styles (what we now call "colonial," such as the salt box, and garrison house) and the native plant and building materials. The result was a unity of architectural and landscape design as valid today as it was in the 1700s.

The pictures on these eight pages show what colonial gardens were like. They were taken in the restored 18th-century town of Williamsburg, Virginia, where there are faithful reproductions of some of the earliest residential gardens in the U.S. The ideas here are presented not to be copied as such but as a source of authentic designs which will create the ambience of a traditional garden when adapted to suit individual landscaping needs.

The original colonial gardens were basically green with occasional splashes of color and usually included an ornamental, divided, or "parterre," garden (examples shown on these two pages), a kitchen or herb garden and a small orchard. Any or all of these would be in keeping with a house of traditional design.

Oval parterre garden is full of color in the springtime when the dogwoods, azaleas and the triangular beds of tulips are in bloom. The garden is also charming when not in flower because of the clearly defined symmetry of the design and the interesting texture of the evergreen shrubs.

◀ **Traditional herb garden** with rosemary, thyme, sage, yarrow, lavender and artemisia is planted in front of the kitchen (right) in the formal manner with a pattern of diamond-shaped beds and brick walkways enclosed by neatly trimmed hedges of yaupon holly. All beds have raised edges of brick.

The basic materials used in colonial gardens are a part of this parterre, or divided, garden: wood, from the nearby forests (mainly pine, cypress, locust and cedar), clay bricks, gravel for the walks and such plants as ivy, dogwood, privet, roses and the Chinaberry, native wisteria and coral honeysuckle on the arbor.

A typical informal *colonial garden included a close-cropped lawn edged with colorful borders of flowers and trees. Among the flowers here are tulips, iris, Sweet William and hostas at the base of a crape myrtle, an oriental import.*

The Influence Of Informality

Not unexpectedly, the colonists' early gardens were modeled on the formal English examples they knew so well and had left behind. (Actually, formal "English" gardens were greatly influenced by the Dutch gardens through William and Mary.) They were located at the side of the house or in the back and were all a similar size. Most Williamsburg homes were built on a half-acre, a lot size that's not unusual in houses today. This uniformity was the result of Williamsburg's being built according to a town plan, among the earliest in the northern hemisphere. Besides the ornamental garden, kitchen garden and orchard, the lots also accommodated several outbuildings—such as the dairy, kitchen, smokehouse and stable. The most obvious restrictions the town planners imposed on the homeowners were that the main house be built close to the street (six feet by law) and that each property should be "paled in" or enclosed; which accounts for the dozens of different fence designs.

Formal topiary *is planted by an informal (unedged) gravel path in this example combining two complementary elements of traditional style.*

52

Thick ground cover of ivy and myrtle in a shaded side garden creates the effect of a naturally overgrown open space in a dense forest. Trimming the paths is the only maintenance required in this forest garden.

Gradually, in the late 18th century, the formal parterre gardens gave way to informal ones. Intricate patterns, elaborate topiary and trim hedges interlaced with walkways were replaced by a wide strip of lawn (called a bowling green) surrounded by a profusion of flowers, shrubs and trees. The picket fence remained, and is to this day one of the key ingredients of a traditional garden.

How to explain the change to informality? A case is made in the United States for the fact that revolution was "in the air." If people feel capable of standing alone politically—so the argument goes—they develop independence in other areas.

The informal style encouraged individual creativity in design and the use of plants. Many varieties of flowers were grown together in a natural manner rather than in symmetrical patterns.

Colonists in many parts of North America also made extensive and effective use of native plants.

53

The plants listed on the facing page were commonly used in Williamsburg. Native plants and others from around the world are included. They all thrived in the mild Virginia climate, but fortunately some grow in various parts of Canada, too. And, of course, the design ideas can be appropriately adapted to any "modern" traditional garden or landscape.

Keep in mind when planning a traditional garden that considerable variation is possible. One area of a basically informal plan could be developed as a parterre garden. A few fruit trees and a vegetable garden can be planted at the edge of a lawn. There are, however, a few things to avoid, such as modern construction materials—concrete, plastic and steel—and "free-form" designs. As the pictures show, there is a basic symmetry in the hard edges of planting beds and walkways in both the formal and informal colonial gardens. If wood, gravel, clay brick and plants—the basic materials the colonials worked with—are used together with restraint and pleasant proportions, the flavor of traditional gardens can be established for modern-day houses built in "traditional" style.

Informal planting beds *border a gravel path. In keeping with natural style, white violet, on the left, grows unevenly over the edge. Plants in raised wooden bed on the right are yellow epimedium and lemon lily.*

Plain wood fence *built of random-width boards becomes a decorative wall with the addition of a border of plants at the base and handsome fox grape growing along the top. Vine also extends height of fence by a foot or two.*

▶**A vine is used** *as an informal espalier to soften the corner of this small outbuilding. Notice how the lower stems are cleared of foliage to make an interesting tracery against the wall. The plant is a coral honeysuckle.*

54

Plants Grown in Eighteenth-Century Colonial Gardens

For Cool Climates:

TREES. Eastern red cedar (*Juniperus virginiana*).
Canada hemlock (*Tsuga canadensis*).
American hornbeam (*Carpinus caroliniana*).
Sugar maple (*Acer saccharum*).
Mountain ash (*Sorbus decora*).
White mulberry (*Morus alba*).
Black oak (*Quercus velutina*).
Scarlet oak (*Quercus coccinea*).
White oak (*Quercus alba*).
Peach (*Prunus persica*).
Sassafras (*Sassafras albidum*).
Babylon weeping willow (*Salix babylonica*).
SHRUBS. Pinxterbloom Azalea (*Rhododendron nudiflorum*).
Tree box (*Buxus sempervirens* Truetree).
Dwarf Box (*Buxus sempervirens* Truedwarf).
American cranberrybush (*Viburnum trilobum*).
Scarlet firethorn (*Pyracantha coccinea*).
American holly (*Ilex opaca*).
Lilac (*Syringa vulgaris*).
Mountain laurel (*Kalmia latifolia*).
Beach plum (*Prunus maritima*).
Privet (*Ligustrum vulgare*).
Flowering quince (*Chaenomeles lagenaria*).
ROSES. Cabbage(*Rosa centifolia*), Damask (*R. Damascena*), French (*R. gallica*), Swamp (*R. palustris*).

Mapleleaf viburnum (*Viburnum acerfolium*).
Winterberry (*Ilex verticillata*).
VINES. Trumpet creeper (*Campsis radicans*).
Tatarian honeysuckle (*Lonicera tartarica*).
Matrimony vine (*Lycium halimifolium*).
Virginia creeper (*Parthenocissus quinquefolia*).
GROUND COVERS. English ivy (*Hedera helix*).
Periwinkle (*Vinca minor*).

For Warm Climates:

TREES. American beech (*Fagus grandifolia*).
Yellow birch (*Betula lutea*).
Red buckeye (*Aesculus pavia*).
Chinaberry (*Melia azedarach*).
Cornelian cherry (*Cornus mas*).
Crape myrtle (*Lagerstroemia indica*).
Dogwood (*Cornus florida*).
Common fig (*Ficus carica*).
Goldenrain tree (*Koelreuteria paniculata*).
Washington hawthorn (*Crataegus phaenopyrum*).
Southern magnolia (*Magnolia grandiflora*).
Medlar (*Mespilus germanica*).
Paper mulberry (*Broussonetia papyrifera*).
Japanese pagoda-tree (*Sophora japonica*).
Pawpaw (*Asimina triloba*).
Pecan (*Carya illinoensis*).

SHRUBS. Japanese aucuba (*Aucuba japonica variegata*).
Indica azalea (*Rhododendron indicum*).
Camellia (*Camellia japonica*).
American cranberrybush (*Viburnum trilobum*).
Cape-jasmine, gardenia (*Gardenia jasminoides*).
American holly (*Ilex opaca*).
Oakleaf hydrangea (*Hydrangea quercifolia*).
Indian currant, coral-berry (*Symphoricarpos orbiculatus*).
Oleander (*Nerium oleander*).
Flowering pomegranate (*Punica granatum*).
Flowering quince (*Chaenomeles lagenaria*).
ROSES. Carolina rose (*Rosa carolina*), cherokee rose (*R. laevigata*), sweetbriar rose (*R. eglanteria*), Virginia rose (*R. virginiana*).
Wintersweet (*Chimonanthus praecox*).
VINES. Crossvine (*Bignonia capreolata*).
Trumpet honeysuckle (*Lonicera sempervirens*).
Common jasmine (*Jasminum officinale*).
Carolina jessamine (*Gelsemium sempervirens*).
American wisteria (*Wisteria frutescens*).
GROUND COVERS. Aaronsbeard, St. Johnswort (*Hypericum calycinum*).
Periwinkle (*Vinca minor*).

Authentic Plan for a Traditional Garden

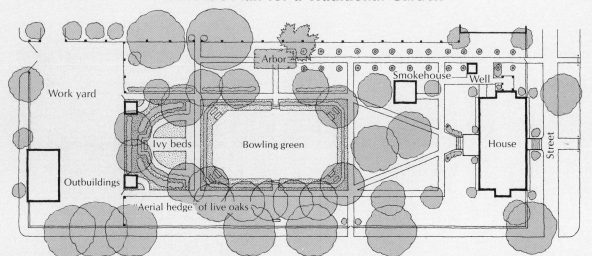

Work yard

Arbor

Smokehouse

Well

Ivy beds

Bowling green

House

Street

Outbuildings

"Aerial hedge" of live oaks

Good Ideas From Traditional Gardens

The decorative ideas shown here, and those found in all of these traditional gardens, can be used to good effect in any kind of garden, even the most modern.

For instance, the clean lines of the topiary seen here might be just the accent for a corner of a raised wooden deck; the straight-backed bench would be inviting set under an old tree on a back lawn. In landscape design, as in interior design, a mixture of periods and styles in one setting can be combined with good effect if one aspect is clearly dominant and the others are used for accent and contrast.

Design impact depends upon a pleasing relationship of size, shape and color of the objects used together regardless of the periods they represent. As you look over these pictures again, consider how the features you especially like might fit in your garden, whatever its style.

Picket fences were a necessity in colonial times and people continued to use them when they were no longer required by law or needed to control stray cattle. They are still an attractive hallmark of traditionalism. They are, however, expensive to install and need considerable maintenance. Below are a few examples of posts, pickets and finials from the dozens of fence designs developed at Williamsburg. The first picture shows a self-closing gate, a good idea for any fence. When the gate is opened, the weight of the ball pulls it shut again. See page 358 for details on setting fence posts.

This **"interrupted cone"** *made of tree box is not difficult to maintain. It is the eye-catching centerpiece in an informal bed planted with day lilies, and other colorful perennials.*

Picket fencing establishes a sense of security in an attractive way. A few styles are

Straight-backed bench is set off by clipped privet hedge behind it. Clean lines of the bench would work well in many settings: on a lawn, veranda, screened porch or deck; by a tennis or basketball court, or, as here, on a patio. If used in a traditional garden the most fitting color is white or cream and the finish should be fresh and clean.

◄ **Shallow steps** on incline in Williamsburg are made of brick and timbers. This combination of materials is still appropriate in informal gardens today.

Dwarf boxwood (near right) forms a dense green border retained by 2-x-4s stained and treated with preservative to prevent decay.

Border of lavender cotton (Santolina chamaecyperissus) adds importance to a planting bed. The gravel path is a complementary texture and gray color.

available ready-made, but fancy designs like those shown here can be made by hand.

3

Inspiration
For Outdoor Living

More people these days are spending more of their leisure time on their own property—and with good reason. As public recreation areas become more crowded and more expensive, and traffic, coming and going, gets worse, there is a real need to create better facilities for outdoor living and recreation at home. Another reason for developing such facilities is the cost of building. As the price of land, labor and materials forces up the cost of every square foot of living space inside the house, the less expensive possibilities for outdoor living become more appealing. And no matter what the size of the indoor room, an adjacent outdoor living area is an inviting and attractive addition.

People in mild climates have learned the pleasure of spending time outdoors—cooking, eating, playing and entertaining. Even a few months of mild weather is enough. Private swimming pools—Hollywood elaborate or backyard simple—are now found in every climate zone of the country.

There's a world of opportunity for quiet pleasures and active pursuits—right in your own backyard.

Terraces and Patios

A small, simple terrace, with an inexpensive gravel floor, has privacy (obtained by a wall of flowers), good sun exposure and a pleasant view to trees beyond. Redwood furniture is tough and durable in all weather.

Almost everyone has enjoyed the freedom that comes from leaving a closed room and walking onto a terrace or patio. The sudden awareness of space, the change of light, the firm ground underfoot, the smell of the earth, the fragrance and color of plants—all give a happy sense of release and escape. Such pleasures are not dependent on the size or luxury of the area. Any terrace or patio, no matter how simple or small, comes to possess this compelling magic. Many people find that after building an outdoor room with trees and plants, walls and fences to assure privacy, bright tables and chairs, no other area of the house is quite as pleasant and interesting or as much used and enjoyed. In addition, such space can be had for a surprisingly low cost in money and upkeep.

The widening of what is actually a cross-walk leading past the house to a garden in back creates a pleasant, intimate place for tables and chairs. The beautifully patterned floor is of brick and gray cut stone. Surrounding planting gives contrast in shape and color. Tree at left gives partial shade, the fence affords privacy and—most important—the terrace is immediately adjacent to the house.

Small and intimate, this sunny spot was made of bricks laid inside a border of old railroad ties sunk in the ground. There is no sturdier wood for outdoor use. The ties were also used to make a frame topped with brick laid on gravel and sand which acts as a platform-step leading from the door to the terrace. Plants and shrubs lend color and also provide pleasant and adequate privacy.

59

The dramatic, vertical lines *of the two trees above are seen to their best advantage in this small, simple terrace. The trees, in turn, are relieved of starkness by the circular border of bright flowers.*

A terrace within the garden *rather than near it or at the edge creates an atmosphere of charm and privacy. It is quiet, too, and should be planned and furnished with these qualities in mind.*

The Advantages of a Deck

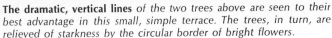

Terraces and patios must be built on level land. A deck, on the other hand (with its system of posts, framing and wooden floor), can be built over an irregular, sloping or otherwise troublesome piece of ground. The construction does not destroy the contour of the land or the drainage pattern and, in addition, hides what is often unsightly or unmanageable terrain. Furthermore, decks are relatively inexpensive to build and are not difficult to maintain. An occasional restaining keeps them attractive and, with cracks between the floorboards, the cleaning is easy. It may well be that a deck is the best solution for some aspect of your landscaping problem. For specific information on building a deck, see page 391.

The ground slopes sharply *away from the house foundations beneath this deck, which creates an attractive outdoor living space on otherwise unusable land. Note how the decking is cut to follow the outline of the bank.*

A large floating deck, *built around a beautiful tree, provides a cool, quiet spot for reading or resting. It also solves the problem of trying to grow grass in the deep shade and in competition with roots of large trees.*

A two-level deck *of western red cedar. The upper platform has good exposure for sunbathing. The lower platform is for lounging. River rocks studded with mugho pines and yuccas lend interest and are easy to care for.*

The most dramatic setting *for a deck is a hillside with a panoramic view. This deck is a good example. But even without a view, a deck is the best of all building techniques to transform unmanageable land into a pleasant living area. As an added advantage, a deck can always be built on the same level as the adjacent indoor area.*

Ideas for Overhead Shelter

While protection from the sun, wind or rain is the usual reason for building an overhead shelter, there are also some pleasant by-products. Even a minimum structure creates a welcome sense of enclosure and security, serves to establish the dimensions of a seating area, and casts interesting shadows on the floor and wall. If the shelter is at a distance from the house, it can be an inviting destination and quiet retreat.

A dropped ceiling *adds spatial interest inside this screened porch and helps to define a central seating area. The split bamboo walls create privacy and provide a backdrop for the play of shadows on the wall.*

Light glows *through the canvas of this shelter and brightens its festive look. Side panels can be closed for privacy and to cut wind. Canvas is laced to pipe frame and can be removed for winter storage.*

Inexpensive sunshade *of wooden slats slopes over a concrete patio. The slats relate nicely to the woven fence beyond. Plantings in raised beds soften the bare white walls of the house and add color.*

◀**Pattern of shadow** *from the lattice overhead offers a pleasing contrast to the open, sunny section at the far end of this long, narrow city garden. Lilac tree is trimmed high to accentuate interesting trunks.*

This translucent roof creates a light and airy outdoor room that is made even more homelike by the "painting" on the fence (which serves as a wall) and the arrangement of the furniture into both a dining and a living area. Note how the plastic panels overhead provide privacy from upstairs windows of the house next door.

This dramatic tent is made with rolls of reed screening over a simple frame. High roofline allows the breezes to come through and trees provide shade. Carpeted platform adds more importance to the setting.

▶ **Soft light** from translucent panel above falls on this patio. Planting of ferns at the base of the tree adds interest. The checkered pattern of the roof is repeated in shadow on the floor and in the chairs.

63

For a Shower in the Sun

Gardens can occur in many forms and places and here is a delightful example, with a shower, that opens off a bathroom. An eight-foot fence of 1 x 4 redwood slats insures complete privacy and is in effect an outdoor extension of the bathroom walls. The eight-foot sliding glass door opens wide to let in the fresh air and sunlight and to make the garden a part of the bath. The door can be locked, and the room, with its protective fence outside, is as safe and secure as any other part of the house.

The lush garden atmosphere is established by the use of bamboo, ferns and a climbing vine that decorates the open beams overhead. A weatherproof hanging lamp illuminates the garden at night. At the base of the shower is a circular slab of exposed aggregate for secure footing and, because a planting of ground cover is difficult to maintain in such an enclosed area, the surface is of gravel. Large rocks are used for their sculptural form. In warm climates a garden like this can be used the year around, but even in colder climates the auxiliary shower can be enjoyed in mild weather.

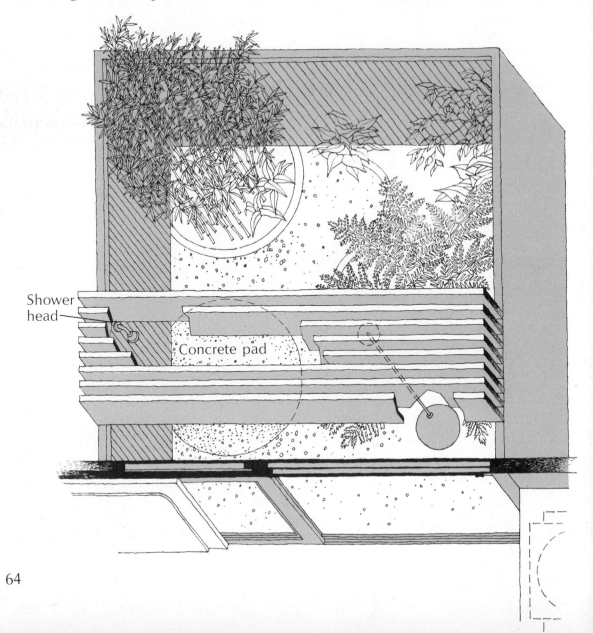

Shower head

Concrete pad

Terrace Furniture and Built-Ins

The qualities to look for in garden furniture are durability and weather resistance, size in relation to the setting, appearance and comfort. Durability is listed first because furniture that is in poor condition by the end of one season is not worth buying. There's a wide choice of outdoor furniture in wood, metal and plastic on the market.

Just be sure that the kind you choose is in proportion to the space you have for it. Also consider the advantages of built-in furniture. It can be designed as a part of the garden's structure, it conserves space and, when combined with a few portable pieces, reduces a "forest of legs" look which too many tables and chairs can create.

Concrete blocks *support this bench on the border of a terrace. Spacing boards on edge is an easy way to construct a curved shape and provides a quick drying surface for seating. Design relates to the shape of the round flower bed.*

Massive scale *of the 8-x-8-inch timbers on concrete blocks develops a sense of strength and stability. The crisp lines of the bench are in good contrast to the gravel, fence and foliage.*

◀ **The tree-house** *atmosphere of this deck that seems to float over the dunes is enhanced by the swinging hammock. The lightweight chairs further add to the illusion. Scatter pillows are a colorful and inexpensive way to increase the seating capacity in limited space; the three in the foreground mark the edge of the deck. Note how native growth on the dunes is important to the design.*

▶ **Combination** *planting box and garden seat is an attractive and useful decoration on this concrete terrace. For a permanent installation the paving under the tree should be removed so that the roots can spread. A self-contained planter is movable but limits the root area and thus the size of the tree. Some drainage through the bottom is required. Note matching bench in background.*

If durability is important, this table is ideal for outdoor use. Made of decorative concrete blocks topped with a sturdy redwood frame, it is the kind of furniture that can be left in place all through the year. The concrete base is practically indestructible and the heavy but removable top is slatted so it will not collect water or melting snow and, thus, resists warping. For instructions on making this table, see page 398.

A built-in kitchen is a luxurious and useful addition to any outdoor area. When the hinged front panel is up, at left, it provides overhead protection. When down, right, it is an attractive wall concealing the sink, refrigerator and outlets for appliances.

Privacy Is
a Two-Way Street

No one questions the use of shades and draperies on the windows of a house to maintain a sense of privacy indoors. But many people would not think of putting up a fence or tall hedge for privacy in the garden for fear of offending the neighbors.

The negative connotation of fencing, which keeps people from establishing the privacy that they and their neighbors would enjoy, is largely a result of our history and traditions.

Those who first came to the New World wanted freedom from limitations and they relished the idea of unclaimed and seemingly unlimited territory.

They had to cut down forests and travel dangerous trails to open up the land.

And now, long after all this has changed, we still tend to equate freedom with open space.

Where the Problem Started

When farmers came to plow the wide-open West, they brought barbed wire to separate the cattle from the crops. The fences, symbol of a new order on the prairie, were a threat to the cattlemen's freedom. The conflict between open land and fencing led to range wars and supplied a standard plot for western movies.

The emotional overtones of this struggle, so widely recognized and dramatized, still exist on the streets of suburbia. In many parts of the country a fence of any kind is thought to be a "spite fence." While understandable, this feeling is unfortunate because it keeps people from getting full use of the land that surrounds their homes and is there for the taking.

It is as true today as in frontier times that acres of land can provide freedom and the privacy that comes with distance. But most of us now live where land is measured in feet instead of acres. In a crowded suburb open space does not mean freedom, it means just the opposite. For freedom of movement and action, outdoor screening of some kind is required in most situations.

Times Are Changing

Where outdoor living has become almost a way of life, fences and screens are accepted. In some housing developments every lot is separated from the neighbors' by a six-foot fence. People in these communities have found that a fence provides privacy on both sides. The family inside has privacy and the neighbors and the public on the outside are spared the details of outdoor cooking and dining, play and entertaining.

But what about those who would like to have privacy out-of-doors but live where people are offended by fences? There are some possible solutions. Most people respond to reason. The best way to start is to talk to your neighbors and explain that privacy can be a two-way street and a fence will give everyone more freedom to get the most possible use of his land without intruding upon the privacy of others.

There are many designs for "good neighbor fences" that look the same on both sides. You'll find some examples on page 360.

If you think your neighbors will be too

offended if you put up a fence of any kind, there are other ways to get screening. A planting of three to five hemlocks strategically placed along the line of sight between you and the house next door is less obvious than a fence but still an effective way to get some privacy. A vine-covered lattice is another friendly device to use where fences are not yet understood or accepted.

Our territorial imperatives being what they are, it is often best to set out a planting or build a screen well within our own boundaries. The closer we get to the property line and a neighbor's land, the more defensive he may become.

Often the problem solves itself. Neighbors come to understand the value of fences through experience. In suburban neighborhoods where outdoor cooking is popular and fences are frowned upon, the first family to set up for a barbecue or a party on a weekend afternoon often has the area to itself—because it is something of an intrusion to use adjoining terraces that are in full view of a party in progress.

Screening Comes in Many Forms

On the following pages of this chapter are many good ideas for fences and screens of various shapes and sizes using a variety of outdoor building materials. And in a later section, on projects you can build yourself, there are specific instructions for making fences as well as how to set fence posts and hang gates. In the section on planting you will find lists of trees and shrubs that when mature serve as hedges and screens.

The ways and means of attaining privacy are many but before making any definite plans be sure you know the rules and regulations concerning fences in your community.

In most places the municipal office can give you the regulations. Checking with the municipality is not always enough, however. In some places neighborhood associations have rules on the subject. Some communities have restrictive covenants as part of the deed to the house and they legally affect what you can and cannot do with your property. Make sure any fences or screens you plan will be legal from all points of view before putting them up. The authorities might object even if the neighbors do not.

Sometimes restrictions in the height and the distance that screening must be set back from the street or property line apply only to fences. If this is the case, plantings, such as a hedge, can often be used for privacy without objection.

The restrictions in height may apply only to the structure itself. If, for example, a four-foot fence is legal, it can be built two feet up the side of a slope, or on a two-foot raised bed, to give it the screening effect of a six-foot fence. In most situations a six-foot screen will provide adequate privacy for outdoor living.

And, finally, if the laws regarding fences in your town do not suit your needs and those of your neighbors, the regulations can be changed.

People can get together and work with the existing system to change the laws on fencing for the benefit of all. The law, after all, is meant for the common good.

Fences and Screens

Fences and screens, if they are tall enough and properly designed and located, can provide the privacy that is one of the most important requirements for outdoor living. If they are used to border your property, they create, at the least, an implied privacy by establishing a boundary between public property and your own. Fences also help define or limit space. They can divide an awkward or overly large area into comfortable, more intimate units, serving attractively as the walls of your outdoor rooms.

Fences and screens are available in such bold, dramatic designs and such imaginative materials—as tinted plastic or bamboo, for example—that they have become decorative elements in their own right, like pieces of linear sculpture. They can be used to create mood, serve as a background for plants, screen an unsightly view, let in or shut out light and air and provide, if necessary, protection for children and pets.

▲**Old-fashioned** *picket fence still has great charm, especially when it borders a pleasant, informal garden or edges a wide sweep of green lawn, as it does here. A fence enclosing your property is useful for keeping small children inside and stray dogs outside. Ivy planted at base eliminates the need to trim the lawn near fence.*

◀**Neat and orderly,** *yet unobtrusive, stockade fence blends well with the luxuriant green foliage on either side. Wooden fences are an excellent natural background for flowers and shrubs and work especially well with climbing plants. The height and tight spacing of the palings create a welcome sense of privacy for this garden terrace.*

▶**Strong decorative pattern** *on the fence is of major interest in this small, stark area of simple gravel and sparse plantings. If the area were more elaborately planted or decorated, the sculptural beauty of the fence might be lost. Movement of sun creates constantly shifting shadow patterns on the surface of the fence.*

71

Strong horizontal pattern of saplings wired together is an interesting variation of the traditional stockade fence, which uses saplings vertically. The linear emphasis of this fence is effective in accentuating the curving drive. Planting at the edge of the drive is an effective means of blending the square end of the fence into the garden.

Small oasis of green enriches a courtyard of gravel enclosed with walls of brick that are of a color complementing both the plantings and the gravel floor. One side of the wall has occasional bricks pulled out to form a decorative pattern. The end wall, made of the same material, is left plain to provide a good background for the statue. Walls of this height and solidity offer maximum security as well as complete privacy.

Dwarf fruit trees *and junipers espaliered against this fence, and a slim planter of ivy, create a green divider along the narrow side yard between neighboring houses. Plantings and fence design must be kept simple in such a restricted area so appearance is not cluttered or cramped. Fence is stepped down where height is not needed.*

From the street side, *this louvered fence (fronted by a green lawn and full hedge) partially hides the forecourt and parking area of the house. It also provides a pleasant decorative accent to an otherwise plain entranceway.*

Above the surface, *on a raised bed of ground, the "screening power" of this fence is increased without adding to its height—which may be limited by law. Panels of translucent plastic are framed with redwood.*

73

This solar screen was constructed in front of living-room windows to reduce intensity of late afternoon sun. Alternating vertical and horizontal panels contrast well with predominantly horizontal lines of house. Zoning bylaws prohibited building any structure more than four feet high between front property line and building line of house. Owners built screen as a kind of test case and, on appeal, the bylaws were amended.

Translucence of plastic screen creates dramatic shadow effects. Here the lovely lines of palms produce a decorative pattern that is particularly well suited to an entryway—more so than if the wall at left were continued.

A narrow screen can often do the work of a much wider one. This screen separates a small area in front of glass-walled living room from the rest of the terrace, thus preserving the important aspect of privacy on both sides.

Split-bamboo screening, *purchased by the roll, is used to cover the back of a neighbor's rather unattractive high fence. The crushed rock in the raised bed at base of the fence prevents the soiling of bamboo by water splashing off bare, muddy ground. Bamboo plants (with their long, graceful stems and delicate green leaves) and the wicker furniture harmonize perfectly in color and in character with the bamboo fencing in the background.*

Garden Steps for Design and Change of Grade

Steps are naturally required in gardens where the grade is steep and there is need to walk from one level to another. But most gardens, even those that appear flat, have changes in grade, and steps can be used to advantage even if they are not a strict necessity. There are also other reasons why steps are a welcome addition to a garden. For example, their materials alone often have a decorative value, constructed as they usually are of weathered stone, old brick, textured concrete or wood, and edged with plants. They offer, in short, an opportunity for adding design interest to a garden.

Steps also lend an air of warmth and hospitality to a garden. If they are properly made they are an invitation to a comfortable stroll from one level to another. In Chapter 10 you will find instructions on building steps. But, first, there are some things to consider in the planning stage.

Garden steps must be large enough in scale to relate to the outdoors. It is not enough to duplicate the size of indoor steps in the garden; they will be much too small. Remember, too, that outdoor steps rarely have handrails. This requires that they be stable under foot, not slippery or too steep or too shallow, with proper proportions of tread and riser. Steps look best when edged with a softening border of flowers and shrubs. Such plantings help reduce the hard "manufactured" look that steps may have and make them more a part of the garden.

Worn flagstones are used here for steps winding gracefully up an embankment. Almost covered in places with low-lying plants, the steps have become an integral part of the garden, seeming to grow out of the ground.

A stone landing is often necessary to break up steps that are too steep or too long. Note the width and depth of the steps. Indoors such proportions would be out of scale, but outdoors they work well.

Slabs of cast concrete are solid and heavy enough to stay in place when set directly on the ground.

A long flight of steps is in itself a decorative vertical accent. These are made of railroad ties.

Railroad ties, with choice plants in the spaces between, make a good transition from terrace to lawn.

Decorative grouping of giant log rounds and well-placed native boulders makes an imaginative design for outdoor steps. The shapes and their relationship are dramatic enough to stand alone as informal garden sculpture. In constructing steps like these, where standard forms and techniques are not used, care must be taken to make the foundation perfectly solid and firm. Power equipment is required for lifting.

77

Pleasures of Arbors, Gazebos and Pavilions

The need for shelter is basic to man and there is always something pleasant and appealing about sitting outdoors, free from the confinement of four walls, and yet partially sheltered by some kind of roof or ceiling from whatever may be going on overhead. Anything will do, from a beach umbrella to a terrace roof, but three of the most charming and decorative shelters are the arbor, gazebo and pavilion.

An arbor is essentially a light, open framework designed to support climbing vines or shrubs. It may be small and free-standing, no more than a graceful trellis arching over a seat or bench, or it may be a simple colonnade with a latticework roof or ceiling covered with a tracery of green foli-age and often attached to the house or other structure where it might double as a cover for a shady path or quiet terrace.

Gazebos and pavilions, on the other hand, are small, ornamental garden houses that are roofed, open on the sides, and usually include seats or benches. A gazebo (also called a belvedere) was originally built as a pleasant shelter from which to view the surrounding landscape, hence the name derived from the verb "to gaze." A pavilion is much like a gazebo except that it may be somewhat larger. In former times on the great estates, it was usually more elaborate or classic in design, often built in the form of a small Greek temple with the familiar domed ceiling resting on a circle of columns.

Dense foliage *cascading over the fence could in time become a problem. A good solution is an arbor like this made of a framework of metal pipe. The vines continue their growth on wires stretched across the top.*

Made of roughhewn lumber *and sturdily built, this arbor is strong enough to take the weight of a mature grape vine. Attached to the side of this one-story house, the arbor, with its covering of green foliage, not only extends the roofline horizontally but also becomes an attractive decorative border that provides shade and gives shape and definition to both house and terrace.*

◀ **Shade for the terrace** *is provided by this classically simple arbor attached to the house. Such a straightforward structure is a visual extension of the house as well as a support for vines planted next to the house or by the posts. The decorative effect of the plants is doubled by allowing them to spill over and eventually cover the latticed arbor ceiling, creating a cool, green canopy for the terrace below.*

▶ **This Japanese pavilion** *with its handsome screens of plastic panels seems to float over this corner of the garden where the interesting pattern of grass and light gravel also has an Oriental character. Japanese simplicity and a "planned bareness" are seen here in the uncluttered lines of the building and in the gracious but sparse furnishings, actually no more than a low table and four cushions.*

This rustic gazebo is perfectly at home in its informal, woodsy setting. Such simple structures of logs and branches were traditional in Canada in the 19th century, often thatched with straw and situated at the end of a long walk through a wooded park or on a hillside overlooking the landscape beyond. The wood should be treated with a preservative, and if the ground stays damp the platform should rest on concrete piers.

Light and elegant, *this high-roofed gazebo or pavilion has an Oriental look without laboring the point. The roof is made more interesting by the extension of the beams, plates, ridgepole and roof cap. Simple benches are set back, leaving adequate floor space for additional seating and tables, and the deck is built so that it floats nicely over the sloping site.*

▶**The designer** *calls this gazebo an "Instant Shade Tree," although the roof has been left partially open to let in some light. For protection from the rain, the roof could be completely shingled. This interesting structure, with its strong architectural form, would be an eye-catcher in any garden. It is built of redwood, and cedar shakes.*

◀**More formal,** *as befits its setting, this handsome gazebo is ingeniously made of metal fencing attached to a framework of pipes. It is charmingly old-fashioned and delicate in design, but sturdy in construction. The entire framework (supported on metal pins) rests several inches off the concrete foundation, which is a good way to reduce rusting.*

81

Free Materials Used with Style And Imagination

This is a garden with a style adapted to the design of the house, the needs and interests of the family and the challenge of finding and working with the least expensive materials. In sympathy with these goals was the landscape architect who helped establish the overall concept and the relative size and location of the interrelated gardens.

Entry introduces materials used throughout the garden. Rough texture of the tie and crossarm fence contrasts with smooth stones of the walkway. Carved in the gatepost is hobo sign for "safe camp."

Railroad-tie walkway leads to the front door. Short timbers set on end mark the route and serve as seats. Problem of what to grow in shaded area is solved by handsome ground pattern of gravel, stones and ivy.

The owners and family did all the work. Most of the materials used were indeed free for the asking and carting away: old railroad ties from the railroad yard and telephone pole crossarms from the telephone company. Flat stones are from the shores of a nearby lake. Brick, concrete block and gravel were purchased.

Fences, edgings, walkways, steps and three small terraces were built with these materials. One is paved with stones at the entry, one with railroad ties and one with crossarms and gravel. The main structural materials, crossarms and railroad ties, relate beautifully. Both are modular, rectangular, weatherworn and informal in character.

While this garden of patterns may not suit everyone, there are many ideas here that can easily be adapted as accents in other kinds of gardens.

Sunken garden *is enclosed by railroad ties used for seating space. Bench made of ties set on concrete blocks at end of rock bed accentuates depth of the area. The railroad ties here relate to the fence of crossarms bordering the property. The rock, cactus and ivy accents are in keeping with emphasis throughout the garden on shape, design and texture rather than color.*

Shallow steps *are made with crossarm risers from the light company. They can be used here without cutting to fit. (Note thickness of lower riser in relation to adjacent railroad ties.) Three crossarms joined together form the bench seat. Holes in these arms, which once held insulators, make a decorative border. Ivy bed shown at right has edge of crossarms with mitered corners.*

The effect of a patchwork quilt on the ground is produced in the rear garden by building a series of walkways, surfaced areas and beds filled with an assortment of low plants and other textured materials. The areas are interrelated to create an overall design of striking composition and muted colors, textures and shapes. Seen in the two pictures of the patchwork garden on this page are beds of ivy, moss, brick crossarms, wood chips, pebbles, stones and grass. Vertical accents are potted plants, found objects (stone pillar and water hydrant behind birdhouse), tree stumps and a round table made from a cable spool.

Crossarm fence *borders property. The pieces are used as they come, without cutting. They are stacked to overlap at the ends so lengths of iron pipe can be dropped through the existing holes which once held the insulators.*

Crossarm bench *is set on concrete blocks in a bed of gravel. The bench is used for sitting in the sun and also as a display shelf for decorative accents such as this clay jug.*

Sandbox *at edge of "patchwork quilt" garden is also a sculptural object. The strong lines of the rectangular box are emphasized by raising it off the ground and placing a low bench on one side. Children enjoy the stand-up play.*

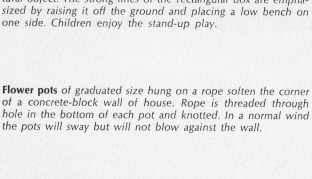

Flower pots *of graduated size hung on a rope soften the corner of a concrete-block wall of house. Rope is threaded through hole in the bottom of each pot and knotted. In a normal wind the pots will sway but will not blow against the wall.*

Outdoor Rooms with Screening

In some climates and at some seasons in most climates, outdoor living can be unpleasant without screening to protect against flying bugs and other pests, especially mosquitoes. Fortunately, modern screening is no longer the coarse, metallic, unattractive, quick-rusting material it used to be. There are now some decorative "fabrics" that offer more than protection from insects.

There is a louvered aluminum screen that lets in light and air but keeps out the heat of the sun. There are screens of vinyl-treated glass fiber that will not stretch, corrode, rust or lose their strength and resiliency upon prolonged exposure to the elements. These "plastic" screens are easiest of all to cut and handle, which is an advantage for do-it-yourself projects.

Galvanized screening was one of the first to be used. It is relatively inexpensive and is satisfactory for dry climates, but it will not hold up well where there is much rain. Copper is a handsome weather-resistant material but, compared to others, is on the expensive side.

Aluminum screening is a popular choice but it deteriorates in salt air or smog. It is also stiff and difficult to repair if dented or bent. A vinyl-coated aluminum is available and, while more expensive, is also more resistant to salt and smog. In choosing material for screening, look for these qualities: ease of handling and installation, resistance to change of color, or attack by mildew, or excess oxidization (which includes rust), and a readiness to withstand shrinking, snagging, stretching and denting. A screen can be a handsome surface when it is on a flat plane stretched tight, but it becomes unslightly when marred by bends or dents.

This handsome, *floating room is raised high above the downward-sloping lot for level access from the house and deck. Screening was used instead of glass in order to take advantage of the height to catch every passing breeze. It is cool as a treehouse, and insect-free.*

◀ **A double patio**—*part screened and part open—provides a pleasant outdoor setting for various times of year. Both areas are easily accessible from the house and from one another. Should the mosquitoes invade an evening gathering, it is easy to move into the screened room.*

▶ **Partial screening** *on opposite walls gives this study or guest house excellent cross ventilation. For more protection from heat and glare, aluminum screens composed of tiny louvers could be used. Sliding glass panels would make it usable all year long.*

◄ **Cool, shady,** *quiet and private, this handsomely designed outdoor room for relaxing, cooking and eating is built over a stream and surrounded by trees. Because such a location breeds a variety of crawling and flying pests, the room needs screening on the top and sides to make it a comfortable and inviting place to be.*

▶ **A deck** *or patio attached to a kitchen is a pleasant and convenient spot for family dining and entertaining. Where flying insects are a problem, it should be screened. Best in hot climates is louvered screening that cools the inside by reflecting the sun's rays and preventing accumulation of heat.*

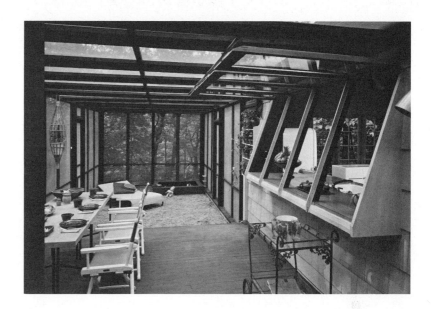

Added Uses for a Greenhouse

The prime purpose of a greenhouse is to provide a controlled climate for starting and growing plants that would otherwise not survive. Such an atmosphere must usually be somewhat on the warm and humid side and not particularly suited to human habitation. This is especially true in the summer when sunlight pours through the glass walls and roof.

In the cooler seasons of the year, however, a greenhouse can provide a lovely, "green" environment in which to spend comfortable hours surrounded by the color and fragrance of plants and flowers. A growing trend, with much to recommend it, is the practice of building greenhouses directly connected to the house, furnishing them as a conservatory and using them as additional rooms for living.

While not the best place for lively parties or large groups, a quiet corner of a greenhouse, with a table and a few chairs, is a charming spot for tea or cocktails, for a leisurely Sunday brunch or an afternoon of reading on a cold but sunny fall day.

A fountain or small pool among the plants can be an evocative addition. There should be a stable, quick-drying floor (brick on sand is good) and weatherproof furniture.

A veritable garden *has been created beneath this glass dome, with rocks, paving stones, a small pool and climbing vines—a far cry from the drab benches and boxes of potted plants found in most greenhouses.*

Attached directly to the main house off the living room, this greenhouse has a door between the two rooms for isolating any problems with heat or humidity that might develop. The workbench does not detract from the appeal of the setting with its attractive brick floor, rattan furniture and two small trees for shade.

The greenhouse sits in view of the terrace like a jewel box filled with lively color. It is connected to the house with a door and windows in the wall. In milder climates the connection could be sliding glass doors which would literally make the greenhouse a colorful extension of the room. In addition to the show it provides, the area can be used for starting seedlings in early spring for later planting in the garden.

Decorative Accents and Ideas

Decorative accents are pleasing arrangements in the landscape that catch the eye by means of contrast. Any material that looks well in a garden can be used: patterned paving, a plant related to its container and setting, such as a basket of vines hanging from a tree branch, sculpture or topiary (made by sculpting plant material). If the accent itself is outstanding, a lovely statue for instance, plants can be used alongside for emphasis and to relate the ornament to the rest of the garden. Put accents beside entries, on pathways or on a terrace to be seen from inside the house. That gardens are full of opportunities for accents is illustrated on the following pages.

A hanging flower pot *displays the graceful form of these fuchsias while decorating the bare wall behind it. Hanging flower pots can also be effectively used on fences, porch railings and on trees in the garden.*

A vertical shape *can be created by hanging baskets of flowers one above the other. As these flowers grow, more of the poles will be covered and so look less obtrusive. The baskets can also be easily rearranged.*

Natural-looking ground cover *is actually carefully planned. Smooth textures of the leaves contrast well with the rough surface of the rock. The clumps of daffodils add seasonal color as well as another texture.*

▶ **Any arrangement** of three different-sized containers looks good. These cast concrete bowls are filled (going from big to little) with geraniums, bedding begonias and pachysandra. Effect is multiplied by the reflection in the window.

Window boxes can create a front garden where no ground space is available for plants. The lamppost balances the planting opposite. These additions to the town house soften its abrupt entry and distinguish it from others on the street.

92

◀ **A special setting** adds importance to this statue. The two urns and ivy on the wall leading to the arbor help to create the focal point. The planting inside the arbor brings the statue into scale with the trellis.

The statuesque quality of these tree trunks is highlighted by concentric circles of flagstone and pachysandra ground cover. The complex patterns of stone and foliage are a pleasing contrast to the tree trunks.

Water falling over a rock into the pebbled concrete basin below is as much a pleasure to listen to as to look at. The yew branch is also reflected here.

Above right: A variety of shapes, colors and textures is used here to enliven the plain wall of concrete block. Particularly effective are the red and white flue tiles serving as a plant container.

Levels of fencing, plants and a statue turn a plain partition into an attractive garden wall. The need to block an ugly view, such as garbage cans or an outdoor storage area, or to fence off a section of garden, can be an opportunity to design a handsome setting. The high fence brings the whole arrangement into scale with the trees and draws attention to the beauty of their branches.

94

A bicycle basket *filled with cut flowers from the garden converts a simple gate into a charming entrance. During the winter, evergreen branches, colorful leaves or clusters of berries are used in the basket.*

▶ This upright juniper *adds new character to the deck corner. The shrub's texture is pleasantly related to that of the concrete planter, and the irregular branching relieves the angularity of the wall and floor.*

An attractive container *can enhance the beauty of the plant it holds and can itself be an important accent. Using pots solves the problem of how to grow plants where there is no ground for planting beds.*

Paint a water tub *and you have an attractive, inexpensive flower pot. A variety of containers are convertible into flower pots: watering cans, sturdy boxes, sections of sewer pipe and buckets, for instance.*

95

A raised planter *doubles as a border for steps that lead to a below-the-ground entrance. The shapely spreading branches of the Japanese black pine make an effective bridge between the two levels.*

A hedge trimmed *into the shape of an animal, or in a geometric design, is a classic decorative touch to use in a formal or informal garden. Simple forms are not difficult to shape and to keep in trim.*

A sundial centerpiece *dictates the circular design of this garden. Sundials have been garden ornaments since ancient times. Their accuracy depends upon careful leveling and orientation.*

Colorful hydrangeas *highlight a handsome Oriental garden lantern and make an eye-catching composition with the graystone steps and tree trunks. As the seasons change, other flowers are used here.*

Beauty of Water in the Garden

When pleasure gardens first began, in Babylon and Egypt 2000 years ago, water played an important role and it has been a treasured part of English, Spanish, Japanese, Italian and Chinese gardens ever since. Water naturally relates to plant life and its characteristics add pleasure to the garden. A placid reflecting pool puts a patch of sky on the ground. Sunlit water has the sparkle of life, and the sound of running water is the music of nature. Water cools the air, attracts birds and has a soothing effect on man himself. No garden is too small to benefit from its use. Even a gallon in a tin bowl on a small patch of grass can be a delight.

A quick and easy way to make a garden pool for water plants and fish is to sink a galvanized washtub into the ground. Camouflage the edge with planting. Another inexpensive method is to mold cut-to-fit plastic material such as a transparent shower liner to the inside of a scooped out hole in the ground. The edges can be tucked under the surrounding turf. Small, inexpensive recirculating pumps are now available. These will shoot water up through a fountain, or will pump it to a higher point to cascade into an artificial stream. You can make a microclimate for a cool green grotto of ferns and moss by letting water trickle down a wall. To do this run a small pipe from a hose bib to the top of a wall and put a well of gravel at the base to take up the overflow that doesn't evaporate on the way down.

This watery jewel *is activated by a submersible pump hidden under the concrete platform, and the sound of the water falling into the pool is as refreshing as the sight. Fountains and decorative sprays are available at garden supply centers, fountain specialty companies and through landscaping services.*

Sculptured waterfall *enlivens a corner of this walled garden. Recirculating pump submerged beneath lilies at far end of pool forces water through a pipe concealed in the middle of concrete blocks set in tiers to create splash and sparkle.*

Reflecting pool *is a charming small accent for a quiet corner of a garden and attracts the pleasurable company of birds. Choice rocks are used for contrast of texture and also to prevent the soil from spattering the water when it rains.*

A hot city garden *is cooled by this shallow brick pool and spray of water recirculated by a submersible pump. For maximum effect pool is full width of garden. Decorative stepping-stones in the water connect the two living areas that are paved.*

99

A woodland waterfall can be simulated with a good design and a recirculating pump. The best design is that which looks the most natural. Thoughtful observation and sketches of existing waterways are the best sources for inspiration. Colorful plants are set in the rich soil between the rocks. Ferns add to the natural effect.

Planting Beds and Colorful Features

In grandmother's day the typical garden was an expanse of lawn bordered with a profusion of annuals and perennials backed by a row of flowering shrubs. Grandmother may also have had a knowledgeable, hardworking gardener to trim and weed the beds and change plants for continual bloom.

The typical home garden of today is confined to a small plot of land, and the maintenance must be done by a husband and wife who seldom have the time or know-how to care for a big display of flowers.

The best way to make a significant show of color in limited space (with minimum work) is to concentrate flowers in small areas that are made for them. Think of the flowers as jewels, and design the planting beds to set them off to best advantage. As illustrated here, the beds may be formal or naturalistic. The first consideration is harmony. Relate the setting to the overall design of the garden—in size, location and character—then choose flowers that are the right height and color for the situation.

Planting beds make it easier to weed and to maintain well-defined edges. Soil in the limited space of a bed can be conditioned to suit the needs of plants. Raised beds make watering more efficient by preventing runoff and holding water in the root area.

A bed of tulips edged with pansies creates a bright panel of color accentuated by the plain surface of the stockade fence. The espaliered pear is an effective point of interest on the fence. The flagstone border of the bed, indented to make a pattern of small areas, is also a mowing strip and establishes an edge that's wide enough to walk on.

This informal planting of hardy flowers, shrubs and vines gives the impression of natural growth. The planting is in keeping with the country-style house, as is the untrimmed grass between the stones in the walkway. When plants are grouped informally, they require little care beyond an occasional trimming, watering and a little weeding.

Two separate areas, one for dining, and one for sitting, are created by the long rectangular planting bed. Keeping the plants low and in the same square dimension as the concrete patio slabs gives the effect of an inset panel of decorative tiles. The ends of the bed serve as edges for the steps and help to unify the overall design.

Most informal, *but nevertheless a planting bed, is this impressive splash of color set among rocks. The rock also serves to retain the upper level and establish a uniquely attractive edge between the two levels.*

◀ **Seats around** *the edge separate bed from patio and are useful as well. The original slope was maintained around the tree to avoid disturbing its roots. Patio in foreground was terraced to minimize the grading.*

Unusual planting of corn in this driveway is attractive and useful. The stalks block sight of driveway from patio during the outdoor living season, enliven the black Tarmac and provide delicious fresh corn for the table.

▼ **Checkered pattern** of alternating gravel and planted beds is, in effect, a decorative extension of the concrete patio. The combined wood and brick edging is an attractive device for keeping the gravel neatly in its place.

◀ **Colorful masses** of lantana, in foreground, and beds of begonias are edged with special rounded brick set on a slant. These flowers bloom continuously for most of the outdoor living season where the climate is mild.

Set like a jewel, *this circular bed, packed with clusters of chrysanthemums in variety, sparkles in the sun against the smooth green of the lawn. The height and placement of the flowers have been carefully planned to create the orderly rounded effect.*

▼**For a big display** *of summer color this bed of perennials is wider than most. The brick edging gives a sense of order and symmetry to the mass of flowers. The brick makes a mowing strip, and the edge of the grass is therefore easy to maintain.*

105

Lighting in the Garden

It is unlikely that the proud possessor of a garden would choose to relinquish the pleasure of seeing it at night, once the opportunities for the imaginative use of electricity were fully understood. The play of light on gently moving leaves, for example, can be endlessly fascinating, and a tree or shrub lit from below, above or from the sides reveals new dimensions of color and form.

Even grass, rocks, a brick wall or path, and especially water, become unusually evocative and beautiful when touched with light. Some gardens, in fact, seem more lovely at night than during the day.

As a general rule, the most successful fixtures for garden lighting are those that are least conspicuous. The exceptions are the rare fixtures that reveal a beautiful form when lit from within.

A well-lit garden can be a pleasure not only out-of-doors or for the summer season. Lighting can be arranged to be seen from inside in all weather and all seasons.

Lighting, of course, is not only decorative.

It is functional as well. Good light is imperative for safety at night. It is required for illuminating steps, paths and those obstacles likely to be stumbled over by unwary guests. Any kind of garden light is some insurance against intruders, although the powerful floodlights recommended are hardly decorative and should probably be independent units controlled from inside the house.

Outdoor lighting systems of 110 volts must be carefully installed with insulated cables properly buried and protected from plunging spades and hoes. This is work that only a professional electrician should do. However, the new low-voltage systems (in which the dangerous 110-volt current is put through a transformer and reduced to a safe 6 volts) are comparatively easy to install.

(Caution: some provinces require that all electrical systems be installed by electrical contractors; all require the work to be checked by an examiner.)

See also page 422.

Overhead lights *in the trees convert this patio into a perfectly lit area for dining. The rather hard planes and angles of the house are also interestingly lit, in contrast to the softness of the foliage and lawn.*

The dramatic quality *of light casting large shadows on a wall is clearly illustrated here. In direct opposition is the quiet beauty of light coming from under water and softly outlining plants and the wall mosaic.*

A pool of light *is what every swimming pool can become after dark. For those who enjoy a night swim—and who doesn't?—such a pool with its sunken lights is a necessity, but the glow of bluish light also has a decorative quality and creates a wonderfully romantic atmosphere for a summer party or quiet rendezvous.*

Strong floodlights *are used to provide adequate light for the approach to this house. The rocks that jut into the driveway could be a hazard in the dark, but when lit their decorative qualities are revealed.*

Versatility of lighting *is illustrated here. Sculptural branches of the tree are dramatically defined and cast decorative shadows, dining area in rear is lit, shrubs are accented as are the three roof beams.*

4

Places for Play and Work

Year-round Family Play Yard

Wherever there are children, they will find a place to play. It may be the public park, the school yard, the vacant lot or the sidewalk or street. But the park may be some distance from home, the school yard may be overcrowded, the vacant lot may be undergoing construction—and the hazards of the street are well known to all. Therefore, the more facilities for play you can provide at home, the more your children can enjoy their leisure hours in safety and comfort. Here on these pages is one family's solution to the problems—a complete playground environment built in a backyard; and used, incidentally, by the adults almost as much as by children.

The overall play area shown in the drawing at right is 30 by 40 feet, which is about half the area needed for a tennis court, but it offers the fortunate youngsters, and adults, almost unlimited opportunities for recreation. In addition to handball and basketball, the hard flat surface is good for bicycle and tricycle riding, dancing, roller-skating, ice-skating (when the surface is flooded and frozen in winter), skipping, hopscotch and all the favorite sidewalk games. There is ample space for developing a pitcher's arm or

Continued on page 112

For skating, *the play area is flooded. To prevent leakage, asphalt surface is joined to railroad ties to form a waterproof joint.*

108

20'

12'

20'

18'

30'

FIRE PIT

HANDBALL COURT

QUARTZ LIGHT

BASKETBALL COURT

GIANT CHECKERS

109

Plants and Houses

One encouraging aspect of moving into a new subdivision or housing project is the fact that your own house and all the others will look better and better as the years go by. They will, that is, if you plant trees and shrubs as soon as you move in.

Suburban houses, which are often at their worst when new, can become beautiful neighborhoods over the years. The good examples range from coast to coast. The trees rise up to soften the skyline, which becomes an undulating panorama of changing colors rather than the stark rectangular edges of the housetops. As the trees and shrubs in the foreground grow and show off their flowers and foliage, the houses seem to move gracefully back from the street and to separate from one another as islands of screening develop. Plants help soften the impact of the elements around a house. They catch the rain, break up the wind, provide shade and help keep the inside of the house cool. Plantings become points of year-round interest to be enjoyed from indoors. In the front yard they are a welcoming sight for family, friends and passersby. There is, on every attractive suburban street, good evidence that plants and houses belong together. Many of the effects you find pleasing in other places can often be adapted to your own. Look for the principles of the design rather than making exact duplications.

These flowering cherries *make a colorful wall for the outdoor terrace. They also create privacy and a lovely view for the screened room behind the terrace. The ground cover of Vinca minor (shown here in bloom) beneath* *the trees looks like a thick, textured rug. Imagine this view without trees: the skyline would be less interesting, the lines of the house would be harsh and it would not seem so well related to the site.*

110

This rock garden *is composed of stones and closely grown small flowers and plants. All of the plants grown here are an intimate part of the house, reminiscent of a country cottage garden.*

A few carefully chosen *elegant plants beside a house can have an effect far beyond their number. The silhouette of bamboo enhances this simple façade and is a pleasure to see from indoors as well.*

View of the garden *from this sun porch shows how the lovely, ancient boxwood (400 years old) becomes part of the interior décor. This added room was sited so the plant could be enjoyed the year around.*

Bold strip of color *parallels the length of the veranda. The zinnias have a long season of bloom and enliven the whole façade. Tree trunks hugging the house add a strong sculptural shape.*

Railroad ties *are used as a retaining wall and for seating on one side of the playground. The playwall also serves as a useful privacy screen. Note the brick firepit as a useful point of reference for the picture at right.*

Brick firepit *for bonfires and casual outdoor cooking has drainage at the bottom to prevent the accumulation of water. Foliage of the white pines on the property line almost hides the neighboring houses.*

sharpening up tennis or squash strokes—all within easy reach of a bandage, a cup of hot chocolate and a sympathetic parent's ear.

The firepit is useful for outdoor cooking of all kinds but is especially handy, on crisp winter and fall nights, for building bonfires and keeping pots of coffee warm. A giant checkerboard offers an interesting version of this game and doubles as a place for a card table and chairs. Outdoor lighting prolongs the use of the yard in the evenings.

The area was built well away from the house so as to reduce the inevitable sounds of active play. A screen of white pines provides privacy and at the same time protects the peace and beauty of the adjacent garden. The hard surface is asphalt—2 inches thick —laid on a 4-inch layer of gravel which rests on a 2-inch foundation of roadbed sand. A beige-colored asphalt paint has been used to seal the surface for winter flooding and to lighten the black color of the asphalt. The central drain can be plugged with a simple rubber cap in winter to retain water. The playwall, made of concrete blocks reinforced with steel rods, has an outer coating of cement which gives it the appearance of solid concrete. Three quartz lights—similar to those used for football and baseball games —are sufficient to simulate bright daylight on even the darkest night. Music can be piped in for dancing or skating.

You may not have the space or budget to create such elaborate facilities, but your children can find much pleasure and satisfaction in a smaller, less expensive project. By putting down a hard surface outside the garage, for example, and then reinforcing the garage wall with tongue-and-groove siding, you have a ready-made practice wall for tennis and handball, as well as a flat surface for sidewalk games. A basketball goal can be fixed to the wall with a metal bracket.

Before planning any such facilities, it is important to consult the local zoning regulations to make sure that outdoor lighting is allowed and that the play yard does not violate any setback requirements. You will also have to decide whether or not you are prepared for your backyard to become a meeting place for neighborhood children, because they are certain to congregate in such an attractive spot. But if you do have the space, the budget and the inclination, you will find that the backyard playground has benefits that far outweigh the shortcomings. In a society that is becoming more and more urban, where open spaces are disappearing, and public parks are sometimes distant and difficult to reach, this play area can become a safe, friendly place for recreation. It encourages the children to bring home their friends and establishes a happy background for childhood play.

More Ideas for Outdoor Fun

The complete play yard, as shown on the previous pages, is probably too expensive for most young families to afford. But, as was pointed out, many of the individual ideas illustrated there can be adapted and used in other situations. The same is true of the ideas for outdoor fun on the following pages. Some of them are simple, yet imaginative, while others are more elaborate and will be more expensive.

No matter how small or modestly equipped a play area may be, a child in the freedom of his imagination can make it into a multitude of faraway and fascinating places. A sandbox and a wading pool become part of the beach and ocean; a bush, a tree and an obliging cat are seen as a forest full of wild animals. The point is to provide something—anything—as a beginning, even though to you it may seem ordinary and unrewarding, and then relax. Children have ingenious ways of making much of very little. Quite often, in fact, they distrust things that are too elaborate or complex. The old cartoon of a child throwing away an expensive toy and playing with the box it came in is not without basis in fact.

Another reason for not investing too much in play equipment for younger children is the pace at which they outgrow it. Some things can be adapted to other uses. A sandbox can become a planting bed or base

A paved "highway" that circles out into the yard adds a whole new dimension for traveling on tricycles, within sight of but not too close to an adult seating corner. It is also a jogging track and an attractive walk.

Swing set, sandbox, climbing bars and, for wheeled toys, a large expanse of surrounding hard surface turn this area into a playground with a variety of amusements that makes it a neighborhood favorite.

Graceful and attractive, a putting green does not distract from, but rather adds to, the charm of the garden. Laid out near a sunbathing spot, the green is an invitation to relaxed play for children and adults.

A magnificent tree, the materials at hand and children's imagination created the unique quality of this tree house. No amount of planning can produce these happy accidents, but parental encouragement can be of help.

Shuffleboard, *the traditional sport of ocean travel, is an excellent game for older children and adults. It requires a space 52 feet long and 6 feet wide. Since it is not a strenuously active game, it does not need much clearance space and, as in the photo, can be bordered by shrubs and flowers without any great danger of plant damage.*

for a cold frame, and a splash pool might serve later as a birdbath. But the permanent equipment must be moved away when the children outgrow it. Such things as large and expensive swing sets, climbing frames and play houses can usually be justified only when there are younger ones coming along to use them.

However, hard surfaces for bicycle and tricycle riding or for a wide variety of sidewalk games are useful for all ages and prove to be well worth the money spent on them.

Also, don't overlook the value of a patch of grass for informal play. It is soft enough to be safe for jumping and falling and good for all kinds of rough-and-tumble games. If the ground is reasonably level and smooth, it will serve for croquet, badminton or volleyball. But don't expect a grass patch to have the finish of a fine lawn. This grass will get a lot of hard use and show it.

Another good idea, if there is space for it, is to allow a back corner of a lot to go uncultivated and let grow what will. This kind of home-grown "wilderness" has universal appeal to children. They can dig up the ground and plant their own gardens, set up

a camping site, have a campfire, put up tents for sleeping, build their shanty clubhouse, or simply enjoy the feeling of having a place that's mostly their own. Such a play area, however, not only requires space, but without parental supervision or group efforts at cleaning up, it may take on the unsavory appearance of a hobo jungle. In which case, the "campground" on the residential lot of average size will probably have to be more civilized than the youngsters would prefer.

At the beginning, it is best to plan and complete only one project at a time—maybe a simple rope fixed to a stout branch, or a load of heavy timbers nailed solidly together for climbing. This will satisfy immediate needs the children may have and, by watching them at play, you can perhaps better predict the kinds of things they will most enjoy in the future.

But if something you buy or build doesn't seem to catch on, don't despair. This month's disaster may be next month's favorite. Climbing, swinging, running and jumping are the proper work of every healthy child. If you give them the elbow room and a few facilities, they will do the rest.

114

A cleverly designed climbing frame (made by nailing together 8-by-8 timbers) offers a variety of challenges for young climbers. In fact, this entire play yard seems designed to test and develop a youngster's balance, strength and agility. A ground cover of tanbark is excellent for softening falls and, in addition, is attractive.

Old pilings, beautifully weathered, have been put to good and imaginative use in the construction of this unusual climbing unit. It is attractive to look at and has an obvious appeal and fascination for youngsters.

Solidly built and supported (as its height demands for safety's sake), this tree house, reached by a conventional stairway, offers a good second choice if youngsters become tired of the elaborate playhouse at right.

115

Swimming Pools and Facilities

A swimming pool can do more to increase a family's enjoyment of leisure hours together than almost any other addition to the garden. It provides a pleasant, healthful place for exercising and relaxation. And when properly planned, a swimming pool can enhance the landscape and serve as a center for entertaining.

While the popularity of pools—they are the fastest-growing home improvement today—has brought the cost within range of modest family budgets, the necessary and optional accessories still make it a considerable investment.

Adding a pool not only brings changes in the landscape and the family life style but there are some new responsibilities as well. It is extremely important to consider all of these factors before deciding to go ahead.

Wherever there is a pool there will certainly be guests—uninvited as well as invited—especially in neighborhoods with young children. Dressing rooms by the pool reduce wear and tear on the house. In cold climates it's worth checking into pool heaters too. For beauty's sake, the filtering and heating equipment is best camouflaged with plants or screened from view. And a pool can hardly be considered complete without a lounging area.

The most successful pools and facilities are carefully planned as a part of the landscape and the family's way of life. As rewarding as a pool can be, it should not be undertaken without full consideration of the original cost and subsequent maintenance.

Brick, gravel and wood *give to a standard rectangular pool the character appropriate to a woodsy setting. Once the pool is installed, the brick patio, planting beds and sundeck can be separate projects.*

Leveling the top *of a sloping site makes space for the pool on high ground well away from the house. This view of the pool at left shows its relationship to the patio on the lower level and to the house.*

To create the effect *of a natural pond this pool was built in an irregular shape with rocks, shrubs and trees overlapping its edge. The pool is a decorative feature in the total landscape as well as an inviting place to swim.*

◀ **A vine-covered hillside** *makes a stable slope and a dramatic backdrop for pool. The stone retaining wall helps keep pool clean by holding back surface runoff. Wood deck extends patio area over the sloping ground.*

A circular pool *beneath a gentle waterfall stepped down over a strata of rocks was inspired by natural settings in the mountains. A submersible pump is used to lift the water back to the top of the fall and keep it circulating.*

The sound of water *splashing from one level to the next complements the visual beauty of this waterfall (a closeup view of above picture). Umbrella-shaped lights by the steps and waterfall illuminate the peaceful scene at night.*

The kidney-shaped pool, *available as a standard from most contractors, fits well into small, uneven plots of land. The irregular shape of the paving and the circular terrace enhance the overall design.*

A small pool, *even in a city garden, can be the most important element in the landscape design. Here it's a cool oasis for sunbathing and relaxing on hot summer days and a pleasant wading place for children.*

Pool in the backyard *of a house set close to the neighbors gains privacy from the planting of thick, high trees and shrubs. These also provide good camouflage for pool equipment (such as a filter and heater) and cut the wind. Paving the area between the pool and house helps to prevent the tracking of debris indoors.*

An above-ground pool is portable, inexpensive and, while not especially attractive, can be improved by pleasant surroundings. Pool on concrete or brick surface prevents the tracking of mud and grass into the water.

A pool house can be a useful and attractive addition to the landscape. It can include storage space for pool equipment and furniture, bath and dressing facilities and space for a poolside kitchen and bar.

The geometric shape used here is a dramatic accent in the cliffside setting. Overhead shelter provides relief from a strong sun, and makes a covered bridge across the pool to the seating area overlooking the view.

This guest house with bedroom, bath, kitchen and open dining area also has space to store pool equipment. Drawing the curtains around the dining area cuts wind and rain and creates an additional private room.

A concrete pool and patio in this country place is the modern replacement of the old swimming hole in a nearby stream. The roof over the screened porch has been extended out to the pool to make a sloping sunshade. Insulation under the wooden sunshade roof increases the protection from a scorching summer sun. Flowers and a vegetable plot naturalize the scene and add color and character to the pool area.

Work Centers and Storage Areas

The clutter of garden tools and equipment on permanent display in most suburban garages is mute evidence of the widespread need for more storage space. And when the storage is built, it takes little more money and effort to provide a bench and a few other facilities for such chores as potting up plants and keeping them in shape. A source of water, even if nothing more than a hose bib, is one useful addition to consider.

A shed for storage can often be attached to the back of a garage or side of a house. It need not be unsightly if the design is in good scale with the setting and if the finish is of the same material as the structure to which it is attached. If a free-standing building is in order, it should also relate in scale and finish but, beyond that, it offers an opportunity for imaginative design.

If the structure is for wheeled goods such as barrows, mowers and carts, the door must be wide enough for easy entry, and there should be a ramp so the equipment can be readily rolled in and out. All wall space can be used for hanging tools, and space under the high part of the roof is good for overhead storage of seasonal things such as seat cushions, hammocks and barbecues.

Unobtrusive storage facility *can be attached to a fence, as here, or to the side of a garage or house. It can be built of any material but is most attractive when made to blend in with the adjacent structure. The roof of this one is waterproof so that power equipment can be safely stored. Picture at left shows openings along the side and at one end. For information on the construction of this storage-fence see page 407.*

Convenient walk-in storage space *is large enough to house not only toys but terrace furniture at the end of the day; or, in case of rain, it's easy to put everything away. The unit is attractively designed to be an integral part of the trellislike structure that borders one end of terrace. Privacy screening can be an added advantage.*

Solid and simple, *this storage unit is large enough for all kinds of garden and lawn tools, including wheelbarrows and lawn mowers. The walks and two double doors give easy access to everything stored inside.*

◀**One end** *of this utility building is used for shallow storage space with easy access from the outside. Garbage cans fit behind louvered doors. Recessed wall keeps firewood orderly and reasonably dry.*

Garbage cans *are excellent containers for needed supplies of loose materials, such as soil, sand, peat or compost. Here the cans are tilted on a notched baseboard to make it easy to reach in with scoop or shovel.*

Plastic containers *fitted through holes of pull-out shelves are handy for storing planting materials. Hinged top lifts to reveal storage space behind pails. The sturdy bench is partially shaded with lath to protect potted plants.*

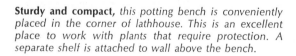

Corner of a paling fence *was put to good use here to form this simple but adequate work area. Bins for peat, soil or sand beneath the table are grooved at sides to accept additional boards and adjust the height.*

Sturdy and compact, *this potting bench is conveniently placed in the corner of lathhouse. This is an excellent place to work with plants that require protection. A separate shelf is attached to wall above the bench.*

124

A work center can be a colorful and decorative addition to a landscape, as illustrated by this combination lath house and potting area. Work benches are screened by the facing of horizontal boards and, as with any open structure, the shadow pattern becomes an important part of the design. Such a building, located strategically, can also serve as a property divider and a screening device for privacy if it is needed.

Spacious, well-designed work center has large wooden bins for potting mixtures, fertilizers and soil amendments. Bins have pins on either side at the bottom so they can pivot out easily from the top. Overhanging roof is partly solid to protect seedlings, cuttings and young plants from direct sunlight, and partly constructed of lath in order to cast a light shade and to allow for the necessary ventilation.

What We Can Learn From the Japanese

Oriental gardens, as originally created by the ancient emperors of China, were rich in the symbolism of philosophy and religion, and when the Chinese concepts of garden design were brought to Japan, many of these religious elements were retained. Although an understanding of the mystical aspects of Japanese design is a rewarding study in itself, the main appeal of Japanese gardens is in their remarkable beauty, in the lessons to be learned from the subtlety and serenity of their composition, and from the Oriental's deep understanding and appreciation of nature.

Even in Japan, the aesthetic considerations are becoming more important than the religious. And in this country it is the charm and character of the design alone upon which the Japanese garden must stand or fall.

Because the forebears of many of our landscape de-

Relate the Garden to the House and Surrounding Scene

Japanese houses and gardens are designed as one unit within a larger setting. The wooden house is usually close to the street with a wall to separate the small entry garden. Upon entering the house, its relationship to the garden is apparent at once. From each sliding door, a carefully arranged natural scene is revealed to the viewer. The garden appears as a tiny world comprising foreground plants to establish a visual point of reference, a strong middle-distance feature of water, sand or rocks, and finally an enclosure of greenery to block undesirable neighboring views. Background planting is often arranged to allow a glimpse of a distant hill or forest which then becomes a part of the "borrowed scenery" of the garden. These principles have universal application.

signers were European, most of our heritage is from the royal gardens and great estates of Britain, France and Italy. The elaborate European gardens are essentially formal in arrangement and show a fascination, if not obsession, with geometrical form. They serve to demonstrate the belief that man is the master of nature. And even the less formal gardens of Britain are so vast as to overwhelm the viewer with their grandeur.

In the Orient, on the other hand, the designs are informal and asymmetrical and are related to the human being in their scale. Man is meant to be a participant in the scene, but he does not dominate it. These gardens, reverently created of plants, stone, earth and water, invite the viewer to come in and then lead him subtly through a series of pleasant discoveries in form, texture, line and muted color. The plantings are never out of proportion to their immediate environment, but are always related to a house or other man-made structure.

Japanese gardens are based on a set of time-tested principles that, when understood as *principles* and not just quaint effects, can be of value in all landscape design.

On the following pages some of these concepts are illustrated and explained. Each picture was chosen to illustrate one particular point, but each picture also demonstrates some of the other principles as well.

Idealize the Natural Setting

The essential elements in nature that appeal most to the human eye are readily recognized by the Japanese. In creating a natural scene in a small garden space, only the most desirable and thoughtfully chosen components are used. Rocks, still or flowing water, river pebbles, sand and plants are selected to express their own essential characteristics. They are then combined to simulate a fondly remembered fragment of nature. Although the scene may be idealized, the elements are naturally weathered and are of proper size for the setting they are in. The Japanese also meticulously avoid exposing any indication of the hand of man in the construction of "natural" settings. Remember that the Japanese garden is never a "miniature," but is designed to have the appearance of a full-scale abstraction of nature.

Dramatize the Nature of Materials

Every garden depends on natural elements, such as rocks, water, pebbles or plants. But from the Japanese we can learn the value of revealing the particular beauty of these elements, either by isolation or display against a contrasting background.

In a Japanese garden, an entire area may be given over to displaying a single rock surrounded by nothing but raked sand. Such a setting accentuates the character of the rock without the distraction of other elements. The same idea is used for favorite plants and pieces of sculpture.

Careful pruning can create a lacework pattern against the ceiling of the sky, as with this Japanese maple.

"Still" water should be placed so it is lively with reflections, raindrops and the wind on its surface.

Another way to dramatize water is to channel the flow for the sound as well as the sight of movement.

Patterns of sun and shade are in constant change and alter the shape and surface of this cone of sand.

Create Pattern on the Ground

In a culture rooted strongly in the belief that the earth and the sea are the source of all things, and in a land of strictly limited space, the Japanese garden designer makes the most of every resource. Even the surface of the ground is looked upon as an opportunity for imagination in design. Low-growing plants are used in patterns on bare ground or combined to make a design of contrasting textures. Stones are used to create intricate figures in paving, and sand is raked with geometrical precision. Such possibilities exist in every landscape.

Lines and circles *raked in a coarse-sand ground cover catch the slanting sun and the shadow of pine.*

Stepping-stones, *spaced to the average step of a man, form an abstract pattern crossing a roof-eave drip block.*

Pattern within pattern *is another means of enrichment, as the linear ridges on the round millstone.*

◀**Suggesting islands** *on a sea, these plantings are beautifully spaced on a panel of swept sand.*

129

Establish a Sense of Line

In almost every pleasing Japanese garden scene, there is a visible or invisible line connecting the strong elements of the overall design. This line, often curved, holds the various parts of the garden together visually. When two or more adjoining materials meet, a line is formed, as in the meeting of water, grass and raked gravel in the Japanese garden at right. By using this meeting point of materials in a strong, continuous, flowing curve, a sense of coherence and pleasing unity is achieved with a minimum of effort. Such a garden "line" can either be seen or sensed in almost all of the photographs on these pages.

Reveal Texture and Form

The Japanese have mastered the principle of combining a diversity of plant forms and textures to achieve interest. All plants have definite characteristics and most can be pruned to accentuate these qualities. Here the formalized rounded azaleas at the water's edge are contrasted with the maple, which is trimmed to accentuate its flowing form. The tight texture of the trimmed azaleas also contrasts with the lacy openness of the tree. The foreground reeds give a unifying "grace note" to the scene. These techniques, along with the use of a limited number of choice adaptable plants, can all be easily applied in any garden.

130

Accent Shape with Light

At certain times of day or in certain seasons a garden scene or object may be highly dramatized by sun and shadow. The basic point to keep in mind is that the form of an object is more clearly defined when viewed from the shadow side than from the sunny side. Reflections from top surfaces and light at the edge of solid objects also sharply define their form. Translucent objects such as leaves are dramatized by the sunlight shining through. By studying the movement of sun and placing plants and sculptural objects in the proper relation to it, the gardener can most effectively utilize the dramatic values of light and shadow.

Slanting sun *lights the translucent leaves of a Japanese cherry in contrast to the shadow side of stonework.*

Pattern *of stepping-stones and their circular shape is accentuated when viewed looking toward the light.*

Invite the Curious Eye

Small gardens have the inherent weakness of revealing all their treasures at a single glance. The Japanese, with stringently limited garden space, have learned from necessity that sustained interest is maintained by screening out the choice views or featured highlights and exposing them only after building up a few moments of suspense. Even walkways of richly textured paving and adjacent foliage patterns, as illustrated in the path at right, are of greater interest when the path turns ahead to suggest pleasures yet to come.

In applying this principle, we must also learn from the Japanese that once such expectations are aroused, there should always be something interesting to see and enjoy as one turns the path. If the scene is set for a visual accent, there can be a sense of disappointment if it's missing.

Display Choice Objects

The Oriental way with sculptural accents is, first, to choose only a few pieces of exceptional quality. These are then displayed in carefully selected settings where they can readily be enjoyed, yet hidden enough to be in quiet keeping with the scene. The Japanese do not use a strong visual axis to emphasize garden features as we do in the West. Pieces are placed after the turn of a path, against a wall similar in color or texture to the piece itself, or partially screened by a handsome planting. Favored objects are made of natural materials that become more beautiful as they age. These are principles to consider in planning any garden.

Through a doorway *framed in cypress, a stone lantern stands slightly aslant—a subtle, planned imperfection.*

In a setting of plants, *this grouping of rocks, stone basin and sculpture is carefully related in size.*

Unusual objects *but certainly choice, these colorful carp give movement and grace to the usually still water.*

On a panel of raked sand, *one treasured rock is displayed, strongly suggestive of an island in the sea.*

Control the Man-Made Accents

The emphasis on nature in the Japanese garden must ultimately be qualified by the intrusion of man. Without the human element there is no garden—only jungle, desert or wilderness. But in Japan the structures are pleasant unobtrusive accents. Natural materials, usually unpainted, are often used for such subtle relationships as this viewing platform and the raked sand, water and old pines.

5

How to Remodel
The Landscape You Have

Improving the Entryway

Most landscaping is actually a matter of remodeling an existing situation. Only brand-new homes offer the challenge (and opportunity) of bare ground to begin with.

Remodeling is a more leisurely process than planning a garden from scratch. There's no urgent need to cover the brown earth. It's better to come to the right decisions slowly than to rush in and make mistakes that will annoy you for years.

While remodeling plans should always be a part of a total landscape project, the work can be done one area at a time. Where better to begin than by improving the entryway? On the following pages are examples of good ways to handle this important part of the landscape. Basic principles of design are shown here, and they can be creatively applied to many situations whether in remodeling a garden or building a new one.

Deck in Front of the House

If there is not enough space for comfortable outdoor living in back of the house, there may be room in front. This generous wooden deck on the street side, for example, has the friendly effect of the traditional narrow front porch with its swing and rockers. The area is rectangular and has the added advantage of space for tables and chairs and plenty of room to walk around them. While a front deck is not as private as a backyard patio, it can be partially screened from view as this one is or, if local regulations permit, can be completely enclosed with fences or planting. If the deck or terrace requires privacy from the front walk, a divider such as the tall wooden panel shown here can be added. This screen also adds architectural interest to a plain façade. Planting helps to supplement the screening and also softens its lines.

This modern version of a front porch is on public view and requires good-looking, well-arranged furniture always kept in order. The deck is slightly raised above lawn and is sloped for proper drainage.

The old walk *forced a procession in single file on a surface that was uneven, cracked and ragged at the edges. Both the walk and drive were paved with asphalt and there was no clear delineation of the entry.*

The new walk *is a welcoming extension of the house. Its width accommodates two people side by side and the edges are clearly defined. The section of brick paralleling the driveway is for stepping out of the car.*

Add an Inviting Entry Walk

This handsome house shared a problem with many others of its era. The undistinguished character of the entryway, above left, did not offer an aspect of welcome. The remodeled version, on the right, is much more inviting. The walk was paved with brick to make it a visual extension of the brick house. It is wide, solid and safe to walk on. The section of brick laid parallel to the driveway clearly indicates where cars are to stop and provides space for getting out of the front and back doors without stepping on the grass. The 2-x-4 edging around the entryway clearly defines the area while also serving as a mowing strip.

Low shrubs and ground cover have replaced the high foundation plantings set too close to the house, and the wide beds increase the mass of the whole entryway so that it is in better balance with the house.

The foundation *required depends on severity of climate. Entry-walk brick is laid on two inches of sand tamped on leveled soil. The 2-x-4s on edge, capped with 2-x-4s laid flat, hold brick securely.*

135

Fencing for Privacy on Street Side

Many houses are built so near the street that there is no room for a proper front lawn or garden. Such narrow frontage can be turned to good advantage by using it for an outdoor living room as was done here.

The façades of the house and fencing become the walls of the "room," and the slope of the hill is graded to establish two levels for the outdoor living area. Using this idea is feasible only where local ordinances permit fencing on the front property line. Check carefully before making plans.

Entryway is indicated *by a light and house number on the fence post. The board-and-batten fence is designed so the bottom slopes with the hill and the top runs parallel with the lines of the house.*

The entry level *carries the hard-surfaced, easy-to-clean concrete of the sidewalk up to the front door behind the chimney. Wood, more appropriate to a living area, is used for flooring on the lower level.*

In this inviting corner *enclosed by a solid fence there's no feeling that a public sidewalk is only three feet away. The raised bed by the steps adds significantly to the height of the tree, which will soon give ample shade. Planting at the base of the fence provides color. The wall decoration helps create the effect of a living area.*

Planting for Privacy on Street Side

A border of small trees or large shrubs in front of a house can establish as much privacy as fencing and usually looks less forbidding. In three or four seasons the hemlocks flanking this entry garden will completely screen it from the street. The tall oak tree gives cool shade, and the informal plantings accentuate the woodsy appearance. In towns where planting is allowed along the front property line, and structures of any kind are not, this may be the only way to achieve such privacy.

Easy maintenance *was the main reason for paving this front garden. A circular pattern of Belgian block was laid around the oak tree, and the adjoining area is plain brick. Both surfaces need only an occasional hosing down. The paving is set on sand so water will reach the tree roots. Plants grow over the edges of the paving and little if any trimming is required.*

The picture at the right, *taken about eight years later, shows how the hemlocks have grown up and formed a high, dense screen that establishes complete privacy from the street side.*

137

Walkway of Brick

The improvement in the remodeled walkway below is largely due to its generous width and the gentle curve extending from the front door to the drive. These changes more clearly define the walkway and make it more inviting. Now with the addition of brick, evergreens, gravel and birch trees there's an interesting variety of textures and color to enjoy on the way to the entrance which is clearly marked by a handsome white planter. Removing the thick high shrubs reveals the attractive façade, lets more sunlight into the house and permits a better view of the front garden. To maintain the needed sense of separation from the street, the low hedge of evergreens has been planted at the left.

A typical problem in front landscaping is overgrown shrubs too close to the house. The ones here are also too varied and planted without thought to creating a sense of order. The walkway is also too narrow.

Inviting curve of the new walk is accented by gravel, which also contrasts nicely with the evergreen foliage of the pines and junipers. As all mulches do, the gravel eliminates rain spatter, keeps moisture in the soil and discourages weeds. Curved planting beds reduce the cold look of too wide an expanse of brick paving.

Flagstone Entry Terrace

A house is sometimes so close to the street that a lawn cannot do it justice. Replacing the grass with a broad entry terrace is a good way to handle such a problem. The generous dimensions of the flagstone terrace shown here provide a solid base in proportion to the house and room for a comfortable seating area. The flagstone terrace relates to the stone trim of the house and it also serves as a link between the sidewalk and front door. The way to the entry is clearly indicated by wide steps paralleling the driveway from the street. To simplify maintenance, the front lawn has been eliminated completely. Low shrubs cover the ground from the railroad ties to the sidewalk and between the terrace and façade.

From the driveway (note car at right) the only access to the front door was across the grass. Since most arrivals are by car, this is obviously impractical. Here, too, the house is overwhelmed by the mass of plantings.

One solution to walking across grass from the driveway to the front door is to replace the lawn with a broad entry terrace. This one is stepped down to the level of the drive. Light at left marks steps up from sidewalk to terrace. and illuminates entire area. The wall and edge of planting bed are railroad ties set vertically.

For Better Outdoor Living

Remodeling for better outdoor living space is perhaps the most rewarding of all landscape projects. It contributes to the whole family's enjoyment of leisure hours in the garden—"garden" here meaning all of the land around the house. This area should be attractive, inviting and accommodating.

Bare concrete platform *looks uninviting, uninteresting and uncomfortable. The raised area is not well defined and it lacks such welcome signs of life as flowers, trees, shrubs or a comfortable place to sit outdoors.*

Quality workmanship, good-looking materials and a design of appropriate size and in keeping with the family's outdoor living patterns all help achieve this effect. While you are still in the planning stage of any outdoor improvements, read again "Solving the Mystery of Outdoor Scale" on page 173.

Enriching an Existing Terrace

Outdoor living has become so popular that the builders of most houses include a patio or terrace of some kind. The problem is that they are almost always too small and the design is usually undistinguished. Fortunately the homeowner can often do something to improve the situation.

These three pictures show the transformation of a concrete platform by the back door into an elegant split-level terrace. The low brick wall and pillars create a sense of enclosure without blocking the view. The rough texture of brick is a pleasing contrast to the smooth house surface. Trees and shrubs adorn terrace and provide shade.

Large split-level terrace *is created from the concrete platform by paving it with brick and adding a gracefully curved expanse of brick at ground level. The steps between the levels can be used for informal seating. Beds of shrubs and a tub of ivy add pleasant accents of color and texture and they require little maintenance.*

Terrace is divided *into an entryway, dining area, and, on the lower level, there's room for relaxing in the sun. A sense of privacy is established for each section by using the shrubs, trees and brick walls as "room dividers." Possible monotony of too much brick is forestalled by the planting beds and the wrought iron table and chairs.*

See What Landscaping Can Do for a Home

"Landscaping" is a broad term that means more than simply improving the appearance or changing the features of "land."

For example, when this old house was remodeled, a deck was added in the back to create more living space, and evergreens were planted around the deck to add permanent color, soften the appearance of the edge and relate the whole to the surrounding trees and shrubs.

In the context of this book, the construction of the deck can be considered landscaping just as much as the planting of the evergreens. In fact, any and all additions or alterations that will affect, change or improve the outdoor life around the house can be properly called landscaping.

A number of changes were necessary here, both inside and out, to make the original house more attractive and livable. Although all these alterations were important to the project as a whole, our primary concern here is the stunning transformation of the back of the house. It is a good example of how design overcomes almost any obstacle.

To begin with, the plain back wall of the house was opened wide to let in light and reveal the pleasant year-round view of the grounds and the trees. The glass wall, with its sliding panel, and the double picture window (all of which somewhat inhibit privacy) are placed at the back of the house rather than at the front where they usually look out on nothing more inspiring than traffic and the similar windows of the houses across the street. This new wall not only extends outward from the house to make additional living space inside, but the central "glass" portion juts out from the house at an angle to enlarge the living room and create an interesting backdrop for the spacious deck. The rounded edge of the deck helps unite the two ends of the house.

Strong character of the roof line and narrow clapboards were the outstanding features of the original house. These characteristics are retained and strengthened by the remodeling. The large and handsome trees on the site (better seen in the adjacent picture) were a major reason for buying the property in the first place. When the new windows and the broad wooden deck were installed these trees became an integral part of the daily scene here—from both indoors and out.

After remodeling, and from same angle of view, the remaining narrow clapboards and the window below the peak of the roof are seen. Mass plantings of juniper help to tie the new façade and deck to the surrounding yard and balance the mass of the trees' foliage. To further relate the house to the ground, its apparent height is reduced by painting the upper area dark and emphasizing the horizontal lines of siding. Shadow pattern enlivens the surrounding surface of gravel.

The deck is an extension of the living room with easy access through sliding glass doors or through the door at right. The curved shape is in pleasing contrast to the angularity of the new addition. Dense planting of junipers at edge of the deck needs only occasional deep watering and clipping. Potted plants are used here for seasonal color.

Deck panels of 2-inch redwood are divided into sections for easier construction. The deck is supported on piers made of two concrete blocks stacked on end and set into the clay sub-soil for drainage and stability during the winter freezing and thawing. Wood is stained and treated with a preservative.

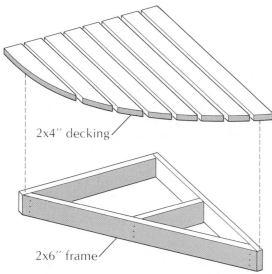

2x4″ decking

2x6″ frame

143

Dividing a small area into two sections makes it seem larger; parallel curves of reed screen and log rounds in foreground unify the space. The room and garden are visually linked by the redwood boards used in related patterns and related horizontal planes in both areas.

▶ **This awkward space** was created by addition of the new room at left. Also shown is the jag at the corner of the house that dictated the curve of the reed screen. Space behind screen admits light into windows and provides access to the hose bib located on the far wall of the house.

144

Taking Advantage of Unused Space

Even the most elaborate plans for landscaping may overlook or simply discount some areas such as a strip between two houses, a bare spot in a distant corner or a weedy place behind the garage. Often this lost space can be adapted later on for use as a play area, patio or a vegetable or rose garden. It becomes important to landscape lost space when the addition of a room or pool brings it into prominence. There's always some way to beautify and make useful any patch of land no matter how unsightly or difficult to handle it may seem at first.

In a U-Shaped Pocket

Remodeling a house can, ironically, create lost space. This is what happened when a screened recreation room was added to an older house, as shown here. The house lacked a cool spot for summer relaxation, and this attractive, airy room is just what was needed. But adding the room brought into prominent view an unsightly rectangular pocket of land and the backside of the house,

which was largely unnoticed before. This outlook was detrimental to the charm of the room itself, and it soon became clear that it had to be improved.

The sides of the house opposite the new room were screened with a high framework covered with high reed fencing. This camouflage was curved to fit the space and set a few feet away from the wall to let some light into the windows of the house. The enclosed area received too little air and sunshine for a flower garden or lawn, so less-demanding materials were used. Sculptured elements—a Kuan-yin statue, rocks, trees, shrubs and pieces of wood were carefully arranged on a bed of soft brown gravel. As a welcome bonus, less maintenance was also achieved. Outdoor lighting is unnecessary because the room lights subtly illuminate the area at night.

While this is not meant to be an "Oriental garden," the handling of the materials in this pleasing composition is patterned on certain design elements that are found in Japanese gardens.

Obtrusive downspout and bare ground typify what little attention is often given to out-of-the-way places around a house. Little was done here until the new room brought this area into more prominent view.

Underground drainage into a dry well was built to hide end of downspout and for more efficient disposal of water. No draperies are necessary in the room because the reed fence screens it effectively.

145

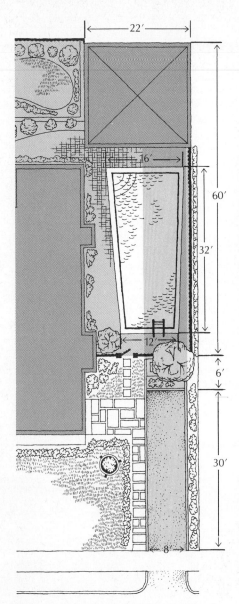

The colored area shows *the length of driveway before the conversion. Square garage at the back is now a pool house.*

From the street *one sees the remaining drive now used for parking. Stockade fence and planting completely screen the pool from public view. Walkway is wide enough to aid in getting out of a car.*

Old Driveway and Garage Into Pool and Cabaña

The garage of many an older house is set inconveniently at the back of the lot, as this one was. This is a remnant of the days when motor access was through the back alley and the days before that when the horse and buggy were kept out back in the barn. Long after land became too expensive for the luxury of back alleys for service, the garage stayed in back and a long driveway led to the street—hardly the best use of the land.

The example on these pages shows how an old garage and driveway were converted to a cabaña and swimming pool. There's still room to park cars in the remaining front half of the drive. And, if needed, there's space for a carport or garage. The pool is set back well beyond the front property line, a

146

From the garage *now converted into a cabaña the view is of pool and back of the stockade fence shown in picture at left. The pool is narrower at the far end to give an illusion of greater length and to provide more seating area at right. Ivy border and other plantings help to modify the somewhat hard, cold appearance of the paving.*

requirement in many communities. It is totally enclosed (also a common requirement) by the stockade fence and plantings on two sides, and by the house and converted garage on the other sides. Be sure to check all regulations concerning swimming pools with local authorities before building on your property. If a pool is not possible (or desired), an unused drive could also be used as a flower garden, patio or play area.

The plan at left shows how "forced perspective" was used to good advantage. Parallel lines seem to converge in the distance, and when lines are purposely narrowed in the distance the apparent length of the area is increased—when looking in that direction. There's more seating space inside the cabaña as well as dressing rooms and storage space. The garage was opened on the left side to link the back garden to pool.

147

6

City Gardens

The design and care of city gardens is rewarding but not without problems. Almost by definition they are small. The variety of plant material and design elements —the shapes, textures and colors—must be carefully planned so the overall effect will have interest without confusion. Soot-fall is a major problem in most cities. Leaves must be sprayed with water regularly and the soil may have to be replenished or even replaced from time to time. Poor drainage can be handled by planting in raised beds and containers. A heavily shaded city garden demands creative use of materials such as brick, wood, stone, gravel, water and shade plants. Ivy, yew and privet have proven to be dependable in even the most difficult city conditions. For advice on what grows best in your own city consult a good local garden store.

A Brick Garden with Plants as Accents

This is a garden of weathered brick in keeping with its attractive old neighborhood, where most houses and sidewalks are of the same material. Its basic form is skillfully enriched with trees, shrubs, vines, plant containers and a small fountain. Essential to the effect of open space in the small tightly contained area is the careful balance of plant material in relation to the overall dimensions of the garden.

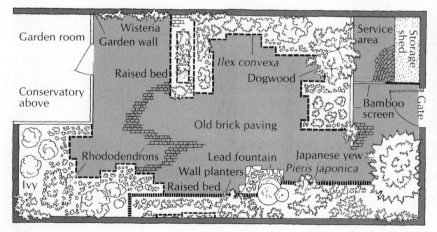

Planting beds, *raised and at ground level, divide the garden into three connecting shapes that are also interesting when viewed from the house above.*

Tiered fountain *splashes down to a rock and moss garden set into the brick paving. The moss is kept green by the water controlled by a faucet at the rear.*

High walls and trees *put the garden in proper scale with the buildings surrounding it. The plants are arranged to create a sense of openness. Adjacent buildings, trees and even the sky are a visual part of the garden itself and carry the eye beyond its confines. The open area is a place for sitting but is not so large that it seems empty in the winter when the chairs and table are put away. Potted plants fill in as needed.*

Wall planters *lower the apparent height of the wall as does the stepped-down top of wall itself. These boxes and the flower bed below relieve the expanse of brick.*

Screens of bamboo *conceal the tool and storage shed at the rear of the garden. Screens are lower than the walls so the space behind is a related part of the whole.*

149

Variations on A Theme

Here are three solutions to the same demanding conditions and limited space.

Each town-house garden is long and narrow, relies on high wooden walls for privacy, has two entrances—through a living-room door opening onto the garden and up a flight of stairs from a lower level—and is overlooked by balconies outside the bedroom windows one story above.

While the character of each garden is different, they all show signs of a landscape architect at work interpreting a homeowner's individual tastes according to his own specialized knowledge of outdoor scale and design. The skills of a landscape architect are particularly helpful in the planning of small spaces. In these city plots even a foot or two could make one section seem too large or too small in proportion to the rest of the area.

An architect's strong sense of design is also helpful when planning gardens in prominent view from above. The delightful patterns seen from the balconies of these houses are clearly shown in the plans on the following pages. Any landscaped area near a tall house is more enjoyable to look down upon if the positioning of planting beds, terraces, outdoor furniture and the like is made with the thought in mind that these areas will be seen from above.

These rectangular spaces were landscaped for minimum upkeep and maximum use as outdoor rooms for parties. All the surfaces are quick-drying; trees and shrubs need little trimming or watering. Potted flowers provide needed accents of color.

City gardens, *along a row of charming old townhouses, as seen from roof of building on adjacent hill, show three different landscapes designed for the same amount and kind of space.*

Four Spaces for Sitting

A narrow rectangle of land was transformed into this lively garden by dividing the space into many sections. There are four seating areas, each one at a different height: the gazebo, sun deck (note the two rock steps up to it), the bridge from house to garden and the landing below the bridge on the stairway from the lower floor. When looking down on the garden from second-story windows, the fencing becomes another section at an even higher level. Rear steps accentuate natural incline of the land.

Each seating area has a distinct geometric shape that emphasizes it as a separate unit. These areas are further defined by the different colors and textures of the

materials used. The multitude of plants on the sides of the garden highlight the plain wooden façade of the fencing and the smooth surfaces of the redwood seating areas. In turn the latter stand out against the rougher textures of the flagstone walkway and the railroad-tie steps. While railroad ties may seem too informal for this garden, they do look appropriate here be-cause their cut and fit is as precise as the rest of the woodwork.

For unity there are railroad-tie steps at both ends of the garden bordered with the same kinds of plants, and umbrella-shaped lamps are scattered throughout. The Chinese tiles on the back fence and pagoda-style gazebo relate the garden to the many Chinese artifacts inside the house.

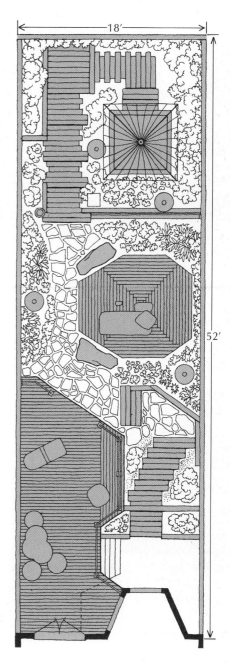

Parasol lamps illuminate *sections of garden (downward cast of light avoids glare) and are charming decorative accents. For softness and scent, flagstones are planted with thyme, moss and ajuga.*

◀ **Bridge from house** *to garden has character of interior room with wood-paneled wall and carefully arranged furniture. Planting along steps to lower level turns the landing into a city grotto.*

▶ **The plan** *shows that the various elements have related forms to unify the design. Notice how the edge of the platform facing the deck is parallel to it and in line with the railroad-tie retainer.*

153

Gravel Terrace and
Seating in the Round

This garden was designed for maximum open space with no objects to obstruct the view from one end to the other. The U-shaped bench makes the garden seem even larger and more open than it is by attracting the eye away from the high, confining walls. The narrow dimensions of the garden are further disguised by dividing the space into two sections with completely different functions: a rounded terrace for conversation and a curved path leading to a closeup view of the sculpture and a place to be alone. An uncluttered garden on two levels (note the rock step up to the path) is good for large stand-up parties. (Gravel surfaces,

however, are not. They're hard to walk or stand on when high heels are in fashion.)

For low maintenance, a basic garden of gravel is excellent. Seeds fall among the pebbles and some surface-rooted weeds do sprout, but they are easy to pull up. The rest of the garden is mass-planted with ivy, which will be practically weed free when it completely covers the ground. Since spreading ivy requires a good deal of hand weeding, it saves labor to set out as many plants as one can afford.

The calm atmosphere of the garden is largely a result of the monotone color scheme of reddish brown woodwork, dark green plants and gray tones of gravel. Places to display potted flowers for accents of color are part of the garden's design.

Lights illuminate *gravel terrace and path at night. Sculpture at rear is lit by spotlight (barely in view), and bonsai plants on the low table are lit by the tubular light on the wall above them.*

◀ **Shelf behind bench** *is attractive place to set potted plants for seasonal display of color. Potted plants are also used to mark steps up to the seating area by the house and down to the lower level.*

▶ **The plan** *shows how the two lounging areas relate for easy flexible use. Small groups tend to congregate on the deck by the house, larger groups also use the built-in bench around the gravel area.*

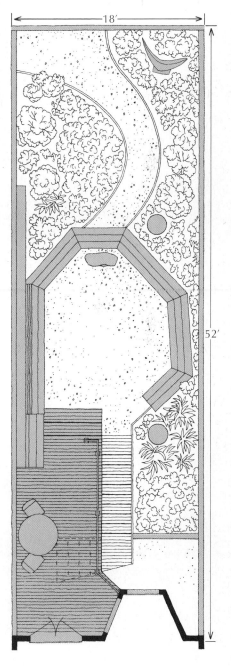

155

Rug of Brick for an Outdoor Room

The brick rug pulls together all the parts of this garden room into one coherent design. Even though nothing else is made of brick, it has this unifying effect: its shape is similar to the curved planting box, and the wooden border around it is in keeping with the wooden planting box, outer frame-work and steps at both ends of the terrace.

The rug also has a calming influence on the garden because of its symmetry, smooth surface and soft earth tones. Without this restful area in the center, the small amount of space here would be overwhelmed by the jungle profusion of foliage and irregular pattern of flagstones. Also, the effectiveness of the splash fountain with a sculpture of a

cupid on top depends on this feeling of quiet.

The garden's generous proportions and the arrangement of plants around the edge create an elegant atmosphere and plenty of space for entertaining. The rug itself is big enough to hold a long dining table and chairs for a sit-down meal or to comfortably accommodate a living-roomful of furniture and people. If the furniture is removed, the garden becomes a cool spot for dancing.

A large part of the success of this garden is due to excellent workmanship and attention to detail. All lines are straight, curves even, joints flush. The trees are clipped, hedges trimmed and flagstones carefully arranged. How well a garden is landscaped and cared for is always important but particularly so in a small space.

Symmetry of paved areas in the garden is maintained by the complete (though narrow) separation from the seating area near the house. Light illuminates steps to lower level at the right of the railing.

◀**Height of fences** is obscured by closely planted Indian laurel figs. Their height is also decreased by clipped yews beside the planting box and the boxes hanging from the trees.

▶**The plan** clearly reveals the pattern of the brick design set into the flagstone paving as it is seen from the second story of the house. This element is accentuated by separation from the deck.

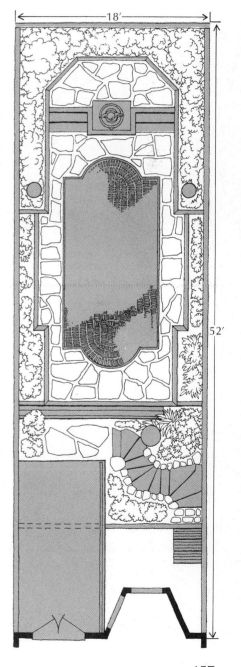

157

Hanging Garden Between Houses

This rooftop garden between two houses grows from pots and boxes. For the effect of luxuriant growth and to conserve floor space the containers are massed together: on the floor, on risers and on top of the fence.

Pots on the balcony, hanging baskets below and rampant growth of a morning glory extend the garden to the top of the house. Using this vertical space increases the size of the garden and creates a colorful retreat.

On top of fence *are petunias planted in a long box. Except for the philodendron by the door and rubber tree in right foreground most of the plants are annuals. Across from the geraniums at left is an impatiens. The display is as lovely to see from inside the house as from the garden itself.*

▶ **Morning-glory plant** *is climbing up strings attached to top of fire escape. It is rooted in a box on the rooftop. Pots of nasturtiums are massed on the lower balcony. The whole garden is easily watered daily with a hose. Excess water drains through the slatted wood flooring onto the roof just below.*

Portable Garden for a Penthouse

A wooden deck interspaced with beds of gravel and planting boxes was used to transform this apartment rooftop into a penthouse garden. It is a portable, low-maintenance design that is easy to install and can be adapted to any small space. The wood panels are separate modules joined together in an interesting design. They are made of fir, pressure treated with preservative. Treated pine or redwood can also be used.

A spectacular view, plenty of space and a good solid surface make this an excellent rooftop for a penthouse garden. Besides camouflaging the sloping parapet and covering the floor, little else is needed except a cool, shaded area and trees to break the wind.

▼ *Overhead for shade in foreground is a framework covered with reed screening which relates well to the wooden fence and paneled deck. The trees are all hardy kinds that survive city conditions. Crab apples line the fence in the foreground, and Russian olives (Elaeagnus angustifolia) are behind them. Black pines are mainly used in the graveled sections.*

Sit Back and Think About the Future

Having seen the examples on the preceding pages you should have more than enough new ideas and inspiration to encourage you to improve your own landscape. Here we have shown solutions to a wide range of problems, conceived by outstanding designers and landscape architects from all across the country. No matter what the style of your own house or the size of your property or budget, you are sure to find ideas here that will suit your needs.

As you spend more time with this book you will find that every good design is soundly based on understandable principles. These principles can be applied in a number of ways using materials of varied price. And, of course, in the sections on landscape construction you will learn how to save by doing some of the work yourself.

These first pages are designed for inspiration. They are meant to show the best and set you dreaming about ways you can use the land around you to enrich your daily life.

In the section that follows, you will find specific help in relating your dreams to the realities of your own land and the budget you have to work with. Here you will learn to analyze your needs, consider the options and decide what you should and should not expect to accomplish by landscaping.

Planning in the Fourth Dimension

The width and depth of your property and the height of the house and trees are the three dimensions that can be included on the plan. But the fourth dimension, the passage of time, is one of the most important factors in a design, and it doesn't show up automatically in the planning process.

The design of a landscape is made up of separate parts. There are walkways, hedges, fences, terraces and plantings of many kinds. Each part must be considered, designed and built as a separate entity. Yet each must also relate in design as well as function to the others, to the total site and to the neighborhood of which it is a part.

This is why an overall plan is important. Even if only a few improvements are contemplated, they will relate better and function better if they are first committed to paper. And because a garden is usually created in a series of events, an order of priorities must be established.

When we decide that the new entry walk will be done before enlarging the terrace, and that the lawn will be installed before the fencing, we are working with the fourth dimension and must keep it in mind.

What Comes First?

Only you can determine the priorities. But we can help by giving you the basis for a definite point of view, by suggesting some of the best options and by showing you how to put your plans on paper.

The sequence of construction is one aspect of the time factor. Another is the changing needs of the family. Even if there are no children, there will be change from the early years of outdoor entertaining and active construction and gardening to the quieter and more leisurely pursuits of later years. But the needs change most when there are children to consider.

Any homeowner who is also a parent

160

knows that children are the fastest-growing element in the landscape.

The changing need for mud pies, sand boxes, splash pools, tricycle paths, swing sets, basketball backboards and parking space for another family car comes in dizzying succession.

It's important to provide for as much as possible when needed, but always with the understanding that nothing is forever. Flexibility and long-range planning are important. An abandoned sand box can become a raised bed for growing herbs. A splash pool can be filled with water lilies. The Indian camp or hobo jungle in the back corner can later be rototilled and used for vegetables and cut flowers. The playlawn marked with worn spots can be reseeded and restored to serve again as an outdoor carpet or a putting green. Interests change whether you have children or not, and the landscape can be designed to change as needed.

How to Work with the Section that Follows

By paging through the next section you can see the kinds of decisions that should be made before a worthwhile plan can be developed.

Included here is basic information on a complex subject and one cannot expect to assimilate it in a hurry. This is a section for leisurely study and reference. But even as you page through the first time you will see some things that immediately suggest ways to make better use of your landscape.

As you find which areas of your garden hold the most promise for improvement you may want to turn back to the previous section on "Great Ideas" and look for specific examples. That will be the time to read the text on those pages that supports the ideas shown in the pictures. In each case you will find the basic principles to consider in planning that aspect of your garden.

The section you have just seen and the one that follows supplement one another. The pictures of existing gardens are meant to reveal the possibilities and stimulate your imagination. The planning section shows how to analyze your needs and decide what you want and can afford in terms of time, space and the amount of money required.

Don't Sell Yourself Short

It's easy to think that landscaping can be too much trouble, too expensive, or take too much time to complete. While this could prove to be true, there's no way to be sure until you have thought about it, roughed out some plans on paper and figured out how much the changes you propose will actually cost.

The quality of outdoor living, recreation and beauty can all be improved by changing the landscape. And often at less cost in time, money and effort than you might think. Even a small project can often make a big difference in the beauty and the usefulness of your garden. Later and larger improvements can be made at your own pace once the overall plan is outlined.

It doesn't cost anything to make plans. And they may very well lead to the pleasant discovery that a modest investment in improving the landscape could pay the greatest of dividends in your daily life.

2

Planning

When the time comes to fit your dreams to the realities
of your budget and the space you have to
work with, this is the information you will need.

7

Basic Principles of Design

How a Landscape Architect Would Approach Your Problem

Professional designers have developed some time-tested techniques for approaching problems and these can be of help to anyone planning a garden. The secret is to isolate various elements, establish a set of priorities and general solutions, and then bring the parts together in a specific plan that integrates the whole. This is easier said than done, and such subtle matters as a good sense of design and proportion can only come with years of experience. But simply following a logical process will help to establish the definite point of view that every good designer must have.

First, decide what to keep. Even if your house is new and no landscaping has been done, there may be some trees or native shrubs you will want to keep, or a boggy place or an outcropping of rock that might be worth improving and working into the design. And if you are planning to improve on an older garden, you may want to retain most of the existing material. In any event this information should be recorded on a rough plan as shown at left. This is, in effect, a visual inventory of established

features that will affect the overall plan. This sketch plan, and others recommended here, should be in the same relative scale. The sketches may be rough, and for this purpose everything need not be in exact scale. Simply estimate the size and distance. The very process of making them forces one to analyze every aspect of the site and form some opinions about the relative importance of things. Note the X-marks on the foregoing drawing which indicate a row of overgrown shrubs that should be removed. This kind of crowding is a common problem in older gardens and should be avoided.

Consider the wind, sun and rain. The patterns of sun and shade, the direction and force of the wind, the rainfall, snow and the way that water collects and runs off the surface all have their effect on plants and people in the landscape. When a landscape architect first looks at a piece of ground he has the impact of the elements firmly in mind. He knows from experience where the sun will warm the ground, where the heat

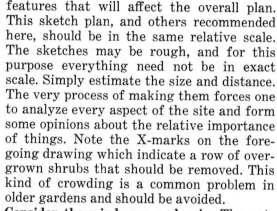

▶**Establishing zones** of activity is one of the first things a landscape architect does in developing a plan. He might not sketch them out but would have them clearly in mind. The entry zone is the place for off-street parking if needed. Outdoor living is for terraces or decks. Recreation is for a pool or play yard and it requires a place of its own as does the utility area for storage, compost or a vegetable garden. If decorative beds are needed they should be given their places. Routes of circulation (the dotted lines) must be established. All the zones may not be needed and may change as the plan develops but they should all be considered at the start.

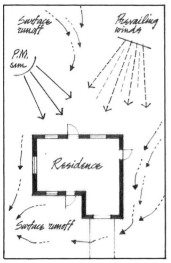

traps are and where all the cold places will be. He will feel out the gusty places and those that are calm. He will know how rain and melting snow run off the ground and where the runoff may go too fast and cause erosion and where it will collect and saturate the soil. You should do the same kind of analysis, and get a feel for the many different micro-climates in all parts of the landscape. This information can be accumulated over a period of time and recorded on a rough sketch as shown above for reference when decisions are made later on as to where to locate a patio or plant a vegetable garden. These sketches can be separate, as they are here, or the information can all be recorded on one sheet and coded with colored pencils. **Looking out from the inside.** In the best of situations the house is sited only after careful consideration of the landscape and all the

effects of the weather mentioned above. The plan for the garden is then coordinated with that of the house so the two work together attractively and conveniently.

But this happens only when an architect and landscape architect work together on the project from the beginning. In most places it is a matter of adapting the landscape to the existing facts of the house. This means that the location of the doors and windows becomes important. A door from the kitchen or dining area is an obvious place for a terrace for outdoor cooking. If a terrace for entertaining and family sitting can open off a living room, so much the better. Sometimes a side door in a bedroom can lead to the building of a private enclosed garden. And if this prospect pleases and there is no door, don't overlook the possibility of having one installed.

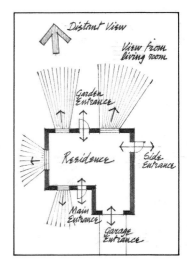

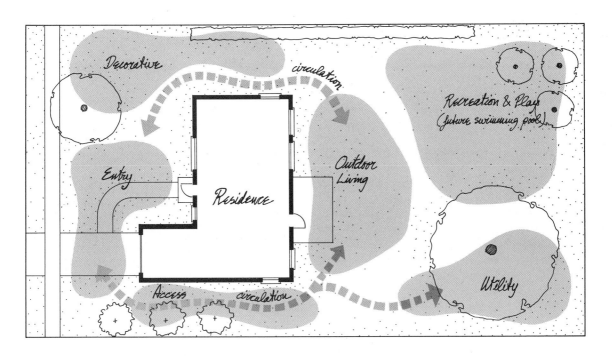

Such features as flowering trees, sculpture or flower beds can often be located where they can easily be seen and enjoyed from inside the house. If there is a good view from the site the house will probably be designed to take advantage of it. In designing sitting places in the garden the view is no less important. The views should be indicated on the rough plan.

Looking in from the outside. Most of the land around a suburban house is usually open to view from the street and surrounding houses. There may, however, be some locations that are screened from outside view. If so, these should be marked on the rough plan as preferred areas for outdoor living, such as area A on the plan below. If the existing private areas are not in the right place for outdoor living, due to sun, wind or their relationship to the house, then appropriate places, such as area B, can be made private by screening on the line of sight between that place and the neighboring house. Such screening is as much a favor to the neighbors as it is to yourself. If a fence is used be sure it is neat and attractive and if the screening is done with plantings they should be well within your property line so you can prune them as required to keep them looking attractive without having to trespass.

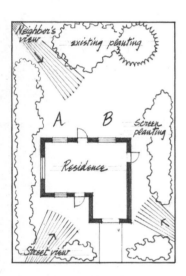

While the need for privacy for outdoor living is the most obvious, it is helpful if views into the house are also obscured. Use screening strategically to separate private and public areas for the benefit of all.

Making sketches as recommended here or, at least, considering the principles they illustrate, is an important first step. But a professional would also make a general plan, a grading and drainage plan, an irrigation plan if needed, a planting plan and drawings of specific construction details.

A Checklist:

Though the foregoing pages will have brought to mind many questions about the design of your landscape, there are still some specifics to be considered. Listed here are the kinds of questions that would come up and be answered if you were working with a landscape architect.

You might like to check off those that apply to your needs and your landscape. Ask your family to look over the list, make their checks and then discuss the problems together. By using the checklist in this way you should be able to consolidate and combine your ideas about the landscape you share. Although these are by no means the only questions that will occur, their answers will put you well on your way toward planning a landscape that will do everything you can expect it to.

☐ **1** Do you need off-street parking for guests and extra cars or can they park on the street?

☐ **2** Is the entry clearly defined from the street so guests can easily see the house number by day and night? Can guests see clearly where to leave their cars and how to get to the front door?

☐ **3** Will you need extra outdoor lighting to mark the way from the cars to the house? If so, it's best to have the wiring installed before the lawn goes in.

☐ **4** Will the walkway comfortably accommodate two people walking side by side? At least five feet of width should be allowed and more is often good for long walks to keep them in relative scale.

☐ **5** Do you plan to make the entryway more interesting with plantings or, perhaps, enhance it with hanging baskets, potted or tubbed accent plants or a piece of natural or man-made sculpture?

21 Questions to Answer Before You Begin

☐ **6** Should the house be somewhat screened from view with plantings on the street side? If so, this would call for the careful location of trees (on the sight lines) and probably an underplanting of shrubs.

☐ **7** Could you use tall trees on the south side to cast shade on the house and help to keep it cool?

☐ **8** If you want a lawn, is there a good open space in full sun for it? If not, it may be better to settle for other ground covers.

☐ **9** Is there enough space to walk or push a wheelbarrow completely around the house? This is a definite advantage in day-to-day maintenance.

☐ **10** Is the soil good enough to give the plantings the best chance for strong performance? If it has to be improved, the roto-tilling is an unsightly job, but the sooner it is done in the process of developing a garden the better.

☐ **11** Have you decided how large the terrace area should be for the kind of outdoor living and entertaining you plan to do? Be sure there's space allowed for the largest gathering you intend to have. Check the space required for furniture on page 188.

☐ **12** Could you use more than one place for dining outside? Perhaps you could create a picnic spot well away from the house. Plantings can be used for screening.

☐ **13** Do you plan to cook out-of-doors and, if so, how complete a facility is needed? This can range from a small space for a portable charcoal broiler (which provides optimum flexibility), a larger space for a built-in cooker with gas or electricity or a complete weatherproof kitchen with refrigerator, sink and range.

☐ **14** Will you want a place for quiet lounging or reading apart from the main terrace? Should it be in the sun or in the shade? Is there a place where relative privacy can be found without too much extra planting or building?

☐ **15** Would it be helpful to have built-in seating? Perhaps this could be in conjunction with a wall or raised bed. It saves space for furniture and it's always there when you might want it even if the furniture is put away for the winter.

☐ **16** Do you have a good place for storing outdoor furniture during the off-season? If not, consider using folding pieces and building a narrow "storage wall" to put them in. This might be added to an existing fence or the side of a building.

☐ **17** Have you considered the outdoor space required for such necessities as garbage cans, clotheslines, storage of heavy equipment and garden tools?

☐ **18** Is more privacy screening needed? If so, you'll need to decide what devices to use, whether plants, fences, walls or panel screens.

☐ **19** Will there be young children in the garden? Have you planned adequate room for their play or for the changing needs of space and equipment as they grow older?

☐ **20** Are you a gardener? Do you need space for a cutting garden or vegetable garden and for a compost pile? These are all best screened from view.

☐ **21** Do you think there might be heavy construction later on, for a swimming pool or large paved area? If so, plan at the beginning to provide access for trucks and other machinery.

Consider the Drainage and Runoff

As surely as the water falls on the land it will flow to the low places in the fastest possible way. If the slope is toward the house, water will build up against the walls and may seep into the foundation or basement. If the low spot is a hollow, the water will collect there and the soggy soil may suffocate the grass and kill the trees and shrubs. If the water runs off too fast it can erode the surface and wash away the good topsoil.

Wherever there is sloping land poor drainage and heavy runoff can be serious problems. To alter the slope or divert the flow, as illustrated here, can be expensive, but it can be even more expensive not to do it.

It Pays to Know Your Soil

If you live where there are heavy rains, it pays to know how much of the water will soak into the ground and how much can be expected to flow off the surface. If you are moving into a new place and planning to do some grading and planting before the rainy season, it would be a good idea to check the porosity of the soil.

Find a natural hollow or dig a wide shallow hole in which to make the test. Add water slowly until the soil is thoroughly saturated and water stands on the surface. If the surface water stays for a matter of hours without soaking in, chances are that during a storm or when the snow melts in the spring most of the water will run off the surface. You should know where and how fast it will go. The steeper the slope the less time for soaking in and the faster the water will move. And when water from a wide area is channeled into a narrower space the rate of flow speeds up. The probability of erosion depends upon the stability of the surface and the rate of flow.

Open garden soil has little stability. Even on a slight slope the topsoil will wash away in the rain. A bed of ivy, on the other hand, will shed water and hold the soil on a steep slope even in a cloudburst.

Don't let brown water leave your land. All erosion contributes to the muddying of nearby streams and lakes.

▶ **You can change the slope.** *When water collects and makes soil too soggy for grass and most garden plants, the surface can be altered by cutting away the high places, as shown in the drawing, or filling in the low. If this is impractical or too expensive, you might prefer to live with the condition and turn the wet area into a garden of bog plants such as marsh marigold, cardinal flower (Lobelia cardinalis) and sweet flag (Acorus calamus).*

▶ **Direct the flow.** *If the water that collects in low places comes from the surface and not up through the ground, as is sometimes the case, it can often be diverted around the hollow by means of an interceptor ditch. The ditch can be made by cutting and filling on the uphill side, as shown at the left of the drawing. Where the ditch will go depends on the terrain. The size depends on the expected rate of flow. Keep in mind that when water moves into a restricted area the rate of flow is increased. To prevent erosion in the ditch, plant with sod or line it with gravel, asphalt or a skim-coat of concrete.*

▶ **Take it under the ground.** *In many gardens, particularly on sloping sites in densely populated suburban areas, this may be the only solution, and it can be very expensive. "Buried treasure" is what one noted landscape designer calls it. If all that's needed is a simple dry well or a run of perforated pipe to spread water underground you could probably do the project yourself. But if a system of drains is needed, especially if tied into storm sewers at street level, it is definitely a job for professionals. Unfortunately, when buying a house, one can't assume that the builder has handled the surface drainage.*

▶ **Use plants to retard the flow.** *A mass planting of dense ground covers such as ivy, Euonymous fortunei, pachysandra or Vinca minor set out in a broad swath across the face of a slope can help decrease the problem of erosion. Low-growing shrubs such as dwarf Japanese yew and the heavily textured low-growing junipers such as J. horizontalis will also do an excellent job of holding back the flow of water. The plants develop a heavy fibrous mat of roots that help to stabilize the soil and also take water up into the plant. The leaves collect rainwater and also take up the initial impact of a downpour.*

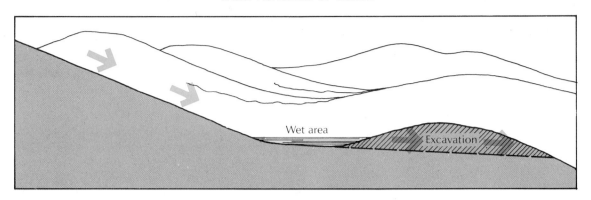

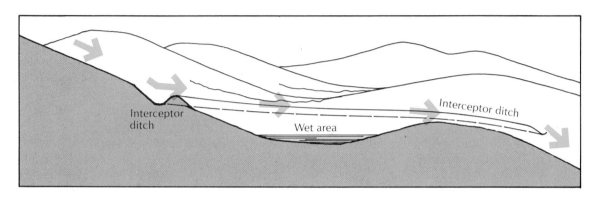

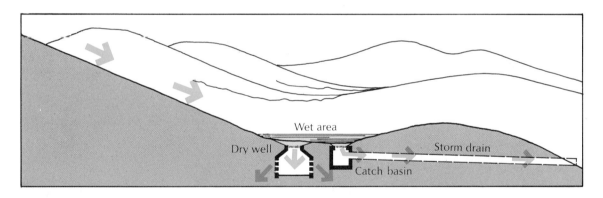

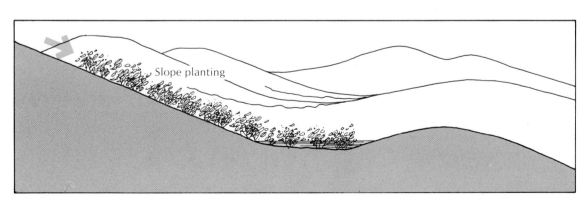

Patterns of Sun and Shadow

One of the most important things a home-owner should know, and often does not, is where there is sun and where there is shade on his property at different times of the day and at different times of the year. To know this requires an understanding of both the (apparent) movement of the sun and how it changes with the seasons in relation to the location and the axis of the house.

This knowledge helps solve many landscaping problems such as choosing the best location for certain flowers, trees and shrubs. Shade-loving plants suffer from being subjected to long hours of hot afternoon sun, and plants that need sun will fail if they are in shade for most of the day.

Knowing how the sun moves is equally important in choosing areas for outdoor living. You may want full sun on a terrace or patio for early morning coffee and cooling shade at midday lunch. You may also want an afternoon sun-bathing spot, and, if the early evenings tend to be damp or chilly, a place where the direct or reflected warmth from the setting sun can be enjoyed. You can create these ideal settings only if you know exactly where sun and shade will fall.

In a house that is already built, the

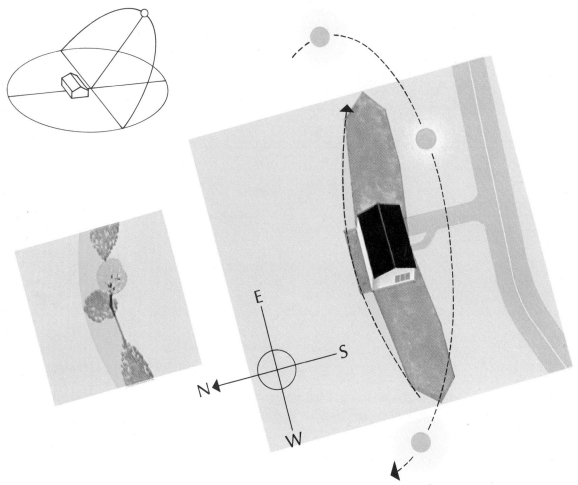

In the summer, *in this hemisphere, the sun rises and sets slightly north of an east-west line. This means, in effect, that the north side of any east-west structure is in shade at midday and receives weak sunlight in the early morning and late afternoon. Plants requiring direct sunlight will not do well with this north exposure.*

basic orientation to the sun has been established, although changes are always possible. But if you are building a house, the sun-and-shadow pattern is a major consideration in deciding how it should be sited.

In the illustration below, the houses are set on an exact east-west axis. This is not a recommended orientation but helps to simplify the patterns of sun and shade as they are related to a house and to a single tree. The illustration at the left shows the sun as it rises and sets on the line of its furthest northern progression and on the longest day of the year, the summer solstice, June 22nd. The sun then begins its steady swing to the south where it reaches the line of its furthest southern progression on the shortest day of the year, the winter solstice, December 22nd. This is shown in the illustration at the right.

As the sun moves from east to west, the shadows it casts move from west to east. These directions are indicated by the pair of dotted lines. The dark areas of shadow in the drawings show early morning shade, midday shade and evening shade related to the fixed positions of the sun as shown. Note that when a house is set, as here, on an east-west axis, there is almost no direct sunlight on the north side of the house and almost no shade on the south side. It is better to set the house on an angle to the east-west line to get some sun and shade on all sides and some sun in all windows.

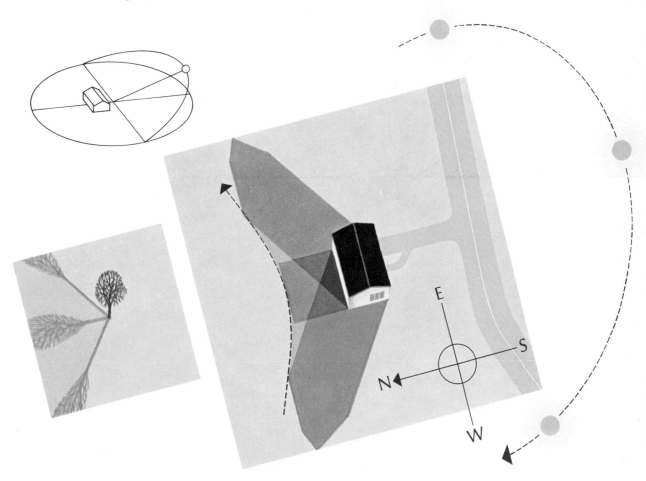

In the winter, *the sun rises and sets well to the south of the east-west line, casting long shadows to the north side of the house and limiting the kinds of plants and trees used in that area. On the south side, the winter sun reaches in under trellises and overhangs. Structures can be designed to take advantage of the sun's low angle.*

171

To infinity

Cloud cover
10,000'

Outdoor dimensions
Indoor dimensions
Property line

Tree cover
20'

150'

9'

12'

75'

Solving the Mystery of Outdoor Scale

The familiar dimensions used in the house
no longer apply where the overhead cover may be foliage 20 feet
above the ground and the "walls" are a distant line of trees.

The mistake most commonly made by homeowners in laying out their own landscape design is in planting trees and shrubs too close together and too close to the house, and in making the steps, walks and outdoor living areas much too small for comfort and attractive appearance. These errors in judgment all stem from one cause—the failure to recognize the difference between indoor and outdoor scale.

The Limiting Sizes Indoors

In the house we spend most of our time under ceilings that are less than 8 feet high and between walls that are 12 to 20 feet apart. In the houses of today a room is considered large if it measures 20 by 30 feet. Stairways are about 30 inches wide and doors are the same. These dimensions are related to the cost of building, not necessarily to the size and needs of people living in the houses. There is good reason to believe that people prefer to live in larger spaces. In days gone by, when labor and materials were relatively less expensive, the houses and all the rooms were much larger. But no matter what the reasons, the fact is that we have been conditioned by our houses to "think small" in terms of living space. This lifelong influence of indoor scale makes it hard to understand the larger dimensions that apply outdoors.

If a 20-by-30-foot living room is large enough for comfort, why, then, won't a terrace 20 by 30 feet be large enough? There are two reasons—one concerns appearance and the other function.

The vertical dimension, or "ceiling," outdoors is not a flat surface 8 feet overhead but is instead perhaps the foliage of a tree 20 feet above, or the clouds at 10,000 feet. The "walls" are not 15 feet apart but perhaps 100 feet between the house and the back fence or 500 feet to a line of trees on neighboring land. Thus it follows that the floor space outdoors must also be on a larger scale. A good way to prove this is to go out on the lawn, stake out an area the size of the largest room in your house. You will see how small it seems in its surroundings.

The property lines establish the legal limits of the floor space you can use in the landscape, but the walls of an outdoor room spread as far as the eye can see. In the illustration on the facing page the neighbor's house, the nearby trees and the distant view of the mountain will all be a part of any outdoor room that has them in sight.

Everything Is Larger Outside

Not only will spaces with indoor dimensions look too small outside, they will be too small for comfort. Outdoor furniture is heavier in scale and larger than most indoor pieces. People are accustomed to more elbow room out of doors; movements and actions are freer and more expansive. Garden steps and paths should be wide enough for people to walk side by side.

In most owner-designed landscapes the question of outdoor scale is not even recognized until the terrace turns out to be too small when finished. But once the problem is recognized it is not hard to solve. On the following page are some ideas that will be of help in making sure the sizes are right.

This is the difference between indoor and outdoor scale. The woman in the house stands between walls and under a ceiling of limited dimensions. The man in the garden is in a vastly larger space extending as far as the eye can see. Dimensions that are generous indoors are too small outdoors. The outdoor living areas, walks, steps and decorative objects must relate to the larger scale of the garden or they will not look right.

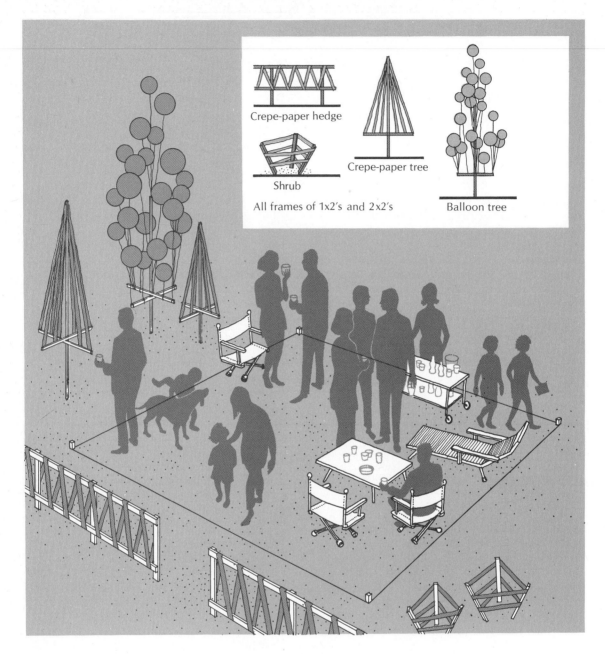

Crepe-paper hedge

Shrub

Crepe-paper tree

Balloon tree

All frames of 1x2's and 2x2's

Try These Ideas for Size

There's no need to guess about how large a terrace should be or where plants would look best. You can make sure with mockups, and also make a party of it, as shown here. Stake out the proposed size with string, set up furniture, invite the number of people you would like the terrace to accommodate and you will soon find out whether or not the size is right. To try another size or shape, simply move the stakes and string. Full-sized models of shrubs and small trees can be made of lightweight materials, as shown, and tried in various locations for size, spacing and screening effect.

8

The Standard Sizes

In certain outdoor areas, such as walkways, garden paths, driveways, parking areas and turnarounds, there are minimum spaces that must be allowed if they are to function properly. In planning any of these projects, it is necessary to know these sizes.

On the following pages, various standard dimensions are given for such facilities. Keep in mind, however, that these are the *minimum* requirements and that all walks or drives can usually profit from being made wider, provided space is available.

Walkways and Paths

Two people walking through a garden or approaching a front door should be able to walk side by side rather than single file. It is indeed an inhospitable entry that puts guests on a walk so narrow that arms and legs uncomfortably bump or an outside foot is forced to take to the grass. In addition to physical discomfort, paths that are too narrow are unattractive. For the sake of good design, a walk leading across a broad expanse of lawn should be considerably wider than the minimum dimensions given below.

Entry Walk

The width shown above is enough for two people to walk comfortably together side by side. Variation from this norm should be toward greater rather than less width.

Garden Path

A garden path can be, if necessary, less wide than an entry walk. But be sure the path is wide enough to accommodate wheelbarrows and other equipment.

Space Required for Driveways and Parking

A definite amount of space is required to park and drive an automobile in and out of a driveway. Skimping on the amount needed leads to frustration, difficult driving and ugly tire marks in the adjacent planting beds or grass. The diagrams on these pages give the minimum dimensions required for a driveway to accommodate a standard-size car. If there is room, these dimensions may be extended but they should not be any smaller. Dimensions for a number of basic driveway designs are given to help the homeowner determine what kind of driveway and parking facilities he has room for.

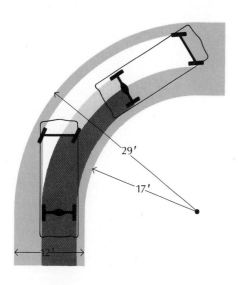

The Turning Radius

The width of any curve in a driveway is determined by the turning radius of an automobile. Because only the front axle of a car actually turns, a driveway curve must be at least one third wider than the width of a car. Turning in a driveway with the minimum dimensions given in the diagram above requires careful driving to prevent the back wheels from going over the curb. All dimensions are for standard cars.

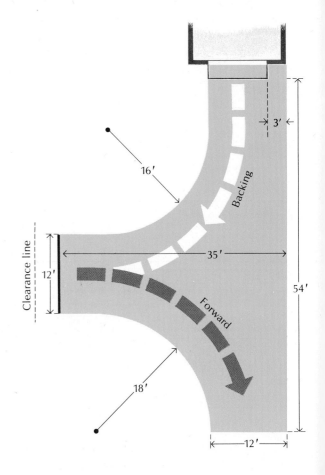

Back-and-Turn

This design is a good one to use in limited space for a driveway that connects a garage to a busy street. It avoids the danger of having to back a car out of the garage directly onto the street. As the arrows indicate, a car can be backed into the first curve and then turned to face the street. The turn-around area also provides temporary off-street parking space for a car or two. More parking and easier turning can be had by increasing the width of the back-up area. Zoning laws should be checked to see how near the pavement can come to the property line. Also keep in mind the need for space to accommodate the overhang—the distance between the end of the paved area in back of the wheels and the rear bumper. A wheel stop is a good idea.

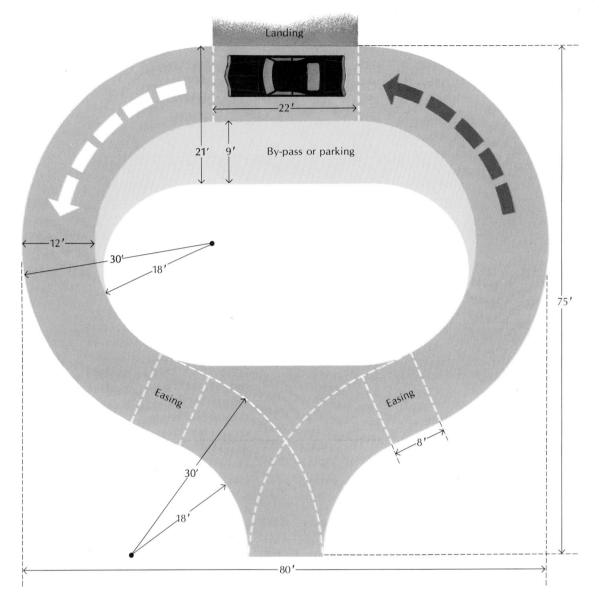

Landing

22'

21' 9' By-pass or parking

12'

30'

18'

75'

Easing

Easing

8'

30'

18'

80'

A Circular Drive with Parallel Parking

A circular driveway is a great convenience to family and guests. It is easy to drive in and out of, has extra room for parking and drawing up parallel to an entry. The drive is an attractive addition too, provided there is enough space to keep it in scale with the house and the rest of the property. Planting an appropriate arrangement of ground cover, trees and shrubs in the center section of a circular drive helps relate it to the rest of the landscape. High shrubs are good to use. They give privacy from the street and prevent a sense of "too much pavement" by blocking any view of the driveway as a whole.

(For year-round effect, use such evergreens as pine, spruce or juniper.)

Note that the parking area can be a by-pass if one car is parked along the straight stretch (which must be 22 feet long to permit a car to pull in without backing). If a U-shaped drive is preferred, it can be accommodated in the same amount of space.

177

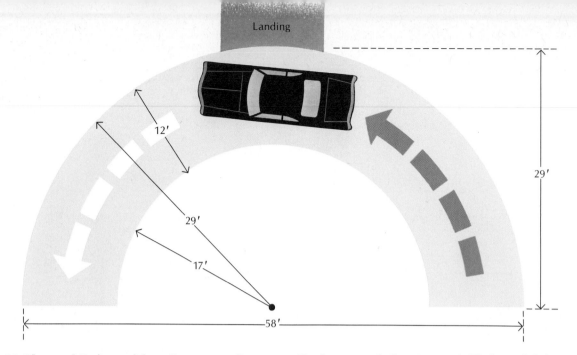

U-Shaped Drive with a Constant Curve

The advantage of a U-shaped driveway is that a car can be driven in and out without backing or turning. Shown here is the minimum amount of space required. The width of the curve given above cannot be reduced but the two ends of the U can be shortened or extended to fit the space between the house and the street. A U-shaped driveway is often a good arrangement to use at a side entrance for the convenience of carrying packages back and forth from the car to the house. If enough space to draw up parallel to the entry without backing is desired, an extra 22 feet in width must be added to this design, as shown in the center-drive diagram on the preceding page.

Saw-tooth

A saw-tooth design is an efficient and attractive way to make room for parking. Because the shape indicates exactly where to park, not even the most casual driver is likely to take more space than he needs. The zigzag lines form an interesting border, an attractive place for a bed of a low evergreen ground cover. In this diagram a three-car saw-tooth is an extension of a driveway. As long as the dimensions given for each parking space are retained, a saw-tooth could be added on to a turn-around in back of a house or used for off-street parking in front, and, of course, the number of spaces can be increased or decreased. Ideally, the pavement of the saw-tooth should be the same as that next to it. For economy a blacktop or gravel surface will suffice. The bumper strips, usually made of railroad ties or concrete, should be firmly secured at a workable level.

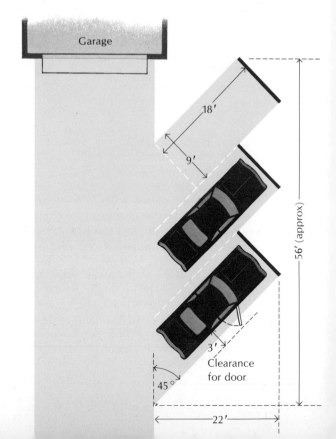

178

Parking Bay

The parking bay at right is set into the sloping front lawn of a house. Usually houses built on an incline have a narrow driveway leading to a garage in the rear. While this design does make pavement a prominent part of the front landscape, in this situation the bay is worth the loss of a few feet of green because it provides off-street parking for guests within view and easy access of the front entrance. One drawback of this arrangement is that cars must back out into the street, a dangerous procedure in heavy traffic. If there is room, on busy streets it is safer to add a parking bay on to the turn-around of a driveway. The dimensions given here allow enough space for the doors of a car to be opened without banging the side of the car next to it. Lines to establish parking spaces should be considered.

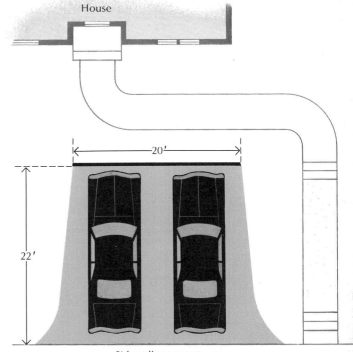

Sidewalk or street

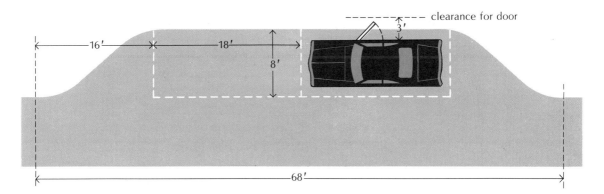

Parallel Parking

Often a parallel parking area will fit into a space too narrow for a saw-tooth or bay. The diagram above shows a straight length of driveway that has been widened to accommodate two parked cars. Each extension of the parking area above by 22 feet will make room for another car.

In a two-car parallel parking area, the first car can drive directly into place but the second must back into position. There is no need to back out of a parallel parking area, unless the cars are jammed together.

And the front car can always pull right out. For this reason a parallel strip is a safe design to use for off-street parking alongside a busy street.

For a unified effect, the parallel strip should be paved with the same material used for the adjacent surface. However, a contrasting material is all right, too. Blacktop is best but gravel is the least expensive. An edging of railroad ties, low shrubs, brick or stones gives a parking strip a finished look and if a gravel surface is used, helps keep it from spreading. Slope the surface so water will not accumulate.

179

Dimensions of Play

Court games in the backyard are a great source of fun and exercise for the whole family. As they require considerable space, it's best to decide on a site for them while planning the layout for the whole garden. In the court diagrams below, official dimensions are given. If there's space for a regulation-size court, by all means use it. If not, mark off a smaller, "unofficial" court. With the exception of a few serious players, everyone will have just as much fun. Surfaces need not be regulation either. An uneven grass lawn will do for games such as tetherball, badminton, croquet and volleyball. And many an asphalt driveway doubles as a hard surface for basketball and handball. If possible the site of lawn games should be moved from time to time to avoid compaction and scarring the surface, especially if it's in a prominent place. Remember too that even a lawn scuffed from heavy play can be aerated, reseeded and brought back to life in a season. With the exception of tennis and deck-tennis courts, all courts illustrated here can be do-it-yourself projects for even the inexperienced.

Volleyball

Volleyball is a game for all ages and any number of people from two to 16 or 20. The court should be located away from low branches to avoid obstructing balls hit high in the air. For optimum play try to maintain a width of at least 30 feet at the net, but the 60-foot length may be shortened. The net can be strung between two trees or attached to poles. Boundary lines can be made with chalk, tape or lengths of lath.

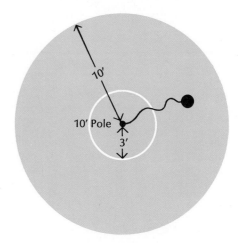

Tetherball

Tetherball is an active game played in a relatively small space on either asphalt or grass. Because the ball is hit hard it's important that the pole, to which it is attached, is firmly secured. The best pole support is a sleeve of pipe in concrete set into the ground. The inner circle in the diagram is the foul line which players may not overstep. It's optional but makes the game more difficult and interesting.

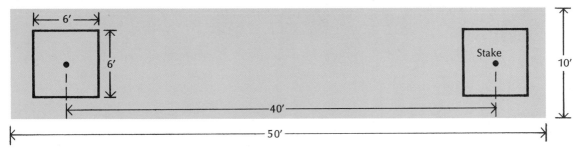

Horseshoes

Horseshoes is essentially a game for teen-agers and adults but children can play too, if children's toss lines are drawn closer to the stakes. Because horseshoes often bounce in unexpected directions, the game should be located well away from cars, buildings and walkways. The area between the stakes gets worn, so choose a place out of prominent view. Grass is the best surface on which to play; there's no noise when horseshoes fall short of the boxes and it's easier to reseed than to repair nicks in a hard surface like asphalt. The square boxes around the stakes can be filled with tanbark, sawdust, spaded earth or sand. For temporary use a pit can be dug for these materials.

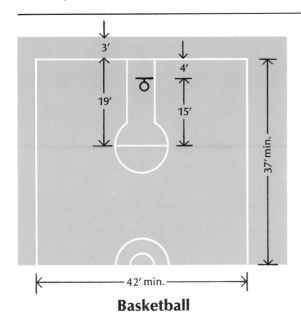

Basketball

The diagram above is an official men's half court with correct measurements for the keyhole, freethrow line and backboard. All that's really necessary for a great game, however, is a backboard and basket attached to a garage door frame, tree, pole or wall. The regulation height of the basket is 10 feet from its top edge to the ground. A flat stretch of hardtop or asphalt driveway can be used as a court or one can be made on any level part of the property by clearing and tamping the earth for a hard surface.

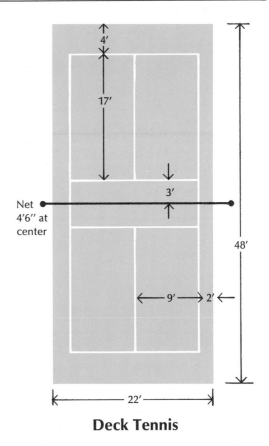

Deck Tennis

Deck tennis is becoming more and more popular with homeowners because it's a year-round sport played in a much smaller area than regular tennis. What's more, the court can be built on sloping ground. The regulation surface is heavy wood decking laid on top of a platform. (The game is sometimes called platform tennis.) Screening or chicken wire is used to enclose the court. Construction really calls for a contractor. Neighbors often build a community court in order to divide building expenses.

stops set at least 15 feet behind each baseline. Choice of a surface material—clay, grass, asphalt or all-weather—depends on individual preference, local conditions and budget. Not a do-it-yourself project.

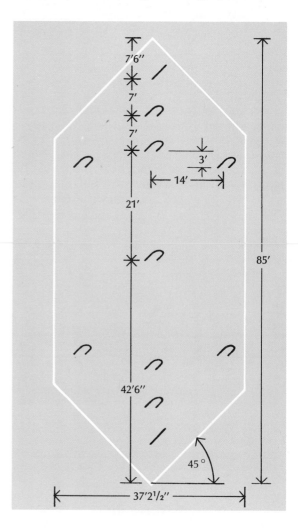

Tennis

Tennis is an exciting sport, good exercise and a game that can be played from childhood past retirement age. As the diagram indicates, it does require considerable (flat) space. Also necessary are high fence back-

Croquet

Croquet is a game of wit and strategy, and a great way to get fresh air and a bit of exercise. It's a fine family game that young people and adults can enjoy together. It requires wickets, wooden balls and mallets and a fairly even stretch of lawn, the thicker and closer cropped the better. Even a front lawn can be used without severe damage to the grass. Exact dimensions needed only for serious players.

182

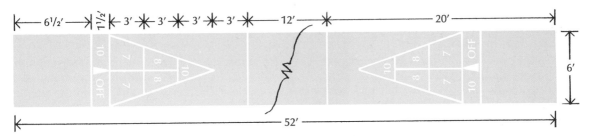

Shuffleboard

Shuffleboard is a family game which requires considerable skill when played on a proper court with regulation dimensions and an absolutely smooth surface. The least expensive, most practical surface is polished concrete. With a terrazzo machine for polishing (which can be rented) and some all-weather paint, a flat section of paving can be converted into a shuffleboard court during a weekend. One popular place for a court is beside a swimming pool where a section of the walkway can be used.

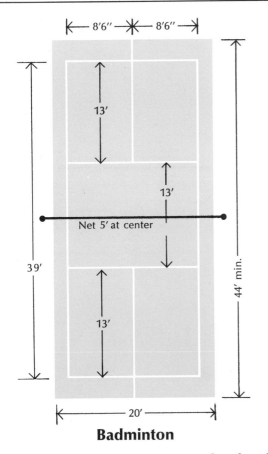

Badminton

Like volleyball, badminton can be played on any lawn big enough to accommodate from two to six or eight players and a net. With the purchase of nets for each game, both can be played in the same area. Serious badminton players, though, will want a proper-sized court as shown here, situated in a place protected from the wind and without overhanging branches.

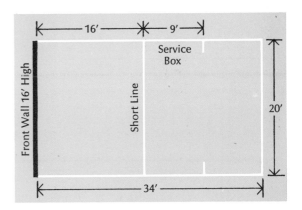

Handball

Handball can be played wherever there's a high wall (preferably smooth) and a hard ground surface (preferably nonskid). In fact, most boys and the few girls who play, learn the game on makeshift courts, such as empty city lots, driveway turn-arounds, or school walls. Almost any wall, if it's big enough, can be converted into a proper court. The wall can be faced with tongue-and-groove siding and the ground tamped down to a hard surface or covered with asphalt or concrete.

183

Sizes and Shapes of Pools and Facilities

A home swimming pool can be any size, really, as small as the above-ground pool seen on a following page or, if there's room and the budget permits, as large as a regulation Olympic pool. But if a family pool is any smaller than the example shown on these two pages, or the free form and round pools that follow, swimming is not the pleasure it should be. Building and maintaining such a small pool is hardly worth the cost and effort.

If you're considering a pool and have space for one larger than minimum size, discuss the cost of a few extra feet with the contractor. The enjoyment of swimming in the pool can be increased tremendously and there may not be a substantial increase in the total cost of building and landscaping.

When figuring a pool-building budget, remember that size is not the only factor affecting cost. Fencing a pool is an expense that must be taken into account in communities where it is required by law. Digging a deep area for diving may become an expensive addition if there's bedrock which must be blasted out. Of course building a pool of non-standard size or shape will also increase the cost. Another luxury well worth considering is a bathhouse. Shown here are minimum dimensions for a combination dressing room and shower. (The shower is optional.) Double these dimensions for dual changing and showering facilities. Dressing rooms will reduce traffic into the house.

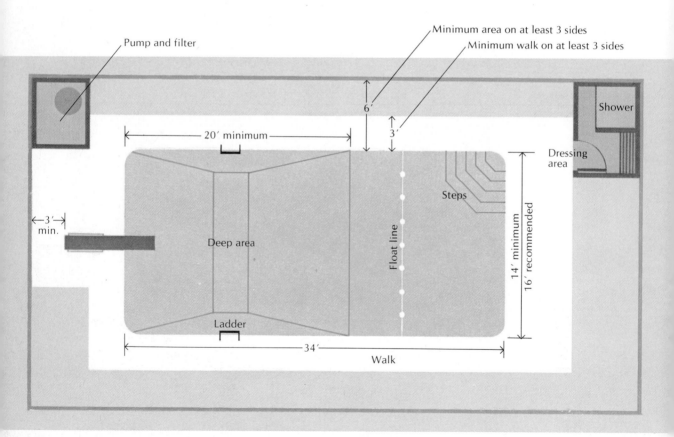

This is the minimum space *recommended for a pool. Anything less is really too small for good swimming. The walkway all around the pool is not a necessity, but it looks good, is a definite convenience and helps keep the water clean. The dressing room and shower are optional too, but the filter is required.*

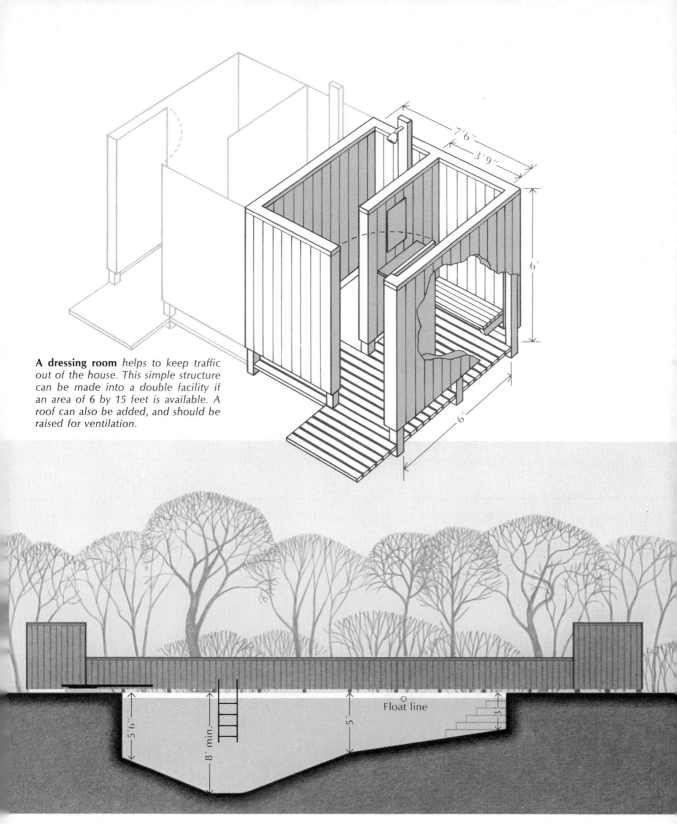

A dressing room helps to keep traffic out of the house. This simple structure can be made into a double facility if an area of 6 by 15 feet is available. A roof can also be added, and should be raised for ventilation.

7'6"
3'9"
6'
6'

Float line

5'6"
8' min.
5'
3'

If a diving board is to be included, the water must be at least eight feet deep in the diving area. If the land is rocky, blasting might be required to get the necessary depth. Blasting is expensive. Probe the ground before making final plans to see how the digging will go. For swimming, a four-foot depth is enough.

185

9

Optional Sizes and Shapes

This chapter deals with sizes and shapes for the garden that need not be as precise as those of the turn-around area of a driveway or the dimensions of a tennis court. The size of a terrace, for instance, is largely dictated by the amount of land available, personal preference and one's budget. But even with such non-prescribed sizes, there are limiting factors. A terrace large enough for only four chairs would seldom be worth building. There's no sense having a pool too small to swim in with pleasure or a planting bed too large to be easily maintained. Use the dimensions here for allocating space in the planning stage. As for the optional shape of a terrace (or bed or pool) it is somewhat influenced by the size, shape and other characteristics of the material used.

At the Edge of a Terrace

Shown below are shapes often used for edges of beds and terraces. Each shape is shown in a material to which it is well suited. For straight edges, brick is attractive and easy to use. For rounded shapes, concrete is easy to work with (though it is good on straight edges, too). The S-curve is shown in flagstone. Irregularly shaped stones are in character with a curvilinear form. Keep these examples in mind when planning a shape to use with the specific materials you have in mind.

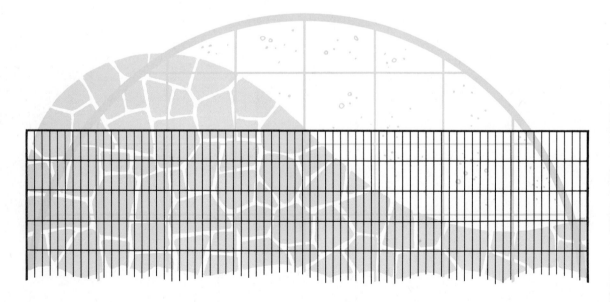

Variations on Swimming Pools

The standard pool shape is a rectangle, but round and kidney-shaped pools are so popular that many contractors have standardized these as well. Shown directly below are the dimensions of the largest standard kidney-shaped pool and, drawn in a dotted line, the smallest standard kidney-shaped pool generally sold. Of course any conceivable shape is possible for a pool, but the cost of designing and building a non-standard shape is much more expensive. Get comparative estimates before you decide.

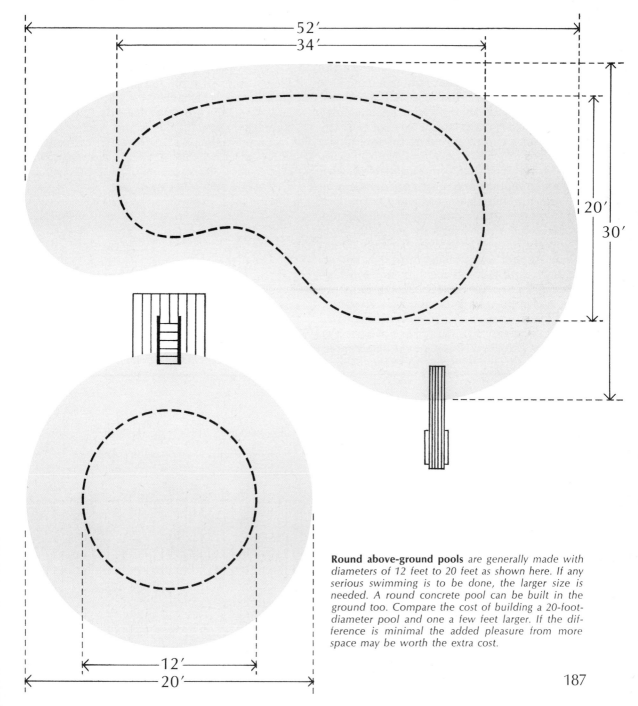

Round above-ground pools *are generally made with diameters of 12 feet to 20 feet as shown here. If any serious swimming is to be done, the larger size is needed. A round concrete pool can be built in the ground too. Compare the cost of building a 20-foot-diameter pool and one a few feet larger. If the difference is minimal the added pleasure from more space may be worth the extra cost.*

187

How to Choose Terrace Furniture

These illustrations are a helpful tool for planning the space required for furnishing a terrace. They show the typical sizes and shapes of outdoor furniture and are drawn to the scale of ¼ inch. Each square on the grid equals one square foot. To use this chart first measure the existing or planned area to be furnished. Using the scale of feet at the far margin, transmit those dimensions to a piece of tracing paper. You now have an area outlined that's in scale with the furniture drawings and you can see how much furniture of what size can be accommodated without overcrowding. The shaded areas indicate extra space needed for circulation and service around the tables and chairs.

There are two ways to experiment with various groupings and pieces of furniture on the scaled plan: Make cardboard cutouts of the furniture shapes and move them around. Or trace the shapes directly onto the plan. If you are interested in furniture styles not shown, simply make scaled drawings or cutouts. This all takes time but it serves an important purpose. Experimenting on paper with different sizes and shapes of furniture avoids making unsatisfactory choices or real mistakes when it comes to buying. The longer you work with a plan the more likely you are to discover the potential problems, and opportunities.

If the plan looks crowded with furniture the terrace will too, but don't worry about a terrace plan that looks bare after all the chosen furniture is in place. An indoor room enclosed by four walls would look empty with one or two pieces but an outdoor terrace does not. A terrace, with or without much furniture, is seen as one decorative element within the larger "room" (landscape) of surrounding trees, grass, house and sky.

Besides size, shape and quantity of terrace furniture, there are other considerations. Color: on a small terrace solids look best. Material: if moved often, lightweight materials make the job easier; and only weatherproof materials should be used. Arrangement: two areas are a good idea if the terrace is used for lounging and dining.

Placement of furniture should not obstruct entry to or movement around the terrace. Don't buy too much at first.

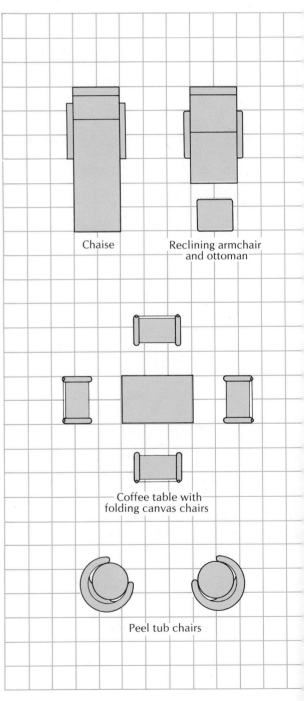

Chaise

Reclining armchair
and ottoman

Coffee table with
folding canvas chairs

Peel tub chairs

The size of a terrace is best when related to the surrounding landscape. However, this is often not possible because of limited property size, building costs and personal preference as to use of the land. As a rule large terraces are more in keeping with outdoor scale than small ones. Build as large a terrace as possible if it's going to be used a great deal for entertaining. Think about the most successful patios and terraces you have seen and get their measurements to consider for your own use.

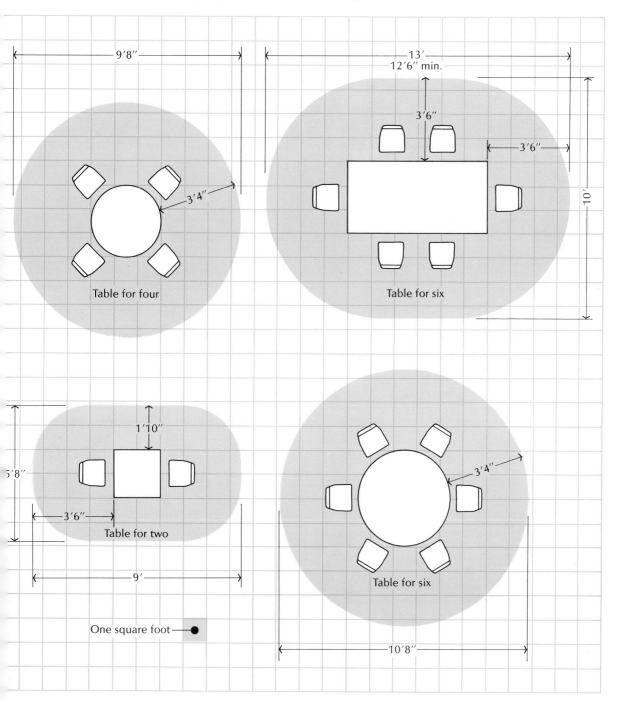

Table for four

Table for six

Table for two

Table for six

One square foot

189

Leave Plenty of Space for Maturing Trees and Shrubs

Before setting out any trees and shrubs in front of your own house, it would be worthwhile to walk down a few suburban streets and have a thoughtful look at the mistakes so commonly made in the name of "foundation planting."

You will see place after place where too many shrubs have been planted too close to the house, where the character of individual plants is lost in a mass of intertwined and overgrown foliage, and where plants push against the walls and obscure the windows. And in many places the remedy for overgrown plants, which is drastic pruning, is as unsightly as the overgrown bush itself.

The only proper solution to overcrowding is to plant trees and shrubs far enough from the house and with sufficient space between them to allow for their proper development. This requires knowledge of how fast the

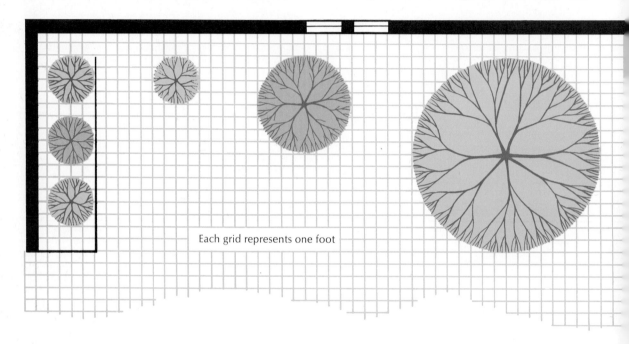

Each grid represents one foot

These common trees and shrubs, and others of similar size, should be planted no closer to the hous

To 4 feet

Boxwood holly
(Ilex crenata convexa)

Dwarf English yew
(Taxus baccata nana)

Dwarf flowering quince
(Chaenomeles japonica)

Dwarf Japanese barberry
(Berberis thunbergii minor)

Mugho pine

Slender deutzia
(Deutzia gracilis)

6 to 8 feet

Medium rhododendrons

Pfitzer juniper
(Juniperus chinensis pfitzeriana)

Pieris floribunda

Leucothoe fontanesiana

Kerria
(K. japonica pleniflora)

Dwarf Japanese yew
(Taxus cuspidata nana)

Shrub roses in variety

10 to 12 feet

Flowering almond
(Prunus triloba)

Common boxwood
(Buxus sempervirens)

Large rhododendrons

Mountain laurel
(Kalmia latifolia)

Japanese yew
(Taxus cuspidata)

Rock cotoneaster
(Cotoneaster horizontali.

plants grow and their ultimate size. In the lists below are the names of various plants commonly used beside a house.

The drawing below shows about how far plants of a certain size should be set from a house. In all cases the distance is enough to allow the plant to mature fully and still leave two or three feet of clearance from the adjacent wall.

In the best of all worlds one would set out mature plants of the size required and there would be no question of how far to plant them from the house. This is possible, but very expensive. Next best is to buy the largest plants you can afford so they won't appear too isolated when planted where they should be. If neither of these alternatives is feasible and young plants must be used, they can be combined with a ground cover or perennials to fill some of the space around them. As the trees and shrubs mature you can remove the temporary plantings and use them elsewhere or, in the gardener's tradition, pass them along to friends and neighbors. Perennials, such as day lilies, tree peonies and iris, are excellent for this use.

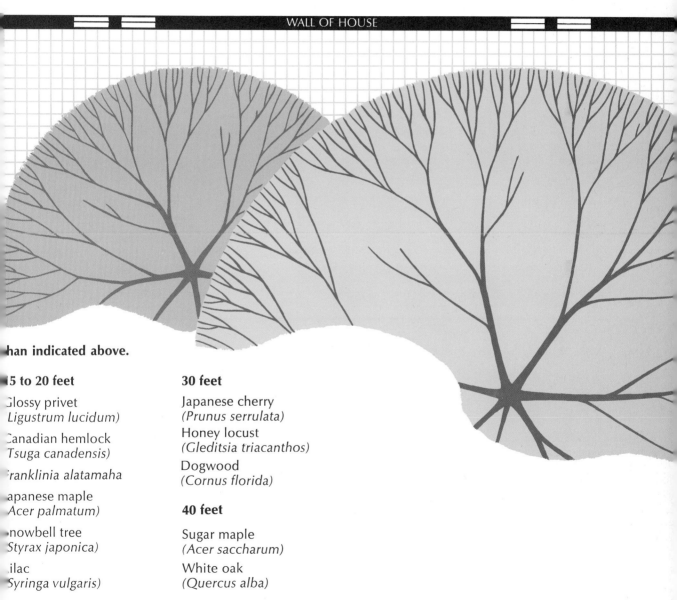

WALL OF HOUSE

han indicated above.

5 to 20 feet

Glossy privet
(*Ligustrum lucidum*)

Canadian hemlock
(*Tsuga canadensis*)

Franklinia alatamaha

Japanese maple
(*Acer palmatum*)

Snowbell tree
(*Styrax japonica*)

Lilac
(*Syringa vulgaris*)

30 feet

Japanese cherry
(*Prunus serrulata*)

Honey locust
(*Gleditsia triacanthos*)

Dogwood
(*Cornus florida*)

40 feet

Sugar maple
(*Acer saccharum*)

White oak
(*Quercus alba*)

191

Minimum Sizes for Other Plantings

Plantings can, of course, be any size; one tree or a forest, one flower in a pot or a field of bloom. But in a home garden there are considerations of maintenance and proportion that affect the size of a planting bed. If a bed is too large, planting, weeding and thinning are difficult. Beds that are too small can be a problem too. Water evaporates more quickly in small areas and they need more sprinkling. Proportion is as important as maintenance in determining the size of beds, if not more so. Considering the magnitude of outdoor scale it is more likely that a gardener would make a planting bed too small rather than too large. Shown here are some minimum sizes for garden plantings of vegetables, trees, flowers and shrubs. Smaller sizes are likely to seem out of scale.

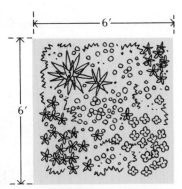

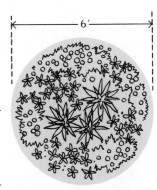

Flower beds *are often too small to be effective. But mass plantings have more impact than the same amount scattered from place to place. There are also fewer edges to trim and maintenance is easier. The three beds shown here are large enough to fit well into the scale* *of most home gardens and yet in each one the gardener is never more than three feet away from a plant. A rectangular bed can be any length, but if it is wider than six feet, a narrow path down the middle is needed to keep all flowers and weeds within easy reach.*

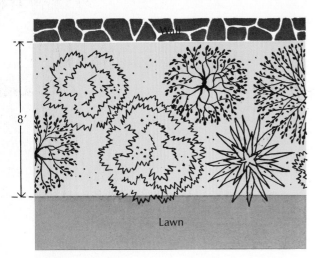
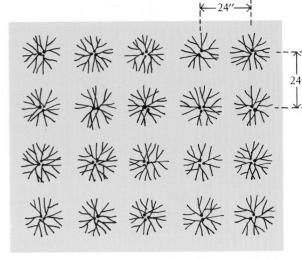

A border of shrubs *beside a house or set apart should be at least eight feet wide to allow each plant space to develop. For appearance the length might well be a module of the house—the length of a porch could well determine the span of a border.*

Roses need space *for roots to grow without competition. For good growth, pleasing scale, easy maintenance and a good show, garden roses (hybrid teas, floribundas and grandifloras) should be 2 to 3 feet apart in beds four to six feet wide.*

192

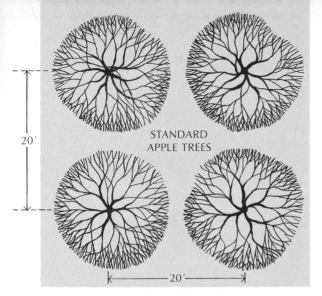

STANDARD
APPLE TREES

20'

20'

8'

8'

DWARF APPLE TREES

Standard fruit trees (above left) require 20 feet between trunks to grow properly, whereas the dwarf varieties (above right) need only 8 feet. In the same space then, you can grow four times as many dwarf as standard trees and get much more fruit. Depending on the selected root stock, dwarf trees reach a height of 8 to 15 feet so they're also easier to prune, spray and pick. In spite of all these assets it's not an easy matter to decide whether to plant dwarf or standard trees. For many gardeners the graceful form of a big apple tree, for instance, is well worth the added time and effort needed to care for it and pick the fruit.

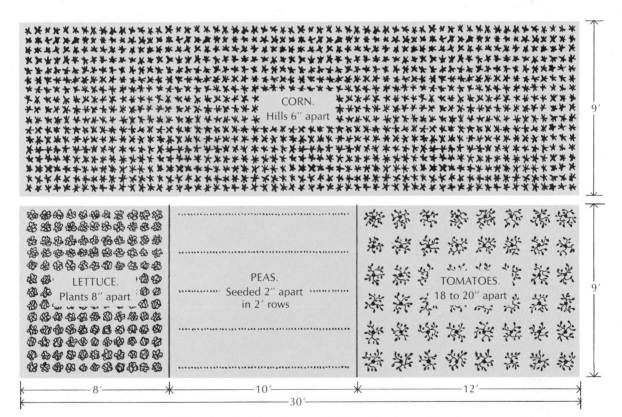

CORN.
Hills 6" apart

9'

LETTUCE.
Plants 8" apart

PEAS.
Seeded 2" apart
in 2' rows

TOMATOES.
18 to 20" apart

9'

8'   10'   12'
30'

A vegetable garden big enough for a family of four is illustrated here, showing the amount of space to allow for four vegetables especially worth growing at home. More space is given to corn than the other vegetables because each stalk produces relatively few ears and, in order for pollination to take place, corn must be densely planted in blocks. Corn should never be planted in a row or two but if you don't have 30 feet, an area 9 feet square will grow well and yield enough ears for a few delicious summer treats.

10

Putting the Plan
On Paper

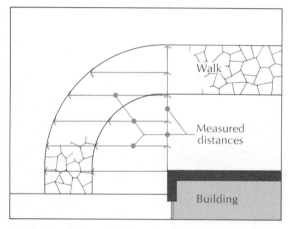

To plot a curve *establish base line with stakes equally set at useful intervals. Measure from each stake.*

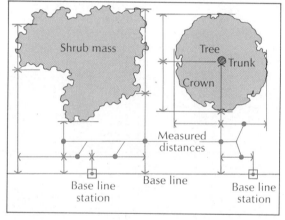

For masses of foliage *these are measurements that should be recorded for plotting on graph paper.*

If you plan to do some of your own landscape design, you will need to know how to measure the site and map certain features in the form of a plot plan. Before deciding where to put a parking area, terrace or play yard you should know the relative size and location of the house, drive, walks, trees and other major elements of the landscape. With the method described here this is not too hard to accomplish.

First, establish a "base line" along the length of the site and parallel to the house or property line. Set a straight row of stakes at 10-foot intervals along this line. A cord running the full length is helpful. Number stakes from front to back.

You now have a point of reference from

which every feature of the landscape can be measured and then plotted on graph paper. An easy scale is to let each square on the graph paper equal 1 foot on the ground. For larger properties the sheets may have to be joined together. To position the house measure from the curb (stake 1) to the front corner. If this is 22 feet, note the distance as $2 + 2$ (stake no. 2 plus 2 feet). If the back of the house happened to be 32 feet further on, the notation would be $5 + 4$ (stake no. 5 plus 4 feet), and so on for all the other key

▶ **Typical measurements** *that might be required for mapping a suburban landscape. Note how the base line parallels the side of the house. Small squares indicate the numbered stakes at 10-foot intervals.*

194

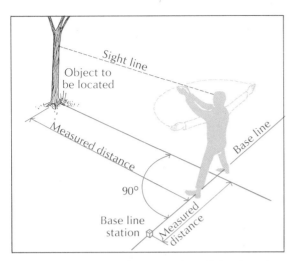

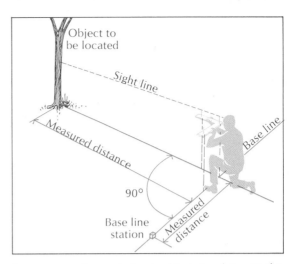

Quick way *to plot an object. Stand parallel to base line for sighting. Measure distance from stake.*

A more accurate way *to locate objects in relation to the base line is by sighting along a triangle.*

elements along the base line. Objects that are off the base line are measured as shown above. Put the stake numbers in a line on the graph paper (10 squares apart) and plot the elements in relation to these.

When this has been done you will have a plot plan on which changes and additions can be outlined, to the same scale. Sizes and shapes can be tried out on an overlay of tracing paper, or cutouts can be made and tried in various positions. In laying out a new garden the plot plan might include no more than the property lines, drive, walks, house and terrace and a tree or two.

When figuring space for various additions, see the dimensions on preceding pages.

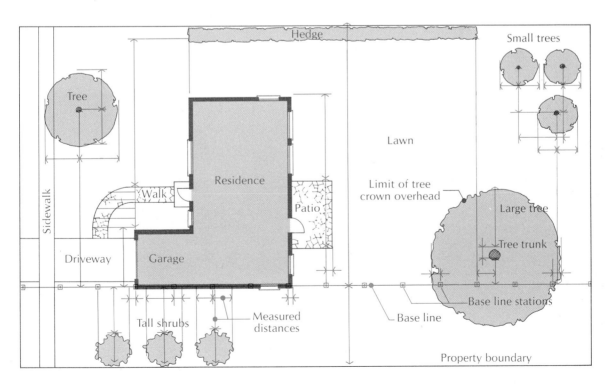

How to Measure the Slope

A hand level, which you can get for less than ten dollars, is a good investment for anyone who is planning to level a plot of irregular land, lay out flight of steps, cut into a slope to make a flat space or build a deck on a slope. The level is a small instrument with a bubble which shows when a line from one point to another is level as you sight through it.

By sighting from a fixed height to a rod of the same height, the difference in grade between the sighting position and the rod is easily determined. Some practical applications are illustrated on the facing page. Once you understand the principle you will see how it can be used to lay out steps (see specifications on page 199), to find how much would have to be cut from a rise or added to a hollow to make a good level space, or to

establish the slope necessary for drainage.

In using this simplified system of surveying, the rod must always be on the uphill side, and the zero must be at the top of the rod. The fixed height of the instrument may be eye-level when standing, or that of a support the height of the rod.

At left, a folding carpenter's rule is used for the rod. The bottom section is folded up to make it 5 feet 6 inches to match the eye-level of the surveyor. A yardstick can be tacked to a piece of 1 x 2 to make it eye-level, or a special rod can be made, as shown. Note the optional support for the level.

Surveyors use a rod marked in 10ths because it is easier to figure percentages of grade and make other transpositions. But for the small projects proposed here it's easier to have the readings in inches.

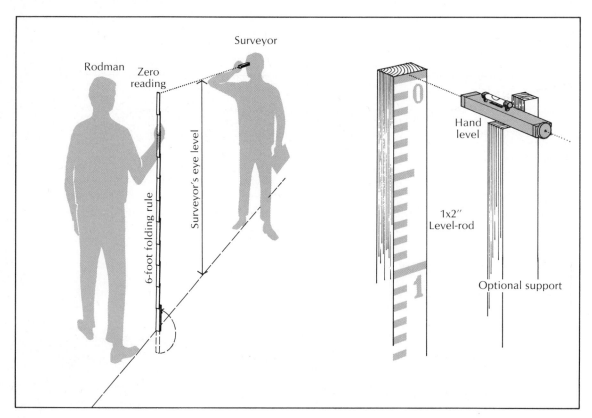

Measuring rod *must be same height as the level when sighting. Rod can be a folding rule or piece of 1-x-2 marked in feet and inches, as shown. Rodman moves finger up and down until level with surveyor's sight line and reads off the dimension. For greatest accuracy, match rod to height of level support as above.*

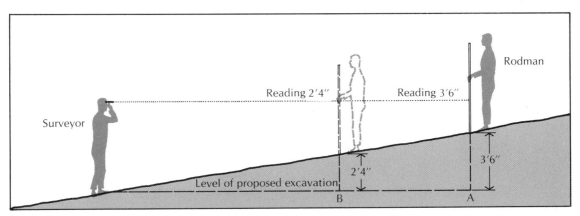

When planning to cut *into a slope, for more level space, stand at grade to be maintained and position rodman up the hill. Reading where a level sight line intersects rod (with zero at top) gives height of the cut required to establish a level area for the distance between the surveyor and rodman: points A and B.*

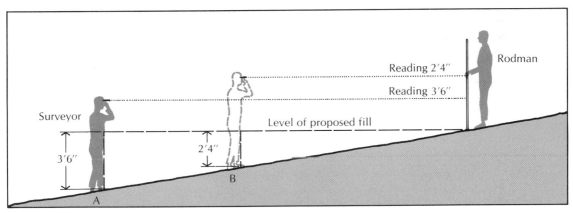

When filling *a slope to make it level, surveyor stands at proposed wall positions, rodman stands where the level will begin. With zero at top, reading on rod gives height of fill required to level an area for the given distance: 3 feet 6 inches for A, 2 feet 4 inches for B. These are also the post heights required for a level deck.*

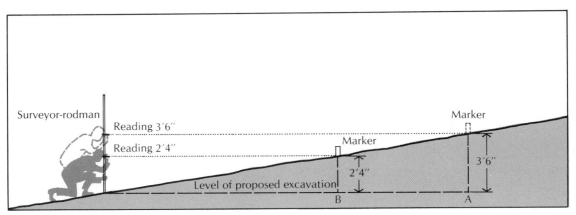

Working alone, *the surveyor holds rod as shown and slides instrument up and down to establish a line level with the stake. Reading on rod, with zero at bottom, shows height of cut (or fill) required to level the area between the surveyor and stake. Height would be 3 feet 6 inches for distance to marker A, 2 feet 4 inches to B.*

Planning for Privacy

Good land planning, from a developer's point of view, makes space for the greatest number of houses. While understandable in the light of rising land costs, it is not the best approach to planning from the home-owner's point of view.

The opportunity for outdoor living and recreation is part of the appeal of a single family house, and to enjoy this fully calls for a degree of screening and privacy. The question is, how much and where?

If you live in a community where complete enclosure of the back yard is an accepted practice, the fencing may be included with the cost of the house. For those who have not lived with it, the idea of total enclosure may seem stark and unfriendly. But fences can be softened with planting, the neighbors also have privacy and everyone enjoys more use of the land around his house.

If total outdoor privacy is out of the question where you live, you can at least plan for partial screening in areas where needed most. The problem may not be as dramatic as illustrated here, where a large window in one house faces the terrace of another, but the solutions shown could apply to a variety of other situations.

Notice in the top drawing that the screen is an extension of the house and creates a second wall for the outdoor room. The same effect could be had with a high hedge and, for privacy on three sides, it could be an L-shape as shown in the second drawing. The other example shows how an informal border planting could be used for the same purpose.

Upper right. *An extension of the wall of the house could be as high as the roof line. Height might be needed for privacy if the neighboring house were on the uphill side. Plants can enhance wall, on both sides.*

Center. *Tall hedge, or vines grown on a high lattice frame, could also be used adjacent to a terrace. If privacy or wind protection is needed on three sides, the screen could be L-shaped as shown.*

Bottom. *Screen planting near the property line reduces the neighbors' outlook but it could improve the view if particularly attractive trees and shrubs were used. For seasonal screening use deciduous plants.*

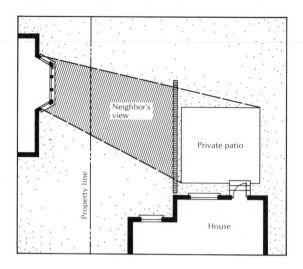

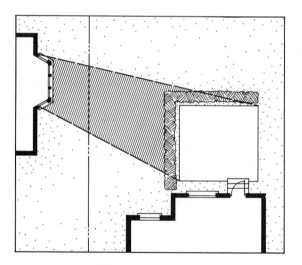

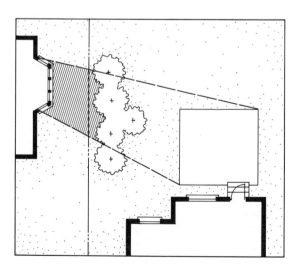

The Magic Formula for Garden Steps

The slope of the land will determine, in part, how steep or shallow garden steps must be. But for ease and safety in walking and for best appearance there are definite restrictions in design. As shown below, a run of five steps may rise as much as 30 inches in a distance of 5 feet 10 inches, or as little as 20 inches in a run of 7 feet 6 inches. And they can, of course, be designed in any mul-

tiple of these sizes. Once you know the rise required for a given distance, use these dimensions to figure the height and number of steps. See page 196 on measuring slopes.

The proper proportion of tread (flat surface) to riser (the vertical) is based on an average length of stride and is simply stated: *Twice the riser plus the tread should equal 26 inches.*

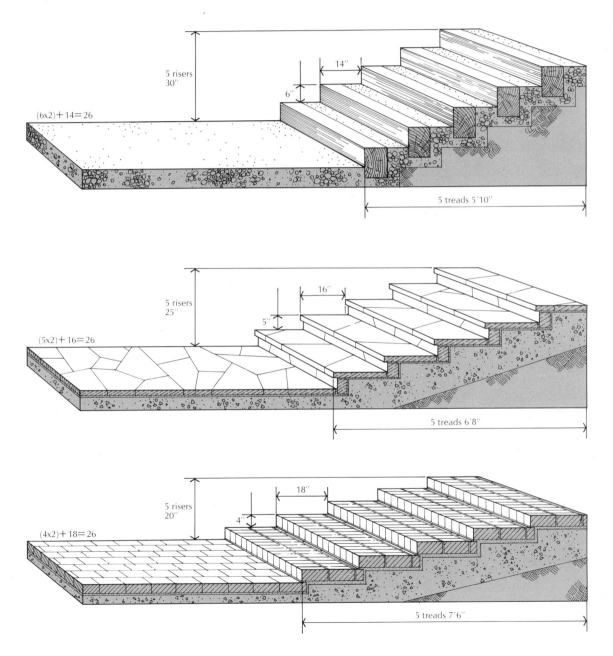

The Graphic Language of Plans

In recording your designs on paper you will find these symbols useful. They are typical of the drawings used by professionals on plan views (a graphic outline as seen from above) to assist in visualizing the finished garden. Of course the names of plants and structures could simply be written on the plan in the space they'll occupy but these symbols indicate texture, size and shape.

Plants are always shown at their mature size and a dot or "X" used to indicate the position of the trunk. Generally the names of plants and their spacing (distance from trunk to trunk at maturity) are also listed on the plan to avoid having to cross check a key with a separate listing of the plants. Try not to put plants so close together that they will be crowded as they mature.

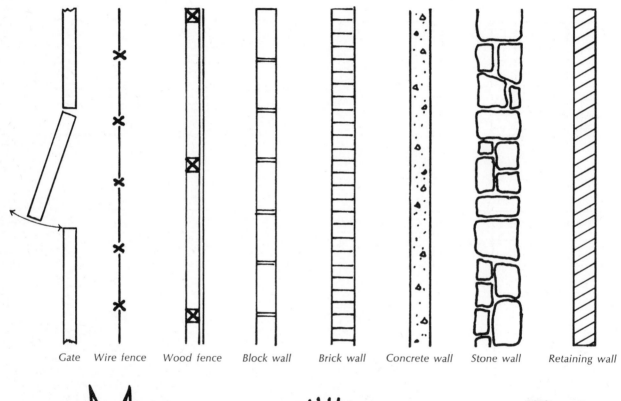

Gate   Wire fence   Wood fence   Block wall   Brick wall   Concrete wall   Stone wall   Retaining wall

Evergreen tree (fir)

Evergreen tree (pine)

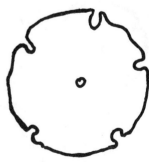

Deciduous tree

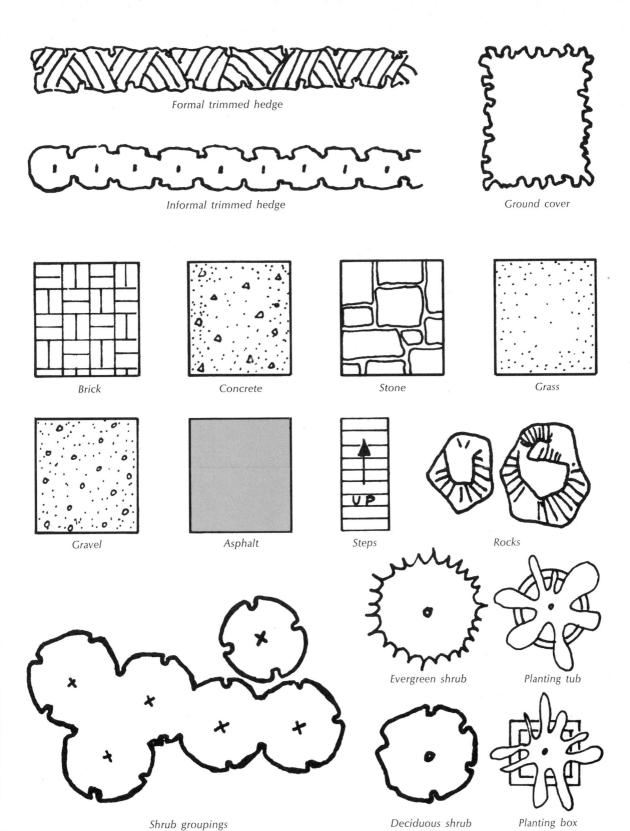

Formal trimmed hedge

Informal trimmed hedge

Ground cover

Brick

Concrete

Stone

Grass

Gravel

Asphalt

Steps

Rocks

Shrub groupings

Evergreen shrub

Planting tub

Deciduous shrub

Planting box

201

Here's the Plan and ...

It is not easy to visualize a finished garden by looking at its plan. But to help you make the transition, a typical plan is shown below and opposite are pictures of the garden developed from this plan. The camera angles for each picture are marked on the plan with blue arrows. You can see that many aspects of the garden are not revealed in the drawing. Color, texture, true shapes (irregular circles outline the spread of trees and shrubs) and, in particular, the vertical dimensions of objects are not shown. The mind must fill in these missing parts. It helps in visualizing the "up and down" of a

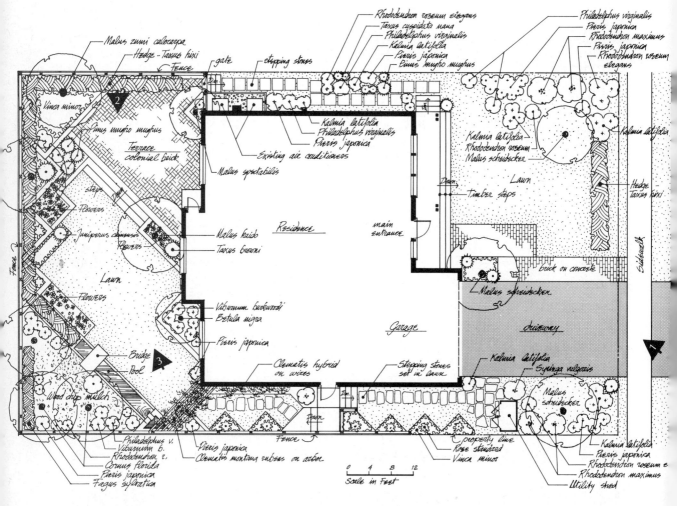

This is the plan of the garden seen in the photographs on the opposite page much as it would be drawn and labeled by a landscape architect. Arrows keyed to the photographs have been superimposed to show the position of the camera when the pictures were taken: 1. on the sidewalk in front of the house; 2. looking across the back lawn from the terrace; 3. looking toward the terrace and back corner of the garden from the far side of

the lawn. Plants are outlined as they will appear at mature growth. Dots indicate where each plant is set in the ground so the distance between plants can be visualized. Botanical names of plants are used to avoid misunderstanding. Common names cannot be depended upon for exact identification. Rather than writing names on the plan, some designers key the plants to a separate list with numbers or letters.

Here's the Finished Garden

garden to separate things on the ground first, such as beds and walks from furniture, flowers and shrubs of middle height. Then think of trees as overhead green masses supported on trunks. Bear in mind, too, that a plan seldom shows what lies just beyond property lines, as is well illustrated below.

1. Front entry *from the street. The shapes of driveway, walk and lawn are easily visualized from the plan; shrubs, trees and steps are harder to imagine.*
2. View of the back corner *from terrace shows how planting is used to screen neighboring houses. In a few years they will be completely hidden from view.*
3. Lawn and terrace *in the actual garden are not as dominant as they appear to be in the plan. This is because the bulk and height of the trees and shrubs, which have a softening effect, cannot be shown on the plan.*

What You Should Know About Costs and Contracts

Landscaping a new house generally costs about 10 percent of the total price of the house and property. This, however, is only a broad rule of thumb.

Such factors as the nature of the subsurface (from loam to rock), what the homeowner wants (terraces, swimming pool, exotic flora or simply a lawn and the basic trees and shrubs) and how much of the work the homeowner will do himself are so variable that exact estimates are impossible.

The best way to determine probable costs is to sit down with pencil and paper and estimate the cost of materials and labor item by item. And even then, no matter how precise the estimate, the real cost may well be more. This is because some items—unforeseen or forgotten—are simply not accounted for. Likewise, the time allotted for landscaping is almost always less than it actually takes. Materials aren't delivered on schedule or a sunny day lures the expected handyman away from his project to go fishing.

But don't be discouraged. It is possible to keep the cost of landscaping within a specified budget despite the problems. The key to success is careful planning.

How to Cut Costs

Since labor is increasingly a greater percentage of total cost, one of the best ways to save is by doing as much as possible yourself. There are other ways too: In general the younger a plant the less it costs. A tree, for example, increases in cost in geometric proportion to its size. Plant small young trees; let them develop on your property rather than at the nursery. Year-old trees come bare-root in bundles of "whips" and cost much less than larger sizes. It's also generally true that faster-growing plants cost less than slow-growing ones. Covering a hillside with myrtle, for example, is less costly than covering it with ivy. Seeding a lawn is hard work but costs considerably less in the beginning than sodding, although sod, in the long run, is comparable in cost.

It pays to use indigenous plant materials; they grow better and cost less. By shopping around for plants you can sometimes save money but be sure to buy from a reputable nursery that sprays and root-prunes its stock to keep it growing well.

Construction Costs Can Also Be Cut

Choose a design solution that works with the given topography and involves little if any earth-moving. This saves money by avoiding the use of heavy machinery. Usually larger modules (concrete block) cost less than smaller ones (brick). Concrete foundations are expensive. If it is feasible to do so, lay your terrace on sand rather than on a concrete base. Once you start thinking of how to cut down on landscaping costs without sacrificing quality you'll probably be able to add to the above list.

A less obvious, seemingly contradictory way of saving money is to hire a professional designer. This may be a landscape architect, landscape designer or a nursery that offers design help. Some nurseries, however, are more interested in selling plant material than in developing a good overall plan.

Most qualified to help is the well-trained, experienced landscape architect. You have to pay for professional help but the services rendered can save you money in both the short and long run.

With his knowledge of plants, structures and design, a landscape architect can develop attractive ways to use less expensive materials and methods of construction.

When there's heavy construction work to be done he can save you time, money and trouble by reviewing contract bids and choosing a contractor who will do a good job for a reasonable amount.

All this can add up to real saving.

A homeowner who wants to do all his own landscaping, but has some questions about the design and construction, can save time, wasted effort and money by paying a professional for rough sketches of various plans or finished plans to work from. In fact, once a homeowner hires a landscape architect his budget can be depended upon. Training and experience enable good designers to adapt a homeowner's landscaping needs and desires to the realities of his budget. This is one of his most important jobs.

What a Professional Designer Can Do for You

If you decide to hire a professional, be sure to discuss your budget and ideas with him in the first meeting. Homeowners with only a general notion of what they want will develop a more precise idea working with the designer. From this information he draws up a landscaping program that includes such things as surfacing, planting, drainage and an estimated budget for carrying out these plans. The program and budget are reviewed by the homeowner, discussed with the designer and changes made if necessary. The designer can then draw a few sketches of his ideas for developing the program. From the sketch approved by the client he'll draw up preliminary plans (the approved sketch drawn to scale and a listing of materials to be used) and a more precise estimate of the cost.

Once this preliminary plan and budget is okayed, contract plans are made. These are detailed drawings used by a contractor (or homeowner) to build the job. If a contractor is needed and the homeowner doesn't know of a good one, the architect will issue and receive contract bids, advise on the best contractor for the job and, if needed, supervise the construction work.

Full or Partial Service?

You can hire a professional for all of the services mentioned above or only certain aspects of a job. You may be able to do without contract plans (and save money) if you have a good contractor who can work from detailed sketches. In this situation be sure to have an agreement that the contractor can call on the designer for help whenever he needs it.

Some people spread their landscaping costs over a period of years by having a landscape architect make a master plan with contract drawings for the complete job that can be used whenever there is money on hand to do another part of the project.

Landscape architects and designers usually charge an hourly rate for residential work, though for a specific project—a sketch or working drawing of plantings around a terrace, for example—a lump sum may be charged. On large projects the fee may be a fixed percentage of the total cost of the job.

Contractors work both on an hourly and set-fee basis. On large jobs it is beneficial for all concerned to determine an upset fee; that is, a figure above which the landscape architect and contractor agree not to go.

A contract between architect and client is not legally necessary but some sort of written agreement—a legal form or letter—is a good idea. It helps insure a clearer understanding on both sides of services, materials and fees. The clearer the understanding on every detail the better it is for all.

205

SECTION

3

Planting

How to choose the right plants for the job at hand
and how to keep them growing at their best.

11

Using Trees
in the Landscape

Climatic Influences

Trees are unquestionably the major elements of landscaping. So you should not plant them without some basic knowledge of your region, especially of its lowest temperatures, because *cold* is plant-life's greatest enemy.

The adjoining map of plant hardiness in Canada indicates the climatic zone in which your region is located. The nine zones are based on minimum winter temperatures. They also take into account factors which influence, although to a lesser degree than cold, plant survival in a given region. These factors include the length of frost-free periods, quantity of precipitation, degree of humidity, and wind velocity. A classification of plants featured in this chapter corresponds to this map. Each graphic symbol bears the numbers of the zones where a plant can be cultivated.

The zones, of course, are not absolutely uniform: in each are regional sub-climates which affect plant hardiness. The map is only a general indicator of climate. Higher altitudes are likely to be colder than indicated on this map. Other geographic and topographic features may also make a specific small area considerably warmer or cooler than the general zone by which it is surrounded. The zones also overlap to some extent. It is wise to respect the limits indicated, but if conditions in your area are not average, consult a local nursery about special requirements.

From data supplied by dozens of experimental farms, the Canadian Department of Agriculture has created a plant hardiness map that divides the country into nine main climatic zones. Our map is based on it.

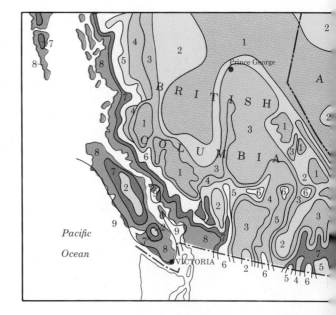

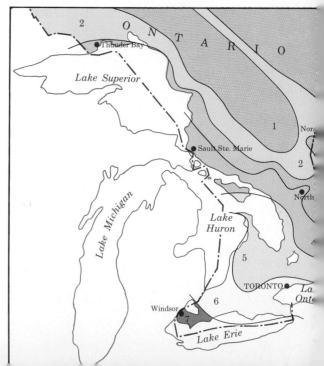

Plant Hardiness Zones

Regions of extreme cold (Mid-North) belong to zone 1 where vegetation is very limited because of low minimum temperatures ($-43°F$). The most temperate region (the British Columbia coast) is in zone 9. Here periods of frost are short and temperatures rarely fall below $32°F$. The Toronto and Montreal metropolitan areas are situated between these extremes. A gardener or a landscaper interprets these zones as follows: Any plant in zone 1 will grow in all zones up to 9, but the reverse is not true. For example, a plant whose hardiness zone is 5 can be cultivated in zones 5, 6, 7, 8 and 9, but not in zones 4, 3, 2 and 1. For easy reference, on the following pages each tree's complete growing range is shown (i.e. Carolina spruce, zones 7-9). Although most plants in colder areas will also grow in warmer ones, there are some plants which need cold winters to do well. If in doubt, consult a local nursery.

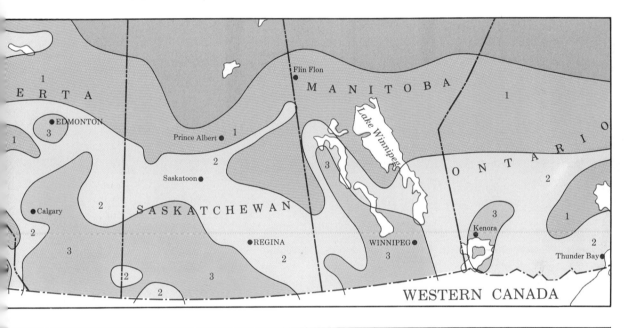

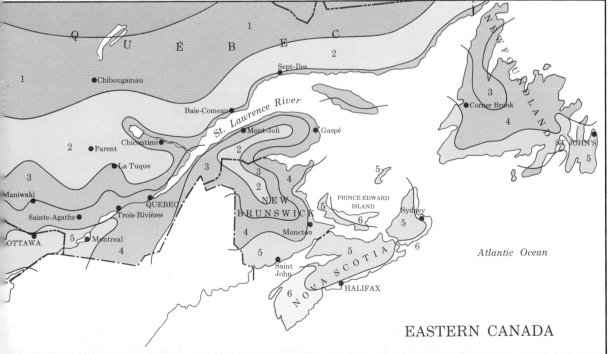

How to Choose Your Trees

Trees not only adapt differently to climatic conditions, they vary in ornamental value. Therefore a landscaper must select them with care, taking into account such considerations as hardiness, shape, size, special features and the purpose for which the tree is planted. It is essential to choose the best trees for your landscaping requirements. On the following pages is a list of excellent garden trees generally available in the nursery trade. To help you se-lect the right shape and kind of tree for your garden, each one in the list is keyed to the symbols below. The key shows you at a glance the tree's general shape, its root system and its foliage and flowering features. Simply match the characteristics of each symbol in the list to those below. Because trees require years to mature they should be planted as soon as possible—but not before you are sure they are in the right places.

The Shapes

Rounded. This symbol represents round and/or spreading trees. It is shown here with shallow roots, indicating that plants will not grow well beneath it.

Pyramidal. Most conifers (or needle-leafed trees) have this general shape. Some are narrower and some wider than indicated by this symbol. Note the shallow roots.

Upright. Most large trees have this shape. Some are wider at the top than at the base (vase-shaped), but all are taller than they are wide. Note again the shallow roots.

The Foliage

Deciduous. Symbols that are bare-leafed with branch structure represent trees that lose their leaves in the winter. In this group are trees with brilliant fall foliage.

Evergreen. Symbols without branch structure foliage correspond to evergreen trees, either broad-leafed or needle-leafed conifers as indicated.

The Roots

Deep-rooted. The green strip indicates trees that have deep roots and therefore don't compete with plants beneath them for food and water.

Features

This symbol represents broad-leafed trees (either deciduous or evergreen).

This symbol stands for conifers (needle-leafed trees).

This symbol represents trees that are outstanding for their flowers.

Large Trees: 40 to 100 Feet or More

These trees are tall enough to dominate the landscape and cast shade on the roofs of houses. In cities they are particularly vital: They emit oxygen, absorb air pollution, act as windbreaks, and, in winter, warm the atmosphere. Oaks and maples are among the best known of this group.

One of the finest of the big shade trees is the American elm, but it has been devastated by Dutch elm disease. It is now so seldom planted that there is as much danger of extinction by disuse as by disease. It would be a worthwhile act of faith for anyone willing to take a chance—and with the space to spare—to plant elms so there still will be some left when a cure for Dutch elm disease is finally found.

zones 1-9

Balsam fir (*Abies balsamea*). This fir is one of Canada's most common trees. Its symmetrical, tapered shape is reminiscent of a church steeple and makes balsam fir a popular choice as a Christmas tree. Distinguished by upright seed-bearing cones, this fir adapts well to practically any soil but is very sensitive to atmospheric pollution. Like all firs, it needs coolness and high humidity and must be planted in the open, where it can get plenty of air and light. Mature specimens require deep, slightly acid soil. Balsam fir is best used in the country or in a natural environment, to create screens and groupings.

zones 1-9

White poplar or trembling aspen (*Populus tremuloides*). Probably the most widely distributed tree in North America, this poplar is useful for quick screening. Although not a true garden tree, white poplar helps to create attractive groupings, especially in cold regions.

zones 2-9

Colorado blue spruce (*Picea pungens glauca*). The spruce is a stiffer tree than the fir and is often prickly to the touch. Colorado blue spruce is a common specimen tree for home gardens. Its blue needles, at right angles to the branches, are striking. Blue spruce is best planted in open areas where one can admire its pyramidal shape. Like all conifers, it grows too large to be planted in the middle of a lawn or in front of a house. An attractive variety is 'Moerheim,' which has an irregular shape and blue-gray needles. Colorado blue spruce thrives in deep, moist soil, preferably with high acid content. It grows in full sunlight or in partial shade.

zones 2-9

Eastern white pine (*Pinus strobus*). For most gardens where a needle-leafed tree is desirable, pines will usually do better than any other conifer. The white pine is a vigorous, fast-growing tree with a soft gray green color. It makes an excellent screen when young, and clipping the top encourages dense growth. The tree eventually develops a tall trunk with horizontal branches held high in the air.

zones 2-9

Carolina poplar (*Populus canadensis*). This tree has a greedy root system, and bright green leaves which stand out in the landscape. It should not be used in cities, except in a large park. Like other poplars, this tree is fast-growing and can be planted in a row to provide a screen. It is easily recognized in winter by its distinctive green buds, and grows in any well-drained soil.

zones 2-9

American linden (*Tilia americana*), also called basswood in Canada. This indigenous tree often grows to 70 feet. When immature it has smooth bark which breaks up into scales as the tree ages. The leaves are simple, large and heart-shaped. In summer it blooms with sweet-smelling yellow flowers. A fast-growing tree, it is easily transplanted.

zones 2-9

Silver maple (*Acer saccharinum*), also called river or white maple. This fast-growing tree grows to 90 feet. Because of its shallow roots it should be planted in an open area. It is highly resistant to disease, and grows well under difficult conditions. One of its varieties, *A. s. laciniatum,* is much in demand.

zones 2-9

Red pine (*Pinus resinosa*). A dark green pine whose needles are clustered, it has spreading branches and reddish scaly bark. The tree is often clear of branches for up to three-quarters of its height. Although red pine thrives in cold climates (as indicated), it will grow in warmer places but is susceptible to a tip disease that tends to spoil its shape. It is best grown in well-drained acidic soil. It tolerates drought to some extent, but requires plenty of sunlight.

zones 3-9

European larch (*Larix decidua*). This unusual tree is a deciduous conifer—it does not retain its foliage in winter. The needles grow to about one inch then turn an attractive shade of yellow before dropping in autumn. In spring the bright green of the new needles is one of the most beautiful of new leaf colors. The tree is graceful and open.

zones 3-9

Yellow birch (*Betula alleghaniensis*). Native to eastern Canada, this tree is characterized by silvery-yellow bark and leaves that smell of wintergreen when crumbled. Best grown in parks, it thrives in a mild environment and can easily be transplanted in spring. It requires no pruning.

zones 3-9

White ash (*Fraxinus americana*). This is a round-topped tree whose autumn leaves range from bright yellow to deep purple. A slender, graceful tree, it is easily transplanted and grows in almost any soil; it does best, however, in moist, well-drained areas.

zones 3-9

Black walnut (*Juglans nigra*). This tree, which grows to 90 feet, has black, deeply ridged bark and downy twigs. Its black nuts are edible and sweet-tasting. A fast grower, the black walnut must be planted in well-drained soil. Because its roots often take very large amounts of nutrients from the soil, it is wise not to plant a black walnut near other plants —particularly a vegetable garden.

zones 3-9

Red oak (*Quercus rubra*). Oaks take decades to mature, and the red oak grows slowly but steadily. It is more upright than other oaks and is noted for its rich fall color. It grows well on rocky, gravelly soils and develops a short, sturdy trunk, divided into several large branches. The red oak commonly grows to 80 feet; under ideal conditions it may exceed 100 feet.

Bur oak (*Quercus macrocarpa*) is a wide-spreading tree that grows to 50 feet. Because it transplants easily and is highly resistant to air pollution, it is often seen in city parks.

zones 4-9

Douglas fir (*Pseudotsuga taxifolia*). In general, Canadians do well to use the Rocky Mountain variety (*Pseudotsuga taxifolia glauca*). One of our very best ornamentals, the Douglas fir takes shearing and can be hedged. The Douglas fir is one of the world's most popular timber-producing trees.

zones 4-9

White poplar (*Populus alba pyramidalis*). This variety features the main characteristics of the species: rapid growth, greedy roots, attractive appearance. But it takes to dry soil better than most poplars and is often used as a windbreak. It grows in most garden soils.

zones 4-9

Hemlock (*Tsuga canadensis*). When young, this is one of Canada's most attractive conifers. The hemlock makes a good tall clipped hedge or a beautiful large tree, with dense gray-green foliage. It is easy to grow but requires moist soil. As a hedge it should be planted in a protected place or sheltered from heavy wind with fencing. It is easy to move from the nursery, where it is root pruned, but very difficult to transplant from the wild.

zones 4-9

Shagbark hickory (*Carya ovata*). This is an erect, open, handsome tree with big sheets of bark of interest year round. The nuts are good eating. It does well in shallow and stony soil, but grows best in moist areas. There are many varieties available. Wheelwrights used to make carriage wheel spokes from shagbark hickory; later it was used for automobile wheel spokes.

zones 4-9

Pin oak (*Quercus palustris*). This attractive upright tree, popular as an ornamental, has a straight trunk, and horizontal branches covered with pin-like twigs. The lower branches droop. The pin oak's glossy green foliage turns dark red in fall and then leathery brown. Leaves are persistent and some often hang on the tree throughout winter. Pin oak grows in any well-drained garden soil.

zones 4-9

White oak (*Quercus alba*). A wide-spreading tree, it has a handsome branch structure and a well-rounded crown. Another attractive tree that shares the white oak's characteristic roots and longevity is the English oak (*Quercus robur*). Only after many generations does it become a tree of noble size and proportion.

zones 4-9

Ginkgo or maidenhair tree (*Ginkgo biloba*). This slow-growing tree has thick, fan-shaped foliage and is a link between broad-leafed and needle-leafed species. Its young leaves, sprouting like small bouquets along the branches in spring, are very attractive. In fall the yellow color of the ginkgo stands out strikingly. The leaves have an unusual shimmering quality, so the ginkgo does not always complement other trees. It is, however, pest- and disease-free, and thrives in city conditions. Usually only male plants are sold.

zones 4-9

Hackberry or sugarberry (*Celtis occidentalis*). Native to eastern Canada, this tree is noted for its wide crown and the pronounced ridges on its bark. Its simple, alternate leaves resemble those of the elm. In fall it displays dark red berries. The tree grows in a variety of forms, some scarcely larger than shrubs. It is well adapted to city conditions and will grow in rather poor soil. Ball planting is done in spring.

zones 4-9

Sugar maple (*Acer saccharum*). This is not a tree for the city or for a small home, but where there is plenty of space it is a good choice—not only for its brilliant orange color in autumn, but for the rustic beauty it lends to the landscape. It is slow-growing but long-lived, with heavy-feeding roots and a heavy branch structure. It grows in almost any soil, needs little sunlight and is ideal for a patio or along a walkway. Sap from the tree is used to produce maple syrup.

zones 4-9

American beech (*Fagus grandifolia*). This is an indigenous tree but one that does not adapt easily to the city. In open areas it grows to 80 feet. It has silvery bark, and bluish green leaves that were used by early settlers as mattress stuffing.

zones 5-9

Norway maple (*Acer platanoides*). An old standby, this is a popular choice as an ornamental in Canada. It is difficult to grow anything under the Norway maple because of the shade it casts and the shallowness of its roots. The foliage of this rapid-growing, long-lived tree turns yellow in autumn. Various forms can be had with varieties. Columnar: 'Erectum'; oval: 'Cleveland'; red-leafed: 'Crimson King.' It grows in moist, well-drained soils.

Shallow   Deep
ROUND DECIDUOUS

Shallow   Deep
ROUND EVERGREEN

Shallow   Deep
UPRIGHT DECIDUOUS

Shallow   Deep
UPRIGHT EVERGREEN

Deciduous   Evergreen
PYRAMIDAL

Broad leaf   Needle leaf
FOLIAGE   FLOWERING

zones 5-9

White fir (*Abies concolor*). An exotic species commonly used in landscaping, the white fir is noted for its long gray-green needles (twice as long as other fir needles). This impressive conifer is easy to grow, and is characterized by a dense crown, and lower branches that touch the ground.

zones 5-9

English oak (*Quercus robur*). A European tree now well known in Canada, it looks like the native white oak but has smaller leaves. It grows slowly and develops best when exposed to full sunlight. It thrives on rocky, gravelly soils.

Sycamore (*Platanus occidentalis*), London plane (*P. acerifolia*). This is an open tree that, until recently, has been among the most popular for city use because it was disease-free. It is now subject to a blight and this use becomes doubtful. Of beautiful shape when mature, it has flaky, brown-and-white mottled bark, and puff balls of seeds that remain through winter. Its bright green leaves resemble a maple's and are shed in fall. It is common practice in Europe to cut back the branches each fall to encourage the spring growth of small, dense heads of sucker branches. These create a low canopy when trees are planted in groups.

zones 5-9

Tulip tree (*Liriodendron tulipifera*), also called yellow poplar. Growing up to 175 feet, it has tulip-shaped leaves, and flowers that resemble yellow-orange tulips (although they are often obscured by leaves). The tulip tree requires lots of space and thrives along streams, near swampy areas or anywhere there is deep, moist soil.

zones 5-9

Pyramid oak (*Quercus robur 'fastigiata'*). A middle-size tree, it has upright branches that form a spindle-shaped crown similar to that of the Italian poplar. Pyramid oak keeps its leaves until late fall, is immune to most diseases and resists air pollution well, making it ideal for city gardens. Like most oaks, it prefers well-drained soil.

zones 6-9

European beech (*Fagus sylvatica*). Perhaps the most regal of all northern trees, it demands plenty of space, both for its roots and its branches. The smooth, gray bark and the autumn leaves (a dark yellow-brown) are very attractive. This tree makes an excellent tall-growing hedge.

Among other European beech varieties is the cutleaf form (*F. s. laciniata*), which has leaves of a magnificent texture. Weeping forms are also available. Beeches require plenty of sunlight and grow well in all but heavy, wet soils. As a rule, beeches are good for screening, either clipped or unclipped. Nothing will grow under low-branched beeches. Specimen trees require no pruning.

zones 6-9

Cucumber-tree (*Magnolia acuminata*). A fast-growing tree, it is upright when young but becomes broadly pyramidal with maturity, and its branches usually touch the ground. Its flowers (yellow-green cups) are concealed by leaf cover and should not be considered an ornamental asset.

Continued on page 216

Horse chestnut

Black walnut

213

See
What Trees
Alone
Can Do

The "before" and "after" pictures seen here demonstrate the near-miraculous effect of trees on the landscape. It's hard to believe that the pictures on the right are of the same view—fifteen years later—as the pictures to their left, but they are. Luckily for the homeowners in this housing development, the builder planted trees along the streets as soon as the houses were finished. If you're in the market for a new house don't leave the addition of trees to chance. If they are not included in the contract, plant street trees as soon as possible. Soon after you've moved in, plant more (the biggest you can afford) where needed. While carpeting or a dining table may seem more important, trees are a wiser first investment in the beautification of a house because they take years to mature. And, as these pictures show so well, without trees to establish a natural setting even a handsome house (and block) becomes an ungainly intrusion upon the land.

But beauty is not the only contribution of trees. Their roots hold the soil. Branches and trunks help reduce noise pollution. They provide cooling shade. The decayed leaves replenish the soil with minerals; live ones freshen the air with oxygen given off in return for the carbon dioxide that trees must take up in order to grow. Trees, in the world of plants, are exemplary citizens.

Trees and shrubs were planted on lawns and by the street as soon as houses were built. Comparison of two pictures shows the lovely, irregular pattern mature trees superimpose on the skyline.

A friendly entry as well as shade and privacy from the street and next-door neighbor are provided by trees and shrubs on this lawn. It's a good idea to include some evergreens for winter color.

zones 6-9

Cryptomeria (*Cryptomeria japonica*). The branchlets and scale-like needles of the cryptomeria cluster in bunches so that much of the reddish brown trunk is exposed. A hardy, fast-growing tree, it is attractive planted singly or in a group. Although easy to grow, cryptomeria does best in well-drained soil in a sunny, sheltered spot. It is an excellent evergreen for home gardens on the west coast.

zones 7-9

Sweet-gum (*Liquidambar styraciflua*). This is one of the most outstanding trees for autumn color: The star-shaped leaves range from bright scarlet to deep purple. The sweet-gum grows slowly unless planted in rich, moist soil. However, only small trees can be moved safely. Its name derives from the amber-colored liquid sweet-gum produces.

zones 7-9

Lawson false cypress (*Chamaecyparis lawsoniana*). This pyramid-shaped tree has flat, scale-covered branchlets that turn downward at the ends. Its foliage is soft-textured and the tree is graceful in appearance. Where a large, narrow-topped conifer is desired for dramatic effect, this is ideal.

zones 7-9

Pecan (*Carya pecan*). Growing to 100 feet, this spreading hardwood has furrowed bark and a somewhat loose, open form. It turns yellow in autumn and bears greenish flowers in spring. The named varieties, which vary according to region, give better nuts than the species. Use nursery-grown stock for success in transplanting. The pecan requires deep, moist soil and lots of space. The tree has limited worth in Canada because the short growing season does not allow nuts to ripen.

zones 7-9

Carolina hemlock (*Tsuga caroliniana*). The Tsuga genus is found mainly in North America and in East Asian forests. Whereas the needles of the Canadian hemlock (*T. canadensis*) grow flat on opposite sides of the twig, those of the Carolina hemlock grow around it. This makes the Carolina hemlock more decorative. It is, however, hard to find. Hemlock thrives in almost all soils and does best in areas of heavy rainfall.

zones 7-9

English walnut (*Juglans regia*). Although nearly as large (up to 100 feet) and imposing as the pecan, the English walnut is generally hardier. As with the pecan, its varieties produce better nuts than the species itself. A loose, open tree with compound leaves that usually drop in early fall, the English walnut requires moist, well-drained soil.

zones 8-9

California incense cedar (*Libocedrus decurrens*). This is a narrow evergreen with bright green scale-like needles on flat, twisting branchlets. It makes a better hedge than an arborvitae or a juniper and is practically disease-free. A handsome specimen tree and a popular ornamental that grows reasonably quickly, it should be planted in sheltered areas with ample moisture. California incense cedar thrives on exposed sites with shallow soil, but subsequently loses foliage near the crown.

zones 8-9

Cedar of Lebanon (*Cedrus libani*). This spreading dark green conifer has low branches that eventually die out to reveal the trunk. It is hardy, long-lived and grows rapidly in well-drained soil. It is particularly suited to seaside gardens. The deodar cedar (*C. deodara*), a similar tree but not as hardy, has a soft green color.

Medium-Sized Trees 30 to 50 Feet.

Included in this group are some excellent trees to use for shade on a terrace or lawn, for streetside plantings or as specimens wherever larger trees would overwhelm the surrounding area.

It is often best to use medium-sized conifers in the garden, and a choice from this list will make a handsome addition to any home landscape. Here too are some flowering trees that will add color and variety to your garden or lawn.

zones 1-9

Laurel willow (*Salix pentandra*), also called bayleaf willow. Although caterpillars will feast on it, this is an attractive tree if properly cared for. Its bright green leaves are similar to those of the true laurel. Laurel willow can be clipped to form hedges.

zones 2-9

European white birch (*Betula pendula*). A slender tree, it has white bark, and fine branchlets that droop slightly. There are several varieties with a weeping form. Although popular, it is short-lived. It is best planted in groups with other trees in the background so that if one or more birches die no unsightly gap will be left.

zones 2-9

Paper birch, canoe birch (*Betula papyrifera*). Although less popular than the European white birch, paper birch provides more shade than its slender relative. The white trunk is larger and the paper birch is much less susceptible to borers. In early spring, the catkins—long, pointed flower clusters—are particularly attractive and in autumn they turn yellow, contrasting with the white trunk. Paper birch does best in rich soil, *Continued on page 218*

Shallow   Deep
ROUND DECIDUOUS

Shallow   Deep
ROUND EVERGREEN

Shallow   Deep
UPRIGHT DECIDUOUS

Shallow   Deep
UPRIGHT EVERGREEN

Deciduous   Evergreen
PYRAMIDAL

Broad leaf   Needle leaf
FOLIAGE   FLOWERING

White pine

Black cherry

Douglas fir

Sycamore

Sugar maple

though native trees often grow on thin, sandy soils. It doesn't take heat well, and should be sheltered from wind.

zones 2-9

Black cherry (*Prunus serotina*). This is the largest of our native cherry trees. Its notable features are a broad, oval-shaped crown and dark brown bark. It bears white flowers in spring and blackish fruit in fall. In exposed areas, it is usually best to support a newly planted black cherry with stakes until it is firmly rooted.

zones 2-9

Scotch pine (*Pinus sylvestris*). This is a narrow pine whose somewhat open branches grow in clumps. The needles are bluish gray and the bark is reddish. Its branches are often trimmed, especially near the top. The Scotch pine is ornamental when planted in groups, but after 40 or 50 years it may become undesirably sparse.

zones 3-9

Arborvitae (*Thuya occidentalis*), also known as white cedar. A native tree whose needles have a yellow-green color, it is ornamental when planted in groups. Arborvitae usually needs damp soil and lots of sun. The low branches never lose their leaves.

zones 3-9

Hop-hornbeam (*Ostrya virginiana*). During youth, this tree is slender and rather like an elm. Older specimens tend to spread and become attractively rounded. Virtually pest-free, hop-hornbeam has grayish brown bark and bears a flattish nut enclosed in an inflated sac. In fall the leaves turn yellow. Hop-hornbeam grows in most well-drained garden soils and will tolerate shade. Its wood is one of the hardest and toughest in Canada, and was once used for sleigh runners.

zones 3-9

Red or swamp maple (*Acer rubrum*). Of all the maples, this is the most open and graceful. Although it prefers moist conditions and thrives near swamps, it grows in almost any garden soil. It is the first tree to show red in spring (with delicate red flowers) and the first to turn red in fall. It is prone to only one disease, leaf blotch, which causes little damage. Among superior varieties of red maple are 'October Glory,' which retains its leaves until late fall, and 'Tilford,' which has a thick branch structure. If desired for its ornamental value, red maple should be planted in sheltered areas, where winds won't strip away foliage.

zones 3-9

Siberian elm (*Ulmus pumila*). This fast-growing tree can reach 25 to 30 feet in a few years. Among the first trees to flower in spring, it has the smallest leaves of all elms. In landscaping, the Siberian elm is used mainly for creating temporary screens to protect more decorative but slower-growing species while they reach maturity. It is a popular shade tree, often planted along streets. The 'Park Royal' variety is noted for its symmetrical form.

zones 3-9

Little-leaf linden (*Tilia cordata*). This deep-rooted, wind-resistant tree requires plenty of fertile soil. The branches of mature lindens often touch the ground, and the tree is a popular ornamental. The flowers, which bloom in early summer, are not prominent and last only a few days, but their fragrance is one of the most pleasant in the garden. The linden is valued for its wood, the softest and lightest of any Canadian hardwood. In autumn, the leaves turn yellow, but if the soil is poor, they tend to drop early. The 'Greenspire' variety has a straighter trunk and a more regular shape than *T. cordata*.

zones 3-9

American hornbeam (*Carpinus caroliniana*), also known as ironwood, blue beech, musclewood. A hardy, slow-growing tree, it is usually multistemmed and is among the smallest of the hornbeams. It thrives in deep, moist soils, especially near swamps.

zones 4-9

Weeping willow (*Salix alba tristis*). A graceful, fast-growing tree, it has a broad round crown and bright yellow hanging branches. It is noted for its ornamental value and is especially attractive when planted near a pool (willows do best in moist soil). It should not be grown near a house because its shallow root system may interfere with the foundations.

zones 4-9

American yellow wood (*Cladrastis lutea*). Slender when young, this tree becomes more rounded, with dense foliage, as maturity approaches. It is characterized by bright green leaves, and fragrant hanging white flowers in early summer. The bark is an attractive light gray and the foliage turns yellow-orange. The American yellow wood is a good terrace tree that offers pleasant light shade.

zones 4-9

Common honey locust (*Gleditschia triacanthos*). Once a thorny tree, it has been bred and selected so there are now several thornless varieties that give good shade. Among the best of these varieties are 'Moraine' (wide-spreading and dense); 'Majestic' (compact, good for a small property); 'Skyline' (a narrow tree with a pyramidal shape); 'Continental' (a spreading tree); and 'Imperial' (compact and dense). Generally pest- and disease-free, the common honey locust grows in almost any garden soil but requires plenty of sunlight.

Shallow · Deep
ROUND DECIDUOUS

Shallow · Deep
ROUND EVERGREEN

Shallow · Deep
UPRIGHT DECIDUOUS

Shallow · Deep
UPRIGHT EVERGREEN

Deciduous · Evergreen
PYRAMIDAL

Broad leaf · Needle leaf
FOLIAGE

FLOWERING

zones 4-9

Austrian pine (*Pinus nigra*). A thick, dark green tree, it is excellent for screening and has firm, pointed needles which grow in pairs. Its broad cones turn yellow before ripening. Like all pines, this species thrives in practically any soil—even on a sandy beach.

zones 4-9

Amur cork tree (*Phellodendron amurense*). This is a small tree with wide-spreading branches. Its outstanding features are a shapely form and heavily textured cork-like bark. In late spring, it bears small, off-white flowers that smell like turpentine. An excellent patio or lawn tree, it grows quickly in almost any well-drained garden soil, is pest- and disease-resistant and can withstand city air pollution. But it does require plenty of sun.

zones 5-9

Dawn redwood (*Metasequoia glyptostroboides*). This tall, narrow redwood has feathery needles which drop in winter. The dawn redwood is not an evergreen. It does best in moist soil (in full or partial sunlight) and grows as much as three feet annually. This specimen tree was known only as a fossil until found in China in 1945. For best results, keep the tree's base free of weeds for several years after planting.

zones 5-9

Crimean linden (*Tilia euchlora*). This popular ornamental has glossy green leaves which give the tree a crisp, neat appearance. Ideal for shade and screening, Crimean linden is attractive planted individually or in close rows. It does best in moist, well-drained soil. Bees are attracted to the nectar in its small yellow flowers.

zones 5-9

Turkish hazel (*Corylus colurna*). A slow grower, it is highly resistant to disease and bears nuts in clusters of three to six. This stately tree has thick green leaves and is recommended for ball planting in spring.

zones 5-9

Ruby horse chestnut (*Aesculus carnea briotii*). This chestnut is smaller than the common horse chestnut (*Aesculus hippocastanum*) and its flower clusters range from bright pink to red. At the turn of the century, the ruby horse chestnut commonly grew to 100 feet, but now rarely exceeds 30 feet. In fall it bears a woody, inedible nut (horse chestnuts or "buckeyes"), often used in children's games. The 'Baumanni' variety of the common horse chestnut has large double flowers but is sterile and bears no horse chestnuts. The ruby horse chestnut grows best in well-drained sandy or gravelly soil; it prefers a sunny or partially shaded site.

zones 5-9

Katsura tree (*Cercidiphyllum japonicum*). This is, in effect, two different trees. When young, it is slender and has beautiful bright green heart-shaped leaves which turn yellow-orange in fall. After 15-20 years, it becomes a wide, open tree with low-spreading branches. Available with multiple trunks (the preferred form), it is often used as a garden substitute for the white birch. The katsura tree is resistant to pests and disease, and thrives in moist soil. If it is planted in lime-rich soils its autumn colors will be subdued.

zones 5-9

Korean pine (*Pinus koraiensis*). This bushy dark green tree is similar to the Austrian pine but grows more slowly; it is ideal where space is limited. It requires plenty of sunlight, thrives on well-drained acidic soils and is relatively drought-resistant once established. The Korean pine is one of the best conifers for a small garden.

Japanese black pine (*Pinus thunbergii*). Wide-spreading, with branches that often grow near the ground, it can be trained into almost any shape. A rich dark green, the Japanese black pine is particularly attractive in winter, when snow settles on its irregularly spaced branches. Also good for screening, it grows in almost any soil, even in dry infertile soil such as sandy seashores.

Japanese red pine (*Pinus densiflora*). The Japanese red, like the black pine,

is a tree of character and makes a fine addition to any garden. It is irregularly shaped, although it tends toward the horizontal.

zones 5-9

Catalpa (*Catalpa bignonioides*), also known as Indian bean tree. The catalpa has heart-shaped leaves, and long brown pods that resemble beans. A good shade tree, it is tolerant of poor, dry soil but grows best on sunny, sheltered sites. The catalpa bears yellow-and-white flowers and its leaves give off a pungent odor when crushed. The 'Aurea' variety has yellow leaves and is known as the golden catalpa.

zones 6-9

Japanese pagoda tree (*Sophora japonica*). This attractive tree, which grows to about 40 feet, has dark green leaves, and clusters of creamy white pea-like flowers that bloom in early summer. An excellent shade tree, it grows best in well-drained soil and should be sheltered from wind; it grows in full or partial sunlight. The 'Regent' variety is the preferred form where available. It grows more rapidly than *Sophora japonica* and is very disease-resistant.

zones 6-9

Japanese zelkova (*Zelkova serrata*). A tall and graceful tree with a rounded, narrow top, the Japanese zelkova has leaves which turn brownish red in autumn. The tree bears red, yellow or blackish berries, also in autumn. The brown bark often flakes, revealing small patches of bright orange. Relatively fast-growing and disease-free, it is useful as a shade tree. Once its roots have found their depth, this species is virtually drought-resistant.

zones 7-9

Flowering ash (*Fraxinus ornus*). This handsome ash has a full rounded top, and fragrant white flowers that bloom in spring. Flowering ash bears greenish fruit, usually about an inch long, which turns brown when ripe. The leaves are full and glossy. This tree is good for large gardens and thrives in well-drained soil.

219

zones 7-9

Sycamore-leafed mulberry (*Morus platanifolia*). Noted for vigorous growth, spreading branches and large glossy leaves, this tree seldom exceeds 30 feet in height. It is sterile, so there are no berries, and there is no yearly crop of seedlings to litter the garden. Easy to grow (it thrives particularly in deep moist soils), it is an excellent tree for cities—where it is often planted along streets—and ideal for gardens where shade is desired.

zones 7-9

Umbrella pine (*Sciadopitys verticillata*). This tree is named for its long, bright green needles, which radiate from the branches and twigs like spokes of a half-open umbrella. The needles resemble a yew's, but are thicker and up to five inches long, making this full-bodied tree one of the most impressive available. Eventually growing to about 30 feet, the umbrella pine is good as a corner accent, in a hedge, or as a formal element in a mixed planting.

zones 8-9

Pacific madrone (*Arbutus menziesii*). This is the only broad-leafed evergreen native to Canada. Its clustered white flowers smell like honey. A scraggly tree, it has thin, twisting branches, and bark that changes from green to brick red, then flakes off. The Pacific madrone thrives in stony, well-drained soil.

zone 9

California laurel (*Umbellularia californica*). This shapely, narrow tree has small branches, and shiny green leaves that smell like bay leaves. In fall, it bears pear-shaped fruit that turns from green to purple. A hardy tree, it is useful for both screening and shade and often has branches close to the ground. It prefers rich, moist soil and, in Canada, grows only in British Columbia.

Small Trees, to 25 Feet.

While small trees are useful wherever space is limited, the ones listed here are exceptional for their colorful foliage and interesting shapes. Although they cast little shade, small trees add accent and variety to any landscape, and their limited root networks do not interfere with house foundations.

zones 1-9

Bird cherry (*Prunus pennsylvanica*), also known as pin cherry. This small, hardy tree has a slim, straight trunk and smooth reddish bark. The simple spear-shaped leaves turn bright red in fall. In early summer, the bird cherry bears clusters of white flowers; about a month later, edible red cherries appear. The tree needs plenty of sunlight and is most attractive when planted in groupings.

zones 2-9

Amur maple (*Acer ginnala*). The hardiest of all maples, this tree has dense branches which make it excellent for shade and screening. Amur maple is characterized by brilliant red foliage in autumn. It grows best in deep, moist, well-drained soils.

zones 2-9

Russian olive (*Elaeagnus angustifolia*). A shrubby, wide-spreading bush, this species can be pruned to form interesting shapes. Like most olive trees, it has twisted branches. Its narrow grayish green leaves have a silver tinge, and the small rounded berries that appear in fall are yellowish. In spring, the Russian olive bears small flowers. It grows best in sandy, well-drained areas (although it tolerates poor, chalky soil) and withstands heavy winds and ocean spray. It should be planted in a sunny

spot. In some areas this tree tends to wilt, so before planting consult a local nursery. Generally pest-free, the Russian olive grows quickly and requires little care.

zones 2-9

Ohio buckeye (*Aesculus glabra*). A smaller, slightly less formal tree than the horse chestnut, it is noted for its yellowish green flowers which bloom in spring. In fall its foliage turns yellow-orange. The Ohio buckeye does well in sunny or in partially shaded areas.

zones 2-9

Nannyberry (*Viburnum lentago*). In spring, this tree's fragrant white flowers bloom in flat-topped clusters. The black, edible fruit for which the nannyberry is named appears in autumn and is favored by birds. The tree grows best in sunny areas with moist soil, and usually bears more fruit if planted in twos and threes.

zones 3-9

White mulberry (*Morus alba*). This tree, native to Asia, has shiny leaves and a crown with many branches. In late summer, it bears pink-white fruit. It is ideal for free hedges. Like all mulberries, this tree oozes a white sap that contains latex; it tends to "bleed" when cut so avoid pruning. It requires deep, rich, well-drained soil and is relatively free of pests. A beautiful variety is the weeping form, *M. a. pendula*.

zones 3-9

Gray birch (*Betula populifolia*). One of the hardiest trees, it is also among the smallest birches, rarely exceeding 30 feet. It has slender branches and a narrow, conical crown. The trunk of the gray birch is usually curved; it has bark that rarely peels. Characterized by triangular light-green leaves that tremble in the slightest breeze, this tree grows

Shallow / Deep
ROUND DECIDUOUS

Shallow / Deep
ROUND EVERGREEN

Shallow / Deep
UPRIGHT DECIDUOUS

Shallow / Deep
UPRIGHT EVERGREEN

Deciduous / Evergreen
PYRAMIDAL

Broad leaf / Needle leaf
FOLIAGE

FLOWERING

quickly but is short-lived. It thrives in sandy, gravelly soils but is highly susceptible to damage by leaf-miners (although these can be fought with Cygon spray). It does well in full sunlight or in partial shade.

zones 3-9

Staghorn sumac (*Rhus typhina*). Although often called a "weed tree," it has much character and is distinguished in fall by orange-red, yellow and purple foliage; in summer, this plant yields hairy pale red flowers. It has a small, rounded form which gives deep shade. Staghorn sumac grows in almost any well-drained garden soil, but needs plenty of sunlight. It is generally pest-free and requires little pruning.

zones 3-9

Hop tree (*Ptelea trifoliate*). This small, spherical, indigenous tree has leaves made up of three leaflets. The fruit—a flat, round samara—appears in fall and remains through much of winter. The leaves and bark give off a slightly pungent odor when crushed. The hop tree, also known as the stinking ash, does well in moderate shade.

zones 4-9

Shadblow or serviceberry (*Amelanchier canadensis*). Characterized by delicate star-shaped white flowers in spring, this tree bears edible dark blue fruit about mid-summer. In autumn, its oval green leaves turn russet yellow. The shadblow requires little pruning and can be grouped for an interesting effect. It grows best in moist soil in sunny or partially shaded areas. Although generally free of pests, it is prone to damage by fireblight.

zones 4-9

Choke cherry (*Prunus virginiana*). A small indigenous tree, it has grayish bark and thick clusters of white flowers. In late summer it yields cherries, which are excellent for jams and jellies. Ideal for groupings or free hedges, it thrives in rich, moist soil. On windy sites, it is best to stake specimen trees. One notable variety is the 'Shubert,' which has thick wine-red foliage. It is hardy but needs plenty of sun.

zones 4-9

Sawara false cypress (*Chamaecyparis pisifera*). A column-shaped tree, it has bright green foliage which gives off a pungent resinous odor when crushed. The 'Squarrosa' variety is distinguished by its feathery blue-green leaves and often is used in Japanese gardens (but will not grow as tall as it does in Japan). Cypress do best in well-drained soils, but without plenty of sun they lose their low branches.

zones 5-9

Devil's walking stick (*Aralis elata*). This unusual-looking tree often has several spiny trunks, which support top-heavy branches with large compound leaves (up to two and a half feet long). It is distinguished by spikes of white flowers, and black fruit on red stems. It is a showy tree but its strange appearance makes it difficult to use. It grows in almost any soil.

zones 5-9

Japanese flowering crab apple (*Malus floribunda*). Many crab apples are actually large bushes, not trees, and several are multi-trunked. There are many varieties, usually distinguished by their color. Among the more colorful, disease-resistant crab apples are: tea crab (*M. kupeheusis*), which has pink to white flowers; 'Snowdrift,' with white flowers; 'Radiant,' with red flowers; the hardy, fast-growing 'Aldenhamensis,' with red flowers and purplish blue foliage; and 'Elryi,' a small, hardy variety which is popular as an ornamental. Although crab apples grow in ordinary, well-drained garden soil, it is best to use manure as fertilizer.

zones 5-9

Bradford callery pear (*Pyrus calleryana* 'Bradfordi'). This fine shade tree bears white flowers in early spring, and its glossy foliage turns a striking crimson in fall. Its tiny fruits are inedible. Vigorous and relatively disease-free, the Bradford callery pear is easy to grow and is becoming increasingly popular. It is resistant to air pollution and is often planted in downtown parks and along city streets. It grows in moist, well-drained soils.

zones 6-9

Hinoki false cypress (*Chamaecyparis obtusa erecta*). This narrow, upright tree resembles the incense cedar and has overlapping dark green leaves. It grows slowly and reaches heights of more than 30 feet only in its native country of Japan. Hinoki false cypress needs plenty of sun.

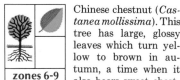

zones 6-9

Chinese chestnut (*Castanea mollissima*). This tree has large, glossy leaves which turn yellow to brown in autumn, a time when it also bears sweet chestnuts. To obtain fruit, however, you must plant two varieties together, for the individual tree is sterile. In time, the Chinese chestnut may exceed 30 feet. Generally pest-free, it grows well in any ordinary garden soil but requires plenty of sunlight.

zones 6-9

Flowering peach (*Prunus persica*). One of the most colorful flowering fruit trees, it is short-lived and subject to diseases and pests. It rarely exceeds 25 feet, and bears furry, red-orange fruit. It blooms profusely—with red or rose-pink flowers—when young. Flowering peach grows well in dry soils but requires full sunlight.

zones 6-9

Oriental cherry (*Prunus serrulata*). One of the more popular flowering trees, it is distinguished by heavy clusters of hanging flowers. Among the best varieties: 'Kwanzan,' the hardiest, has pink flowers, is upright and vase-shaped when young, and becomes wide-spreading; 'Shirotae' has fragrant white flowers but is not as full as 'Kwanzan'; 'Shirofugen' has fragrant pink flowers turning to white; 'Amanogawa' has fragrant, light-pink flowers; 'Jo-nioi' is noted for its spreading form, 'Takinioi,' for its drooping, fragrant flowers.

Japanese flowering cherries require rich, well-drained soils with adequate water.

Oriental cherry trees are particularly susceptible to damage by birds.

Continued on page 224

SPRING

CORNELIAN CHERRY (*Cornus mas*). A dogwood, not a cherry. This rounded tree-like shrub with dense dark green foliage has clusters of small yellow flowers that appear before forsythia and are very effective when provided with a solid background. (Zones 5-9.)

FLOWERING CRAB APPLE (*Malus floribunda*). Small bushy tree or shrub with spreading branches. Flowers are deep carmine to red in bud, white when fully open. Rewarding, but difficult to maintain because of susceptibility to insects and disease. (Zones 5-9.)

FLOWERING PLUM (*Prunus cerasifera pissardii*). This small, dark-trunked, purple-leafed tree is outstanding for foliage which contrasts with other plants. Showy pink and white flowers last for only a few days. There may be infestations of tent caterpillars. (Zones 5-9.)

ENGLISH HAWTHORN (*Crataegus oxyacantha*). Shrubby, low-branched and round-topped with stout one-inch thorns. Clusters of 6 to 12 white flowers become scarlet nutlets in the fall. Varieties include red and pink and a double white. (Zones 6-9.)

STAR MAGNOLIA (*Magnolia stellata*). This slow-growing, dense tree has small dark green leaves. White flowers with 12 or more ribbonlike petals bloom for a week or more unless touched by frost. Produces starlike flowers when only three feet high. (Zones 5-9.)

SHADBUSH (*Amelanchier canadensis*). Slender treelike shrub with ascending branches found in the wild in wet places. Its delicate white flowers last less than a week. Trunks gray. Autumn color bright red. Best used against a dark background. (Zones 4-9.)

REDBUD (*Cercis canadensis*). Small tree with wide irregular crown. Clusters of half-inch stalkless, rosy-pink, pealike flowers appear on branches and trunks before the heart-shaped leaves. Winter injury may occur in the North unless protected. (Zones 6-9.)

CAROLINA SILVER BELL (*Halesia monticola*). A small tree or large shrub, with a short stocky trunk that may divide into several branches to make a rounded, broad crown. The white bell-shaped flowers droop in clusters of two to five. Needs shelter from cold. (Zones 6-9.)

FLOWERING CHERRY (*Prunus serrulata*). Most varieties are upright, 20 to 25 feet with spreading branches. Flowers white, pink or greenish yellow; single, semi-double or double. The early, late and medium varieties bloom for about three weeks, depending on weather. (Zones 6-9.)

WASHINGTON THORN (*Crataegus phaenopyrum*). Large upright treelike shrub with clusters of white flowers with green centers. Bright orange-red leaves in the fall, persistent scarlet fruits in winter and long thorns. Subject to blight, borer and scale, resistant to rust. (Zones 5-9.)

SAUCER MAGNOLIA (*Magnolia soulangeana*). Small low-branching tree with rounded head. Flowers are rose to purple inside, and white outside, to six inches across. If attacked by scale insects, spray with dormant oil before buds open. (Zones 5-9.)

GOLDEN-CHAIN TREE (*Laburnum watereri* 'Vossii'). Large upright shrub or small tree. An improved variety with dense growth, and vivid greenish yellow flower clusters to 20 inches long. Will need a protected spot in the North. All parts are poisonous to eat. (Zones 6-9.)

FLOWERING DOGWOOD (*Cornus florida*). Stately small tree with a crown of spreading branches. Tiny flowers have white or pinkish petallike bracts giving the impression of one large flower. Tight clusters of scarlet fruit and red leaves in the fall. (Zones 6-9.)

JAPANESE TREE LILAC (*Syringa amurensis*). This small tree has cherrylike bark, a round form and dark green foliage. It can be grown as a large shrub. This is the tallest lilac, with six-inch clusters of creamy white flowers and the fragrance of privet. (Zones 2-9.)

Trees—in Order of Bloom

NORTHERN CATALPA (*Catalpa speciosa*). Big, conspicuous panicles of white and yellow flowers. Fruit is a long, brown pod, the "indian bean." A big tree with big heart-shaped leaves, for big areas. Stiff-branching. Takes heat and dry conditions. (Zones 5-9.)

CASTOR-ARALIA (*Kalopanax pictus*). A heavy-branched, open, spreading tree with lustrous red-maple-like leaves. Tiny white flowers are arranged in small spheres which in turn are in big loose clusters; same spheres turn black at fruiting time. (Zones 5-9.)

JAPANESE DOGWOOD (*Cornus kousa*). Small compact tree. Flowers are inconspicuous but the showy bracts (modified leaves) are green changing to white, and finally to pink. They last up to a month in cool weather. Autumn color is a soft red. (Zones 6-9.)

PEEGEE HYDRANGEA (*Hydrangea paniculata grandiflora*). A very large shrub that can be trained to tree form. Flowers are big, foot-long cones of white changing to pink and purple and often remaining dry on the plant after the leaves have fallen. (Zones 3-9.)

GOLDEN-RAIN TREE (*Koelreuteria paniculata*). Grows no more than 30 feet, with spreading branches. Upright clusters of half-inch bright yellow flowers have an orange-red blotch at the base. One of the few yellow-flowering trees. The fruit is tan or yellow. (Zones 6-9.)

DEVIL'S WALKING STICK (*Aralia elata*). White flowers in huge panicles sometimes two feet long. Dark green compound leaves can be three feet long. A very different, exotic-looking plant, to be used carefully. Red color in autumn. Suckers. (Zones 5-9.)

JAPANESE PAGODA TREE (*Sophora japonica*). Medium size, to 30 feet, with a short trunk and ascending and spreading branches forming a rounded crown. Creamy white pealike flowers in 15-inch clusters. Fruit is a long rounded pod. (Zones 6-9.)

FRANKLINIA (*Franklinia alatamaha*). Small tree or shrub with leaves to six inches long. White flowers with yellow stamens grow to three inches across. Plant in full sun for best orange-and-red fall color. Dies back in the colder North and may not produce flowers there. (Zones 7-9.)

SOURWOOD (*Oxydendrum arboreum*). Small tree with a spreading form and drooping branches. The glossy leaves are a leathery dark green and turn to brilliant red in the fall. Hanging clusters of white urn-shaped flowers change to tan-colored fruit. (Zones 7-9.)

WITCH-HAZEL (*Hamamelis virginiana*). Large shrub or small tree. Yellow flowers with four twisted petals. Fruit ripens the following autumn so that this is one of the few plants having fruit and flowers at the same time. Autumn foliage yellow-orange. (Zones 4-9.)

How to Use this Chart

Although trees will flower earlier in the year in warmer climates, the *order* of bloom shown here is quite dependable. Thus you can study this chart to find which trees to plant for a continuous show of color from earliest spring to latest fall. The chart will also help you choose specific trees to fill in where needed. The flowering dogwood, for example, blooms in mid-spring and the Japanese dogwood in mid-summer but their flowering does not overlap. As you can see on the chart, a Washington thorn or goldenchain tree will bridge the gap. The length of the color bar represents the length of bloom time which is another important factor in choosing trees. Weather affects flowering time from season to season but some trees, as shown, bloom longer than others. For trees that are not hardy or not available in your area consult your local nurseryman for adaptable substitutes.

zones 6-9

Redbud (*Cercis canadensis*). In spring this tree bears red-purple round flowers on black branches. 'Alba,' a white-flowered variety, has heart-shaped leaves and an irregular form. Redbud is best grown on a sunny site sheltered from wind. It does well in almost any well-drained garden soil.

zones 6-9

Japanese snowbell (*Styrax japonica*). This small, spreading tree has dark green leaves and a graceful form. In spring its white bell-like flowers hang below the branches. Generally pest-free, it has a tendency to reseed easily. Although sometimes listed as a shrub, with careful pruning it can be shaped into a tree. It grows in well-drained soils, in full sunlight or in partial shade.

zones 6-9

Higan cherry (*Prunus subhirtella*). It is noted for the masses of pink flowers that bloom before its leaves appear in early spring. The 'Autumnalis' variety is more fully flowered. However, the most attractive variety is the weeping form. It must be sheltered from wind and requires reasonably rich soil, preferably with a trace of lime.

zones 6-9

Japanese maple (*Acer palmatum*). This maple often has several trunks and, with its star-shaped leaves, is an excellent shade tree. It is attractive planted individually or in a group. Japanese maple grows slowly but does best in rich soil and where protected from wind. It is usually free of pests and disease.

Other attractive small maples include several varieties available with green or reddish foliage. Trident maple (*A. buergerianum*) grows well in drier areas; hedge maple (*A. campestre*) makes a good screen.

zones 7-9

Japanese apricot (*Prunus mume*). This tree bears fragrant pink-and-white flowers in early spring but the named varieties have the brightest colors. This is a fine small tree for a bright spring accent. One of the most attractive named varieties is 'Alphandii,' which bears rose-pink flowers in spring.

zones 8-9

Silk tree, 'Mimosa' (*Albizzia julibrissin*). A fast-growing tree, it is distinguished by fine, soft, feathery leaves that close with the cool of night. Also notable are the fragrant pink flowers which first bloom in June and continue through most of summer. An excellent shade tree, it does well in dry or poor soil. When the leaves drop, the branching is somewhat open. The silk tree is relatively short-lived but its attractiveness makes it a popular ornamental. It lends a distinctly tropical effect to the landscape, and should be used with discretion in non-tropical areas.

In cold climates, the slightly smaller 'Rosea' variety is best. It is hardier, especially if protected for the first winter or two.

Good Fruit Trees Small to Medium In Height

Some fruit trees, such as cherries, apricots and plums, provide a bountiful harvest with little if any extra care. Others, such as the apple tree, require considerable care to bear good fruit. But they all offer promise of productivity, while lending character to the landscape. For the best results, plant fruit trees in sunny places. Most fruit trees are shallow-rooting and should not be planted too deeply, and the soil around them should not be cultivated too often. Make sure you plant fruit trees in early autumn while the soil is still warm.

zones 3-9 Apple. Apples are the classic fruit tree. Usually with crooked, gnarled trunks, they become wide-spreading, grow to 20 or 30 feet and have shapely branch structures. The supply of fruit often greatly exceeds the demand. In autumn it is wise to gather fallen apples; rotting fruit attracts bees and can harbor disease through winter. Apple trees thrive in well-drained clay soils. The fruit of trees grown in damp, low-lying areas is generally inferior. For the best fruit, a thorough regimen of spraying and pruning usually is required.

zones 4-9 Cherry. A fruiting cherry grows to about 30 feet, has pink flowers in spring, slender twigs and offers cooling shade. Although disease may kill an entire branch (it can be cut off), the tree itself has a reputation for longevity.

zones 4-9 Plum. An attractive tree for a small garden, it has white or pinkish flowers. They bloom in spring and are slightly fragrant. This tree bears good fruit for many years.

zones 4-9 Pear. Often overlooked, the pear is possibly the best fruit tree for home properties. It is upright and narrow, long-lived (to 100 years or more) and deep-rooted, thus permitting other plants to grow at its base. The yellow-to-green fruit is attractive and usually remains on the tree until late fall, when the insect season ends. White flowers bloom in early spring, offering a striking contrast to the dark brown of the branches and trunk. The pear grows best in well-drained loam soils.

zones 6-9 Apricot. Also recommended for the small garden, it never exceeds 20 feet. It has dark green foliage and generally blossoms earlier than the peach or plum.

zones 6-9 Peach. A small tree, 10 to 15 feet high, it yields fruit only two or three years after planting. An attractive garden tree, the peach blooms with pink flowers in spring. It thrives in sandy, gravelly areas but will grow in heavier soils if they are well-drained.

| Shallow Deep | Shallow Deep | Shallow Deep | Shallow Deep | Deciduous Evergreen | Broad leaf Needle leaf | |
| ROUND DECIDUOUS | S ROUND EVERGREEN | UPRIGHT DECIDUOUS | UPRIGHT EVERGREEN | PYRAMIDAL | FOLIAGE | FLOWERING |

White birch

Common honey locust

Flowering dogwood

Arborvitae

Weeping cherry

225

Trees of Special Interest

Upright and Columnar

zones 2-9 Simon poplar (*Populus simoni*). Similar to the Lombardy poplar, this deciduous tree is smaller and resists the canker that kills Lombardys. It has dark green leaves and grows to 40 feet.

zones 4-9 Bolleana poplar (*Populus alba pyramidalis*). One of the most attractive poplars, it has an interesting whitish trunk, and leaves that are green above and white below. This deciduous tree is long-lived and grows to about 50 feet.

zones 5-9 Maples (*Acer*). The Norway (*A. platanoides*), sugar (*A. saccharum*) and red (*A. rubrum*) maples are available in upright form. All deciduous trees, they are slow-growing, long-lived, and reach about 50 feet. They require moist, cool soil.

Small trees

zones 2-9 Upright crab apple. Among the most interesting columnar crab apples are the Strathmore crab (*Malus strathmore*) and the Siberian crab (*M. baccata columnaris*). These deciduous trees are popular as ornamentals, have colorful flowers and grow to about 25 feet.

zones 3-9 Upright juniper (*Juniperus virginiana*). This branching, slow-growing species makes a good narrow evergreen screen but is less effective planted singly. It has pale green leaves and is the hardiest of the columnar plants.

zones 3-9 White cedar (*Thuya occidentalis*). This attractive upright conifer is a slow-growing, short-lived tree with an open, often irregular crown. Slender and straight, it can grow to more than 50 feet.

zones 5-9 Hawthorn. The pyramidal Washington species (*Crataegus phaenopyrum fastigiata*) is a good street tree. It bears white flowers in spring, followed in summer by red fruit.

zones 5-9 Upright yew (*Taxus*). Hick's yew (*T. media hicksii*), often among the hardier yews, is very narrow and dense. Although this evergreen grows to only 15 feet, it has a thin form which can be sheared for formal effects.

zones 6-9 Japanese cherry (*Prunus serrulata*). This upright, columnar deciduous tree bears light-pink flowers in spring. Round-headed, it has copper-red leaves and commonly grows to about 20 feet.

zones 8-9 Italian cypress (*Cupressus sempervirens*). A hardy, columnar evergreen, it adds a formal accent to the landscape, but its roots require good drainage. Italian cypress grows to about 60 feet but is found only in British Columbia.

Weeping and Pendulous

Large trees to 50 feet

zones 3-9 Weeping silver maple (*Acer saccharinum laciniatum*). Although this fast-growing tree does not exhibit a fully weeping form, the tips of its branches droop attractively. A deciduous species, it grows to 30 feet and has leaves that are bright green above and silvery-white beneath. Weeping silver maple requires well-drained but moist, cool soil.

zones 4-9 Golden weeping willow (*Salix alba tristis*). Because this deciduous tree grows so quickly (reaching a maximum of 25 feet) it often becomes too large for small gardens. It has green leaves, borne on bright yellow twigs, and is particularly attractive on a wide lawn.

zones 6-9 Weeping beech (*Fagus sylvatica pendula*). Like the weeping willow, this slow-growing, deciduous tree has a beautiful shape but greedy roots. It grows well in all except heavy, wet soils, but requires lots of space.

Smaller trees, of garden size

zones 2-9 Cutleaf European birch (*Betula pendula gracilis*). This deciduous species combines a weeping form with the traditional beauty of the birch and is attractive summer and winter. It is wise to choose a cutleaf European birch tree at a nursery to get the best form. It is best for screening or as a windbreak, and grows in thin, acidic soils.

zones 3-9 Weeping European mountain-ash (*Sorbus aucuparia pendula*). Distinguished by its yellow-orange autumn foliage, and bright orange-red berries which ripen in late summer, this deciduous species is one of our most attractive trees. Suitable for ornamental planting, it grows to about 25 feet and is sensitive to bacterial burn.

zones 3-9 Weeping Siberian pea-shrub (*Caragana arborescens pendula*). A hardy, deciduous tree, it bears pea-like yellow flowers in spring. This species grows quickly and makes a good screen or windbreak.

zones 4-9 Weeping mulberry (*Morus alba pendula*). This small ornamental tree has branches that touch the ground. It is ideal for small gardens.

zones 4-9 Umbrella elm (*Ulmus glabra camperdownii*). Characterized by an attractive umbrella shape, this tree has horizontal branches with drooping branchlets.

zones 5-9 Weeping crab apple (*Malus* 'Oekonomierat Echtermeyer'). A fine decorative tree, it yields a profusion of purplish flowers in early spring, and mauve fruit throughout summer. Its branches usually touch the ground.

zones 6-9 Weeping higan cherry (*Prunus subhirtella pendula*). This small weeping tree grows to about 25 feet. In spring it is notable for clouds of pale pink flowers. It has shiny green leaves, an interesting winter form, and smooth bark.

Small Trees With Multiple Trunks

Zones 2-9 Amur maple (*Acer ginnala*). This deciduous tree has heart-shaped leaves which turn bright crimson in fall. In summer it yields red fruit. Amur maple grows to 20 feet and has a spread of about 10 feet.

Zones 3-9 Gray birch (*Betula populifolia*). The multiple white trunks of this deciduous tree make an excellent semi-screen. One of the smallest birches, it rarely exceeds 35 feet. The gray birch is short-lived, seldom surviving for more than 50 years.

Zones 3-9 Hornbeam (*Carpinus caroliniana*). This deciduous tree has ridged gray bark, and finely textured leaves that turn red in autumn. It yields a small, ribbed nut. Seldom exceeding 20 feet, hornbeam has extremely hard, strong wood.

Zones 3-9 Black haw (*Viburnum prunifolium*). This small tree is native to eastern Canada and bears edible black fruits. In fall, it is distinguished by brilliant red foliage.

Zones 4-9 Shadblow (*Amelanchier canadensis*). Almost as showy as the birch, this deciduous species blossoms with white star-shaped flowers in early spring. These are followed by round, sweet-tasting black berries which ripen in early summer.

Zones 5-9 Corkscrew willow (*Salix matsudana tortuosa*). This slow-growing erect tree has twisted and contorted branches. A deciduous species, it grows to 20 feet.

Zones 5-9 Umbrella pine (*Pinus densiflora umbraculifera*). A many-trunked, round-topped evergreen, it is ideal for small gardens.

Zones 6-9 Japanese maple (*Acer palmatum*). Both the red- and green-leafed varieties are available in this form. They grow to about 20 feet.

Trees and Shrubs for Hedges and Screens

Although fences and other structures used as screening require less time, space and care than trees and shrubs do, plants lend more character to the landscape while providing the same amount of privacy. In addition, they influence one's sense of scale, and help to define space and frame views. Here is a list of plants that are especially good for screening. There's a description of each plant in the foregoing list of trees and in the shrub list on page 238.

Dense evergreen trees for screening

Narrow
Upright juniper
White cedar
Hemlock (trim tips)
Douglas fir (clipped)
Upright white pine
Hick's yew
Italian cypress

True laurel (clipped)
Strathmore crab
Washington hawthorn

Wider
Colorado spruce
Douglas fir
White fir
Hemlock (massed)
Austrian or white pine
Rhododendron
European holly
Choke cherry
Shadbush

Shrubs to 6 feet and under
Hick's yew (clipped)
Scarlet burning-bush (clipped)
Tartary honeysuckle (clipped)
Korean boxwood (clipped)
American cranberry bush
Caragana
Winged spindlewood
Rough rose
Ninebark

Attracting Birds to Your Garden

A well-stocked feeder and some fresh water placed out of the way of cats and other predators is the surest way to attract birds. If you position feeders, bird baths and bird houses properly you can observe birdlife from the comfort of your home. And because birds can be highly dependent, with regular feeding some species may adopt your property for long periods.

Birds require trees and shrubs for nesting. Evergreens provide plenty of protection—especially in winter when adequate cover is scarce.

Trees and shrubs with berries also attract birds. Remember: Although birds will flock to feeders in winter, during the rest of the year they prefer natural foods.

However, berries may provide food for a few days but plants are on display the year round. It is best to use plants that both enhance the landscape and appeal to birdlife.

Trees
Crab apple
Mountain ash
Cherry
Hawthorn
Juneberry

Shrubs
Saskatoon berry
Oleaster
Burning-bush
Snowberry
Bluebottle
Black currant
Dogwood
Honeysuckle
Holly

Using Trees to Best Advantage

Trees are among the most beautiful of plants and the largest, most permanent additions to a garden. Because they may be in place for a lifetime, or for generations, they should be set out with this in mind.

Really big trees are often at their best when they can be seen in their full majesty, outlined against the sky, and it is almost always best to plant them where they will never seem cramped or overgrown.

Graciously planted *outside the stone wall, this crab apple tree can be enjoyed by the passersby as well as the homeowners. The absence of plantings nearby allows this tree to be admired for itself alone.*

This flowering dogwood *stands out clearly from its background of larger, greener trees. In the summer, when the dogwood is green, the contrast will be lessened but will return with the dogwood's fall colors (and berries).*

The perfect placement of this flowering cherry along a garden path allows the translucent blossoms to glow against the light. The scattering of fallen petals on the ground only enhances a leisurely afternoon stroll.

Both for the sculptural quality of its multiple trunk and the brilliant color of its pendent flowers, the golden chain tree (Laburnum anagyroides) is seen to best advantage when it stands dramatically alone.

The flowering Hopa crab apples lining this street of a new residential area confer an almost instant charm and graciousness. Without the trees, such communities often have a bare or overly manicured look.

A flowering tree against a blue sky, while almost a photographic cliché, is still a recurring delight in actuality. Such a tree is most enjoyed when its beauty can be easily seen from various places in the garden.

In locating a tree of any kind or size, its position should be considered from the viewpoints inside the house as well as in the garden. Consider positioning a flowering tree so its bouquets of bloom can be enjoyed from a favorite chair in the living room. In the garden a graceful arch over a pathway or a canopy of green to provide shade for a terrace can easily be created by putting the right tree in the right place.

Small trees are often seen against a background of larger trees or a house or a fence. Their color and form should be chosen to separate well and stand out clearly in con-trast to the background. Plant light against dark and dark against light, put linear shapes where they will be seen against the flat surface of a fence or house or against the open sky. Sometimes the contrast is only needed during a particular season to accentuate early spring foliage, summer flowers or bright color in the fall. Sometimes trees can be grouped to make a small grove and further increase their impact.

While these principles of planting can enhance their usefulness, the beauty of the trees themselves is the most important, and the sooner they are started the better.

Strategically located, *this cherry tree provides a breathtaking view when in bloom. It not only helps screen the view from the street but its wide form relates well to the low, horizontal lines of the house.*

▶ **Just one such noble tree** *can be the highlight of an entire neighborhood, and a row of them could be overwhelming. This maple, an impressive specimen the year around, is magnificent in the glory of its autumn colors.*

12

Using Shrubs
In the Landscape

Basic Sizes and Shapes

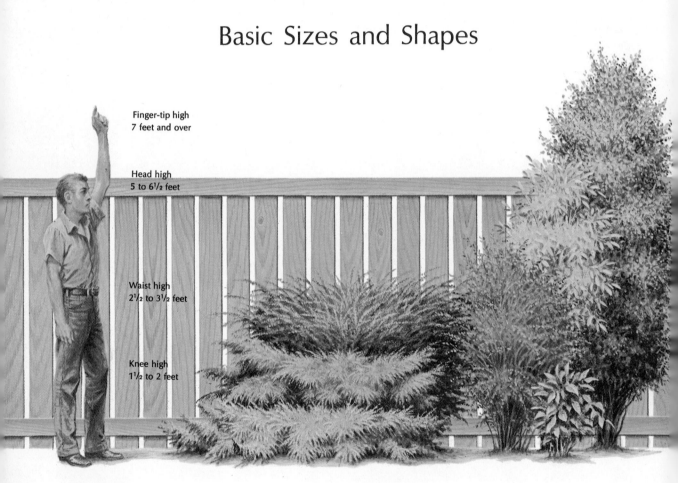

Finger-tip high
7 feet and over

Head high
5 to 6½ feet

Waist high
2½ to 3½ feet

Knee high
1½ to 2 feet

Spreading

Shrubs of this shape are useful for large-scale ground covers and to fill horizontal spaces. Shown here from low to high: spreading juniper (Juniperus chinensis sargentii), compact juniper (J. pfitzeriana compacta) and the Japanese yew (Taxus cuspidata densa).

Upright

Included in this category, to simplify selection, are columnar shrubs as well as upright forms. From front: upright ivy (Hedera helix conglomerata), upright barberry (Berberis thunbergi erecta), heavenly bamboo (Nandina domestica), upright shrub holly (Ilex crenata microphylla).

Of all the plants used in landscaping the shrubs have the most intimate appeal. Unlike the trees and flowers, their size is easily related to man, as illustrated here. The wide-ranging beauty of their foliage and flowers makes them attractive to have close at hand. And they are traditionally planted close to the house (often too close), where they are readily seen. At their best they are used to separate areas and define spaces.

There are hundreds of good shrubs in such a variety of shapes and sizes that deciding which to use is a forbidding problem for all but an experienced plantsman. The purpose of this chapter is to help you organize the material into comprehensible units that can be easily related to specific places in the landscape. The sizes and shapes shown here are purposely simplified. There are shrubs of every gradation in height from shoe-top to above the upraised hand, but for use in the garden they can be logically divided into four sizes as illustrated. The same is true of shape. There are shrubs of every shape, from narrow to spreading, but if you think of them in the four general groupings as shown they can be easily related to the spaces you want to fill in the landscape.

These examples are typical as to form and size but any plant can be reduced in size and changed in shape by careful pruning. In general, however, the plant will look better and require less work if it is pruned only to enhance the natural form.

Rounded

This is the form with greatest mass. Some can be pruned to be spreading, upright or vase-shaped. From the front: warty barberry (Berberis verruculosa), slender deutzia (Deutzia gracilis), common myrtle (Myrtus communis) and rhododendron (which comes in many other sizes).

Vase-Shaped

Some of these are graceful and others tend to be leggy and bare at the base. It so happens that many of the best-known flowering shrubs are this shape. From the front: Floribunda rose, mock orange (Philadelphus lemoinei), beauty bush (Kolkwitzia amabilis).

233

The Three Basic Kinds of Shrubs

The shrubs you choose for your garden will be either broad-leaved or needle-leaved, evergreen or deciduous, and are indicated as such on the lists that follow.

The broad-leaved evergreens have the advantage of attractive foliage the year around and some, such as the rhododendrons, pieris and azaleas also have magnificent flowers in their season. While the foliage is called "green" it does, in many cases, take on variations in color that slowly change from chartreuse to bronzy green with the seasons and add to its interest.

Needle-leaved shrubs are all evergreens although some of the trees, such as larch, are deciduous. They all bear seeds in woody cones and are classed as conifers. For all the similarity of the foliage for which they are grown there is great variation in shape, texture and the shade of green.

Deciduous plants are those that lose their leaves in winter. Some are semi-deciduous and hold their foliage in mild climates. These shrubs are most valuable for the fullness of their bloom. Forsythia, mock orange, spirea and hydrangea are familiar examples.

Broad-Leaved Evergreen

The Oregon grape is used here as a colorful accent. When massed together, broad-leaved evergreens make graceful space dividers in the garden. Most of the broad-leaved evergreens are limited to mild climates, though some such as bearberry, cotoneaster and upright ivy will grow in colder climates. Many have flowers of exceptional beauty.

234

Deciduous

Lilacs are among the most popular deciduous shrubs, valued for appearance and fragrance. There are many varieties ranging in height and size of blossom and ranging in color from white through purple. Like most deciduous plants lilacs are hardy in cold climates and require full sun to flower. Some deciduous shrubs have lovely branch patterns and are attractive when branches are bare in winter. Pyracantha, for example, with its orange berries and twiggy branches is handsome against a plain wall.

Needle-Leaved Evergreen

This spreading juniper has the qualities of most needled evergreens—good green color the year around and sturdy form that makes it a dependable basic planting. It is also a handsome, low-maintenance groundcover. Many needled evergreens such as hemlocks and yews are used for hedges and topiary because they are easily shaped.

235

Easy Ways To Do Heavy Work

Gravity and friction are the natural enemies of easy work. Once this is clearly recognized, such ancient inventions as rollers and wheels, to reduce friction, and inclines and levers, to offset gravity, can be brought into play. Shown here are eight basic ways to make work easier. With these principles in mind, the quest for other techniques that will make heavy work less difficult to do can be a challenge as well as its own reward.

Use wheels whenever possible. The hand truck, above, which is both a lever and a wheel, has a carrying platform that sits flat on the ground and is easy to slide under the load. When tilted back, the load stays in place. On soft ground, or up a slope, it is easier to pull than push. A wheelbarrow is indispensable for work around the house. Buy a good one, preferably with pneumatic tires. For heavy work, get the contractor's model with straight wooden handles attached directly to the axle. The solid steel body can be used for mixing concrete and wheeling it to the job. A child's wagon is a surprisingly useful tool. Its flat bed and the stability of four wheels make it especially good for carrying small heavy objects. The rolling surface, however, must be fairly hard and smooth. Boards can be set across the edge to make a larger platform.

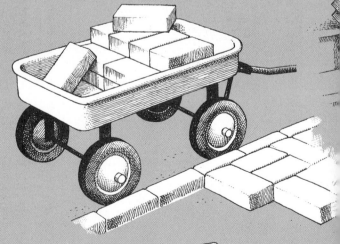

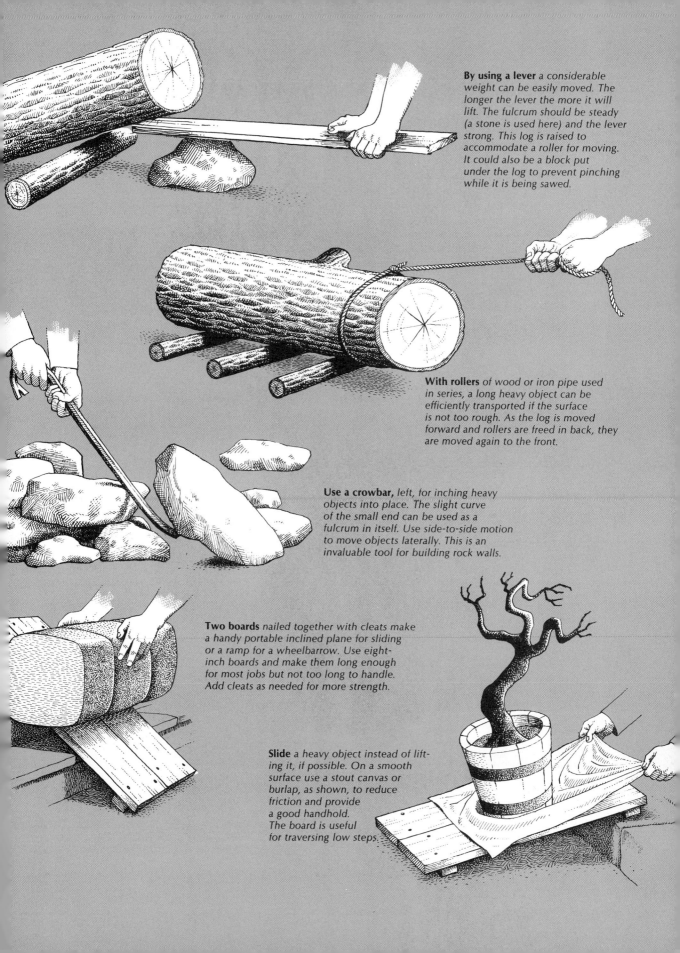

By using a lever a considerable weight can be easily moved. The longer the lever the more it will lift. The fulcrum should be steady (a stone is used here) and the lever strong. This log is raised to accommodate a roller for moving. It could also be a block put under the log to prevent pinching while it is being sawed.

With rollers of wood or iron pipe used in series, a long heavy object can be efficiently transported if the surface is not too rough. As the log is moved forward and rollers are freed in back, they are moved again to the front.

Use a crowbar, left, for inching heavy objects into place. The slight curve of the small end can be used as a fulcrum in itself. Use side-to-side motion to move objects laterally. This is an invaluable tool for building rock walls.

Two boards nailed together with cleats make a handy portable inclined plane for sliding or a ramp for a wheelbarrow. Use eight-inch boards and make them long enough for most jobs but not too long to handle. Add cleats as needed for more strength.

Slide a heavy object instead of lifting it, if possible. On a smooth surface use a stout canvas or burlap, as shown, to reduce friction and provide a good handhold. The board is useful for traversing low steps.

Choosing the Right Shrubs for the Right Place

Although trees are perhaps the most prominent features of a landscape, shrubs and bushes play an important role when planted close to homes—for they greatly enhance the appearance of buildings. Because of their size, shrubs are balancing factors: they form a middle element between a house and trees on one hand, and flowers on the other. Moreover, their different shapes, colors and blooms lend variety to the landscape.

On the practical side, shrubs are used to make formal or informal hedges. They separate various parts of the garden, screen off unattractive objects and indicate property boundaries. And certain species anchor terrain along slopes and banks, thus helping to retain natural surroundings.

Most nurseries carry hundreds of attractive shrubs in such a variety of shapes and sizes that deciding which to use is difficult for all but an experienced landscaper. The following list offers a good selection of handsome, easy-to-grow shrubs. As with trees, they are classified by zones according to hardiness. Remember that species in zones 1 to 5 are more resistant to cold than those in zones 6 to 9, although they will grow in more temperate areas. For further details, see pages 208-209.

The shrubs below also are classified according to shape, and foliage and flowering type. Generally, any plant can be reduced in size or changed in shape by careful pruning. However, it is best to prune plants only to enhance their natural forms.

The Shapes

 Spreading. This symbolizes plants that spread their branches close to the ground. Such shrubs are best in rock gardens and for ground cover.

 **Upright.** This indicates plants with ascending branches and branchlets that give an erect, even columnar shape. Such shrubs are good for hedging and are attractive displayed individually.

 Rounded. This symbolizes ball-shaped plants. They can be displayed singly or blended into beds.

 Vase-shaped. This indicates plants with a spreading crown and slightly curved branches. Some are graceful; others tend to be bare at the base.

The Foliage

 Evergreen. This symbolizes plants that keep their foliage year round. Evergreen leaves come in various shapes and sizes. Coniferous plants bear needles.

 **Deciduous.** This indicates plants that lose their foliage in autumn. The leaves of deciduous plants often turn vivid colors before they drop.

The Features

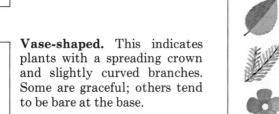 **Outstanding foliage.** These plants are noted for the shape, texture and color of their leaves.

Needles. This symbolizes plants with attractive needles.

 Outstanding flowers. These plants are noted for their blooms, growing singly or in clusters.

Knee-high: 1½ to 2′

Sheep-laurel (*Kalmia angustifolia*). This rather open, loose shrub has clustered lavender-red flowers and spreads to about four feet. A hardy shrub, it does best in wet, peaty, lime-free soil. It should be partially shaded, and is most attractive grouped with rhododendrons or mountain-laurel on semi-wild sites.

zones 1-9

Mayflower (*Epigaea repens*). A trailing evergreen shrub, it has sweet-smelling pale pink flowers which bloom in early spring. Because it needs moist, acidic soil and a semi-shaded environment, the mayflower is difficult to transplant. It yields small berries.

zones 1-9

Garland flower (*Daphne cneorum*). A creeping shrub, it is used mainly in rock gardens. In early summer it bears masses of fragrant pink flowers. Garland flower grows well in chalky, well-drained soil and needs full sunlight.

zones 2-9

Broom (*Cytisus decumbens*). A drooping shrub, it blooms with a profusion of yellow flowers in spring. Broom thrives in poor soil; however, it needs plenty of sun and its roots are particularly sensitive to disturbance.

zones 2-9

Junipers (*Juniperus*). This group varies in shape and height. Some have rising, others creeping branches; some are pyramidal, others broad in form. But all are good landscaping shrubs. Here are some varieties hardy enough to grow in less temperate regions:

zones 2-9

Waukegan juniper (*J. horizontalis douglasii*). This has gray-blue foliage which spreads to four feet. It is excellent for covering slopes, and for massing and wide edging. It thrives where there is plenty of sun, and does well in most well-drained soils.

Wilton juniper (*J. h.* 'Wilton'). This plant is fuller than the juniper listed above, and its spreading branches are more upright. Its foliage is a bluish gray-green.

'Blue Danube' juniper (*J. sabina* 'Blue Danube'). This hardy, spreading variety has bushy branches, with scaly blue needles. It is ideal planted in large beds and attractively complements other conifers.

Common juniper (*Juniperus communis*). This low-spreading evergreen shrub has sharply pointed leaves, and aromatic berry-like fruit that turns from bluish black to white when ripe. It thrives in exposed, rocky areas.

All junipers prefer open, sunlit sites. Although slow-growing, they must be pruned annually if planted in small groups or along borders. They are prone to damage by caterpillars, which eat the leaves and spin the foliage together.

Bumalda spirea (*Spiraea bumalda*). Spreading to five feet, this hardy shrub bears bright purple-red flowers in flat-topped clusters. The 'Anthony Waterer' variety is a particular favorite, and does well in dry soil. It blooms intermittently for nearly a month in summer. 'Froebelii' is a little taller and its second bloom hides the brown skeleton of the first.

zones 2-9

Dwarf viburnum (*Viburnum opulus nanum*). Thick and upright, this shrub has small three-lobed leaves, grows to two feet and bears neither flowers nor fruit. It is best planted in beds or low hedges, and thrives in any moist soil.

zones 2-9

Dwarf ninebark (*Physocarpus opulifolius nana*). Its dense foliage makes a mound of dark green, and the reddish fruit in fall has a papery texture. The dwarf ninebark is excellent for edging. Hardy and drought-resistant, it grows well in poor soils.

zones 2-9

Dwarf evergreens. Several of the needle evergreens such as spruce, pine and fir are available in dwarf varieties. They are often planted together to form an arboretum. They also can be used among flowers for summer accent, and for winter interest when beds and borders are bare. Size varies, but they are all slow-growing, extremely hardy and do well in most well-drained soils. They will grow in full sunlight or in partial shade.

zones 3-9

Kalm's Saint-John's-wort (*Hypericum kalmianum*). A small, indigenous shrub which produces attractive yellow flowers in midsummer, this plant likes moist soil and full sunlight. It is best planted in beds.

zones 3-9

Cotoneasters. These hardy shrubs are highly ornamental. The 'Skogholm' cotoneaster (*Cotoneaster dammeri* 'Skogholm') is a low-lying evergreen shrub ideal for carpeting banks and low ground beneath taller shrubs and trees. Its glossy dark-green leaves are round and it bears white flowers in early summer. A hardy plant, the 'Skogholm' cotoneaster grows quickly, and can spread to a width of ten feet.

zones 4-9

The adpressed cotoneaster (*C. adpressa praecox*), also a creeper with round, evergreen leaves, grows slowly. It produces solitary flowers and in early summer bears red fruit, which remains until fall. The adpressed cotoneaster is ideal for rock gardens.

Savin (*Juniperus sabina tamariscifolia*). A creeping juniper with horizontal branches and upright twigs, it has feathery green foliage. It is best planted in beds and rockeries, and is prized as an ornamental. No staking is necessary and heavy pruning will limit its size. It grows best in full sunlight.

zones 4-9

Heather (*Erica* or *Calluna*). Small, narrow, evergreen leaves on irregular, spreading, spiky shoots create an interesting feathery texture. Upright clusters of bell-like pink or white flowers appear in late spring or early summer. Heather requires acidic soil and dry, sunny growing sites. It is excellent as hedging or for ground cover. Watering is essential on all soils during spring and during dry spells.

zones 5-9

Fortune spindle tree (*Euonymus fortunei*). A creeping or climbing evergreen shrub, it produces red-and-orange fruit in pink pods. The fortune spindle tree is highly shade-tolerant but should be sheltered from wind. Its shoots should be thinned out in late winter.

zones 5-9

Chenault coralberry (*Symphoricarpos chenaultii*). Originated in Cooksville, Ont., this shrub bears an attractive red fruit with zones 5-9 white on the shaded side. Because it is smoke-resistant, it is ideal for city gardens.

Yellowroot (*Xanthorrhiza simplicissima*). Excellent as ground cover under larger shrubs, yellowroot grows well in shade and requires almost no maintenance. It forms a dense mass, spreading by means of underground stolons (stems). The plant's shiny, showy green leaves turn a brilliant orange in fall. It grows in most well-drained soils.

Spiraea arguta (*Spiraea arguta compacta*). The most beautiful of the spiraeas, it has thin, drooping branches and produces zones 5-9 early-blooming white flowers. It resists insects well and is easy to grow from cuttings. It does best in deep, fertile soil in open, sunny areas.

Purple broom (*Cytisus purpureus*). A spring-blooming shrub, it forms a mat of dark red flowers. It prefers well-drained sunny zones 5-9 sites and is ideally suited to beds and rock gardens.

Miniature rose (*Rosa chinensis minima*). This rose plant grows to about a foot and has pink or rose-red flowers. Like most roses, it zones 6-9 requires good drainage and plenty of sunlight. It also needs considerable attention to watering, feeding and pest control. Some popular varieties are 'Oakington Ruby,' 'Red Elf,' 'Perle d'Alconda,' 'Pompon de Paris,' and 'Roulettii.'

Rock cotoneaster (*Cotoneaster horizontalis*). Spreading to four feet, this deciduous shrub has flat branches growing in layers. zones 6-9 It usually makes a mound up to two feet or more but can be cut back. It is best planted by steps or with junipers. The small, rounded green leaves of the rock cotoneaster turn red and drop in the fall. In early summer white or pink flowers bloom; red berries follow in fall.

Japanese holly (*Ilex crenata*). The female plants of this densely branched shrub bear small black berries in autumn. The variety zones 6-9 *helleri* is a dark green mound with tiny rounded leaves. It should be planted in rows as front edging, or massed as ground cover.

Upright ivy (*Hedera helix arborescens*). This hardy evergreen climber grows to 12 inches and has closely packed, pointed ivy leaves. zones 6-9 A good plant for edgings, it grows well on the ground or on a low support. It thrives in full sunlight or in partial shade.

Dwarf English box (*Buxus sempervirens suffruticosa*). This is the standard dwarf boxwood for edging, and may be used in continuous rows or with spacing zones 7-9 between plants. It can be trimmed into neat globes no more than four feet high and does well in sunlight or in partial shade.

Spreading English yew (*Taxus baccata*). This evergreen has dark needles, and branches whose ends droop slightly. The spreading zones 7-9 ing English yew thrives in chalky or limy soils and is tolerant of drought and, to some degree, polluted air. When it reaches maximum height (about 15 feet), it is ideal for large-scale plantings.

Reeves skimmia (*Skimmia reevesiana*). The common skimmia (*S. japonica*) grows to about four feet, but this variety is half the zones 7-9 height. It has shiny green leaves, white flowers and red berries. Reeves skimmia grows best in lime-free soil, requires partial shade and is relatively free of pests.

Small-leafed cotoneaster (*Cotoneaster microphylla*). This cotoneaster's small white flowers bloom in early summer and are zones 7-9 soon followed by red berries. Extremely hardy, this shrub is useful for covering walls and unsightly ground. Although it survives in cold conditions, it grows too slowly to be useful in zones colder than indicated.

It does best on sunny sites and in well-drained garden soils.

Many ground cover plants can be used in the above category, including the 'Max Graf' rose, 'Raubritter' rose, 'Confederate Jasmine' (*Trachleospermum*), 'Christmas' rose (*Heleborus niger*), creeping euonymus, English ivy, pachysandra, myrtle (*Vinca minor*), red osier dogwood, creeping jenny and Canada blue plox.

Waist-high:
2½ to 3½'

Bristly or prickly rose (*Rosa acicularis*). A hardy native rosebush, it blooms with beautiful pink flowers, which give way to red zones 1-9 pear-shaped fruit. The prickly rose is best planted in beds and requires plenty of water.

Mugho or Swiss mountain pine (*Pinus mugo mughus*). Usually gnarled, this plant has dark green needles, brown cones and varies zones 1-9 from almost flat to five feet tall. It is best to buy from a nursery so you can choose the shape. This pine prefers sandy, slightly alkaline soil and plenty of sunlight.

Bush cinquefoil (*Potentilla fruticosa*). An attractive compact shrub, it bears small yellow flowers in clusters of twos and threes zones 1-9 through much of summer. An excellent variety is 'Gold Drop' which has larger yellow flowers. Most gardeners in northern climates prefer to plant evergreens for winter interest, and use annuals or perennials for flower effects. Cinquefoil and its varieties should be grown in sunny areas that have light, well-drained soil.

Golden flecked juniper (*Juniperus communis depressa aurea-spica*). This thick green juniper has attractive flecks of whitish zones 2-9 gold on the tips of the branchlets. It grows to about three-and-a-half feet and is usually wider than it is high. It grows best in full sunlight or in light shade, and should be planted in well-drained soil.

Dwarf Russian almond (*Prunus tenella*). In spring its spreading branches bear an abundance of pinkish red flowers. One of the hardiest and most prolific flowering trees of the cherry family, it is recommended for beds.

zones 2-9

 Basket willow (*Salix purpurea gracilis*). This very hardy willow has thin, flexible branches, and gray-blue leaves. It is excellent planted in beds or used as hedges, and is easily cultivated from autumn cuttings.

zones 2-9

 Rounded occidental thuya (*Thuya occidentalis woodwardii*). A dwarf variety, this cedar has dark green foliage and retains its shape without trimming. It blends well with beds of bushes or evergreens, and grows best in moist, deep soil.

zones 3-9

 Canada yew (*Taxus canadensis stricta*). A decorative upright shrub, it has pale green foliage, and spreading branches that droop at the ends. The yew grows slowly, needs shade and is recommended for beds. It grows on all but swampy sites.

zones 3-9

 Alpine currant (*Ribes alpinum*). This hardy shrub is best trimmed into hedges. Green-yellow flowers bloom in early spring, followed by red berries. Alpine currant grows in poor soils in shady areas. The female is prone to white pine blister blight.

zones 3-9

 Dwarf Japanese yew *(Taxus cuspidata nana).* This small plant has dark green needles and is highly tolerant of wind and drought. If it becomes too large for a small garden, simply cut back the leaders (main stems). The dwarf Japanese yew grows in almost any garden soil in full sun or in partial shade.

zones 4-9

 Golden thuya (*Thuya occidentalis ellwangerian aurea*). This conifer has thick, golden foliage which is easily damaged by snow. It grows best in moist, deep soil and needs plenty of sunlight. Golden thuya can be trimmed into hedges.

zones 4-9

 Red chokeberry (*Aronia arbutifolia*). A native shrub with white or purplish flowers, it produces decorative red berries which persist until winter. The 'Brilliantissima' variety's foliage becomes bright red in fall. Red chokeberry grows best in wet, boggy places.

zones 4-9

 Floribunda roses. These are excellent shrubs for creating edgings, barriers and bright patches of color. Flowers are borne in clusters all summer long. Floribunda roses are troubled with fewer diseases than the hybrid tea roses. They require plenty of sun.

zones 4-9

 Snowmound spirea (*Spiraea nipponica* 'Snowmound'). This forms a green mound of small leaves covered with white flowers in spring. Most spireas are not suited to garden growing as their leaf structure is too small. Snowmound spirea is better than most and very hardy. It requires deep soil in a sunny place.

zones 4-9

 Bird's nest spruce (*Picea abies nidiformis*). This spruce has dark-green needles and a dense form that varies from spreading to vase-shaped. It is one of the hardiest dwarf spruce varieties and is ideally suited to northern climates, although it grows slowly in cold.

zones 4-9

 Gold-tipped juniper (*Juniperus chinensis pfitzeriana aurea*). This juniper's foliage is golden in summer and yellow-green in winter. A slow-grower, it blends well with other conifers and is ideal for beds.

zones 4-9

 White flowering almond (*Prunus glandulosa alba*). A bushy shrub, this has small, light-green leaves, and pinkish white flowers which bloom in early spring. For best results cut out dead branches each season. Plant white flowering almond in a sheltered, sunny site, preferably in well-drained, slightly limy soil.

zones 5-9

 Chinese juniper 'Blaauw' (*Juniperus chinensis* 'Blaauw'). An upright dwarf shrub, it is attractive displayed individually and is well suited to beds and rock gardens. Spreading to two and a half feet, it has thick blue-green foliage on drooping branches. It grows in most well-drained garden soils.

zones 5-9

 Burkwood's daphne (*Daphne burkwoodii*). This evergreen daphne has light-green leaves and a graceful open structure. The fragrant flowers, which appear in spring, range from white to pink. Burkwood's daphne requires plenty of sun. Although little pruning is required, trim off straggly growths in early spring.

zones 5-9

 Oregon holly-grape (*Mahonia aquifolium*). This plant has upright branches, and glossy dark green leaves. Fragrant yellow flowers bloom in spring followed by clusters of blue berries. In cold regions its foliage turns purple in winter. Oregon holly-grape is a fine underplanting for a shady place and does well in any garden soil.

zones 5-9

 Dwarf flowering quince (*Chaenomeles japonica*). This thorny shrub has an irregular shape that can be accentuated by pruning. In spring it bears orange-red flowers, sometimes followed by fragrant, apple-shaped yellow fruit. Recommended are such named hybrids as 'Knaphill,' a scarlet shrub that grows to 16 inches, and the salmon-yellow 'Aurea' which reaches three feet.

zones 5-9

 Spreading
 Upright
 Rounded
 Vase-Shaped
 Evergreen
 Deciduous
 Outstanding for Flowers
 Outstanding Broad leaf
Foliage Needle

Carles viburnum (*Viburnum carlesii*). In June this handsome, slow-growing shrub is covered with fragrant white flowers. It should be planted in full sunlight and in a protected spot.

Korean boxwood (*Buxus microphylla koreana*). The hardiest of all boxwoods, it has small leaves that are more pointed than those of the English boxwood. The Korean boxwood can be grown as hedging or as clipped specimen plants. It does well in full sunlight.

Korean azalea (*Rhododendron yedoense poukhanense*). This deciduous or semi-evergreen plant has long leaves and purple-violet flowers. One of the hardiest of the rhododendrons, it will grow in temperatures as low as 15°F. It thrives in well-drained sandy soil.

Dwarf hybrid rhododendrons. One of the most attractive small rhododendrons is the 'Boule de Neige' variety, which forms a dark compact mound, with white flowers in spring. However, there are dozens of other fine varieties, and it is best to choose them in bloom at your local nursery. Rhododendrons thrive in partial shade and in slightly acidic, well-drained sandy soil. They will not tolerate chalky or limy soils, and must be sheltered from wind.

Compact pfitzer juniper (*Juniperus chinensis pfitzeriana compacta*). This fine-textured shrub has gray-green foliage on spreading branches. Similar to the common pfitzer juniper, it is more compact in form.

Snow azalea (*Rhododendron mucronatum,* also known as *R. ledifolium*). This spreading plant has evergreen leaves up to three inches long and white fragrant flowers. It is extremely hardy and survives to 0°F. Snow azalea requires little pruning, but in spring it can be cut back to within one foot of the ground. It grows best in well-drained soil.

Slender deutzia (*Deutzia gracilis*). A compact plant with delicate light-green leaves, it bears pinkish white star-shaped flowers in early spring. Slender deutzia grows best on well-drained soil in full sunlight. It requires sheltering from wind.

Tree peony (*Paeonia suffruticosa*). This attractive flowering shrub has an irregular open form spreading to five feet, and shapely green leaves. Large flowers appear in late spring and range in color from magenta-purple to rose-pink. Its branches remain bare through winter. The tree peony should be planted where it is shaded from early morning sun. It thrives in moist, well-drained soil.

David's viburnum (*Viburnum davidii*). Suitable for ground cover, this evergreen has long leaves with prominent veins. Pinkish white flowers bloom in early summer and are followed in fall by metallic-blue berries. If grown for its decorative berries, plant this species in groups of two or three.

Dwarf Hinoki cypress (*Chamaecyparis obtusa gracilis*). An attractive, slow-growing plant, it has deep green scale-like needles, and upright branches that grow in dense clumps on a central stem. Dwarf Hinoki cypress eventually grows to about five feet. Although it thrives in any ordinary, well-drained soil, it is intolerant of limy or dry areas. It is generally free of pests, but is prone to honey fungus, a disease that can be fatal. Little pruning is required; fertilizers are rarely necessary but a light dusting with a nitrogenous type in spring improves leaf color.

Japanese skimmia (*Skimmia japonica*). This plant is characterized by round to pointed glossy evergreen leaves, and small whitish flowers which bloom in early spring. On female plants they are followed by red berries that ripen in late summer. Both male and female plants are required for production of fruit. An ideal hedge plant, Japanese skimmia is tolerant of air pollution, thus making it a good choice for city gardens. It needs deep, rich soil.

Abelia (*Abelia grandiflora*). This hardy, spreading evergreen has small reddish leaves, and may be trimmed into hedges. An open plant, it bears slightly fragrant pink-and-white flowers through summer. It should be planted on a sunny site, protected from wind. No regular pruning is required.

Sarcococca (*Sarcococca ruscifolia*). This spreading plant has pointed shiny leaves that grow to a dense mass of dark green. Small fragrant white flowers bloom in spring and are followed by red berries. This variety reaches slightly more than three feet. Himalayan sarcococca (*S. hookeriana*) is shorter and has black berries. Shade-loving plants, sarcococcas do well in any ordinary well-drained garden soil, in full sunlight or in partial shade.

Kurume azaleas (*Rhododendron obtusum*). These handsome medium-sized azaleas have small glossy evergreen leaves on dense branches. In spring they bear masses of funnel-shaped magenta-pink flowers. Like all rhododendrons, Kurume azaleas require slightly acidic, well-drained sandy soil and partial shade. They must be sheltered from early-morning sunlight and from wind. The 'Amoenum' variety has purple to magenta flowers; 'Hinodegiri' is a bright magenta red; 'Mme Auguste Haerens' has pale pink flowers with a darker base; 'Princess Beatrix' is a rich pink; and 'Coral Bells' a double pink.

Bay-leaf rock rose (*Cistus laurifolius*). This spreading to mounded shrub has pointed olive-green leaves and is usually covered with poppy-like flowers in summer. The color of the flowers (and the size of plant) varies with the species: they range from white or purple to white with yellow blotches at the base of the petals. All species grow well in hot, sunny places and prefer poor, well-drained soil. Young plants are more frost-resistant than older specimens.

zones 8-9

Butcher's-broom (*Ruscus aculeatus*). Growing on a stiff upright trunk, the small pointed "leaves" of this plant resemble flattened twiglets. In autumn female plants bear red fruit, often as large as cherries.

zones 8-9

Imperial veronica (*Veronica imperialis*). This evergreen plant has smooth oval leaves, and purple flowers which bloom in summer. It thrives in most well-drained soils (including chalk) and in full sunlight. No pruning is required, and it is generally pest-free. This species may also be found under the name *Hebe speciosa*.

zone 9

Coriaceum privet (*Ligustrum japonicum rotundifolium*). The closely packed leaves of this privet grow on upright branches, and are heart-shaped, dark green and leathery. Its dense, narrow, compact form makes it a good edging or accent plant. It has a shape unlike any other privet.

Head-high: 5 to 6½'

zones 1-9

Canada buffaloberry (*Shepherdia canadensis*). A hardy native shrub with a spreading structure, it has flowers that are green outside and silver-gray inside. In late summer it produces red to orange fruit. Buffaloberry grows in rocky or sandy soil.

Siberian dogwood (*Cornus alba siberica*). This attractive wide-spreading shrub has bright coral-red bark that is particularly striking in winter. It has greenish leaves, which often turn red or orange in autumn. A hardy plant, it is relatively free of pests, grows in any good garden soil and requires plenty of sunlight. Siberian dogwood requires no regular pruning.

zones 2-9

Shrub roses. These hardy deciduous plants are highly decorative and require a minimum of care. Among those that grow in zone 2 are Harisons yellow, which has handsome, bright yellow flowers, and the red-leafed rosebush, notable for its colorful leaves.

zones 2-9

Eastern ninebark (*Physocarpus opulifolius*). In spring this shrub bears clusters of white or faintly pink flowers. The 'Luteus' variety has yellow spring foliage. Eastern ninebark is extremely hardy and an excellent plant for borders.

zones 2-9

Pointed cotoneaster (*Cotoneaster acutifolia*). This hardy dark green species produces black fruit in late fall. Widely used in beds and for hedges, it is prone to attack from insects and bacterial disease. It grows in most garden soil and requires full sunlight.

zones 3-9

Sweet mock-orange (*Philadelphus coronarius*). A dense, bushy shrub, it is notable for fragrant white flowers which bloom in spring. The 'Aureus' variety is popular and displays bright yellow leaves in spring. It retains its color best when grown in shade or semi-shade. The mock-oranges are ideally suited to dry soils.

zones 3-9

Dwarf white pine (*Pinus strobus nana*). This white pine grows as a wide rounded bush and has clusters of long needles. It may grow taller than seven feet but can easily be trimmed to size. It requires plenty of sunlight.

zones 3-9

Mountain or wild holly (*Nemopanthus mucronatus*). This native shrub prefers humid conditions and is distinguished by purplish blue leaf stalks. It bears red fruit in summer and is best planted in woodland settings.

zones 3-9

Black alder (*Ilex verticillata*), also called winterberry or holly. In the spring, this native deciduous shrub blooms with white flowers; they are followed by red berries, which last into winter. Black alder prefers moist, loamy soil.

zones 3-9

Winged spindle tree (*Euonymus alata*). This evergreen shrub is characterized by spreading branches, with two to four cork-like wings. The leaves, simple and delicately toothed, turn scarlet in fall. The winged spindle tree is excellent for beds and hedges. It is highly resistant to disease and easily grown from cuttings.

zones 3-9

Lorberg caragana (*Caragana arborescens lorbergii*). This attractive variety has yellow flowers, and does best in full sunlight. It is less hardy than the species as a whole. Lorberg caragana should be planted by itself.

zones 3-9

Rugosa rose (*Rosa rugosa*). This spreading shrub almost forms a thicket when allowed to spread. It has prickly, hairy branches, and dark green wrinkled leaves which turn orange in autumn. Pink flowers up to three inches across appear in early summer and are followed by orange-red fruit (rose hips) in early autumn. A vigorous plant, rugosa rose is easy to grow and free of pests and diseases. It does best on sunny sites and in sandy soil. Varieties include 'Alba' (white) and 'Sir Thomas Lipton' (white).

zones 4-9

Tea roses. Despite the need for considerable maintenance and care, the beauty of these roses makes them worth the effort. They have a long flowering season (from early summer to late fall) and are excellent as cut flowers—and the plant itself is a satisfactory shrub even without the flower. For more about roses, and ways to use them, see page 276.

Spreading

Upright

Rounded

Vase-Shaped

Evergreen

Deciduous

Outstanding for Flowers

Outstanding Broad leaf

Foliage Needle

Weigela florida varieties. These are grown mainly for their profuse red, pink or white blossoms, which open in early summer. Relatively free of pests and diseases, they grow best on well-drained sites where there is plenty of sunlight. The 'Bristol Ruby' variety is noted for large red flowers, 'Variegata' for its yellow-edged leaves.

zones 4-9

Purpleleaf sand cherry (*Prunus cistena*). This plant has thick foliage, and small white flowers which bloom in early spring and are followed by dark purple fruit. Beach plum (*P. maritima*) has similarly colored flowers but with green leaves and delicious fruit. Both shrubs make fine low hedges.

zones 4-9

Mock-orange (*Philadelphus lemoinei* 'Innocence'). One of the most desirable mock-oranges because of its fragrant single white flowers, which bloom in early summer, this full-bodied plant spreads to five feet. Popular varieties include: 'Enchantment' (white flowers); 'Minnesota Snowflake' (pointed white flowers on long arching branches); and 'Manteau d'Hermine' (tiny-flowered, rarely exceeds two-and-a-half feet). All grow well in full sunlight or in partial shade. They should be planted in well-drained soil.

zones 4-9

Dwarf Alberta spruce (*Picea glauca* 'Albertiana Conica'). This dense, conical shrub has finely textured soft-gray foliage. A rich-looking specimen, it grows best in full sunlight and in sandy soils. It requires little pruning, but must be screened in winter.

zones 4-9

Grandiflora roses. These are upright roses which bear clustered heads of flowers. Taller than tea roses, they are not so susceptible to disease. Grandiflora roses are excellent as a background hedge. Some typical varieties: 'Spartan' (orange-red and fragrant) and 'Carrousel' (red). One of the most popular varieties is 'Queen Elizabeth,' an erect rose with long stems and few thorns. It grows to six feet and has shapely clear-pink flowers.

zones 4-9

Blueberry, highbush (*Vaccinum corymbosum*). An open-growing shrub, it is irregular in form and almost oriental in character. In spring, bell-shaped white flowers hang gracefully from the shrub's branches. Edible blue berries appear in late summer and the leaves turn brilliant red in fall. It requires acidic soil and a shady site.

zones 4-9

Morrow honeysuckle (*Lonicera morrowii*). A dense, wide-spreading plant, it has white flowers which bloom in spring. In summer a blood-red translucent berry appears. Like most of the honeysuckles, it is a vigorous grower. Morrow honeysuckle is ideal for covering unsightly slopes.

zones 4-9

Pfitzer juniper (*Juniperus chinensis pfitzeriana*). An evergreen with grayish green needles, it is too distracting for foundation planting, but useful as an accent further from the house. Pfitzer juniper requires plenty of sunlight and does well in dry soils.

zones 4-9

Diels cotoneaster (*Cotoneaster dielsiana*). This graceful shrub features arching branches, and glossy foliage which turns reddish in fall; red berries appear shortly after. This species should be planted singly.

zones 4-9

Other Catawbiense hybrid rhododendrons. The evergreen catawbas are the hardiest of the hybrid groups and grow to five or six feet. Popular varieties include: 'Nova Zembla' (red); 'Charles Dickens' (red); 'Mrs. C. S. Sargent' (pink); and *Catawba alba* (white). Like most rhododendrons, they grow best in light, well-drained soil.

zones 5-9

Early forsythia (*Forsythia ovata*). One of the hardiest of the forsythias, it has yellow flowers which appear in spring. It should be clipped regularly after blooming; its branches are prone to damage by heavy snow. Early forsythia is ideally suited to city gardens and does well in partial shade.

zones 5-9

Butterfly-bush (*Buddleia davidii* varieties). Blooming in profusion and arching gracefully, this showy shrub has honey-scented flowers which range in color from white through pink to red. Butterfly-bush should be cut to ground level each spring. Although tolerant of limy soil, it requires full sunlight.

zones 5-9

Corkscrew hazel (*Corylus avellana contorta*). This shrub variety of the European hazel tree is distinguished by its contorted spiral-shaped twigs. It is slow-growing, has soft-yellow leaves and reaches eight feet. It should be planted in a sheltered area.

zones 5-9

Japanese kerria (*Kerria japonica pleniflora*). An upright plant, it bears bright green, serrated leaves on long stems that remain green year-round. It looks best when clipped or tied flat against a fence. Its yellow flowers bloom in early spring.

zones 5-9

Mountain laurel (*Kalmia latifolia*). This wide-spreading plant has oval leaves which grow in clusters at the end of the previous season's shoots. Young plants are rounded but with age develop an irregular upright form and may reach eight feet or more. Mountain laurel bears clusters of cup-shaped pink flowers in early summer.

zones 5-9

Do not remove specimens from the wild; buy nursery-grown plants with a good root system. Mountain laurel requires peaty, acidic soil, and grows in full sunlight or in partial shade. Little pruning is required but faded flower clusters should be trimmed off. Mountain laurel is generally free of pests.

Scaly-leafed Nepal juniper (*Juniperus squamata meyeri*). A spreading conifer with a drooping branch system, it has grayish blue needles which are rough to the touch; the needles tend to turn brownish in winter and as the plant ages. This conifer thrives in ordinary well-drained garden soil and in full sunlight or in partial shade. It is prone to juniper scale, which encrusts stems and leaves. No staking is required.

zones 5-9

zones 5-9

Sargent's crab apple (*Malus sargenti*). This crab apple has a broad spreading form but no trunk. It grows to about six feet and bears small white flowers in spring and tiny red crab apples in fall. It is best grown in full sunlight. Sargent's crab apple does not spread juniper rust disease as some crab apples do.

zones 5-9

Hybrid quince 'Spitfire' (*Chaenomeles*). Narrow, upright and thorny, the 'Spitfire' has rounded dark green leaves and red flowers. It makes a good hedge. There are several other hybrids of varying sizes with bright orange, red, yellow or white flowers that bloom in early spring. They require full sunlight.

zones 5-9

Old-fashioned roses. These are larger, more spreading and more informal in character than other garden roses. They include the bluish red Damask rose (*Rosa damascena*); the white-and-pink York and Lancaster rose (*R. d. versicolor*); the cabbage rose (*R. centifolia*), distinguished by fragrant pink flowers; and the moss rose (*R. moshata*), which has large pink blooms.

zones 5-9

Cut-leaf stephanandra (*Stephanandra incisa*). The soft-green leaves, to two-and-a-half inches long, have edges serrated as deeply as one inch. In summer it blossoms with clusters of tiny star-shaped green-white flowers. It makes an attractive hedge that can be clipped to almost any height.

zones 5-9

Rhododendron roseum. The leaves of most rhododendrons curl and droop in temperatures below 20°F. This hybrid is probably the hardiest rhododendron available and is the last to begin drooping. It bears four-inch rounded leaves on a round to upright form. The flowers, which appear in spring, are purplish with green flecks. Like all rhododendrons, it requires a humus-acid soil and does well in full sunlight.

zones 6-9

Shrub holly (*Ilex crenata*), also known as Japanese holly. This group of handsome, wide-growing evergreens has form and foliage like that of boxwood. However, shrub holly grows faster and is hardier. There are several rounded varieties. Convex-leaf (*I. c. convexa*) has shiny green leaves arched in the middle; the 'Bullata' variety is attractive; round leaf (*I. c. rotundifolia*) has shiny rounded leaves on a full rounded plant. Hetz boxleaf (*I. c. hetzi*) is densely textured and more hardy than those listed above.

zones 6-9

Father Hugo's rose (*Rosa hugonis*). An excellent specimen, this is in bloom by early summer. The leaves are simple and tinted a delicate yellow. This rosebush grows particularly well in sunny areas and needs little care compared with such species as the hybrid tea roses. Like most roses, Father Hugo's rose requires good drainage; it will die if planted in waterlogged soil.

zones 6-9

Pinkshell azalea (*Rhododendron vaseyi*). This North American native has pale green leaves which turn orange and red in autumn. In spring, it blossoms with funnel-shaped pink flowers. Evergreen azaleas grow in well-drained sandy soil and in partial shade.

zones 6-9

Dwarf Japanese maple (*Acer palmatum*, bush form). In Japan, more than 100 varieties of this maple have been cultivated, with leaves of varying shapes, textures and colors (ranging from green to red to purple). Although many of these varieties are unavailable in Canada, nurseries in this country stock a good selection. The dwarf Japanese maple is attractive grown individually or massed in a border. In group plantings it should be placed on the sides, not in the center. It requires partial shade and ample protection from wind. When sheltered, it is often among the last trees to lose its fall color and drop its leaves.

zones 6-9

Deciduous azaleas (both *Rhododendron* species and hybrids). These have upright main stems with short, horizontal branches and long, narrow, rounded light-green leaves. They require humus-acid soil and partial shade. Hardiest are the Ghent azaleas, which blossom from late May to early June. Their tubular flowers are up to one-and-a-half inches long. Typical varieties include: 'Altaclarene' (orange-yellow); 'Nancy Waterer' (yellow); 'Irene Koster' (pink and yellow); and 'Daviesi' (cream-white with orange-yellow blotches). The Mollis hybrids have scentless, funnel-shaped flowers that vary in color according to variety. Among the most popular are: 'Miss Louisa Hunnewell' (orange-yellow); 'Hugo Koster' (orange-red); 'W. E. Gumbleton' (cream buff-yellow with orange markings); 'Lemonora' (apricot-yellow flushed with pink); and 'Snowdrift' (white). The Exbury hybrids are improved Mollis, hardy down to 0°F. The number of named varieties increases annually. Among the best are 'Balzac,' which is deep orange-red, and the blood-red 'Devon.'

Torch azalea (*R. obtusum kaempferi*). The name is its best description: Colors range from red to orange and copper. A sturdy upright plant, it is ideal in a woodland setting or as a background.

zones 6-9

Burkwood viburnum (*Viburnum burkwoodii*). This shrub's evergreen leaves are dark green on the upper side, light green below. In spring it bears fragrant pinkish white flowers. Reddish berries follow in fall. In northern areas it may drop its leaves. Burkwood viburnum thrives in moist garden soil where it can get plenty of sunlight. The 'Park Farm' hybrid has larger flowers and spreads more than the species.

zones 6-9

Corylopsis pauciflora (*Corylopsis pauciflora*). This handsome shrub blooms in spring, with bell-shaped pale yellow flowers. It grows in most garden soils but needs full sunlight and a sheltered site.

Spreading

Upright

Rounded

Vase-Shaped

Evergreen

Deciduous

Outstanding for Flowers

Outstanding Foliage Broad leaf

Needle

245

Japanese andromeda (*Pieris japonica*). This bushy upright plant is characterized by narrow leaves that turn from pale green to bronze to deep green in fall. zones 6-9 Pendants of bell-like white flowers appear in spring. With age, the Japanese andromeda reaches about eight feet and becomes more open; the twisted trunks are visible through clumps of foliage, giving the tree an oriental look. This plant should be planted in moist, lime-free soil, in a sheltered position that offers partial shade. For best results, do not let the soil dry out during summer.

Cherry laurel (*Prunus laurocerasus*). This dense, vigorous laurel has narrow, pointed dark green foliage up to three inches long. It zones 7-9 can be clipped into a hedge or left unclipped. This shrub requires full sunlight or partial shade, and should be grown in well-drained, slightly limy soils. Two outstanding varieties of cherry laurel are 'Schipkaensis' (low spreading, with white flowers and narrow green leaves) and 'Zabeliana' (has low, horizontal branches, making it excellent as ground cover).

Boxwood (*Buxus sempervirens suffruticosa*). This bushy plant has glossy dark green leaves, requires little care and often grows zones 7-9 for centuries. It is clipped into hedges or edging or left to make gentle masses reaching six feet. The 'Myrtifolia' variety has smaller pointed leaves than the species. Boxwood thrives in most well-drained garden soils in full sunlight or in partial shade. Pruning of hedges and topiary specimens should be done in late summer.

Sacred bamboo (*Nandina domestica*). This plant has many upright stalks, with green leaves that may turn red and drop in cold climates. It bears creamy zones 8-9 white flowers in spring, followed by red berries in fall. In warmer climates the sacred bamboo may reach eight feet. It should be planted in rich, moist, well-drained soil, in a sheltered, sunny area. Sacred bamboo is generally free of pests and disease. Regularly prune out dead wood and weak shoots after flowering. In Japan this plant is traditionally set beside a doorway.

Rosemary (*Rosmarinus officinalis*). Spreading and irregular, this fragrant shrub has narrow leaves (up to one inch long) which zones 8-9 are dark green above and gray below. Its light-blue flowers appear in late spring and persist through summer. Rosemary thrives in full sunlight and tolerates dry soil. It does best in well-drained areas.

Gold dust tree (*Aucuba japonica variegata*). This plant is named for the gold flecks that appear on its leathery, dark green leaves zones 8-9 (often up to eight inches long). Star-shaped olive-green flowers appear in early spring, and red berries follow in fall. Gold dust tree grows in full sunlight or in partial shade. An easily grown evergreen shrub, it is ideal for town and seaside gardens.

Old-fashioned roses for warmer climates. These varieties are typical of the "species" roses. They are larger, more vigorous and zones 8-9 more shrub-like than better known garden varieties. Musk rose (*Rosa moschata nastarana*) has single pink flowers up to two inches across which appear in early summer. Tea rose (*R. odorata*) ranges from white to crimson and is notable for its fine fragrance and abundant blooms.

Fingertip-high: 7' and over

Saskatoon serviceberry (*Amelanchier alnifolia*). This plant has oval green leaves, and upright branches that form a dense zones 1-9 thicket. In spring, it bears white flowers. It grows in any well-drained soil, but must be kept moist.

American cranberry bush (*Viburnum trilobum*). A sturdy shrub with three-lobed leaves, the American cranberry bush yields zones 2-9 white flowers in late spring, followed in summer by edible red berries. It is ideal planted in large beds or in parks. It resembles the European cranberry bush (*V. opulus*), also known as the guelder-rose, which has evolved into many varieties.

Amur honeysuckle (*Lonicera maackii*). One of the largest honeysuckles, this plant has fragrant white-yellow flowers that appear zones 2-9 in late spring, and bright red fruit that lingers into autumn. It grows in most well-drained soils.

Ninebark (*Physocarpus opulifolius*). This shaggy-looking shrub has green foliage, shredding bark, and small red or purplish fruits. zones 2-9 It grows in a wide range of soil and moisture conditions, in full sunlight or in partial shade.

Amur maple (*Acer ginnala*). This graceful small maple has slightly heart-shaped green leaves which turn brilliant red in fall. zones 2-9 It grows in moist, well-drained soils, and makes a good screen or barrier.

Tatarian honeysuckle (*Lonicera tatarica*). Commonly cultivated in Canada, this hardy deciduous shrub has upright branches zones 2-9 and hollow stems. In late spring, it blooms with pale pink to red flowers; red to orange-yellow fruit follows in late summer. The Tatarian honeysuckle makes thick hedges and requires little care. It grows well in full sunlight or in partial shade, in any well-drained soil. Among several decorative garden varieties are 'Arnold Red,' 'Hack's Red' and 'Zabelii.'

Nanking cherry (*Prunus tomentosa*). This spreading bush form of the cherry tree has medium green foliage, and small white flowers zones 2-9 which bloom in early spring. The sour red cherries follow in summer. It makes an excellent informal hedge or screen planting. Nanking cherry should be planted in well-drained, slightly limy soil.

Common indigobush (*Amorpha fruticosa*). A sturdy plant of the leguminous family, it has long, dull green leaves and, in early zones 2-9 summer, blooms with attractive violet-purple flowers. Common indigobush bears small fruits in late summer. It is very hardy and usually grows in open, dry areas.

246

Russian olive (*Elaeagnus angustifolia*). Like other olive trees, this large shrub or small tree is character- zones 2-9 ized by twisting branches and silvery gray leaves. Its small, fragrant silvery flowers blossom in early summer and are followed by edible silver-amber fruits. Russian olive thrives in dry or sandy areas. The related autumn elaeagnus (*E. umbellata*) branches to the ground. It is more silvery and almost as hardy as the Russian olive.

Caragana (*Caragana arborescens*). This extremely hardy shrub has green leaves of 2 to 18 leaflets, borne on distinctive zones 2-9 brownish yellow boughs. The caragana's flowers blossom in summer, then turn into attractive pods. This shrub is often planted for its resistance to winds and tolerance of dry soils. It makes good hedges and needs little care.

Elder (*Sambucus canadensis*). A hardy deciduous shrub, it bears small, flat- headed white flowers in large clusters. They bloom zones 3-9 in mid-summer and are followed in autumn by edible blue-black berries. A large compound-leafed plant, it is not generally suited to small properties but is ideal for semi-wild borders. The 'Maxima' variety has flower clusters a foot across; 'Aurea' has red berries and attractive yellow foliage. Elder requires plenty of sunlight, but thrives in any fertile garden soil. It is prone to damage by aphids.

Pencil cedar (*Juniperus virginiana*). A slender, pyramidal conifer, it has an ascending branch system, and prickly, sea-green zones 3-9 needles. Because it is very hardy, grows quickly and can be trimmed easily, pencil cedar is often used for hedges. Among the more attractive garden varieties are the steel-blue 'Burkii'; 'Canaertii,' which bears myriads of pale blue fruits; the wide-spreading 'Glauca'; and the column-like blue-gray 'Skyrocket.' These coni-

fers thrive in well-drained soil and in full or partial sunlight.

Alternate-leafed dogwood (*Cornus alternifolia*). In time this native bush grows to tree size. It has tiered branches, striped bark and zones 3-9 a rounded crown. In spring, it bears small white flowers, followed by deep blue fruit. Ideal for beds, it prefers semi-shaded areas and grows in any good garden soil. It requires little pruning, and is generally free of disease and pests.

Lilac (*Syringa vulgaris*). A classic tall shrub or small tree, it has clustered fragrant flowers ranging from white to purple or lilac. Its zones 3-9 heart-shaped leaves are loosely held on slim, shapely, upright trunks that grow to 20 feet. Although not serious, the white mildew that affects the leaves in summer usually can be controlled by spraying with fungicide. Lilacs can be planted as specimens or grouped for screening. For hedges and screens set young plants 6-10 feet apart. Lilacs are long-lived and do well in most fertile soils. Large plants may be cut back severely; faded flowers should be removed in late summer. Hybrid varieties have larger flowers on smaller plants than the species. All require plenty of sunlight.

Upright juniper. The fine texture of its foliage makes this an excellent shrub to use for background or screen planting. Most nur- zones 3-9 series have some variety of upright juniper. The bright green 'Canaert' is recommended. It grows in dry soil, but prefers well-drained areas. It should be planted in full sunlight or in light shade.

Spindle tree (*Euonymus europaeus,* var. *aldenhamensis*). This wide-spreading bush is almost a small tree. Like the common zones 4-9 winged euonymous or burning bush it turns brilliant red in fall, but its leaves are longer and more elegant. The narrow, pointed leaves

remain until late fall. Spindle tree is attractive planted at fence corners and can be clipped as a hedge.

Canadian hemlock (*Tsuga canadensis*). The needles of this shrub are medium to dark green. It becomes a tall tree, but can easily be zones 4-9 clipped to make a thick soft-textured hedge of almost any height. It prefers moist soils but will grow in dry areas. It requires full sunlight or partial shade but should be protected from wind. Canadian hemlock is generally free of pests and disease.

Buttonbush (*Cephalanthus occidentalis*). In summer this rounded native shrub is covered with round, fragrant white flow- zones 4-9 ers. It needs moist soil and a semi-shaded location, and is ideal planted near small ponds. It is best set apart from other plants.

Viburnums variety: *Viburnum sieboldii* has bold six-inch leaves, and flattish white flowers which bloom in late spring. In summer it zones 4-9 bears red to black berries. It thrives in most well-drained soils.

Sea buckthorn (*Hippophae rhamnoides*). An upright shrub, it bears yellow flowers in early spring. The inside of its spiny zones 4-9 leaves is silvery gray. In early fall, it yields orange-yellow fruit which remains for several months. To obtain fruit, plant males and females together. This plant is ideal for hedges, for windbreaks and to anchor sandy soil. It requires full sunlight.

Linden viburnum (*Viburnum dilatatum*) is one of the fullest and most attractive of the many bush viburnums. It bears creamy zones 5-9 white flowers in spring, followed by clustered red berries. Its red fall foliage makes it a desirable screen or background plant. It requires little care and grows in any moist garden soil.

Spreading   Upright   Rounded   Vase-Shaped | Evergreen   Deciduous | Outstanding for Flowers   Outstanding Broad leaf   Foliage Needle

The Japanese viburnum (*Viburnum plicatum mariesii*). This rounded shrub has round to pointed green leaves with parallel veins. White flowers similar to the dogwood's are borne on horizontal branches. A handsome shrub that branches to the ground, it is easily grown in all garden conditions, preferably in partially shaded areas.

Lover's privet (*Ligustrum amurense*). This specimen, with its attractive dark green foliage, is the hardiest of the wax trees. Ideally suited for even, level hedges, it thrives in any ordinary garden soil.

zones 5-9

Five-stamen tamarisk (*Tamarix pentandra*). A bushy plant, it has sturdy stalks covered with delicate drooping branchlets. Clusters of pink flowers are borne in late summer. Five-stamen tamarisk should be planted in full sunlight. If grown as a hedge, it should be trimmed to the ground each spring.

zones 5-9

Star magnolia (*Magnolia stellata*). A slow-growing deciduous tree, it has dark green leaves when mature and branches that touch the ground. Star-shaped fragrant white flowers appear before the leaves in spring. Star magnolia thrives in loamy, well-drained areas, especially where it is protected from wind.

zones 5-9

Cornelian-cherry dogwood (*Cornus mas*). Although this shrub's yellow flowers are inconspicuous, it has edible scarlet fruit, and shiny green leaves that turn red in autumn. One of the earliest plants to flower in spring, cornelian-cherry dogwood requires plenty of sun.

zones 5-9

Smoke tree (*Cotinus coggygria*). A large, attractive shrub, with branches and leaves fragrant when crumbled, it has small purple flowers that bloom in early summer. It is easily grown in chalky, well-drained soil, preferably on a sunny site. The 'Atropurpureus' variety has deep purple foliage in autumn. The smoke tree requires little pruning, although straggly growths should be removed in early spring.

zones 5-9

Rhododendron hybrids. These evergreens thrive in mild climates, so the best hybrids grow on the west coast, on rainy mountain slopes in the southeast U.S., and in southern England. The catawbiense hybrids are included in the six-foot listing. Among the best rhododendron varieties are the Dexter, Fortune and Griffith hybrids.

zones 5-9

Goat willow (*Salix caprea*). An attractive shrub, with long stems and large brown buds, it displays bright yellow catkins in early spring. It grows in moist soil, preferably where there is plenty of sunlight. An indigenous variety, the diamond willow (*S. descodor*), is recommended for colder regions. It is easily grown from cuttings.

zones 5-9

Spring witch-hazel (*Hamamelis vernalis*). This early blooming shrub has yellow flowers which appear in late winter. It has spreading, ascending branches, and rounded leaves that are green above, slightly gray-green below. Spring witch-hazel grows in partial shade or in full sunlight and requires fairly moist soils. Chinese witch-hazel (*H. mollis*) is larger than the species. Common witch-hazel (*H. virginiana*) blooms with yellow flowers in late fall.

zones 5-9

Beauty bush (*Kolkwitzia amabilis*). A vigorous, easy-to-grow plant, it has a rounded top but is bare at the base. It is characterized by small, pointed green leaves, and pink flowers which appear in early summer. Beauty bush grows in well-drained soils.

zones 5-9

Rosebay rhododendron (*Rhododendron maximum*). This is the tallest and hardiest of the rhododendrons. It has long evergreen leaves that are densely or sparsely grouped depending on growing conditions; in cold climates the leaves wilt and curl. Rosebay rhododendron is hardy to −25°F but flower buds die at about −20°F. It can be safely cut back and will regenerate. The species has pinkish purple flowers. Rosebay rhododendron grows in partial shade or in full sunlight. It requires

zones 5-9

peaty-acid soil. Light soil should be enriched, or heavy soil lightened, with peat or hop manure.

Redbud (*Cercis canadensis*). This small tree has a straight trunk, and strong, ascending, delicately twigged branches. Its heart-shaped leaves, bright green in summer, turn yellow in fall. The magnificent pink flowers which appear before the leaves in late spring make this an attractive addition to the garden. Redbud needs moist, well-drained soil and should be sheltered from wind. It requires little pruning.

zones 6-9

Purple-leafed European hazelnut (*Corylus avellana purpurea*). Named for its deep purple leaves, this plant has hanging yellow catkins which appear in spring. It bears brown nuts which grow in clusters of two to four. Purple-leafed European hazelnut requires partial shade for the deepest leaf color.

zones 6-9

Forsythia (*Forsythia*). Often overused because it is so easy to grow, this hardy plant is prized for the yellow flowers which bloom in early spring. Some good varieties: 'Beatrix Ferrand' (large yellow flowers with orange markings); 'Spring Glory' (pale yellow); and 'Lynwood Gold' (deep yellow).

Forsythia suspensa is a weeping form often used at the tops of banks or walls. It grows upward to 10 feet, then hangs down.

zones 6-9

Pyracantha (*Pyracantha coccinea lalandii*), also called scarlet firethorn. In early summer, it bears white flowers, followed by bright orange-red berries. It may require winter protection but is hardy once established. Pyracantha is excellent as an informal espalier.

zones 6-9

Willowleaf cotoneaster (*Cotoneaster salicifolia floccosa*). This plant features willow-like leaves on gracefully arching branches. In fall it yields red berries. Although an evergreen, in cold climates it has leaves that sometimes drop in winter. Willowleaf cotoneaster prefers sunny areas, but grows in any well-drained garden soil.

zones 6-9

Common privet (*Ligustrum vulgare*). This species often reaches a height of 15 feet and is noted for its attractive dark green foliage. Like other privet varieties, it makes a good hedge or a background plant.

zones 6-9

American holly (*Ilex opaca*). Growing to more than 30 feet, this plant has sharply pointed dark green leaves. Although not as shiny as the leaves of the English holly, they are hardier. American holly bears white-green flowers in early spring and will produce red berries if females are planted near males. Hollies thrive in moist well-drained soil. In heavy shade, leaf color tends to be poor, so sunny sites are best.

zones 7-9

Japanese snowbell (*Styrax japonica*). This easy-to-grow plant is characterized by spreading branches, deep green leaves, and white bell-like flowers which bloom in early summer. It is best to transplant Japanese snowbell before it grows higher than three feet. It sprouts easily from seeds and grows to 20 feet. Free of pests and diseases, this plant grows in any well-drained garden soil. It does well in full or partial sun light.

zones 7-9

Franklinia (*Franklinia alatamaha*, also called *Gordonia alatamaha*). This plant has narrow leaves to eight inches long, and white rounded flowers (with yellow centers) which bloom in late fall. Its leaves turn orange-red before dropping in autumn. Franklinia becomes a small tree in warmer climates and is particularly interesting because it blooms so late. It thrives in most garden soils.

zones 7-9

English holly (*Ilex aquifolium*). This upright, rounded evergreen plant has spiny rich-green leaves. It is ideal as a background plant or as an unclipped tall hedge; it can also be used at the corners of buildings. If males are planted nearby, female plants bear bright red berries in fall. English holly grows in full sunlight or in partial shade. It does best in damp acid-humus soil. Burford holly (*I. cornuta*) differs from the species by having only one spine at the leaf tip.

zones 7-9

Portugal-laurel (*Prunus lusitanica*). Excellent as a background screen or hedge, this plant has stiff evergreen leaves on red stems. Portugal-laurel may reach tree size; it can be shaped by pruning, or kept as a hedge. It grows best in limy, well-drained soil and prefers plenty of sun.

zones 7-9

Wax myrtle (*Myrica cerifera*). A wild plant related to bayberry, the wax myrtle has a full irregular form and grows to 35 feet. It makes a sturdy background plant but may be short-lived. It is the taller and more tender form of *M. pensylvanica*.

zones 7-9

English yew (*Taxus baccata*). Although this wide-spreading yew grows to 50 feet, it can be clipped to almost any size. It may live for hundreds of years. English yew grows in all but swampy soil, and is tolerant of exposure, drought—even air pollution. It does well in full sunlight or in partial shade.

zones 7-9

Chinese photinia (*Photinia serrulata*). This excellent background plant has large evergreen leaves on an oval bush. It bears white flowers in summer followed in fall by clusters of bright red berries. It grows in most well-drained garden soils, and in full sunlight.

zones 7-9

Osmanthus. This group of evergreens has toothed shiny green leaves and small but fragrant flowers. Extremely hardy, osmanthus makes a good screen or background. *O. fortunei* has rounded leaves on a full dark green bush to six feet high. Holly osmanthus (*O. ilicifolius*) is a rounded, spreading shrub with leaves that range from prickly to spine-tipped; it bears small fragrant white flowers in clusters. Holly osmanthus grows to 20 feet, and tolerates almost any growing conditions. It does well in well-drained soils, in full sunlight or in partial shade. It is easy to care for, free of pests and diseases and requires no pruning.

zones 8-9

Camellias (*Camellia japonica, C. sasanqua, C. reticulata*). Among the most popular evergreen shrubs, the japonicas exhibit attractive dark green four-inch leaves on a full-bodied plant. Although camellias require little care, they need cool nights to bloom. Typical varieties include: 'Adolphe Audusson' (upright, red); 'Daikagura' (peony-shaped, rose color, on a spreading plant); and 'Frau Minna Seidel' (pink, long-blooming.)

zones 8-9

The sasanquas have smaller leaves and flowers (often single instead of the common double form) than the japonicas. They range from white to rose-pink.

The reticulatas are large upright plants with bigger flowers than the other varieties. Flower color ranges from soft rose or pink to turkey red.

Evergreen privets (*Ligustrum*) are available in numerous varieties. These are so similar they are often confused. All make good hedge or background plants. They are listed in order of size (both plant and leaf): glossy privet (*L. lucidum*), to 20 feet; common privet (*L. vulgare*), to 15 feet; Japanese privet (*L. japonicum*), to 12 feet.

zones 8-9

Sweet bay or laurel (*Laurus nobilis*). This full columnar plant grows to 25 feet and has narrow, closely packed evergreen "bay" leaves. It makes a good background or screen. This plant can also be clipped into a formal hedge or into almost any topiary shape. It should be planted on a sunny, sheltered site. It is generally free of disease.

zone 9

 Spreading   Upright   Rounded   Vase-Shaped | Evergreen   Deciduous | Outstanding for Flowers   Outstanding Broad leaf   Foliage Needle

13

How to Plan, Plant and Care For Your Lawn

Few indeed are the landscape plans that should not include a lawn of some kind. Nature abhors a vacuum and every bare spot will eventually cover itself with something green. This may be called lawn or grass patch, weeds, wildflowers or ground cover depending upon what's planted, or not planted, and the owner's point of view.

In the final analysis, a lawn is one of the easiest and least expensive ways to keep the ground neatly and attractively covered. Professional garden designers have discovered this truth over the years. When a homeowner wants "a low-upkeep yard," he should think first of grass for all areas level enough to mow with today's efficient power equipment.

Grass provides a smooth, living carpet and it is the least expensive ground cover to install. It is delightful to look at, walk on or play on. It is ready in just a few weeks, or even "instantly" if sod is laid down. But there are places where grass is not the best material to use.

If, for example, the neighbors repeatedly have trouble with lawn pests and diseases, it might be well to consider one of the many other ground covers.

The first cost of ground covers such as ivy, creeping euonymus, myrtle (*Vinca minor*) or pachysandra will be higher, and full coverage of the ground may take years instead of weeks. Weeds will also be more of a problem during the first few years. So will raking up tree leaves, and picking up papers and other wind-blown debris. The weeds, at least, are green and sometimes the easiest course is to pull as many as possible and live with the rest until the ground cover finally takes over. But once the shrubby ground covers are completely filled in, they are the easiest of surfaces to care for.

Five Common Mistakes in Planning a Lawn

If lawns have a bad name for being "too much work" it's usually because of five mistakes that most people make when planning and putting them in:

1. Cutting the yard into small areas, say six feet wide or less. These are more difficult to water and mow, and the grass isn't likely to grow as well as when in one large turf.

2. Making the lawn four square, with tight corners. Mowing is the most demanding chore in caring for a lawn. It is required 25 to 30 times a year in general and more often in warmer, more humid regions of Canada. It's easier to mow a lawn having no square corners that force stopping, backing and lining up again. Easiest to mow are lawns with free-flowing curves, outlined with a border strip of concrete or brick. Then one wheel of the mower rolls on the hard edge and mowing is a rapid, nonstop operation. And there is no need for tiring and time-consuming hand trimming.

3. Trying to grow the wrong grass for the climate, or for the use the lawn receives. On the following pages are descriptions of all the major lawn grasses, noting those that are best for various parts of the country.

A clean sweep *of well-kept lawn is a cool and lovely setting for the display of trees and shrubs. The rhododendrons in matching colors on opposite sides of the lawn add a welcome warm hue and help to unify the scene.*

4. Starving the grass. Grass doesn't necessarily die when underfed, but it is more easily damaged by weeds, bugs or blights. The usual excuse for failing to fertilize regularly is: "I already have to mow too often so why speed up the process?" While it's true that fertilizing increases the amount of clippings per mowing, it does not increase the frequency of mowing. Lawns, even when starved, must be mowed regularly or they look ragged and unkempt.

5. Trying to grow grass where grass can't grow easily. This means in deep shade, on steep slopes, in dry spots, flooded areas, or where there's excessive traffic. There are no true shade grasses, although some have more tolerance for partial shade than others. And there are no real desert lawn grasses.

The Basic Needs of Every Lawn

While there are other requirements, such as pest and disease controls that can be applied as needed, the following are basic factors that should be considered before the lawn is planted.

Morning sunlight. Sun is required at least for the morning hours. If shaded until noon, grass won't survive more than a year or two. This is because the sudden exposure to the heat of the sun in midday or afternoon, after a cool, shaded morning, scalds the grass, closing the stomata, or minute openings, in the leaves. This stops the life-giving process of photosynthesis. Without the sugars created by photosynthesis the roots stop growing and the grass will wilt and die.

Warm soil. Grass seed won't sprout unless the soil is 50° or warmer, but grass roots grow best when the soil is between 35° and 60°F. More about this will be found on the following pages.

Moist but not wet soil. The soil must be moist enough to support the growth of the roots, foster the development of new leaves and replenish the chlorophyll that gives leaves their attractive green color. But it should not be too wet, or too salty. Soggy soil keeps the roots from getting the air

they need, and salty soil dehydrates them.

Good surface drainage prevents water from collecting in puddles. The lawn should always slope *away* from the house on all sides. But the slopes should be gentle enough for easy mowing and to keep water from running off before it can soak into the root area, and to prevent surface erosion.

Crumbly soil. This is necessary so rains and irrigation water can sink in instead of running off. Easy test: Squeeze a handful of soil tightly. If you can't crumble it easily when the pressure is released, it is too sticky. If it falls apart on its own, it is too sandy. For either condition—sticky clay or loose sand—the remedy is the same: Put two to four inches of peat moss or other humus on the soil and work in with a tiller.

Deep soil. The top layer of good soil should be four to eight inches. This is deep enough to provide for the storage of one inch of moisture. This is about a three-day supply for lawns in hot climates and a week's supply in cooler areas. It can be topsoil, which always contains weed seeds, or subsoil, which is weed-free. Both produce excellent lawns. Make the choice on the basis of local availability and cost. The subsoil, however, should be broken up to meet the requirements of "crumbly soil" mentioned above.

Proper pH (the letters stand for potential of hydrogen). The soil must not be too acid on the pH scale or too alkaline. Most lawn grasses grow best when soil is slightly acid (pH 5.5 to 6.5); pH 7 is neutral and anything above that figure is alkaline and discouraging to lawn grasses. Your County Agricultural Representative probably can make the necessary soil tests. For soils that are too acid, add ground limestone. For soils that are too alkaline, add gypsum.

Regular feeding. Because a lawn is harvested (mowed) so often, regular replenishment of plant food is required. Use a "complete" lawn fertilizer containing nitrogen, phosphorus and potash. Apply at a rate that provides one pound of nitrogen per 1000 square feet of lawn in each application of fertilizer.

Choosing the Right Grass for Your Climate

A lot of time and trouble can be saved in maintaining a lawn if the grass is naturally adapted to the climate. This is relatively easy to ensure since most "cool-climate" grasses do well in most parts of Canada. (Some "dry-climate" grasses thrive in the plains of mid-continent.)

There are of course limitations. For example, many micro-climates are considerably warmer or cooler than the surrounding norm. In areas where temperatures differ significantly from the average, the best recommendations are those of local experts and authorities: perhaps an established seedsman, a County Agricultural Representative—or a friendly neighbor with an outstanding lawn.

"Cool-climate" grasses—bluegrass, fescue and bent—thrive in the northern half of the United States and all are appropriate to Canadian lawns.

Needing considerable water as they do, they may require irrigation in the mid-plains. However, if the attractions of bluegrass, fescue and bent can be foregone, the buffalo grass or gramas native to the plains will survive dry and on their own, albeit a good deal less luxuriantly.

Bluegrasses

Bluegrass was already widespread through Europe for hundreds of years before it got its scientific name *Poa pratensis,* in 1753. French missionaries carried seeds to the Great Lakes country before 1700. The grass came to be called June grass, and after 1830 or so, Kentucky bluegrass.

Canadian homeowners plant hundreds of thousands of pounds of bluegrass each year. Much of it is wasted in the annual ritual of reseeding. Bluegrass is by nature self-renewing. It can live "forever" if properly cared for. Seeding into an existing lawn is almost always a waste. If seed does sprout, it is soon choked out by the established grass.

The luxury bluegrass

For years common field-run Kentucky bluegrass has been the mainstay of Canada's lawns and golf courses everywhere except in the far north. Now there are many selected bluegrasses vastly superior in one or more characteristics. These have the advantages of being low-growing, broad-bladed and deep-rooting, which makes them drought- and heat-resistant.

Bluegrasses on the coarse side

'Merion.' Long record of good performance, although it has a tendency to mildew.

'Windsor.' Goes off color in cold weather, regains green slowly in the spring; quite susceptible to striped smut disease.

'Nugget.' Dark blue-green, fine textured. Keeps color right up to snow.

'Delta.' Has an immunity to mildew and hence is useful in damp, shaded areas.

'Park.' Exceptionally vigorous upright-growing grass originally selected as a hay crop.

Bluegrass of finer texture

'Fylking.' Superior summer and fall color; seeds twice usual size (calls for twice as much seed).

Requires sustained fertilization and watering, but can then be cut quite short. Light in color.

Exceptionally fine-bladed bluegrass

'Prato.' Texture so fine that the lawn resembles a thick carpet.

Two bluegrasses you don't want

Roughstalk bluegrass (*Poa trivialis*) used to be recommended for shady places. Although it does tolerate more shade than other bluegrasses, it is extremely susceptible to heat and disease and seldom lives more than a year.

Annual bluegrass (*Poa annua*), known widely as "bunch grass" or "winter grass," is a useful species or a weed depending on the point of view. On Canadian prairie golf courses, if well tended, it makes excellent greens tolerant both of drought and of heavy soils with low fertility. Formerly badly hit by fungi and not recovering until late June, it now is made fungus-resistant by mercurial fungicides.

Fescues

Red fescue (*Festuca rubra*) starts as a fine-textured bunch grass, slowly develops into a solid mat in sunny, dry locations. It won't survive in heavy clay soils, or if mowed shorter than $1\frac{1}{2}$ inches, or if overirrigated. Skip fertilizing in midsummer to avoid encouraging severe injury by fungus diseases.

Luxury fescues

These are more expensive than ordinary red or Chewings fescue.

'Pennlawn.' Spreads rapidly, forms thick turf. Not as green as *Chewings*, but neither is it so bunchy and wiry to mow.

'Highlight Chewings.' The only fescue that forms a thick sod when mowed under $1\frac{1}{2}$ inches.

'Dawson,' 'Golfrood' and 'Ruby.' Vastly superior in the Netherlands but not yet thoroughly tested here.

Coarse fescues

Meadow fescue (*Festuca elatior*) is quick to sprout, quick to grow, and thus a favorite of people in a hurry. But it makes a coarse, bunchy turf intolerant of mowing to lawn height.

Tall fescue (*Festuca arundinacea*) is a coarse and unattractive weedy grass, immune to all the selective weed killers. But when seeded heavily by itself, it serves well for playgrounds and highway banks. Varieties 'Alta' and 'Kentucky 31' (not to be confused with bluegrass) are licensed in Canada.

Coarse fescue is present in almost all cheap grass seed mixtures. Even though not listed on the label it will probably be there. And only a 1.0 percent weed content spreads 50,000 coarse fescue seeds on every 1000 sq. ft. of lawn. Wait until the seeds sprout, then pull up the plants. This is easier to do when the soil is soft, after a rain or sprinkling.

Hard fescue (*Festuca ovina*) makes rough turf. It has poor color. Most people find it very difficult to mow.

Ryegrasses

Perennial ryegrass (*Lolium perenne*) has long been favored for getting a passable "lawn" quickly and cheaply. The seed costs little. It sprouts fast. In 5 to 10 days there's a green "fuzz" that can pass as a lawn to the unsuspecting. It may survive 3 to 4 years, but cannot be considered a permanent lawn. It will always be a stand of small, bunchy plants and not an interlocking turf such as bluegrass or red fescue.

'Manhattan' is somewhat leafier and lower growing. It is probably the most dense-growing of the ryegrasses, although some of the new Dutch varieties such as 'Barvestra,' 'Reveile,' 'Barlatra' and 'Taptoe' may develop to be worthy challengers.

Italian ryegrass (*Lolium multiflorum*) supposedly lives just one year, which would make it useful for temporary lawns. But the seed is usually contaminated with some perennial ryegrass and a few plants survive for 3 to 5 years. In a bluegrass, fescue, or bermuda lawn, it's a weed.

Most of the luxury bluegrasses described above, as well as the fescues and ryegrasses, will do well where the soil temperature at night seldom gets up to 60°F. The fescues (above) can also be used where summer nights are cool. 'Pennlawn' or tall fescues are most adaptable.

Bentgrasses, which are described below, also do well in much of Canada for special, high-upkeep uses, such as home "golf greens."

Bentgrasses

These are the traditional golf-green grasses. They are fine-textured and most attractive, but require careful attention and more mowing than most other grasses.

Colonial bent (*Agrostis tenuis*) is best known by its varieties— 'Astoria,' 'Highland' and 'Exeter.'

Creeping bent (*Agrostis palustris*) has hundreds of varieties. Almost every golf course uses its own favorite. Best-known varieties are 'Seaside,' 'Penncross,' 'Congressional' and 'Old Orchard.'

Redtop (*Agrostis alba*) is included in cheap seed mixes labelled "Contains bentgrass!" Has none of the habits or attractiveness of the golf-green bents and is crowded out by Kentucky blue.

Zoysias

Manila grass (*Zoysia matrella*) resembles good bluegrass turf, if heavily fertilized. But it is slow to become established. It requires 3 to 4 years in most areas and the weeds can take over before it makes a lawn.

Japan grass (*Zoysia japonica*) is a hot-weather grass widely promoted as a panacea for crabgrass-plagued lawns.

Usually sold by mail, it comes as 2-inch "plugs" to be inserted into a lawn, "about a foot apart." It is realistic to expect these to fill-in and make a zoysia lawn in about 5 years. Or maybe never, if crabgrass and weeds are already rampant. And it must be remembered that where there is frost the zoysias brown from early fall until late spring.

Bermuda
(Cynodon dactylon)

This is the toughest, most durable, most pest-resistant of all grass for warm climates. But it turns an unattractive brown when the air temperature drops below 35° and stays that way until after the last cold spell in the late spring. This limits its usefulness in frost-prone climates. Some people dye their bermuda each winter but this is expensive and has an artificial look.

Bermuda is for sunny locations only. It gets thin and leggy in the shade. It does tolerate alkaline soils, but to keep bermuda thrifty in any soil it must be mechanically renovated at least once a year. This involves mowing as short as possible, then slicing through the turf with a power aerifier to clear away the mat of dead stems and leaves that builds up quickly.

Common bermuda is often seeded but most of the improved kinds do not produce seeds, so must be set out as sod or sprigs.

Bahia
(Paspalum notatum)

Drought-resistant, it grows well in hot, dry climates. Not especially attractive as a lawn grass, but the easy care is a definite advantage. Also resistant to disease and insects.

St. Augustine
(Stenotaphrum secundatum)

This grass has all but replaced bermuda for quality home lawns in Florida and Texas. Plantings are increasing rapidly in Southern California. At first, homeowners tend to resist its coarse texture. It is a close relative of crabgrass—and looks it. But when grown either in full sun or partial shade it does make a beautiful, thick lawn. Not injured by salt spray, but cannot survive drought or heavy wear.

Dichondra
(Dichondra repens)

Dichondra is not a grass. It is a low, creeping cloverlike member of the morning glory family. Hugs the ground if kept mowed at 1 inch and grows 6 to 10 inches tall if left unmowed.

Originally introduced into Southern California as the "no-mow lawn," but that claim proved false. It requires more care, more food and more water than a grass. It is a useful substitute where summer soil temperatures are too high for bluegrass. And it is a worthy competitor for bermuda grass. Seed the dichondra into the bermuda and in time they will come to a stand-off. It is handsome as long as fertilized monthly, and protected from bugs and blights. A luxurious highcost ground cover.

254

How to Make Your Grass Behave

Most home lawns are ailing, if we are to judge by the questions that pour in to agricultural representatives and lawn-supply companies. For one thing, homeowners are perplexed by the bewildering array of products for lawn care. There are chemicals to make grass grow, to keep it from growing, to kill crabgrass before it comes up, to kill it after it comes up, to wipe out any number of encroaching weeds and grasses, to kill dozens of kinds of invading bugs and grubs, and to counteract grass diseases. There are even colorants you can use to keep grass green the year round.

Grass, however, is a relatively rugged, undemanding plant which, on its own, and in different varieties, will grown almost anywhere. A simple plant, it can also be simple to grow. One resident of an eastern suburb turned a stubbly hayfield into a respectable bluegrass lawn merely by mowing and fertilizing it.

Turf experts preach simplicity, and usually stick to basic procedures for fertilizing, mowing and watering when they work on their own lawns.

The lawn-conscious homeowner, primed by advice from neighbors, dealers and garden columns, frequently punishes himself and his lawn unnecessarily—and the things people do to grass are often horrible indeed. They scalp their lawns because they think it "strengthens the grass." (Cutting more than a third of the leaf hinders growth; and the shorter the grass the more the crabgrass sprouts, because it likes the sun.) One lawnsman decided that twice the amount of fertilizer would make his lawn grow twice as fast. He got fast action, in reverse. His lawn burned out in two days. Another homeowner, when fungus attacked his lawn, poured on the water, and the fungus thrived happily.

For those who want the best lawn with the least trouble, the first step is the correct choice of seed. This means picking a good quality and the *right* seed for your area. Bargain bags of seed are likely to be mostly ryegrass or other temporary grasses with a liberal mixture of chaff and perhaps weed seeds.

Getting the right seed means, basically, planting Kentucky bluegrass and red-fescue mixtures. The main "choice" problem you run into involves picking a grass for shady areas. The best answer is to plant a mixture of 75-percent fine-leafed fescue and 25-percent Ken-

tucky bluegrass in the shade. Reverse the proportions for sunny lawns.

A major point to remember in choosing your seed is to avoid the fancy grasses that require increased attention. Bentgrass, especially, can create a problem. It demands frequent mowing, watering and fertilizing.

Of the basic phases of lawn care—fertilizing, mowing and watering—the average homeowner tends to do too little of the first, too much of the second, and the third too often and too little. The basic principles of mowing are to keep your mower sharp to prevent tearing and browning of the grass and to mow bluegrass "long," from $1\frac{1}{2}$ to 2 inches.

Watering a lawn is a different problem in different areas. But a good rule of thumb, suggests one grass authority, is to watch for a "blue, hazy look" in the grass and for footprints. These signs mean that the grass needs watering. Less frequent but longer waterings, which soak in at least six inches, are better than regular, shallow waterings, because they help the grass establish a deeper root growth. Contrary to popular belief, lawns can be safely watered in sunlight.

If you follow the standard procedures—and simplification—that the experts advise, all that remains is to learn to recognize the most common ills suffered by grass. Weeds are the worst pests, and crabgrass tops them all. Grubs that feed on the roots, and chinch bugs are the most-encountered insect enemies of grass. Fortunately, antidotes are available for nearly every trouble. The tips given above should enable you to solve a lawn problem quickly and efficiently. But you must learn to diagnose your trouble.

One homeowner, for example, found that new seedlings were yellowing and stunting. The trouble? Lack of fertilizer. He stepped up the amount of nitrogen he was providing, and now has a fine lawn.

Another man got rid of his crabgrass by merely setting his mower up to a two- to three-inch setting. He had been scalping his lawn before, and the crabgrass had been thriving. Now that he has given his bluegrass the chance to fight its own battles, it has the crabgrass almost whipped—just as it will whip other enemies when given the chance to reach its maximum strength.

Eight Steps in Making a Lawn

The process of making a lawn can be staggering to contemplate unless it is considered one step at a time. Preparing the ground can be done in easy stages. Only the seeding and the immediate aftercare must follow the fixed schedule that is naturally imposed by growing plants.

The first consideration is when to seed. In the cool climates where bluegrasses and fescues are best, the fall is recommended. Days

1. Grade *the soil so there is a gentle slope away from the house in all directions. Then spread topsoil evenly. Use a sprinkler to check for low spots that collect water. Also check for high spots that might be scalped in mowing. If possible make the grade level with any hard surfaces that can serve as a mowing edge.*

2. Till *the soil, but not too much. Most beginners overdo it. Grass seed can't start in loose fluffy soil. It should have pea-sized lumps and many crevices to catch the seed. Additions to the soil (see text above) should be tilled in. After grading, wet the soil to firm it down, wait a day or so and then plant the seed.*

3. Spread *seed evenly, but not too thickly. Almost everyone uses too much. Seedlings need space for developing roots and leaves. If too crowded the new plants may thrive for a few weeks and then fade as the seedlings compete. Use one or two pounds of the best quality seed per 1000 sq. ft. (for bluegrass or fescue).*

4. Rake *lightly. Do not smother the seed. Use the back of a bamboo rake to barely cover about half the seed with soil. Then roll once only with an empty roller to press the seed into contact with the soil. Keep in mind that grass seed must have light as well as moisture, oxygen and warmth in order to sprout.*

are cool and the soil does not dry out as in summer. Second best is the spring, but early enough for the grass to develop in time to withstand the heat of summer. Spring rains can cause slope or terrace seeding to erode, and mulching with straw or fabric may be necessary.

If the soil needs amending, the magic in-gredient is peat. If soil is too sandy to hold water in the root area, adding 4 inches of peat will provide for this. If soil is too heavy and clayey to admit the required water and air, the peat will alleviate that problem too. If lime or gypsum is needed to change the pH, it should also be added and worked into the soil before seeding.

5. Fertilize generously. Grass seeds are tiny and contain only enough nourishment to push out the initial sprout and roots. Their continued growth depends upon the nutrients that are applied. Spread the fertilizer on the same day either before or after the seeding is done. Use amounts as recommended on the bag.

6. Water a new lawn two or three times a day, say at 10 a.m., 1 p.m. and about 4 p.m. In order to sprout, the seeds need moisture. The top layer of soil should not be allowed to dry out for the first two weeks or so or until the grass is well up. Set sprinklers so they will cover the entire area without having to move them.

7. Mow as soon as the grass (and weeds) are more than two inches tall. This checks upright growth and helps the grass to stool out and knit into a sturdy turf. Do not delay the first mowings, or cut shorter than two inches the first year. Bermuda and bent should be cut at one inch. Catch and remove all the clippings.

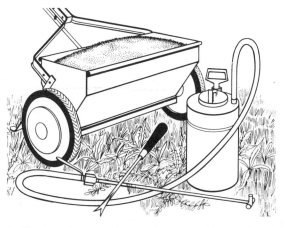

8. Don't panic when the weeds appear. Almost all soil, including expensive screened topsoil, is full of weed seeds. Many weeds succumb after a program of weekly mowing has begun. The rest can be cleared out the second year by using a "weed and feed" mixture, or prevented by using pre-emergent controls in early spring.

Other Ways to Start a Lawn

Following are three techniques other than seeding for starting grass. They have proven their worth when properly done in the right climate.

Sodding. This is the process of lifting an existing lawn and re-laying it in a new place. The sod should be grown especially for this purpose, then "peeled off" in strips of uniform thickness and size. These are easily laid, like rolling out a carpet. Because the sod is cut *thin* —about ¾ inch thick—it immediately sends new roots down into the soil on which it is laid. Within 10 days the sod is so firmly knit to the soil that it can't be lifted. Sod, of course, must be in firm contact with the subsoil and it must be watered and fed generously to insure good rooting. Amateurs usually fail because they cut the sod thick, mistakenly thinking this will help it survive the transplanting. Good commercially grown sod is best.

Sodding is the quick, sure way to a thick, weedfree turf. Truly an "instant lawn." The total cost is only slightly higher than for a comparable lawn from seed, which usually requires 15-18 months of feeding, watering and mowing—and weed control.

Sprigging. Sprigs are little sections of established lawn, usually bentgrass in Canada, which are chopped or pulled apart. They are then scattered on the prepared "seedbed" much as if they were seed. One bushel of plants covers about 200 sq. ft. To insure the all-important firm contact with the soil, they are rolled several times, then a ¼ inch topdressing of half soil and half peat is applied. The aim is to cover 75 percent of the sprigs. The area is rolled again, and watered to keep the soil moist at all times for at least 10 days, or until the sprigs are well-rooted. The new lawn can be expected to fill in completely in 3 to 4 months. With frequent watering, the grass may be ready to cut in 2 weeks.

A number of superior strains of bentgrasses are produced in the trade and may be bought for vegetative planting. Most of them, incidentally, are actual growth (not from seed) of turf, generally golf greens, that have proven themselves to be outstanding over the years.

The Basic Points of Lawn Care

Mowing *is what converts a collection of individual grass plants into the tightly knit turf we call "lawn." Mowing should be repeated as soon as the grass has grown 1 inch beyond the height of its last cut. To allow grass to grow more, then to clip it back in one cut, is to risk severe and permanent injury by the sun scalding the tender growing points in the "crown." A good general rule is to mow once a week whenever there is anything to cut at 2 inches.*

Feeding *makes the lawn green, thick and weed-resistant. Nitrogen is the key. How much nitrogen to apply depends upon the kind of grass. How often depends upon the kind of fertilizer and how much of it is nitrogen. 20-10-5 fertilizer has only 20 percent nitrogen. It takes 5 pounds at this concentration to net 1 pound of actual nitrogen.*

For fescue, bahia or centipede use 2 pounds of actual nitrogen per year per 1000 sq. ft. (This requires 10 pounds of 20-10-8 for an area 20 x 50 ft.)

For common bluegrass, Fylking bluegrass or carpetgrass use 4 pounds per year per 1000 sq. ft.

For Windsor bluegrass or zoysia use 6 pounds per year.

For Merion bluegrass use 8 pounds per year.

For St. Augustine use 10 pounds per year.

For bermuda or dichondra use 12 pounds per year. Caution: 1 pound of nitrogen per 1000 sq. ft. is all that can be applied at one time without grave risk of burning or killing the grass. Even this is too much at once, for most grass, unless immediately watered-in thoroughly. But see note below on new IBDU and the sulfur-coated ureas.

If the fertilizer is a "quick-greening" type, feeding lasts 1 to 3 weeks. (This includes ammoniacal, nitrate, or urea-nitrogen fertilizers.)

If it is a typical "long-lasting" fertilizer, feeding lasts 4 to 6 weeks. (This includes UF or ureaformaldehyde or "organic" nitrogen.)

Note: If it is a IBDU or sulfur-coated urea, the newest and most long-lasting fertilizers, a feeding lasts 2 to 6 months. An entire year's needs for nitrogen can be applied in a single spring application. The particles gradually erode at a pre-set rate, releasing the nitrogen day by day.

Watering *is essential to keep grass green and healthy when rainfall fails to provide the minimum 1 inch of water needed each week. In desert areas, 2 to 3 inches are required.*

The usual home-lawn sprinkler must remain in one spot for 4 to 8 hours to apply 1 inch of water. Check your sprinkler by setting out empty tin cans and checking to see how long is needed to collect an inch. On steep slopes or in hot dry places it may take more than 1 inch to get penetration to the full root depth.

Many soils, especially in dry areas, are so "tight" that they can absorb less than 1/4 inch of water an hour. The excess runs off the surface. Water may also be wasted in sandy soils that retain only 1/2 inch at a time and must therefore be watered frequently.

Best time of day to water is early morning. Midday is next. Late afternoon, or in the evening, is risky because fungus diseases are encouraged when grass is wet at night.

Any water that is safe to drink is safe for lawns. Water from swimming pools may be too high in chlorine, but the amount of chlorine (or fluorides) in city water is harmless to grass.

Weeding should no longer be a chore. Modern weedkillers remove weeds, or prevent their emergence from seeds buried in the soil. But the presence of weeds indicates that something is being done incorrectly in mowing, feeding or watering—or in all three. Thick, healthy lawns have few if any weeds.

Read weedkiller instructions carefully. Be sure you are applying the right chemical to the right grass at the right rate and at the right time of year. Weeds must be growing actively to absorb enough chemical to be killed. Wait until dandelions are in bloom before using weedkillers in the spring.

In dry weather, water the lawn deeply. Then wait 2 to 3 days. By then the weeds will be growing actively enough to absorb the necessary amount of weedkiller.

Late-fall applications may not result in any visible killing action—except that the treated weeds fail to survive the winter.

Light raking can be done after weed control, but deep raking pulls buried weed seeds up where they can sprout. Heavy raking can also tear holes in the chemical "barrier" set up in the soil by the use of crabgrass preventers.

Using "Weed and Feed." Any weedkiller is more potent when used at the same time as fertilizer. Thus the "weed and feed" products are real time-savers. But since all weedkillers are somewhat hard on the grasses, don't use a "weed and feed" unless there are weeds to be killed. Don't think of it as simply a "lawn fertilizer plus a shot of weedkiller." It is really a superpower weedkiller plus fertilizer.

Also, check directions. Is the product safe for use on lawns above tree or shrub roots? "Weed and feed" containing excessive dicamba can be deadly to large trees with even one root under the treated lawn.

Treating pests and disease. These seldom become serious enough to warrant control—unless the lawn is unhealthy because of a bad mowing, fertilizing or watering program. Exceptions: White grubs; inocu-late the soil with spores of the milky-spore disease, its natural predator. Sod webworms (lawnmoths) and cutworms; use preventive chemicals if there was a serious problem the previous year. Rust; step up frequency of fertilizing.

De-thatching. This involves mechanical slicing and tearing through the thatch of dried-out, undecomposed dead clippings that sometimes builds up on top of the soil.

It is, in effect, a thatched roof, keeping water and nutrients from soaking down into the soil. The result is that the grass soon has all its living roots confined to the thin layer of thatch. Naturally the grass then is weak, quick to wilt on a hot day, an easy victim of fungus diseases and hungry insects. Machines designed to slice and tear through thatch can be rented.

De-thatching is best done after the heat of midsummer. Then the grass recovers quite quickly from the tearing, bruising action. Spring is a poor time to de-thatch because summer heat catches the grass before it has recovered its strength.

De-thatching usually removes an unbelievable amount of "duff." There may be a layer 2 inches thick to haul away. Also, an explosion in the weed population is common. Chickweed appears after fall de-thatching, crabgrass after spring de-thatching.

Aerifying mechanically slices through compacted soil so that needed food and water can penetrate deep enough to encourage deep rooting of the plants. The usual cause of compaction is traffic on soft ground. Never walk on a lawn when the soil is soft enough to give underfoot.

The most effective aerifiers are power-driven, equipped with a series of sharp knives plus a series of springy teeth that rip through any thatch layer atop the soil.

Spiked rollers and hole-punching gadgets are considered less efficient.

Liming. There is something about the messy, gritty, hot work of liming that makes lawnowners swear it must do some good. Also, liming provides a highly visible "benefit" for all the neighbors to see—and the cost is low.

Just keep in mind that lime is a chemical soil sweetener, not a fertilizer in any sense of the word.

Unless a soil test shows a pH below 6.0, lime is not needed for at least another year. Public agricultural agencies and commercial firms can make soil tests for you, or an inexpensive home test kit can be acquired. The best material to use is dolomitic limestone.

Alkaline soil can profit from an application of gypsum, which supplies calcium and "opens" the soil without increasing the alkalinity. Or 40 lbs. of agricultural sulfur per 1,000 sq. ft. will drop a pH by about one point.

259

Other Good Plants to Cover the Ground

While grass is the traditional ground cover for large areas, it is by no means the only one. English ivy, myrtle, pachysandra are well known, but there are many others, including flowering plants such as lily of the valley, alyssum and nasturtium. In fact, any low-growing, sturdy, rapidly spreading plant can be an effective ground cover.

As most homeowners have learned by experience, under certain conditions grass simply does not grow, or the difficulty and expense of maintaining it is not worth the effort. This is true in places with intense sun or heavy shade, where the soil is very wet, rocky or dry, on a slope, under trees, around stones, in beds too confined to mow. There are ground covers that thrive in these conditions. A list of some of the most popular is on the facing page.

Ground covers require less maintenance than grass once established but care is required in planting. Buy as many plants as needed to fill in the space and be sure they have good root systems. Set them out in early spring (fall, in mild climates). Regular weeding and watering are necessary the first two or three years. And an application of fertilizer in the spring will help get them established. They require considerable care at first, but less as they fill in.

These wild strawberries, *the everbearing type, make a thick, textured ground cover, a good contrast to the smooth stone walkway. To grow well they need plenty of sun and soil that has good drainage.*

Pachysandra grows beautifully *on this deeply shaded area where grass would not do well. The soil needs regular fertilizing to supplement the nutrients used up by the surface roots of the trees.*

Ivy on a slope *is a good solution for a place too steep to mow easily and safely. It is attractive and prevents soil erosion. In this situation a rotary mower will keep the edges neat so no hand trimming is necessary.*

Popular Ground Covers

Listed here are some of the most dependable, readily available, and most attractive ground covers.

Evergreen Yarrow (*Achillea millefolium*). Grows well in poor, dry soil. Two to three inches high. Full sun.

Thrift (*Armeria maritima*). A tufted plant with pink flowers in spring. Good for sandy soil. Requires full sun.

Wild ginger (*Asarum canadense*). Has lovely heart-shaped leaves. Grows well in rich, moist soil and shady places.

Heather (*Calluna vulgaris*) Many varieties differing in color, foliage and height, from six inches to two feet. Needs moist soil on the acid side, and full sun.

Euonymus fortunei radicans. A vine-like plant good for ordinary soil in sun or shade.

Ivy (*Hedera helix*). This old favorite needs rich, loamy soil, not too dry, and shade.

St. Johnswort (*Hypericum calycinum*). Lovely foliage and in summer, yellow flowers. Very good for sandy, fertile soil in sun.

Pachysandra terminalis. Popular low cover, six to eight inches high. Needs good soil, part shade. Fills in beautifully.

Myrtle (*Vinca minor*). A hardy plant with dark green leaves, white or blue flowers. Needs shade. Deciduous.

Bishop's weed (*Aegopodium po-*

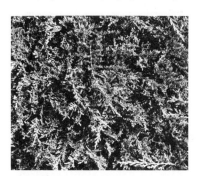

The Wilton juniper *is a low, flat blue-green cover that needs sun or light shade and well-drained soil.*

dagraria). A fast-growing plant with large leaves and white flowers. Grows in either sun or shade.

Bugleweed (*Ajuga reptans*). Has glossy leaves and blue flowers in spring. Grows fast in sun or shade. Needs good, moist soil.

Dwarf plumbago (*Ceratostigma plumbaginoides*). A six- to ten-inch plant with blue flowers and green foliage that becomes bronze in fall. Grows in ordinary soil.

and takes the sun or light shade.

Lily of the valley (*Convallaria majalis*). Known for its fragrant white flowers. Grows in light shade. Needs moist, rich soil.

Creeping cotoneaster (*Cotoneaster adpressa*). Has small foliage with red berries. Needs ordinary soil, sun or light shade.

Dwarf broom (*Cytisus albus*). Six to twelve inches with pea-shaped white flowers. Grows in full sun and well-drained soil.

Rose (*Rosa* 'Max Graf'). Low-growing roses are good for large banks. This one needs ordinary soil, full sun. It has pink flowers and grows one to two feet high.

Potentilla tridentata. *It has white flowers and grows two to eight inches high in acid soil and full sun.*

261

14

Using Flowers
To Best Advantage

To a landscape designer, the annuals, perennials and bulbs are the brightest colors on his palette and he uses them boldly for seasonal accent. This calls for massed plantings of relatively few kinds and colors. The traditional gardener, on the other hand, likes to grow a few flowers of all kinds and have a selection for cutting and bringing into the house. These are two separate points of view and to do them both justice requires two different kinds of plantings.

It takes lots of flowers to make a worthwhile impact on the landscape. If possible, annuals and perennials should be planted by the dozens, and bulbs by the hundreds. And the color should be concentrated in drifts and beds where it will make the best show.

While the full flush of bloom will be the highlight of the planting, the entire process of new growth, development of the buds and the fading of the flowers is a pleasure to observe. It is unrealistic for home gardeners to expect "continuous bloom" in a flower border. This is possible only on estates and in public display where there are full-time gardeners to constantly pick off dead blooms, replace whole plants and otherwise give the

plants their undivided and expert attention.

When a gardener speaks of having "bad luck" with a plant it is usually because he has put it in the wrong place. Every plant thrives somewhere. It's the gardener's job to know what situation is best suited to each variety and give each what it needs. Armed with an understanding of the elements required for growth—which include the right combination of ventilation, temperature, humidity and light—you can grow good flowers.

On these pages is a selection of perennials, annuals and a few biennials that are among the most hardy, dependable, trouble-free all-around performers. On page 264 there is a flower-finder's chart with the plants organized by color and height with the seasons indicated. Use the chart to find the flowers that interest you, then refer to the alphabetical listings for annuals and perennials for a more complete description of each.

If some of your favorites are not listed, it is probably because they are relatively difficult to grow, or do not have the qualities required for optimum impact in the landscape. The bulbs, roses and flowering vines are covered separately on following pages.

Perennials: Years of Dependable Color

Plants that bloom, die down to the ground, revive after a few months of rest and then repeat the same cycle year after year are the herbaceous perennials and make up the permanent floral structure of a garden. If cared

for properly and lifted and separated every few seasons they will continue to grow from 3 to 20 years or more, depending on the kind.

Some perennials are notorious for spreading out and taking up space in the garden.

The foliage of others tends to die down after they flower and leave a void. Some are very tall. Some are attractive only when in bloom and some are undependable as to color. Such characteristics can be objectionable in some places, and an advantage in others. If you know what to expect, you can use them where they will serve the garden best.

They need not be planted only in a border devoted exclusively to perennials. And there's no need to strive for a continuous blaze of color from early spring to hard frost—simply enjoy them in their season.

A garden is seen from the inside as well as the outside of a house. Consider the areas seen from key windows, and when these windows are most used. Perhaps you have breakfast on a screened porch in summer and in the kitchen in fall. Choose plants for each area that will be in bloom when they are most often seen.

You might want to mass one kind of perennial in each of the most prominent areas so the main displays of color will change all through the flowering season. Such a plan could start in early May with naturalized daffodils. Then, when their leaves are ripening, before they are cut to the ground, primroses of the polyanthus, auricula and japonica varieties could be the main attraction.

A bed of bearded iris in a marvelous array of their mixed colors in early summer is worth the space in any garden. Sections of astilbe in different colors could be planted so that each group would bloom a week or so apart. The different-colored foliage of each variety will create an area of special interest for the remainder of the summer.

Liriope is an exceptional perennial whose neat, low, variegated foliage is attractive for two months or more before it flowers in midsummer. Later on the rudbeckia 'Goldsturm' comes into its own and will brighten any sunny area with its quantities of bright daisy-like flowers.

There is no such thing as an irreversible mistake in a perennial garden. Almost all plantings can be moved, even in full flower. Moisten the soil in advance, dig with a generous soil ball to protect the roots, water in immediately when replanted, and shade from the direct sun for three or four days. Many gardeners rearrange plants year after year to change color schemes and relative heights. Don't be afraid to try out your ideas and change your mind later if necessary. The following list is not all-inclusive but it is selective. When properly situated and cared for, these will give you the best all-around results with the least trouble.

Best Varieties for All-Around Garden Use

Achillea millefolium is always dependable. The variety 'Coronation Gold' produces large flat flower heads just above finely textured foliage. A mature clump will generate a mass of bright color in the midsummer garden.

Alyssum saxatile, the easy-growing basket-of-gold, is an excellent edging plant that creeps close to the ground. It covers itself with bright golden flowers in early spring and increases each year. Use it where the spreading can be an advantage.

Anchusa myosotidiflora is a short forget-me-not that flowers in early June. Delicate blue flowers stand out against the large leathery leaves. *Anchusa azurea* variety

'Dropmore' blooms through the rest of June and well into July. It's a good background plant that grows to four feet or more.

Japanese anemone (*Anemone japonica*), in spite of its two foot height, is a good foreground plant because the foliage is not too dense. Several bright white or pink single flowers stand above the leaves on erect stems during September and October. It tolerates shade and needs regular moisture.

Arabis alpina is a six-inch high early spring plant useful for edging and interplanting with bulbs. Takes full sun and literally covers itself with small white flowers. Most useful in its season.

The asters become more varied every year. The michaelmas daisy, for instance, has been bred to grow tall and short, yellow and white with every variation in between. Of the *A. amellus* hybrids the most outstanding is 'Frikartii', a blue flower with a neat, single row of narrow petals. Frikartii will not grow in damp, cold places. The asters flower in the fall when their bright colors are most welcome in the garden.

Astilbe is a plant with spires of pink, white or red flowers that do equally well in sun or shade. Most bloom in early summer, reaching two to three feet, but there are six-inch fall-blooming varieties and four foot hybrids that can be selected for bloom from early to

Continued on page 266

Easy Guide to Flower Color

This chart is arranged by color and height to aid in selecting and displaying to fullest advantage the flower colors that will do the most for your landscape. The 'best known' names are used, whether common or botanical. For maximum information in

Height	White	Yellow	Gold	Pink
To One Foot	A Forget-me-not (E) P *Arabis alpina* (E) P Candytuft (E) A Petunia (M) P Snow in summer (M) B Sweet William (M) A Zinnia (M-L) P *Campanula carpatica alba* (M-L) A China aster (L) A Impatiens (L)	P▲ *Sedum acre* (E) A Gazania (M) A Petunia (M) A Snapdragon (M) A Dahlborg daisy (M-L) A Marigold (M-L) A Zinnia (M-L) A China aster (L)	P Alyssum (E) A Matricaria (M) A Petunia (M) A Snapdragon (M) A Gazania (M) A Marigold (M-L) A Zinnia (M-L) A China aster (L)	A Petunia (E) B Sweet William (E) A Snapdragon (M) P▲ Astilbe (M) A Zinnia (M-L) A China aster (L)
To Two Feet	P▲ Astilbe (M) P Coralbells (M) P Shasta daisy (M) A Salvia (M-L) A▲ *Vinca rosea* (M-L) A Zinnia (M-L) P *Veronica maritima* (M-L) A China aster (L) P▲ *Hosta subcordata grandiflora* (L)	P *Euphorbia polychroma* (E) P▲ *Trollius europaeus* (E-M) A Calendula (M) P Shasta daisy (M) A Seedling dahlia (M-L) A Zinnia (M-L) P *Helenium autumnale var. pumilum* (M-L)	P▲ Geum (E-M-L) A Calendula (M) A Seedling dahlia (M-L) A Zinnia (M-L)	P Coralbells (M) P *Achillea millefolium* (M) A Impatiens (M-L) A Seedling dahlia (M-L) A▲ *Vinca rosea* (M-L) A Zinnia (M-L) P *Physostegia virginiana* (L)
To Three Feet	P Iris (E) P Lupine (E-M) A Flowering tobacco (M) A Spider plant (M) P▲ Astilbe (M) P Baby's-breath (M) P▲ *Hosta sieboldiana* (M) P▲ Monarda (M) A Zinnia (M-L) P Phlox (M-L) P Japanese anemone (L)	P *Baptisia tinctoria* (E-M) P Iris (E-M) A Flowering tobacco (M) P Achillea (M) P▲ Daylilies (M) A Marigold (M-L) A Snapdragon (M-L) A Zinnia (M-L)	P Iris (E) P Achillea (M) P▲ Daylilies (M) A Marigold (M-L) A Snapdragon (M-L) A Zinnia (M-L) P Coreopsis (M-L) P Rudbeckia (M-L)	P Lupine (E-M) A Scabiosa (M) P▲ Astilbe (M) P▲ Daylilies (M) A Snapdragon (M-L) A Spiderplant (M-L) A Zinnia (M-L) A China aster (L) P Japanese anemone (L) P▲ *Physostegia virginiana* (L)
To Four Feet	P▲ *Physostegia virginiana alba* (E) P *Campanula lactiflora* (M) P▲ *Cimicifuga racemosa* (M) P Delphinium (M) P Hollyhock (M) A▲ Cosmos (M-L) P▲ Liatris (L)	P *Thermopsis carolinianum* (M) A▲ Cosmos (M-L) A Marigold (M-L)	A Marigold (M-L) P Helenium (M-L)	P Lupine (E-M) P Hollyhock (M) A▲ Cosmos (M-L) P▲ Liatris (M-L) P▲ Aster (L)

the least possible space symbols are used before each flower name to indicate perennial (P), annual (A), and biennial (B). All of these plants will grow and flower in the sun, but those marked with a triangle will also flower in the shade. Following each name is a letter to indicate whether the flower blooms in spring (E), in early summer or midseason (M), or late summer into fall (L). Two letters indicate that flowering time is extended.

Red	Orange	Purple	Blue	Height
A Petunia (E) B Sweet William (E) A Snapdragon (M) A Zinnia (M-L) A China aster (L)	A Petunia (E) A Gazania (M) A Snapdragon (M) A Marigold (M-L) A Zinnia (M-L)	A Petunia (E) B Sweet William (E) A Lobelia (M) A Zinnia (M-L) P *Campanula carpatica* (M-L) A China aster (L)	A Forget-me-not (E) P *Anchusa myosotidiflora* (E) A Ageratum (M) A Petunia (M) P *Campanula carpatica* (M-L) A China aster (L) P Plumbago (L)	**To One Foot**
P▲ Geum (E-M-L) P▲ *Achillea millefolium* (M) P▲ Astilbe (M) P Coralbells (M) A Seedling dahlia (M-L) A Zinnia (M-L) A China aster (L)	P▲ Geum (E-M-L) A Calendula (M) A Seedling dahlia (M-L) A Zinnia (M-L)	A Zinnia (M-L) A China aster (L)	A Ageratum (M) A Cornflower (M) P *Veronica maritime* (M-L) A China aster (L)	**To Two Feet**
P Lupine (E-M) A Scabiosa (M) P▲ Astilbe (M) P▲ Daylilies (M) P Iris (M) A Flowering tobacco (M) A Snapdragon (M-L) A Zinnia (M-L) P Phlox (M-L) P Japanese anemone (L)	P Butterflyweed (M) P▲ Daylilies (M) P Iris (M) A Marigold (M-L) A Zinnia (M-L)	P Lupine (E-M) P Iris (M) P▲ Monarda (M) A Marigold (M-L) A Salvia (M-L) A Zinnia (M-L) P Phlox (M-L) A China aster (L) P▲ *Physostegia virginiana* (L)	P Meconopsis (E) A Scabiosa (M) P Baptisia (M) P Iris (M) B Canterbury bells (M) P Lupine (M-L) P▲ Aster (L)	**To Three Feet**
P Helenium (M) A▲ Cosmos (M-L) P Hollyhock (M-L) A Italian sunflower (L)	P Hollyhock (M) A Marigold (M-L)	P *Salvia haematodes* (M) A *Salvia farinacea* (M-L) P *Pennisetum alopecuroides* (L)	P Anchusa (M) P Baptisia (M) P *Campanula lactiflora* (M) P Delphinium (M) P Globe thistle (M) A *Salvia farinacea* (M-L) P▲ *Aster frikarti* (M-L)	**To Four Feet**

late summer. Clumps increase in size annually and can be divided to extend mass plantings. Astilbe has masses of attractive, prominent seeds after flowering. Many new specimens of various heights, colors and blooming periods are currently being developed.

Baby's breath (*Gypsophila paniculata*) adds a special lacy quality to the garden. Up to four feet high, it has delicate foliage and equally delicate small white flowers which relieve the monotony of more overpowering plants. Given plenty of sun and room (four feet for each clump) good bloom will continue for two months in midsummer.

Baptisia tinctoria, a member of the pea family, has a flower similar to the lupine. *B. tinctoria* flowers are yellow; *B. australis* are blue. Both varieties grow in tall clumps and bloom in late spring and early summer.

Butterfly weed (*Asclepias tuberosa*). This is a familiar roadside weed. Its beauty is best displayed when several plants are grown together as a loosely formed clump. The bright, showy clusters of orange flowers *do* attract butterflies and in late summer or fall form ornamental seed pods. Butterfly weed grows in sunny locations in soil with good drainage.

Campanula carpatica is short-lived but most attractive in a border. The flowers are large single-bell shapes held erect above the foliage on foot-high stems. There are blue and white varieties. *Campanula lactiflora* has blue or white flowers in July and August. In large clumps, the bell-flowers of this four-foot plant are displayed against a background of excellent heavy foliage. Both varieties are best in full sun.

Candytuft (*Iberis sempervirens*) retains a dark green mass of small leaves throughout the year but is at its best from early May through June when flower clusters cover the tip of each stem. An excellent edging in full sun. Available in pure white, pink and lavender; the white form is most attractive.

Cimicifuga foetida simplex and *C. racemosa* are prominent because of their three to five foot height and arching flower stalks topped with crisp white spires in September and October. The cut-leaved foliage is attractive all summer. Both varieties do well in shade and sun especially in a moist place.

Coralbells (*Heuchera sanguinea*) is a reliable midsummer plant with small flowers loosely held on spikes just above the eighteen inch foliage. They're good for interplanting or in the foreground of a sunny garden. White and pink are the best colors.

Coreopsis is good for informal summer gardens with its golden daisy-like flowers and ragged petal tips. It starts to bloom in June and continues until frost. Because the finely cut foliage does not hide any of the bloom, *coreopsis* is a good flower for display in the garden and for cutting. Although they grow to three feet, staking is not required.

Day lilies (*Hemerocallis*) are perhaps the most dependable, most effective, and easiest to grow of all perennials. Their fleshy roots increase each year. Some varieties bloom from early summer to fall. Day lilies range in color from yellow through many shades of orange and red. The profuse, trumpet-shaped flowers last only one day, however, they bloom in succession and there's a good display of color throughout the season.

Delphinium hybrids are among the most dramatic garden flowers. They start blooming in June and continue as long as the weather does not get too hot. Varieties range in height from three to six feet and come in solid colors of white, blue, purple, red and yellow. Many have a darker colored eye. They love sun but can't take heat. They require good ventilation to keep the temperature down.

Euphorbia polychroma is outstanding in early May when each stem tip bursts open with a yellow green rosette of flowers. Its upper leaves also turn bright yellow

green and add to the floral effect. Each plant is about two feet high, and forms a clump about the same size across. Does best in a sunny, dry location.

Geum is valued for its long season of bloom, from May to October. Yellow, orange, gold and red varieties grow to about 18 inches high on multiple stems. There are enough flowers to provide color in the garden and a few cuttings for indoor use.

Globethistle (*Echinops ritro*) is a tall, sun-loving plant with thorny stems topped by steel-blue globular flowers in midsummer. It grows easily and a clump a few feet across makes a striking display. Fine for cutting and attractive as a dried flower in winter arrangements.

Helenium autumnale is a bold plant that forms a broad clump up to three feet covered with daisy-like flowers from June through September. Colors are usually in the red-yellow-orange range. The smaller variety, *H. a. pumilum*, is about 18 inches tall. Grow Helenium in the sun and root additional cuttings each spring to offset possible attrition.

Hollyhocks bloom in a full range of colors (except blue) throughout the summer on tall stems four to seven feet high. Flowers open progressively along the single stalks. Because hollyhocks are tall and narrow they are best when planted in groups. Give them well-drained, sunny location.

Hosta subcordata grandiflora, a wonderful plant for sun or shade, has rich green leaves about 18 inches high. They make a rich textural bed, before, during and after the spikes of drooping white flowers bloom in late summer. *Hosta sieboldiana* is taller, up to three feet, with large, bluish gray leaves topped by lavender-tinted white flower spikes in July.

Iris is a flower of many species and varieties. Every color in the rainbow is represented and some are perfumed. The big bearded iris, the stiff Siberian and the majestic moisture-loving Japanese

Continued on page 270

Only a garden of flowers *could create such a pleasant glow of soft color. This midsummer display of perennials includes day lilies in the left foreground backed by rudbeckia. The billows of white and pink are summer phlox, which comes in lavender, orange and red. Removing spent flowers helps to increase the time of bloom.*

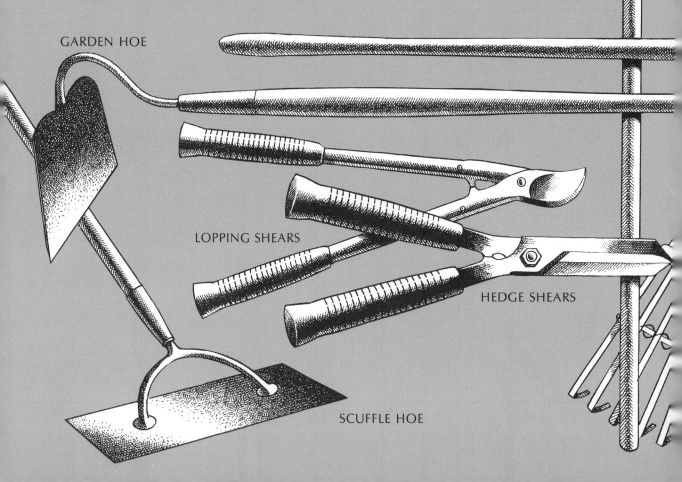

Selection, Care and Use of

The Basic Garden Tools

When it comes to tools in the workshop, kitchen or garden it pays to buy only the best. Tools that are not well designed and well made will waste your time and effort and may fail when needed most. Never buy cheap tools no matter how bright the paint, shiny the chrome or attractive the price. Cheap tools, in the long run, are the most expensive.

The best local source of advice on the specific tool you should have is an honest and experienced hardware dealer. In some categories there are brands of such established quality as to dominate their field; in other cases there's room for comparison. In any event you should know what to look for.

Start with the handle. It should fit the hand with obvious comfort and, when in working position, the tool should have the unmistakable feel of good balance. Look carefully at the way the handle is joined to the working end. This is the weakest point. Round wood handles should be fitted into long metal shanks and riveted firmly in place. Cutting edges should be solid, sharp and well aligned. And keep in mind that Teflon-treated blades reduce friction and make cutting much easier. Good tools deserve good care: A drop of oil will do wonders for moving parts. Use a solvent and steel wool to remove rust, use a file to smooth out nicks as soon as they occur and tighten anything that begins to loosen. And, finally, use only the right tool for the job. This means you will need most of those shown here.

GARDEN HOE

LOPPING SHEARS

HEDGE SHEARS

SCUFFLE HOE

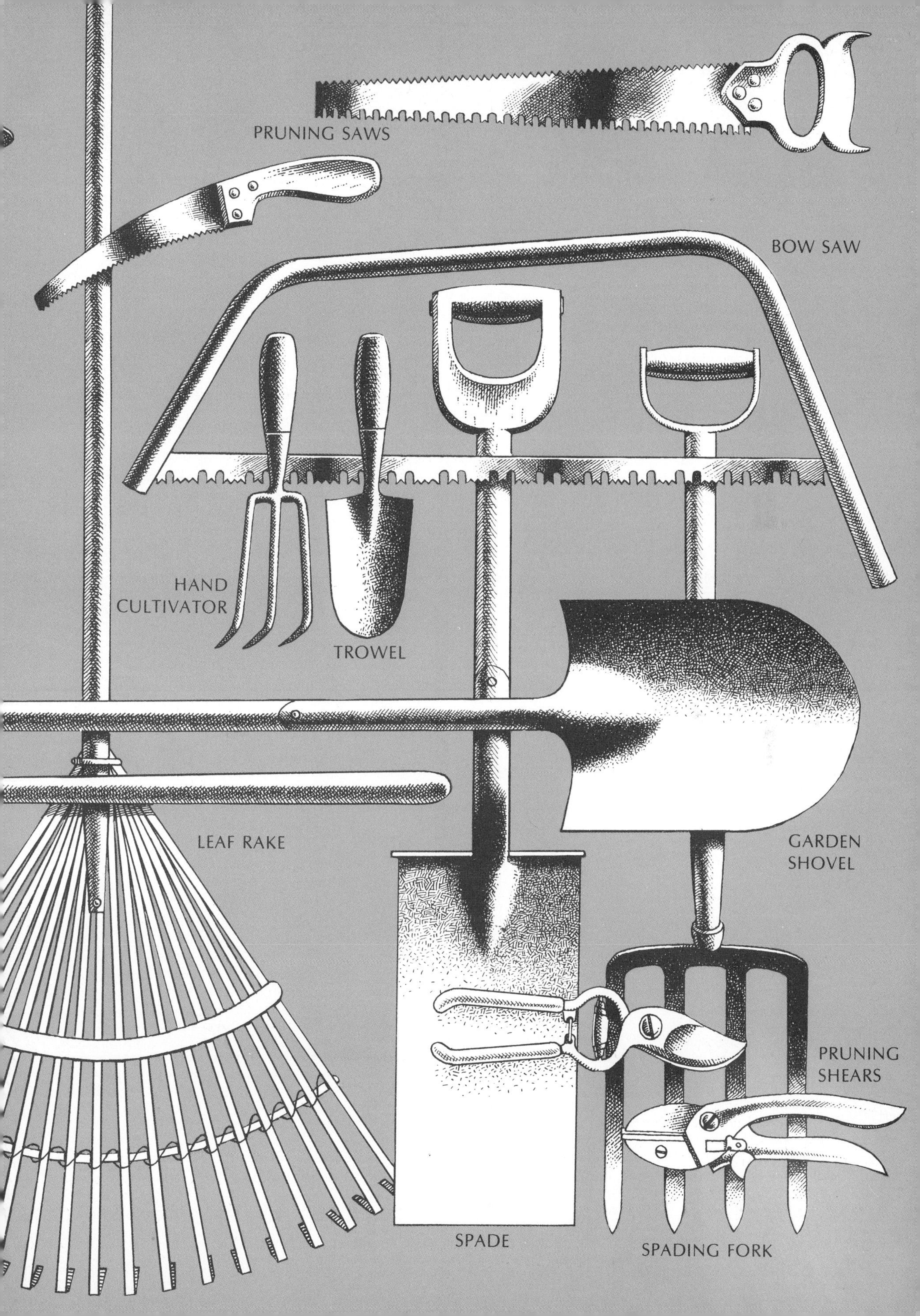

PRUNING SAWS

BOW SAW

HAND
CULTIVATOR

TROWEL

GARDEN
SHOVEL

LEAF RAKE

PRUNING
SHEARS

SPADE

SPADING FORK

are but a few of the taller kinds that grow to three feet or more and are well worth fitting into the sunny portion of your garden. *I. cristata* is about four inches high and starts blooming in late April. The others continue the bloom until early summer.

Liatris, a plant with a narrow, feathery stem, capped with a spike of closely held florets, adds a special texture to the garden during August and September. It reaches heights of over four feet. The usual color is purple, but it also comes in white, pink and rose.

Lupine grows from two to five feet and sends up long spikes of pea-like flowers to stand above the foliage. Available in a great variety of hues, it blooms during May and June. Lupine enjoys the sun, but will tolerate light shade, and needs plenty of water.

Meconopsis, the Himalayan poppy, flowers well into the summer and is similar in form to the Oriental poppy. Three or four species are cultivated. Be sure to purchase those that are grown locally to insure their hardiness. The blue Himalayan poppies have the most dramatic color.

Monarda didyma is easy to grow and forms a heavy-foliaged clump to three feet tall and blooms all summer in sun or shade. When planted in a dry place, water liberally for best results. While the brilliant red 'Cambridge Scarlet' is the most dramatic, *M. didyma* is also available in white, pink and lavender.

Phlox is a mainstay of the perennial garden. Its large heads of florets, in a broad range of colors, light up any border. Strains of many varieties have been developed to extend the season of bloom throughout the summer. Hybridizers have concentrated on producing a host of named varieties for midseason and on overcoming its susceptibility to certain viruses and fungi. While there are early summer kinds only four inches high (*P. subulata*), most hybrids are two to three feet tall. Good sunlight is essential for good bloom through the summer.

Physostegia virginiana starts blooming in midsummer and continues to produce spikes of snapdragon-like florets of pink, lavender or white on stems about three feet high until frost. Watered well, it will thrive in full sun or in the shade.

Plumbago (*Ceratostigma plumbaginoides*) is a hardy, creeping plant with wonderful blue flowers that bloom in the fall. If the underground stems that spread beyond the plant's territory are dug up annually, it is easily contained.

Rudbeckia of which the old-fashioned favorite black-eyed Susan is one, also includes a new group of hybrids. The best of these is *R. goldsturm*. When it blooms in late summer for several weeks the abundant three-inch daisy-like flowers cover most of the foliage. Plants grow to a height of two feet or so.

Salvia uliginosa is a perennial that can also be raised each year from seed because it blooms the first season. The flowers are blue with a white throat. *S. farinacea*, another good blue, is a bit tender

Shasta daisy (Chrysanthemum maximum) *comes in a variety of flower forms and sizes. Takes sun or light shade. Divide plants when crowded.*

but it does well when the roots are stored in a cool cellar during winter and replanted in the spring. *S. farinacea* is difficult to grow but worth the trouble. Both of these salvias are tall but not particularly dense and they can be planted in the middle or back of a border in sun or shade.

Sedum acre is a wonderful, golden-yellow, ground-hugging plant. Its light green leaves seldom grow above three or four inches. In early summer the plant is covered with small bright flowers. It does best in sun but will perform in half shade.

Shasta daisy (*Chrysanthemum maximum*) is a two to three foot plant with large, often double-flowered, yellow and white daisies. Predominantly a midsummer bloomer, the Shasta daisy does well year after year if clumps are divided every two or three years. Needs full sun.

Snow-in-summer (*Cerastium tomentosum*) forms a low six-inch mat of white flowers amid silver foliage. It flowers for a few weeks in June and will tolerate very dry conditions as long as full light is available.

Thermopsis carolinianum grows to a height of four feet and has long racemes of bright yellow, pea-like flowers which bloom in June and July. These flowers add a bright note to a border and a single clump makes a bold anchor for the corner of the garden. They need full sun but will tolerate dryness. Don't overdo it, however.

Trollius looks like a giant buttercup. It blooms from late April to late summer. The butter-yellow flowers rise above foliage that grows to two feet. Hybrids are now available (not from seed) in many shades of orange and yellow.

Verbascum. This cultivated hybrid of the tall woolly-leafed wild mullein is actually a biennial but in sunny locations it self-sows and will serve nicely as a perennial. The yellow flowers in late June and early July are carried in terminal clusters on stems to four feet high. It does best in sun but will perform in half shade.

Veronica maritima will brighten a garden with white or blue flower spikes during July, August and September. It is about two feet tall. Rich green foliage, below the flowers, makes a good foil for shorter flowers in a summer perennial border.

Annuals: Quick, Certain and Easy

The plants we call annuals start from seed, grow to maturity, produce flowers and return to seed all within one growing season. A plant that can complete this cycle of growth in such a limited time obviously has tremendous energy within its seed. An annual can produce flowers in a matter of weeks and this can be of great value in the garden. It is a pleasure and a practicality in landscape design to have a show of color within a reasonable time.

The colors range from brilliant, vibrant hues to soft pastels. In size they vary from the Dahlborg daisy, 3 inches high with flowers no larger than a dime, to the Russian sunflowers 20 inches across.

If started indoors on a window sill, many varieties will be ready for transplanting into the garden after the last spring frost and some will bloom all summer long until the first frost in the fall.

An easy and effective way to use annuals, is to plant them for splashes of bright accent in a green garden of shrubs and ground covers. They are also good to use as "insurance" plants, for you can grow quick-flowering tall-stemmed varieties such as marigolds, zinnias or impatiens in an out-of-the-way location and use them primarily for cutting. But should any spot in a bed or border need replacement these plants can be transplanted to fill in and save the day, even while in full flower. Dig around the plant so all the roots can be lifted. Firm the soil down well around the roots in the new planting hole and water in thoroughly.

Choose varieties that will be compatible with the site they will occupy. Some of them do well in full sun, others can take the shade. Some thrive on little moisture and many are at home in moist situations. There is no point in putting plants in places where they cannot do their best.

Keep the plants growing continuously from the time the seed is sown until they flower. This means waiting to plant seed in the garden until the soil and atmosphere are warm enough to help them germinate easily and grow steadily. Or you can sow seed indoors and transplant the seedlings to the garden when the weather is right.

If the plants get chilled, not only will the immediate growth slow down but the physical structure will be toughened so the cell division (plant growth) cannot resume its normal pace even when the temperatures rise again.

Following in alphabetical order is further information about the annuals on the color chart on page 264.

Best Varieties for All-Around Garden Use

Ageratum grows to about eight inches high with blue, lavender blue, or white furry flowers that create a handsome textured effect when the plants are set about six inches apart. They take sun if it is not too hot. In light shade the plants grow a bit taller. Ageratum blooms from mid-June to frost.

Calendulas are now being greatly improved by hybridizers. The yellow, daisy-like flowers are borne on plants about two feet tall with apple-green foliage. They tolerate a little shade, dislike intense heat, and bloom from late summer until frost kills them in the fall.

Canterbury bells (*Campanula medium*) is a biennial that flowers the first summer if sown early but blooms even better the second season from a midsummer sowing. About three feet high, the plants are covered with large bell-shaped flowers of blue or white, although also available in pinks and purples. Flowering starts in May and, if not too hot, will continue through June. Be sure to water every few days while in bloom.

China aster (*Callistephus chinensis*) is of medium height (one to three feet) with daisy-like or pom-pom flowers available in every conceivable color including green. Successive planting will provide flowers for both cutting and garden bloom.

Cosmos is an outstanding flower with large-petalled blossoms in pure bright colors held above the foliage to a height of three or four feet. If sown outdoors early they bloom from July until fall.

Seedling dahlias (*Dahlia mercki*), not to be confused with the tuberous varieties, can be started easily from seed sown indoors a month or two before the last frost date. They flower profusely and continuously from mid-June until frost on neat, bushy plants 18 inches high. The individual blossoms are single or semidouble-petalled and, in either the Unwin or Coltness hybrids, come in white, yellow, orange, red, or gradations in between. Morning sun is essential and plenty of water on hot days to keep them in good growth.

Dahlborg daisy grows well in a very dry, sunny situation. Only six inches high, this native of New Mexico will be covered with half-inch yellow daisies from June to frost. Sow seeds as early as possible in the spring. In succeeding years it will sow itself.

Feverfew (*Matricaria parthenium*) is an annual chrysanthemum whose hundreds of dime-size flowers bloom throughout the summer. Its shrubby growth makes it good for cutting and for flower borders.

White forget-me-not (*Myosotis alpestris alba*) is technically a biennial and therefore sown in August. This low-growing white variety will bloom in early spring and continue into autumn even where heavy foliage creates shade later in the summer.

Gazania is a bright-colored daisy that blooms on a plant about one foot high. It does well in the hot sun. The orange or yellow flowers, which have a dark eye, are not recommended as cut flowers since the petals close up at night.

Impatiens is dependable in sunny and shady gardens. It blooms continuously from June until frost. Pink is the predominant color but red, white and purple kinds (both single and double flowers) are also available. Single blossoms are best. The one to two foot height makes them useful in many situations. Water well at the first signs of wilting.

Lobelia erinus, a neat, compact plant about six inches high, is excellent in a border. Its blue, white, purple or red flowers bloom throughout the summer. Light shade is desirable if your summers are very hot. Otherwise, it does well in full sun.

Marigolds have often been described as the backbone of the annual garden. Seeds can be sown in place or started indoors and the plants, which range in height from six inches to four feet, bloom from June until the first frost. Flowers are in various shades of yellow, orange and mahogany red. The tall varieties make excellent cut flowers but should have their growing tips pinched off when six inches high in order to promote branching. The bushy smaller varieties are perfect as edging plants.

Petunias need a very sunny location to cover themselves with flowers. A creeper of sorts, the petunia is available in almost every color. Blooms all summer and is an invaluable colorful filler.

Salvia is a member of the mint family, an indication of how easy it is to grow. Height varies from one to three feet; the colors range from soft pastel pink through fire-engine red to deep purple. Some tall varieties (*S. farinaceae* and *S. patens*), are tender perennials, but can be grown annually from seed started indoors during winter. A sunny location is best.

Scabiosa is a plant two feet high with a pincushion of florets atop the stem. It comes in many colors and helps brighten the garden for several weeks in June.

Vinca rosea alba. *Tender perennial usually grown as an annual. Handsome foliage from spring to frost and a bonus of crisp white bloom.*

Snapdragon is becoming a more and more versatile flower than ever. A bedding variety only six inches high in a wide range of all colors except blue has been developed. The taller ones (two to three feet) have been bred for fuller flower spikes and to tolerate more heat. Now they will bloom in full sun or light shade for about six weeks up until hard frost. Sow seeds outdoors in early spring.

Spider plant (*Cleome spinosa*) is easy to grow. In some locations it self-sows year after year. White and pastel flowers bloom from midsummer to frost on plants to three feet tall.

Italian sunflower is smaller than the familiar giant sunflower. It is a bushy plant to four feet high with a great number of brownish yellow flowers and, in a sunny location, blooms from July through September.

Sweet William (*Dianthus barbatus*) will flower the first season from seed if started early. Varieties reach six inches to two feet in height and come in a wide range of colors. Bicolored varieties are the more common. Full sun is a necessity.

Flowering tobacco (*Nicotiana alata*) is one of the best annuals: it is easy to grow from seed, has beautiful blossoms in a wide variety of colors and a pleasant evening perfume. Two to three feet tall, it flowers for a few months in midsummer. Good for cutting and for garden bloom. Stems seldom require staking.

Vinca rosea is good for bedding because it blooms through the summer and is one to two feet high. Seeds should be started indoors and placed in the garden after frost. White with a red eye and pink are the two most popular colors. Tolerates shade and sun.

Zinnia is an important plant in the annual summer garden. Heights vary from six inches to three feet, the flower size varying proportionately. Colors run the gamut, with the exception of blue. Easy to grow. Sow them successively for longest bloom.

Marigolds, *in all their sunny brilliance, are the perfect color accent for this cool green planting of shrubs. They have a long season of bloom and require little maintenance.*

▶ **Terraces** *hold the soil on this sloping site and show off the colorful ranks of petunias (foreground) and snapdragons. The terraces are watered from above by gravity.*

◀ **The zinnia** *has many forms (this is a cactus type) and most have attractive foliage in addition to the rich colors of their bloom. They are easy annuals to grow from seed.*

273

Using Bulbs for Colorful Accent

Bulbs provide one of the most satisfying sources for garden flowers. Because of the way they grow, many varieties can be permanently planted in a lawn under trees, or on a hillside in the shade or in the sun.

Bulbs must complete a cycle of events in order to bloom each season and continue to do so year after year. Such a concentrated use of energy calls for a renewal of strength for the following year. For several weeks after flowering in spring, the leaves gather food to pass along to the bulb, then they yellow, wither and die. The bulb must rest for several months until fall, when the roots begin to grow. Activity is suspended again during the winter months. If this energy-building cycle is not interrupted, the bulb will again flower in spring.

In the garden, use bulbs boldly. Too many varieties, especially in terms of color rather than form, result in a weak display that neither exhibits itself well nor carries the design of the garden. This is as true for a small dooryard plot as it is for a hillside.

An interplanting of low, early-flowering plants such as English daisies, pansies or violas will help to tie a planting of different bulbs together. If you live in a cool climate where wallflowers will grow, they are a useful means of consolidating an overall planting. In such mass plantings, "anything goes" when it comes to color; the most delicate pastel or strongest red. Bright blues, reds, yellows or whites are best for accent.

With the great variety of kinds the choice is sometimes difficult. To narrow it down, decide whether the planting is to be formal or informal. Bulbs that do not multiply readily (hybrid tulips and hyacinths) are seldom as informal as a drift of daffodils, snowdrops, crocus or blue bells. But tulips, such as the tall, upright, large-cupped Darwins or pointed-petalled lily flowering varieties, are dramatic in their crispness. These can be softened by interplanting with pansies, alyssum, daisies or other low-growing spring flowers. Parrot tulips and the double-flowered kinds create a softer effect by themselves. Hyacinths, the most fragrant of all, are best in formal beds.

A few brightly colored crocuses go a long way. These early bloomers with low-growing foliage can be planted right in the lawn and the leaves will have ripened and can be cut by lawn-mowing time.

Daffodils bloom later in the spring and most varieties must grow until their leaves yellow in mid-to-late May. In a naturalized planting the grass would be a foot high before cutting, so a meadow or an unmanicured area is best. Daffodil varieties extend from the large trumpet type 'Mt. Hood' and large-cupped 'Fortune' to double 'Yellow Cheerfulness' and down to such miniatures as 'Dawn,' 'Elfhorn' and 'Frosty Morn.' Also, there is considerable variation in the Narcissus (the botanical name for all daffodils), such as double-petalled and multi-flowered.

Some of the small bulbs will bloom and multiply year after year without any attention. The very best include: Grape hyacinth (*Muscari armeniacum*)—when planted an inch or two apart they produce a carpet of brilliant blue. English bluebells (*Scilla nonscripta*) is best planted in the light shade of a sparsely wooded area. It has helped to make the Irish and English countryside famous. Snowdrops (*Galanthus nivalis*) push their flower stems through the snow and open their green-tipped white petals in March. This, along with snowflakes (*Leucojum vernum*), a similar but later flowering and larger genus, helps start the pleasure of gardening even before the soil can be worked.

These few bulbs, along with another, the winter aconite (*Eranthis hyemalis*), flower at about the same time as the perennial, Christmas rose (*Helleborus niger*), winter jasmine (*Jasminum nudiflorum*) and the Chinese witch-hazel (*Hamamelis mollis*), which are both shrubs. In concert, these six plants can put on a first-rate winter flower show in your garden.

When you add such bulbs as the autumn flowering crocus (*C. speciosus albus, C. pulchellus*), meadow saffron (*Colchicum hybrids*) and hardy cyclamen (*Cyclamen neapolitanum*) which are all fall flowering varieties, the great diversity of these plants becomes apparent.

For clarity of color and stately flower form the tulips stand alone. Here at the base of a birch tree is the pink 'Smiling queen' and yellow 'Sweet harmony' plus a few others. Bulbs look best when the colors are limited in number and when grouped closely together. The 16 pinks could make a good showing alone with the tree.

For the Classic Beauty of the Rose

Rarely has there been a time in history when roses were not widely cultivated by all manner of man. Though much time and effort has been spent in changing the color and form, a rose still remains, happily, a rose, and part of the pleasure of growing them is the nostalgia for gardens of the past.

There are many theories as to the "best way" to grow them. Most logical is the concept that careful attention to their basic needs pays off in fewer troubles and greater success. These needs include: **Good ventilation.** This means a good, gentle flow of air, not a wind-tunnel situation. **Free water drainage.** While moisture is helpful, and even necessary, roses do not thrive with water-soaked roots. **Full sunlight.** This is good for most flowering plants and essential to a successful rose garden. **Dead-heading.** This means snipping off each flower after its peak has passed. It prevents the loss of energy by seed production and directs strength toward further flowering. Dead-heading also brings you in direct contact with the plant, which is the only way to catch mildew or black spot (both fungus diseases) early enough for easy and effective

The classic beauty of a rose rambling along a sunny fence is a welcome addition to almost any landscape design. The one shown here is the coral pink climber 'Aloha.' Tie the canes loosely to the fence.

treatment. Insects are also readily seen when working with the plants at close range.

Soils which are only slightly acid (pH 6.5 to 7) will support good rose growth, especially if well laced with compost and rotted manure. The latter is rarely available today, except in the dehydrated form, but peat moss, to which some lime has been added (to help neutralize acidity), is a substitute.

While roses are seldom interspersed in a perennial border, they are used in almost every other conceivable way. The highly prized hybrid tea roses are often planted by themselves in geometric beds.

The climbing rose grows from about 6 to 15 feet and is quite spectacular when used against a trellis or the side of a building.

The floribunda is much like the hybrid tea, with more shallow flowers borne in clusters. The overall effect of large quantities of these flowers is quite colorful.

Often lumped together as floribundas, the tall-growing varieties are also known as grandiflora. The outstanding grandifloras are: 'El Capitan' and 'Carrousel,' both red; 'Queen Elizabeth,' pink; 'Mt. Shasta,' white; and 'Yellow Queen Elizabeth.'

Tree roses, grown on 3-foot trunks, are excellent accents in an otherwise flat bed.

Whether grown on a terrace wall, trained along a railing, formally spaced in a neatly edged bed, or allowed to clamber casually, framing a doorway, there is always a beautiful rose to call upon. While the search is often for the largest or fullest flower, do not overlook the hybrids developed from the species *Rosa rugosa*.

A fine example of these vigorous hybrids is the small single-flowered 'Max Graf.' It is suited to large areas where a colorful summer ground cover is needed.

The following selections include only those varieties that are "easy to get along with." They are strong growers, dependable bloomers and no more susceptible to attack by insects or disease than any others. However, no rose is so self-sufficient that it can be ignored. To retain vigorous new growth, they should be dusted with a fungicide after rain and pruned as the season progresses. This includes thinning out a few of the old woody stems. Such care will also provide the necessary ventilation which makes the bush less attractive to insects and more easily accessible for thorough spraying.

Good hybrid teas. Red: 'Chrysler-Imperial,' 'Americana,' 'South Seas,' 'Crimson Glory.' White: 'Matterhorn,' 'Garden Party.'

Yellow: 'Peace,' 'Sutter's Gold.'

Good floribundas. Red: 'Frensham.' 'Red Glory.' Pink: 'Gay Princess,' 'Saratoga.' Yellow: 'Gold Cup,' 'Golden Fleece.'

Good climbers. Red: 'Blaze,' 'Don Juan.' Pink: 'Dr. J. H. Nicolas,' 'Pinkie.' White: 'Aloha,' 'City of York.' Yellow: 'Royal Gold,' 'Mermaid' (in a protected place).

Flowering Vines for Color on Another Plane

The climbers in the garden often produce the most dramatic effects of all. Most plants are rather static subjects that grow and bloom right there in one spot. However, the climbers can be trained to follow the path the gardener chooses, by means of a trellis, rope, chain, wire, post or even a tree.

The following have proven, over the years, to be most useful, dependable and beautiful: Clematis probably should be given the first place in any listing. A vine 30 or 40 feet long can be trained across the eave of a cottage, spilling its thousands of flowers during a blooming period of three to four weeks. This would be true of *Clematis montana rubens* in June, and *C. paniculata* would accomplish the same feat in August. Whether selecting the yellow, August flowering *C. orientalis* or the bright purple *C. jackmanii* which blooms during July and August, they will all follow the direction in which you train them and add a colorful architectural note.

While the clematis demands considerable sunshine in order to perform, such is not so with *Hydrangea petiolaris.* This climbing hydrangea will produce its numerous, large, flat flower clusters even on the north side of a building. By definition, a climbing plant must have something to climb upon and, while it might choose a tree in its natural state, in cultivation we must provide the proper structural support.

A heavy, strong wisteria vine, for example, requires an equally sturdy pipe frame or a 4 x 4 wood support. If allowed to climb directly on the house, it can literally pull it apart. For this reason a sturdy gazebo, portico or a trellis is ideal. The clematis is quite a different kind of climber. While it is vigorous, it is also rather delicate and can be allowed to come into contact with a house wall without causing serious damage. A light wire or wood strips are all that is necessary to direct its course.

The best of the heavy vines are climbing hydrangea (*Hydrangea petiolaris*), Japanese wisteria (*Wisteria floribunda*) and Trumpet vine (*Bignonia radicans*).

Vines of lighter weight, although they may be dense in foliage, include *Thunbergia alata*—a delicate annual with small, flat, black-eyed, orange flowers. *Actinidia arguta* and *A. kolomikta* are particularly useful for their attractive foliage. The leaves of the latter variety begin the season as variegated shades of pink, white and green, before turning more fully green later in the season.

The Silver lace vine *Polygonum aubertii* covers itself with masses of delicate white flowers late in the summer.

Cobaea scandens is another annual, well suited to a moist situation. Its purple cup-like flowers bloom in midsummer.

The morning glory (*Ipomoea purpurea*) almost needs no introduction. The variety 'Heavenly Blue' is still the best and, in a sunny position, will be a pure delight. It will put on a show within a few weeks.

Dutchman's pipe (*Aristolochia durior*) looks more massive than it is because of its large heavily textured leaves. The brown flowers are worth looking for in early summer, as they really do resemble the old-fashioned Dutchman's pipe.

A plant that really doesn't qualify as a climber, but does manage to clamber up a tree or trellis, is the winter jasmine (*Jasminum nudiflorum*). It is excellent for holding the soil on a bank and delivers the bonus of numerous yellow flowers in March.

15

A Natural Touch or an Exotic One

White daisies (Chrysanthemum leucanthemum), *with yellow centers, have an unassuming grace. These perennials adapt readily to a garden environment and propagate by seeding.*

It is surprising that many of our attractive native species are not grown more often in Canadian gardens. Such plants contribute as much freshness and color to the landscape as foreign varieties.

Think, for example, of the discreet charm of the daisy or the natural grace of forest ferns. Because such plants grow naturally in your area, they usually require minimal care when planted in a garden. Some indigenous species thrive naturally in forest undergrowth, others are found in water or near it, still others grow in full sunlight. Although decorative planted singly, their beauty is highlighted by a well-chosen background.

However, it is unwise to transplant a wild tree to a garden. The plant rarely survives because it is difficult to disentangle its roots from the ground without damaging the plant. Buy from a nursery that stocks native species.

While native plants often are overlooked by Canadian gardeners, exotic varieties are very popular. Some are particularly striking because of their unusual shapes or rich colors. Before buying an exotic plant, make sure you can provide suitable growing conditions. In general, they should be prominently displayed: near a doorway or bench, along a pathway or grouped beside a patio or pool. Some can be cultivated in hanging baskets, others on wall trellisses. Still others are suitable for bonsai gardening.

On the following pages you will learn about these plants—and about their outstanding decorative features.

Native Plants

Forest Varieties

Among the species growing under trees and on forest floors, some are ideal for public parks and private gardens. Here are a few:

Adder's tongue (*Erythronium americanum*) is a hardy plant, which blooms with attractive yellow flowers in late spring; it has green leaves, often with blotches of gray or maroon. **Checkerberry** or wintergreen (*Gaultheria procumbens*) bears white flowers on shiny green leaves in spring, followed by bright red berries. It is excellent as ground cover or in rock gardens. **Canada maianthemum** (*Maianthemum canadense*), a relative of the lily-of-the-valley, bears clusters of white flowers in spring; they are followed by red fruit. This plant can be used as wall or ground cover in shaded areas. **Prairie crocus** (*Anemone patens*) is Manitoba's floral emblem. It has early blooming light-lavender flowers, and hairy yellow leaves.

◄ **Trilliums** *are fine covering plants. The large-flowered trillium* (Trillium grandiflorum), *seen at left, yields white flowers which turn pink. The painted trillium* (Trillium undulatum) *bears flowers with white petals streaked with red.*

◄ **Ferns** *need acidic soil and partial sunlight. Moisture must be retained by covering the ground with leaves. The most beautiful native varieties are the maidenhair, the Virginia grape-fern, the crested fern and the flowering fern.*

▼ **Bunchberry** (Cornus canadensis), *a herbaceous plant, grows abundantly on the floor of fir and spruce forests. It has attractive light-green leaves surrounded by white bracts (modified leaves). It yields edible red berries in summer.*

Aquatic or semi-aquatic sunlight plants

The beauty of water plants is obvious. If your garden does not have a pond, you can grow semi-aquatic plants in humid areas. Here is a brief list of such plants. **Calamus** or sweet flag (*Acorus calamus variegata*) is an aquatic plant, well suited to marshy terrain. It has green-and-white leaves and blooms in summer. **Flowering rush** (*Butomus umbellatus*) yields graceful clumps of pink or white flowers throughout summer. **Cowlip** (*Caltha palustris*), a herbaceous plant, thrives in moist, slightly acidic soil, in full sunlight or in partial shade; in spring it blooms with golden-yellow flowers, simple or double. **Arrowhead** (*Sagittaria latifolia*) grows in humid soil or in shallow water. As its name implies, the light-green leaves are narrow and arrow-shaped. Its clustered white flowers bloom in summer. **Huntsman's cup** (*Sarracenia purpurea*), a native specimen, is a carnivorous plant, with urn-shaped, green or purplish leaves, and a single drooping flower which blooms in spring. It thrives in marshy ground. **Papyrus** (*Cyperus papyrus*) is a hardy plant that grows at the margins of pools and lakes. It has dark green stems that rise from woody rootstocks.

Water-lilies (Nymphaea *sp.*) *thrive in pools, ponds and lakes. They have large, shiny, heart-shaped leaves and fragrant cup-shaped flowers which float on water. Water-lilies come in many sizes and colors.*

Blue flag or wild iris (Iris versicolor) *has sword-shaped leaves. Carried at the end of a long stem is a violet-blue flower flecked with yellow. This perennial blooms in late spring.*

Sunlight plants

Below are native and ornamental varieties that require plenty of sun. **Everlasting** (*Anaphalis margaritacea*) has pearly-white blooms that appear toward the end of summer. The small blossoms have a papery texture, and therefore are well suited for dry-flower arrangements. Everlasting grows in most well-drained soils, and prefers plenty of sun, but will grow in partial shade. **Aster** (*Aster* sp.), a superb perennial, is suitable for rock gardens or borders. Its daisy-like blooms have yellow centers and are excellent as cut flowers. It grows in an open position, in any fertile garden soil (that does not dry out in late summer). **Fireweed** (*Epilobium angustifolia*), ideally suited to Canadian gardens, blooms at summer's end with long clusters of mauve or magenta-red flowers. It prefers slightly humid surroundings and is generally free of disease and pests. **Day lily** (*Hemerocallis fulva*) is a perennial with linear, pointed leaves from which emerge spikes of large dark-orange flowers. They open in the morning, close at night and die the following day. Day lily is generally pest-free, but its leaves are prone to leaf spot disease, which causes them to wither and die. It should be planted in moist soil. **Black-eyed Susan** (*Rudbeckia hirta*), a brown-yellow daisy, is a widely used ornamental plant. It thrives in any well-drained soil. If planted on an exposed site, it should be staked.

When autumn comes, *the Canada goldenrod (Solidago canadensis) brightens the garden with its numerous yellow flowers. To heighten the effect, it can be planted with other perennials of contrasting colors.*

Canada columbine *(Aquilegia canadensis) is one of the jewels of Canadian flora. The beautiful scarlet flowers droop slightly and bloom in spring.*

Bonsai Gardening

Bonsai (Japanese for cultivation in flat containers) is the art of creating dwarf trees and shrubs by pruning and restricting the roots. True bonsai plants are not natural dwarfs. This type of culture requires special gardening techniques, such as daily trimming of roots, and pruning and shaping of branches. However, the characteristic weathered look, so desirable in bonsai, can be obtained by using plants that need less care than authentic bonsai species. Some container plants with the "bonsai look" are on the following page.

This dwarf tree *shows characteristics of maturity: a gnarled trunk and partially exposed roots. Deciduous species follow the normal cycle: they blossom, bear fruit and shed their leaves.*

Although this mugho *pine does not have the refined elegance of a true bonsai, it has the advantage of requiring only occasional trimming and watering. It has been in the iron pot for 10 years.*

Buff-colored bowl *conforms to the wide, rounded shape of the tree, a dwarf form of an ornamental spruce. In bonsai, the plant and its container must harmonize in shape and color, much as a painting and its frame.*

An illusion of age *is one of the aspects of bonsai most treasured by the Japanese. It is encouraged by careful pruning of the branches and shaping with wire to give the appearance of exposure to a windy site.*

Plants for Containers

Almost any plant can be grown in a container, but the most useful and rewarding choices are those with exceptional interest in form, color or texture. A handsome container and the plant within is essentially a piece of sculpture and serves the purpose of sculpture as a point of special interest for an entryway or terrace. So choose both plants and containers as related parts of an overall composition.

Cluster of colorful plants *bracketed to the garden wall serves as a floral tapestry or painting. When one plant in a design like this fades or dies it can be easily replaced with a fresh one. And the color scheme can be changed at will.*

Bold, unusual shapes *of these interesting plants are perfectly suited in character to their handsome containers which seem to be organic extensions of the plants themselves.*

Good Plants for Containers

TREES
Black haw (*V. prunifolium*)
Black pine (*P. thunbergii*)
Dogwood (*Cornus florida*)
Dwarf citrus (orange, lemon, calamondin)
Japanese maple (*Acer palmatum*)
Russian olive (*Elaeagnus angustifolia*)
Star magnolia (*M. stellata*)

SHRUBS
Boxwood (*Buxus microphylla*)

Dwarf bamboo (*Plieoblastus pumilis*)
Sacred bamboo (*Nandina domestica*)
Japanese andromeda (*Pieris japonica*)
Japanese skimmia (*Skimmia japonica*)
Mountain laurel (*Kalmia latifolia*)
Oregon holly-grape (*Mahonia aquifolium*)
Rhododendrons and azaleas
Swiss mountain pine (*Pinus mugo mughus*)

BONSAI
Azaleas (*Rhododendron*) in variety
Dwarf spruce (*Picea abies* 'compacta')
Firethorn (*Pyracantha coccinea*)
Dwarf flowering quince (*Chaenomeles japonica*)
Hornbeam (*Carpinus betulus*)
Swiss mountain pine (*Pinus mugo mughus*)
Trident maple (*Acer buergerianum*)

Hanging Baskets

There is something lovely and refreshing about a plant hanging and swaying gently in midair. It seems to exist in a medium other than earth and lends a distinctive decorative touch to a patio or terrace.

The best plants for hanging baskets have long, gracefully arching or trailing branches and, in some cases, bright blossoms and handsome leaves. (See the list in the box above.) Single plants make bright accents and a group of them hanging side by side can be effectively used as a space divider.

A spider plant (Chlorophytum) *at left in the foreground hangs together with a Boston fern. The contrasting textures of these handsome pendant plants provide a graceful, interesting display. Hanging baskets in the picture above are filled (from top to bottom) with petunia, lantana (L. camara) and wandering Jew (Tradescantia) to make a pleasing combination.*

Fuchsias *are among the most successful and colorful flowering plants for hanging baskets. They can take a little shade, but not too much, and require daily watering. The showy one in the center is called The Phoenix.*

Using Espaliers for Decoration or Fruit

The French word "espalier" means the trellis or other flat framework or surface on which small trees or shrubs are trained. The trees or shrubs so trained are also called espaliers. In France, this technique of growing (mostly pears and apples) has been in use for centuries. The technique originated not for its decorative effect, but as a means of producing a better and more abundant harvest of fruit—which it does. The careful pruning and rich feeding the trees are given develops extra strength and vigor that is channeled less into luxuriant branches and leaves than into the production of unusually fine fruit.

In this country, espaliered trees are not as common as they are in France. Home gardeners are not usually interested in producing great harvests of fruit, or in waiting for the five or six years it takes the trees to come to maturity. Then, too, the formal and controlled patterns these plants assume have not in the past seemed entirely appropriate for Canadian gardens.

This, however, is beginning to change. Nowadays, when privacy is becoming more important and more gardens are enclosed by

Pear tree *is espaliered to a lath trellis attached to horizontal braces on the side of the house. Use a framework to keep the tree a foot or so from the wall. Pear and apple trees are best for complex designs.*

walls or fences, an espalier is proving to be a useful decorative device. Few trees can be more strikingly beautiful than a richly blooming pear trained to form graceful formal patterns against a wall. Nor need the patterns be formal. A shrub or tree can be trained to grow in any design that is pleasing to the eye or that satisfies one's decorating needs.

Since espaliers are essentially two-dimensional, they take up very little space on the ground. But they do require considerable attention. Plant in good soil and then add a mulch and keep the ground free of weeds. If they are fruit trees and you want a good harvest, all the recommended sprays must be applied. Also, espaliers must be pruned frequently and carefully—depending on the intricacy of the design.

In planting, set the tree or shrub about 8 to 12 inches away from the supporting wall or trellis. Tie the branches firmly with raffia or heavy twine to a framework on the wall or to ring bolts in the wall itself.

Luxuriant evergreen *firethorn (Pyracantha) forms a decorative cover for this large chimney wall. Pyracantha is popular for espaliers because of its thorny foliage and bright red or orange ornamental fruit.*

An espalier *can be as informal in design as this vine attached to fence. If the vine were allowed to grow freely, it would cover the fence like a blanket. But judicious pruning and shaping make it an espalier as decorative as those that are more formally shaped. Here it is used to extend the contained bed of miniature ivy at base of fence. Such a vine could also form an interesting background for flowers or low-growing shrubs.*

16

Herbs, Vegetables and Fruits For Limited Space

Herbs for Food and Beauty

Anyone interested in cooking and with even a little plot of land to use ought to have a garden of fresh herbs. The difference in taste between fresh basil, thyme or mint and their dry-as-dust counterparts found in the supermarkets is considerable. It more than compensates for the little time and effort an herb garden requires. And the effort is very little indeed, because most herbs are remarkably easy to grow. To begin with, an herb bed need not be large. An area measuring only four by eight feet is sufficient for all the herbs most often used in the kitchen—which includes parsley, mint, thyme, bay leaf, fennel, chives, basil, dill, marjoram and tarragon.

Herbs are not too fussy about the kind of earth they grow in. Any patch of sunny, well-drained, friable soil that is not too rich in fertilizer works well. Sow the seeds thinly, cover with a light scattering of earth, and in two or three months you can begin your harvesting. Most herbs require little watering since many of them are native to hot, dry climates. Mint, however, is an exception and does best in moist places.

When the seedlings are large enough to handle, thin them out to make space for growth. Keep beds weed-free and water when soil seems dry.

Fresh herbs are best, but dried herbs, when correctly prepared, are excellent too. The time for harvesting your herbs is just before the plants have begun to bloom, when the concentration of oil is highest in the leaves. A sunny day is best for this and the stems should not be picked until the dew is off the leaves. Then pick the plants, spread them loosely on trays or wire mesh (or hang them in small bunches) in a warm, dry place indoors out of the sun. Make certain that the air can circulate around the leaves and stems. After three or four days, when the leaves have become crackly dry, strip them from the stems, reduce them to a powder or to small particles, and store them in airtight containers.

In addition to being useful in the kitchen, herbs also lend a kind of old world charm to any garden. However, they must be used imaginatively, since a plot of nothing but herbs presents a rather uniformly gray appearance. Traditionally, herbs are planted in small, individual beds surrounded by other flowers or separated by attractive walks of brick or paving-stone. Plan the layout of the beds so the herbs can be easily picked. Herbs are also used as decorative border plants; basil, dwarf lavender, thyme, rosemary and germander in particular. The medieval "knot" gardens, which were made up of carefully trimmed herbs to simulate a border of loosely knotted rope, are worth trying.

A modern version *of the medieval "knot" garden in which the edges are not made of herbs but of interlacing strips of brick paving. It's an effective way to create beds of interesting shapes for growing herbs.*

286

Practical and decorative, *these charming herb beds are made of large chimney flue tiles measuring about two feet square. This is a good size for growing herbs. Several varieties can be grown successfully in a single tile.*

This "herb wheel" *is proof that herbs require little space for growing. During a summer season, such a bed ought to provide an adequate supply of fresh herbs (each one clearly defined) for a family of four.*

Vegetables for the Backyard

In these days of improved refrigeration and rapid transportation, when everything edible seems to be shipped from afar, it is increasingly rare to find vegetables that have come to full maturity in the garden. While such shipping techniques can be a boon during the winter months, nothing is more rewarding in the summer than having instantly at hand a supply of vine-ripened tomatoes, succulent spears of fresh asparagus, tender young peas and Bibb lettuce, baby carrots and, above all, corn which, as the saying goes, shouldn't even be picked until the cooking water is boiling.

Growing vegetables is not difficult. All you need is space (and surprisingly little space is necessary), sunshine (the more the better) and a modicum of time. In a garden of ordinary size, you can certainly find space for such vegetables as carrots, lettuce, radishes and asparagus. But if your garden must be small, one of the best ways to save space is to plant things that can be trained to grow vertically on stakes, a trellis or fence, such as tomatoes, beans, squash or cucumbers. Another space-saving technique is to plant late-maturing crops—cabbage, beets, broccoli or cauliflower—in the beds left vacant by early-maturing plants, such as lettuce and radishes, although radishes, which mature in as little as twenty-three days, grow throughout an entire summer if planted repeatedly.

Also, to save both time and space, start (or buy) such vegetables as tomatoes, peppers, broccoli, cauliflower and cabbage in cold frames or in a flat. No valuable ground is taken up as they develop from seeds to small plants. Raised beds, about a foot high, are good for vegetables. The beds concentrate water near the root area of the growing plants, and also make weeding and feeding easier. When the vegetables are gone, the beds can be neatly mulched to avoid that ragged, half-empty look so characteristic of vegetable gardens at the end of summer.

For detailed information on gardening techniques and problems, consult your local **Agricultural Representative.** If he's not listed in your telephone directory, a local nursery may have his address. All kinds of good advice is available from the "Ag Rep."

The classic vegetable garden *is laid out in orderly rows complete with a cold frame for giving seedlings an early start. This kind of garden takes up considerable space, but the freshness of the vegetables makes it all worthwhile.*

In limited space, *large crops can be grown vertically against a wall, fence or, as above, on specially constructed frameworks. These tomato vines are tied to bamboo poles that can be dismantled later for storage.*

Fishnet on poles *supports this planting of peas, giving foliage maximum exposure to sun and making the harvest easy to pick. Deep mulch, six to eight inches, eliminates weeds and holds moisture in the root area.*

289

A row of dwarf fruit trees *can be a productive and decorative feature for a backyard garden. They can be planted close together to make a pleasant mass of foliage for screening or as a windbreak. Pears, apples and cherries grafted on "dwarfing rootstock" are the most dependable, but peaches and plums are also available.*

Fruits for the Home Garden

The same pride and pleasure can be had from growing your own fruits as from growing your own vegetables. Basically the requirements are similar—a plot of ground (larger for fruit trees or bushes than for vegetables), plenty of full sunlight and a reasonable amount of care and effort.

In suburban gardens, dwarf fruit trees are the most practical. A single dwarf needs a circle of land about 10 ft. in diameter to develop properly, as compared with the 15 to 35 feet required by standard trees. Dwarf trees produce full-sized fruit, are easy to prune, spray and harvest, and usually bear fruit more quickly than the two to eight years required for standard trees.

Dwarf apples, peaches and pears (and lemon, grapefruit and orange trees in other countries) are the readily available varieties. Pruning must be done annually, and spraying or dusting at least five to seven times a year. In addition, most fruit trees require cross pollination (peaches, apricots and sour cherries are exceptions). Since some varieties are not compatible with other varieties, be sure to check your local Agricultural Representative for proper pollinating techniques.

Homegrown red or black raspberries are so delicious that they are well worth the careful pruning they require. Grapes also demand attentive care for fruiting, but the vines make such delightful arbor shade that the fruit may be an extra bonus. Blueberries —decorative plants with spectacularly colorful fall foliage—do well in northern climates and, in fact, need a period of winter cold. And strawberries are an elegant, delicious fruit and make an attractive ground cover.

▶ **The strawberry barrel,** *a garden classic, consists of a soil-filled wooden barrel with holes out of which grow strawberry plants. This version, in a decorative planting pot, adds succulents for year-round interest.*

Fruit is often a striking decorative accent in itself, as illustrated by this luscious cluster of pears. Be sure to plant these visual treats where they can easily be seen.

◀ **Grapes,** with their gnarled vines bearing pendant bunches of fruit, are one of the most decorative of all plants. It is a delight to walk or sit in the green shade cast by the translucent leaves.

▼ **Raspberries** don't ship well. Therefore a patch of this elegant fruit planted in your own garden is well worth every bit of space (if you have it) and the careful pruning these plants require.

17

How to Plant, Prune and Keep Things Growing

What You Should Know About Soil, Food and Water

Many plants thrive with little attention, but a general understanding of the process of growth can be helpful in caring for those that do not. All plants with roots, from a blade of grass to the tallest redwood, grow by the same process and have the same basic needs. Above ground they need light, water and air. Below ground they require air, water and nutrient. Although the nutrient can be applied through the leaves in liquid form, this is done more for a quick pick-up than for regular feeding.

Sunlight on the foliage reacts, through photosynthesis, with the green chlorophyll and other elements in the leaves to make food for the plant. As part of this complex process, carbon dioxide is taken in and water vapor and oxygen are given off through the leaves. The manufactured food moves down the stems to the root area where it helps promote growth. The roots take water and nutrients from the soil and this is transported up the stem or trunk to the leaves as raw material for photosynthesis. It is this liquid that gives the leaves their substance. When it is in short supply the leaf wilts and the whole process slows down.

Some plants have leaves that can support photosynthesis with relatively little light and will grow in shady places. Others must have a sunny site. All plants require good air circulation, clean foliage (so the pores can "breathe") and some protection from insects and disease. Pruning is needed from time to time, but more about this later on. These are the above-ground considerations. Below the ground there are others.

Working with the Soil

The drawing below shows the typical components of garden soil, although the amounts of the material will vary. In the order of

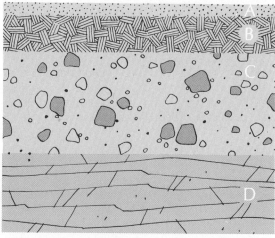

Cross-section of soil in its natural state would reveal humus A, which is decaying animal and vegetable matter; topsoil B, a mixture of humus and the heavier subsoil C. D is an impervious layer of rock or shale and the deeper down this is the better.

density, soils can be classified as sandy, loamy or clayey. The best all-around composition is a sandy loam. Sand helps let in air and water, as illustrated below. The loam has both humus (decayed vegetable or animal material) and clay (microscopic mineral particles). Humus holds water in place so roots can take it up before it drains through. It also helps to sustain the necessary soil bacteria. Clay gives substance to the soil and provides the density needed for roots to hold

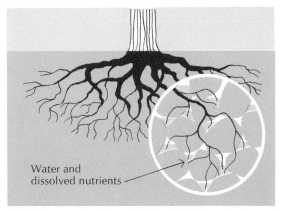

Only the root tips *have the fine hair-like cells that assimilate plant food. They take it up only in solution, which is why the space for air and water between the soil particles is so important.*

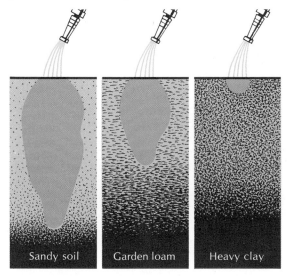

Water must be applied *directly above roots because it goes straight down, as illustrated, with little lateral movement. Relative depth of penetration for a given watering time is shown for various soil types.*

a plant firmly in place. By adding components soil can be adapted to a plant's needs.

The alkaline and acid balance of soil is determined by chemical test and indicated by a numerical value of the symbol pH. For details on measuring and controlling the pH see page 252 in the lawn chapter.

How Plants Take Up Food

The only way plants can take food and water from the soil is through the tiny hair-like cells at the ends of the roots. Granular fertilizer applied to the surface must leach down into the root area in liquid form.

There are about 16 elements required for plant growth, and good garden loam contains them all. Some are readily soluble and others must be released by action of the billions of

living micro-organisms in the soil before they become available to the plant. Most soils have enough of the "trace elements," such as boron, zinc and magnesium. But the three major elements—nitrogen, phosphorus and potassium—are usually required in

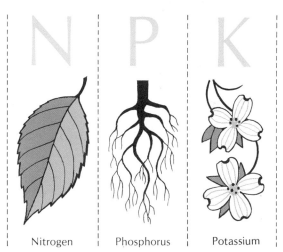

Three major elements *in a "balanced" fertilizer work together but each has a specialty, as shown. The percentage of each, indicated by name and symbol, is always marked on the container.*

larger amounts than is normally released and must be added. A "complete" chemical fertilizer includes all three as explained above. The organic fertilizers, such as manure and compost, are diluted and slow-acting but they include humus, which greatly improves the texture of the soil.

Getting Plants off to a Good Start

There are three ways to start plants in the garden: planting seeds, bulbs or tubers; setting out seedlings that are already growing; and transplanting trees and shrubs with bare roots or roots growing in a ball of earth.

In all cases the first days of growth are the most critical. The time and effort invested in preparing the ground, careful planting and proper aftercare will pay off in strong healthy plants. Vigorous plants are the most resistant to pests and disease, require the least care and will look best.

Setting Out Seeds, Tubers and Bulbs

When conditions of temperature and moisture are right, a seed will break open and start to grow. To sustain growth the roots need moisture and plant food, which means they must be in close contact with the soil. If the tiny roots of a seedling emerge in an air pocket, it will wilt and die. Water the soil a day or so before sowing seed so it will

Plant bulbs *in the fall with the flat (root) end down and firm the soil well. Dig deep enough to cover large bulbs such as tulips and daffodils with 4 to 6 inches of soil, small ones with 1 to 2 inches.*

give them the proper planting depth, location and soil. But for continued growth they need added fertilizer, which is best put below the planting hole where roots will develop.

Transplanting Seedlings

For quick and dependable color in the garden you can grow or buy small plants in containers and set them out when they are in flower or just ready to bloom. The plants may come separately in pots, bands or plastic baskets or may be grown together in a

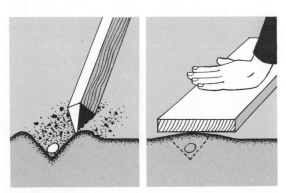

Plant seeds *to the depth and spacing specified on the packet. Furrows can be made with a stick or the corner of a hoe. After planting, firm down well so the new roots will have good contact with the soil.*

be moist but not soggy. Depending on size and kind, seed can be broadcast on the surface or set out in furrows or planting holes. Follow instructions on the seed packet as to spacing and depth of planting. As soon as seedlings come up, thin them out to make space for the development of mature plants.

Bulbs and tubers which have food stored within can grow for a season or so if you

Dig the holes *for seedling plants large enough to put them in place with minimum root disturbance. Firm soil down well and water thoroughly as soon as they are planted. Keep moist to prevent wilting.*

flat. In any event, have the planting holes ready as shown here, remove the plants from the containers or cut them apart in the flat and set them out with as little damage to the roots as possible and minimum exposure to the air. In the process of transplanting, some of the root hairs will be exposed to drying air. The hot sun can put further strain on the plant's respiration system. This inevitable shock can be reduced if transplanting is done on a cloudy day or in the cool of the evening and is accomplished as quickly as possible.

Setting out Shrubs

If a few seedlings are lost in transplanting they are easy and inexpensive to replace and little harm is done. But if a good-sized shrub should fail, it can be expensive and it also leaves a noticeable void in the garden.

First choose a healthy shrub from the nursery. Give it the sun, shade, air circulation and the soil it needs and it should continue to grow well from the day you set it out. It takes a little more time and effort to

Balled and burlapped *shrubs and trees should be set in the hole to the same level they grew before. Tamp soil thoroughly around ball, leaving burlap in place. Open top as shown before the final leveling.*

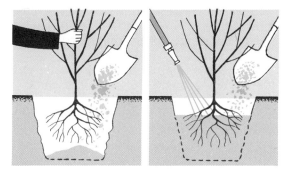

Planting hole *should accommodate roots with space all around for topsoil. Mound at bottom and position plant so ground level will be the same as before it was dug. Use water to settle soil around roots.*

do the job right in the first place but it's a saving in the long run. There's truth in the old gardener's saying that it is better to put a five-dollar plant in a twenty-dollar hole than the other way around.

Make the planting hole large enough to accommodate the roots or root ball with extra space all around. Shrubs and trees of any kind may come with roots in a ball of earth wrapped in burlap "B and B." Deciduous plants may be handled "bare root" if dug up and replanted during their dormant season. The space around the roots can be filled with topsoil enriched with fertilizer so the feeder cells at the end of the root system

will have a good medium for growth. When planting in poor soil make the hole even larger than the one shown here and mix in humus and fertilizer as needed to make a good growing medium with which to refill the holes. Think of the hole as a container and fill it with the soil the plant needs.

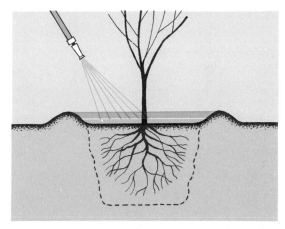

Always make *a watering reservoir by mounding up the soil in a circle at perimeter of the root area. If the water doesn't penetrate in a reasonable time the soil is too dense and humus should be worked in.*

If the planting is done in very poor soil break up the sides and bottom of the hole with a pick and put compost or peatmoss all around. This makes it easier for the roots to penetrate beyond the planting hole. If roots do not grow into the surrounding soil the plant may become root-bound and cease to grow well.

Planting Trees

Trees are handled essentially the same as shrubs and may come either bare root or balled and burlapped. Because of their size, trees usually need staking to hold them secure for two or three seasons until the roots are firmly anchored in the soil. If not staked firmly in place, a tall tree full of foliage will rock back and forth in the wind and the fine feeder roots may be torn away. If these roots are damaged the tree has no means of sustenance no matter how much food and water is applied to the planting area.

Trees are often root-pruned as they are grown at the nursery to keep the root area small and make them easier to dig and to force development of more feeder roots. Some are also grown in containers. If you

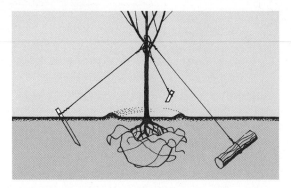

For large trees three guy wires may be needed. Where soil is too light to hold stakes a "deadman" can be buried as shown at lower right. Cover wire with lengths of rubber hose where it goes around tree.

Keep the soil of balled and container plants moist until planted. If you have a bare-root tree to plant soak the roots in water and set it out immediately. If there are too many for immediate planting dig a ditch and heel them in. Lay the trees with trunks at right angles to the ditch and as close to the ground as possible to keep them out of the wind. Cover the roots thoroughly with soil. Bare-root plants must be set out before new growth starts in the spring. Balled plants can be transplanted any time if done with care.

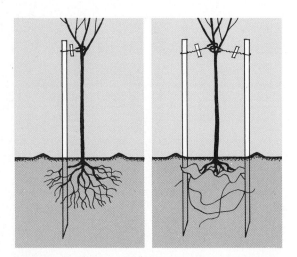

To hold a bare-root planting, a single stake can be driven close to the trunk and will often suffice for small trees. Balled plants tend to rock back and forth and it's better to use two stakes as shown.

are planning to transplant a good-sized tree, it is best to dig a narrow trench around the root area to make as large a root mass as you can handle. Do this a year or so before moving and fill the trench with light soil. Trim the roots again before the move.

When roots are cut back, the top growth must also be cut back to keep the two in balance. For more on this see page 298.

To add plant food or water where soil is compacted use a soil auger to make holes down to the feeder roots. Most of these are near the drip line of the foliage. Fill holes with sand to keep them open.

How to Change the Grade
At the Base of a Tree

Changing the height of the ground around a tree is often necessary when a sloping site is being leveled. The leveling may be done by digging out or by filling in. In either case if there are tree roots under the area they may require some special protection.

Many trees have most of their feeder roots near the surface, and if soil is added, as required for filling, they may be denied the oxygen they need and die back. When excavation is done, feeder roots may be damaged or exposed to the open air, and cease to function. If so, the tree may die.

Physical damage to roots will affect any tree, but there are some that can take a foot or so of soil above the roots with no harm

done. These, in general, are trees such as apples and willows that freely develop sucker growth and water-sprouts.

But most trees will suffer if the level of soil is changed by a few inches or so. Most feeder roots develop at the "drip line" around the perimeter of the foliage. More rain falls here than under the umbrella of leaves. To maintain the soil level within reach of some of these roots when excavating around a tree, a fairly wide raised platform is required.

But when filling, a narrow well can hold the level at the base of the tree, and oxygen for feeder roots can be admitted in other ways, as shown at right below.

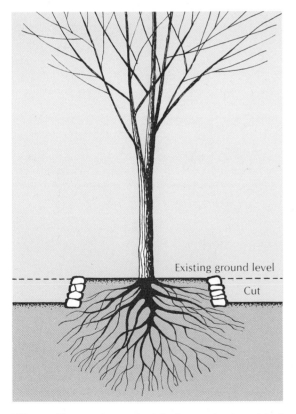

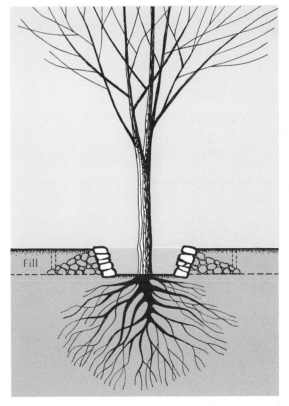

When cutting, *make a raised bed to maintain original soil level to about half the spread of the foliage. Water and feed new roots regularly for a season or two after changing level. Feeder roots develop where cut.*

When filling, *build tree well to maintain original level for 4 to 6 feet around the trunk. To let more oxygen into the root area use rubble behind wall, as shown, and make holes around drip line.*

Principles of Pruning

There are four good reasons for taking saw and pruning shears in hand: Pruning is done to improve the structure or "scaffold" of large trees and give them greater strength. It is done to improve overall appearance, from a light trimming to the complete control required for topiary or bonsai. It is done to remove diseased or damaged wood; and to increase the production of flowers, foliage or fruit.

For landscaping, as compared to growing grapes or apples, relatively little pruning is required. Most of the necessary details follow. For proper timing see the pruning chart following these two pages.

Pruning When You Plant

When a tree or shrub is transplanted, the size of the root ball is reduced, sometimes severely. To maintain the critical balance between the foliage and root areas the top growth should be cut back (as illustrated below) in roughly the same proportion to its total size as were the roots. Also shown are other improvements that can often be made when planting or at any other time. Accord-

ing to the time-honored gardener's adage, the best time to prune is "when the shears are sharp." While this is not always true, it does apply for pruning when planting.

Cutting to Control Growth

Plant growth is the process of leaves taking raw material from sunlight and air and roots taking them from the soil to make solutions of food which are circulated through the plant. A healthy plant establishes a working balance between roots and foliage and when either is cut back the "pressure" in the circulatory system forces new growth.

Pruning the roots develops more root ends for feeding, and top pruning develops more

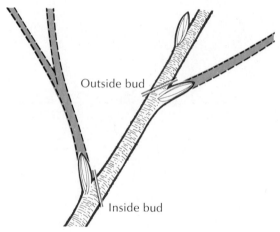

Control direction *of growth by cutting to an outside bud or inside bud, as illustrated. This precaution only applies to relatively large limbs.*

stems and leaves. This is the way pruning helps to promote growth. But if too much is cut at one time, either above or below the ground, the manufacture of food will be impaired and growth will slow down.

Some plants, such as forsythia and lilac, grow vigorously after pruning and develop many new stems to replace those that are removed. Others, such as magnolia and camellia, grow back slowly and should be pruned lightly. To find out how a plant will respond, cut back a few branches in varying amounts and watch through the growing

Keep a balance *between top and bottom growth, as shown at left. If one is cut back, the other should be reduced in proportion. Also, cut out all crossing branches A, narrow crotches B, crowded limbs C, limbs that are too low D, and broken branches E.*

season to see what happens. The following year you can prune with understanding and assurance. Try pinching out the tip growth of evergreens and see how they bush out.

Pruning for Shape

This kind of pruning is more a matter of esthetics than horticulture and is the most rewarding to do. Light pruning, such as illustrated here, can be done at almost any time. Heavy pruning such, for example, as reducing a plant by one third or more, should be done by stages over a period of two or three years. Except for hedges, formal plantings and topiary, it is best to prune to accentuate the natural form of a plant rather than to shape it into a ball or pyramid.

Three typical kinds of pruning: Trimming or shearing to give symmetrical form to an irregular plant; shaping a hedge by making the base wider than the top so low branches will get sun; and accentuating natural form while reducing size (at right).

When to Cut

Details for pruning specific plants are explained on the chart on the following page. But there are general seasonal rules.

Winter, during the dormant season, is the best time to work on most deciduous trees and shrubs. The exceptions are those that ooze sap freely in winter, such as maples and flowering cherries. If these need much cutting, wait until early spring when new leaves come out, or do it in the fall.

Spring is a good time to shape lightly for overall appearance and to prune many flowering shrubs, as shown on the chart.

Summer pruning, when plants are in the full flush of growth, is usually limited to light cutting to force new growth on espalliered trees and force wisterias to bloom. They may otherwise produce foliage at the expense of flowers.

In the fall do no more than necessary to clear out obviously dead and diseased wood.

How to Cut

No matter what tool is used, the cutting edge should be razor sharp. Ragged cuts and tears in the wood can lead to rot and disease. Make all cuts close to the base of the piece being removed, as shown in the illustration below, but not so close as to damage the larger limb. All cuts of appreciable size should be sealed with tree paint to protect the wound until it can heal over naturally. Use the right tool for the job. If it is too large or too small for the size of the limb, it will make a jagged cut.

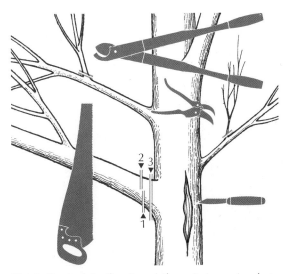

Match the tool to the size of the cut. In sawing large limbs make three cuts in the order numbered above. Remove the limb with cuts 1 and 2. With the last cut shorten the stub, as shown.

Pruning Chart

For the kinds of plants listed at the left, the blocks of copy tell what's to be done in each season. Exact dates may differ in your climate, but the sequence of growth is the same. The shaded panels indicate the primary pruning season. The blank squares indicate that

	Jan.	Feb.	Mar.	Apr.	May
Spring-flowering Deciduous Shrubs These include forsythia, flowering quince, early spirea, early viburnum and such.	Branches can be brought indoors to force into early bloom.		Cut branches for shape and for indoor flowering.		
Summer-flowering Deciduous Shrubs Korean lilac, mock-orange, late deutzia and pearl bush are typical of the kind.				Cut caryopteris and buddleia back to terminal bud cluster, or "knob." Cut crape-myrtle back to uninjured wood.	
Small Flowering Trees These include dogwood, redbud, hawthorn, tree lilac, and trees for berries such as mountain ash.			Branches can be brought indoors for forcing into early bloom.		
Fruit Trees Apple, pear, cherry and peach as well as the ornamental kinds and flowering crab apple.	Cut out ⅓ to ½ of the year-old wood completely. Reduce the remainder by ⅓ to increase size of fruit. Plan cuts to improve structure.				
Deciduous Shade Trees Typical examples are maple, oak, beech, linden, ash and walnut.	Improve structure (work on mild days). Dress wounds with tree paint.				
Broad-leafed Evergreen Flowering Shrubs Best-known are rhododendron, pieris, leucothoe and camellia.			Reduce height of old plants—shorten new stems by 6-10 inches. Pinch off shoots to start low branching.		
Needle-leaf Evergreen Trees and Shrubs A large group including pine, spruce, hemlock, yew, arbor-vitae and juniper.			Cut new growth to shape as it expands but before new wood forms. Pinch out upright "candles" on pines as desired.		

no pruning should be done at that time except to remove damaged wood. It should be emphasized that the dates shown here are not absolute, but don't prune too far out of season. Winter pruning stimulates new soft growth. Summer pruning retards growth.

Use sharp tools: pruning shears for twigs, loppers for branches, and a pruning saw for limbs. Use hedge shears for hedge plants, retain natural contours in pruning other shrubs. Make clean cuts and seal with tree wax. For big jobs, call an arborist.

June July Aug. Sept. Oct. Nov. Dec.

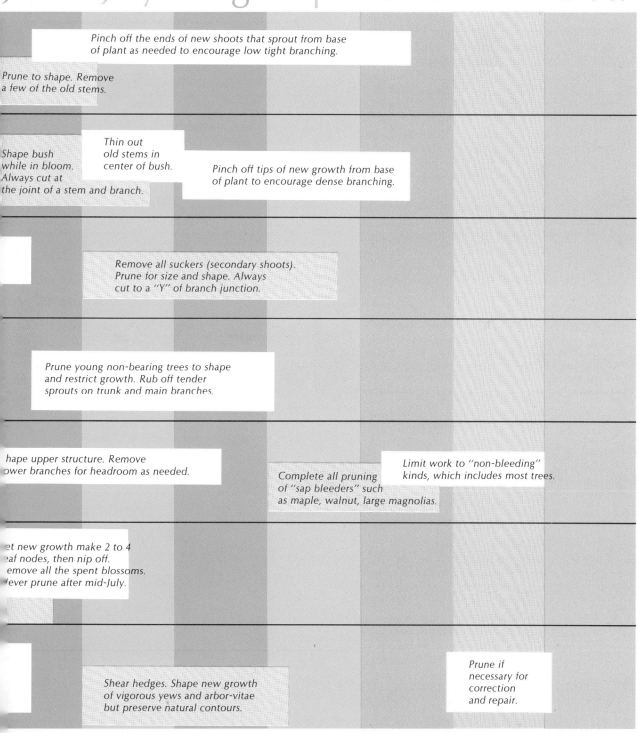

Pinch off the ends of new shoots that sprout from base of plant as needed to encourage low tight branching.

Prune to shape. Remove a few of the old stems.

Shape bush while in bloom. Always cut at the joint of a stem and branch.

Thin out old stems in center of bush.

Pinch off tips of new growth from base of plant to encourage dense branching.

Remove all suckers (secondary shoots). Prune for size and shape. Always cut to a "Y" of branch junction.

Prune young non-bearing trees to shape and restrict growth. Rub off tender sprouts on trunk and main branches.

Shape upper structure. Remove lower branches for headroom as needed.

Complete all pruning of "sap bleeders" such as maple, walnut, large magnolias.

Limit work to "non-bleeding" kinds, which includes most trees.

Let new growth make 2 to 4 leaf nodes, then nip off. Remove all the spent blossoms. Never prune after mid-July.

Shear hedges. Shape new growth of vigorous yews and arbor-vitae but preserve natural contours.

Prune if necessary for correction and repair.

The Garden in Winter

The concept of gardens is so closely linked with summer and with plants in full bloom that one often forgets what gardens look like in winter. Although gardens may lack some of their summer charm, in winter they have their own special beauty. Especially if the gardener has selected plants with an eye to how they enhance the winter landscape.

Evergreens are more noticeable in winter, when not obscured by the leafy trees and shrubs of summer. Weeping willow, horizontal juniper and yew are striking when covered with ice or snow.

When choosing bushes and trees, consider not only their shape but the color and texture of their bark. For instance, the gray bark of maple, shadbush, Korean mountain ash and red oak is particularly pleasing in winter. Scotch pine is notable for its red-brown bark, sycamore for grayish bark with patches ranging in color from yellow-green to orange.

Shrubs are attractive grouped around a bird feeder or used as a contrast to larger plants. In addition, some shrubs are outstanding for winter fruit. Excellent choices are holly, checkerberry and high-bush cranberry, which all bear bright red berries in winter.

When planting a garden for year-round use you should bear in mind practical as well as aesthetic considerations. You must take into account such aspects as prevailing winds, snowdrifts, ice formations and lessening sunlight. Here is some advice for those who want to adapt outside areas to the rigors of winter.

Wind and Snow

Less snow accumulates in places that are open to wind than in sheltered areas that are subject to turbulence. In other words, wind slows when it meets an obstacle (a building, plant screen or other vertical structure) and snow immediately starts to build up behind the obstacle.

As shown in the illustration at right, when exposed to wind, a plant screen with a thick base will induce turbulence and create a snowdrift on its leeward side. Thus, if you plant a row of shrubs along a driveway, on the side facing prevailing winds, the snow will build up not on the driveway but to leeward of the shrubs. Yet the driveway still will be swept clear by the wind.

If you want to shield pedestrians from wind while preventing snow from accumulating on a walkway, plant a row of open-based shrubs facing prevailing winds. Such a screen allows winds to sweep away snow while providing shelter several feet above the ground.

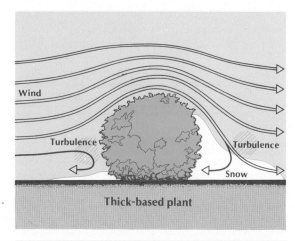

Thick-based plant

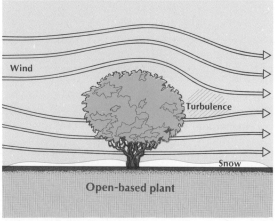

Open-based plant

The picture at the bottom of the preceding page shows how an open-based tree exposed to wind acts as a screen without causing drifting in the immediate area.

In landscaping, one or both methods can be used, depending on the lay of the land, the prevailing winds and the results desired. In the drawing at right, both methods are used.

What is the most efficient arrangement in winter? It is best to experiment during the first winter. For instance, before the first snowfall, use wood panels as screens; in the following months, watch where the snow tends to drift. Based on your observations, plan for the following spring, when the wood screens can be replaced by plants and ornamental hedges.

Some plants must be protected from wind in winter. Stake newly planted trees, and shield tender shrubs such as azaleas from wind by encircling them with wire fencing.

Sun and Trees

Trees near a house can provide shade where required or they can make a spot gloomy year round. The angle of the sun is the governing factor. In winter, the sun rises to about a quarter of its summer height. Moreover, the sun's path through the sky is much shorter in winter than in summer.

To get the full benefit of trees, you must plant them in the right spots. If you want to cool an area in summer and warm it in winter, plant deciduous trees immediately to the south of it. Rooms with large south-facing windows tend to overheat in summer, yet need the warmth of sunlight during the cold months. Deciduous trees outside the windows provide cooling shade in summer but don't obstruct the sun's rays in winter. Deciduous trees planted between a house and the low winter sun reveal the boldness or delicacy of their branch patterns, yet are perfectly lit in summer.

On the other hand, it is best to plant evergreen trees to the west and north of planted

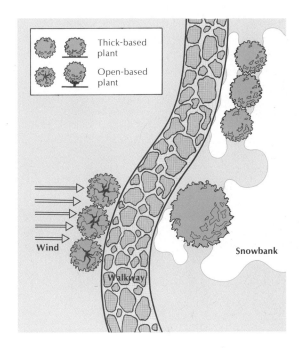

areas that must be sheltered from violent winds; this also reduces heat loss.

Icing Conditions

When ice melts, water often collects in hollows, thus damaging grass. To eliminate standing water, create a small grassy mound at such spots, or plant a decorative arrangement (it should not include conifers if the water is salty).

The weight of ice on trees is a vital consideration in winter. Such species as oak and elm can support great quantities of ice. But fast-growing trees like weeping willow and Siberian elm become brittle in winter and their boughs often break under the weight of ice.

Small shrubs are particularly prone to damage by ice and snow. Periodically shake the branches of such plants to remove any accumulation; it may be necessary to wrap small shrubs in burlap or enclose them in a box (make sure there are airholes to ventilate the inside).

4

Construction

There are projects here for all parts of
the landscape and for anyone who can saw a board
and drive a nail. The techniques are
clearly explained and the plans easy to follow.

HOW TO HANDLE THE

The properties of each building material are different and so the methods of working with each material—the shaping, fastening, preserving, maintaining and finishing—are also different. Before starting to work with any material it pays to have a thorough understanding of its essential qualities and characteristics. Most projects entail the use of more than one.

This first section on construction contains information concerning the basic building materials, which are listed below, together with an illustration of the common tools needed to work with them. It's not meant to be read straight through but rather to be used as a reference source on building procedures with which you're unfamiliar. Whenever you need to know such things as

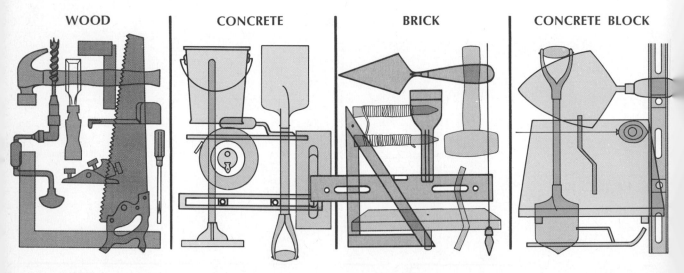

WOOD   CONCRETE   BRICK   CONCRETE BLOCK

BASIC MATERIALS

how to put a grommet into canvas, how deep a foundation should be for a stone wall, how to bond onto old concrete or how to make the strongest wood joint, you'll find the answers here. This section is here to be used as necessary, in conjunction with the following section which contains plans for more than 100 specific projects you can build with these materials for the garden and also, of course, when working on home repairs or building projects not shown here. There's a separate chapter for each material. Each chapter is arranged in essentially the same manner—a discussion of the nature of the material is followed by the shapes and sizes it comes in and then explanations of how to fasten, finish, preserve, maintain and shape it to the purpose at hand.

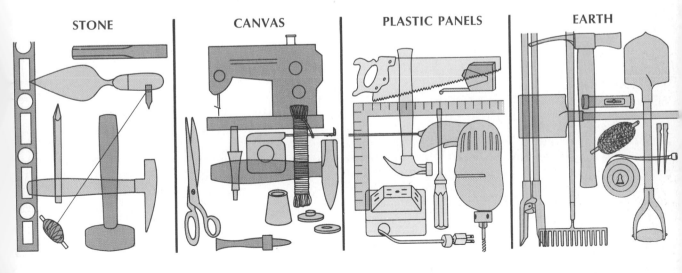

STONE   CANVAS   PLASTIC PANELS   EARTH

18

Working With Wood

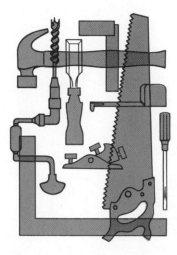

Basic tools, *clockwise: claw hammer, brace and bit, wood chisel, try square, handsaw, tape measure, screwdriver, plane, framing square.*

Wood, which is as appropriate to the landscape as earth, stone or water, is one of the most attractive and versatile building materials that you can use in your garden. It is strong and durable for its weight, beautiful in its natural color and pattern of grain, and of all the available materials it is the easiest for most homeowners to work with. The different kinds listed on the facing page include those that are most widely used for outdoor work. Your personal choice will depend to a great degree on local supplies.

Kinds, Sizes and Shapes

Heartwood, Sapwood and Grain Structure

Heartwood, the darker core of a log, is more resistant to decay than the outer ring of lighter colored sapwood, although decay is not, as some think, an inevitable or natural process in wood, as many ancient wooden structures will attest. Plain- or flat-sawn boards (cut so that the grain runs parallel or almost parallel to the board) cost less but tend to warp more than quarter-sawn boards (cut so that the grain runs more or less at right angles to the board).

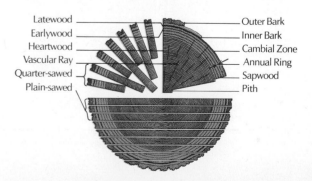

Latewood — Outer Bark
Earlywood — Inner Bark
Heartwood — Cambial Zone
Vascular Ray — Annual Ring
Quarter-sawed — Sapwood
Plain-sawed — Pith

Nine Good Woods to Use

You'll find the nine species listed here best suited to outdoor projects. All are softwoods, which means conifers or evergreens. Hardwoods come from deciduous, or leaf-shedding, trees such as oak, maple and ash. "Soft" does not necessarily mean weak, nor "hard" strong. Carpenters coined the words centuries ago because they found pines, cedars and firs easier to work than the so-called hardwoods.

Bald Cypress. Generally called cypress; also tidewater red cypress, yellow cypress. Its heartwood is one of three most resistant to decay (red cedar and redwood are the others). Color: yellow-brown to brown-red; weathers to light silvery gray. Relatively heavy and strong. Fairly easy to work.

Cedar, Red. Western, the most common, is best known for shingles and shakes; eastern, for fencing. Both have heartwood highly resistant to decay. Color is reddish brown; weathers to silvery gray. Very easy to work; relatively low strength. Western red cedar is light in weight; eastern is heavier.

Fir, Douglas. Has very high tensile strength; good for load-bearing construction. Orange-red to yellow; weathers to dark gray. Above-average weight; heartwood moderately resistant to decay; somewhat difficult to work.

Hemlock. Eastern and western species are moderately strong, with the western variety somewhat more so. Eastern hemlock is a pale brown; western is almost white; both weather to a light silvery gray. Heartwood is low in resistance to decay. Both species relatively light; easy to work; structural.

Larch, Western. Another good species for construction. Moderate to high strength; quite heavy; somewhat difficult to work. Color is a yellow-brown; weathers to a dark gray. Heartwood is susceptible to decay.

Pine, Eastern White. This is also known simply as white pine. Relatively low in strength; lightweight. Species is used in light construction; sometimes as siding. Belying its name, color is light brown; weathers to a medium gray. Heartwood is moderately resistant to decay; wood is easy to work. Western and Idaho white pine are similar.

Pine, Southern Yellow. A high-strength species, used extensively in load-bearing construction. Wood is rather heavy, tough and coarse-grained; somewhat difficult to work. Its color is reddish brown to yellow-white; it weathers to a dark gray. Heartwood resistant to decay. Also called longleaf pine.

Redwood. Perhaps more than other species, redwood is used for outdoor projects. Two reasons: moderate strength and heartwood highly resistant to decay. Moderately heavy, it is fairly easy to work. True to its name, the color ranges from almost a cherry red to a rich mahogany; weathers to a medium-dark gray, sometimes to a driftwood gray.

Spruce. The three varieties—eastern, Engelmann and Sitka (or western)—all fall roughly in the same category as white pine: relatively low strength, lightweight, easy to work. Mostly white; weathers to medium gray. Low resistance to decay.

Hardwood

Poplar, oak and chestnut are sometimes used outdoors, but their relatively high cost restricts them mostly to indoor jobs.

Plywood for Outdoors

Plywood for outdoor projects must be "exterior" or "marine" grade. Ordinarily, plywood is stocked in 4-x-8-foot sheets in thicknesses of ¼ to 1 inch. Alternating grain

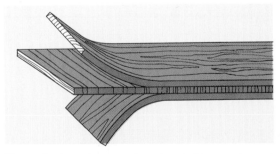

Plywood's strength comes from bonded layers of wood in which the grain of adjacent layers runs at right angles.

direction on each veneer makes the finished material dimensionally stable and quite strong. Douglas fir, redwood and southern yellow pine are the most widely used species. Faces are plain, or, for siding, rough-sawn, grooved, grain-raised or resin-coated.

Using Hardboard

Hardboard is made of wood fibers that are first separated from the log, then matted under heat and pressure, and bound during the process by lignin, the natural adhesive found in wood. This process produces a dense, heavy and surprisingly strong board. For outdoor use, specify tempered hardboard, which is treated to resist moisture and weathering. Hardboard cuts easily with a crosscut saw. Its dense composition will hold screws, but special ring-shanked nails are best. Normally, one surface of the board is smooth, the other rough. The smooth side takes paint well. Prefinished board is also available. It is used for soffits, fascias, siding, outdoor cabinetry and fencing; scraps are used for making concrete forms. Standard size: 4-x-8-foot sheets, ¼ inch thick.

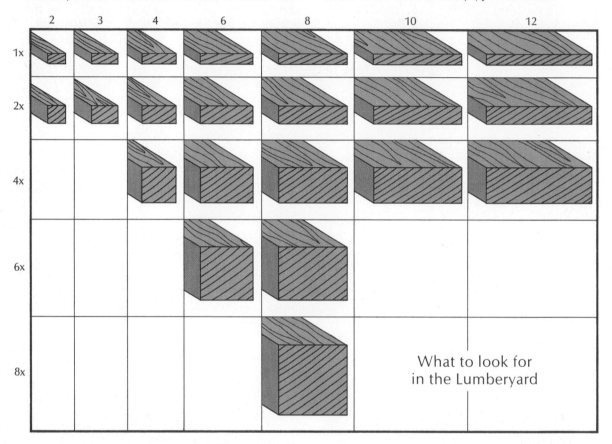

What to look for in the Lumberyard

Standard Sizes and Shapes

In the chart above, you will find the lumber sizes most readily available in local yards. Sometimes a lumberyard will carry odd sizes (½ x 2 inches or 3 x 6 inches). Those that do not can cut them from existing stock or order them from the mill. But you will rarely need a special size. The lumber sizes illustrated are the standard ones used for most outdoor jobs. They are shown here in relative scale.

As you may know, the sizes by which lumber is sold in the yards are *nominal*. The so-called 2 x 4 actually measures only about $1\frac{5}{8}$ x $3\frac{5}{8}$ inches. The nominal size is based on rough-cut lumber, straight from the log. When planed and sanded, or dressed, the size is slightly reduced. You can plan on a reduction of $\frac{3}{8}$ inch for any dimension (width or thickness) from 3 to 6 inches; for sizes 6 inches and up, subtract ½ inch from the nominal size. One-inch boards actually measure $\frac{25}{32}$ or $\frac{3}{4}$ inch thick.

The Right Lumber for the Job

Lumber in contact with well-drained soil should be heartwood of redwood, red cedar or bald cypress; or pressure-treated Douglas fir, southern yellow pine or western larch. For premium strength in dimension lumber (from 2 to 5 inches thick), order #1 or "construction" grade; for larger pieces order "select/structural." Boards less than 2 inches thick are graded on looks. "Construction" or #1 common grade is the first grade.

How to Compute Board Feet

Lumber is priced and sold by the board foot. A board 1 inch thick, 12 inches wide and 12 inches long (using nominal measurements) equals one board foot. To determine the number of board feet in a piece of lumber that doesn't measure 1 by 12 inches, multiply thickness in inches times width in inches times length in *feet* and divide by 12. Thus, a 2 by 8 ten feet long has 13.3 board feet. At 40 cents a board foot, cost is $5.32.

Techniques of Joining

"Joinery," an old name for carpentry, is still in use today. It's a sensible word, since nothing much happens until the boards and planks are somehow put together. Below, and on the next two pages, are the joining methods best suited to outdoor projects, plus advice about cutting and fastening. If you're new to woodworking, it is often advisable to practice first on scrap lumber. You will find that accuracy in cutting is imperative.

Corner Joints

Here are three easy joints for a right-angle corner between like members, or between a plank or board and a post, as in the case of the overlap joint, upper left. You'll be using these in fencing, decks and framing.

Overlap joint, *above left, is easiest but may warp in time. Notched or rabbeted joint, above right, is the strongest. Mitered joint, left, is weakest but best-looking. Use nails or screws and glue all joints.*

Reinforced Corner Joints

Adding a block or plate to the overlap joint greatly increases its strength, especially against racking forces (lateral pressure on the upright). Blocks in upper drawings can also be attached from inside.

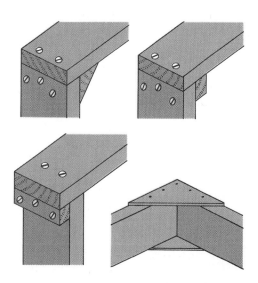

For extra strength, *blocks can be used on corner joints where they will not detract from appearance. Plywood plate, lower right, is fitted flush to the edge on both sides. Glue all joints for added strength.*

Metal Brackets

On the next page: three ways to reinforce an L or T joint with metal brackets. In examples like this, the wood members are

311

usually nailed and glued, but brackets must be fixed with screws. Bore guide holes about half the length of threaded part of screw.

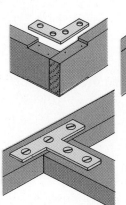
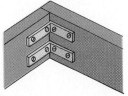

First attach pieces, *then add brackets. Recess bracket when appearance is important. Use at top and bottom for double strength. Mark and drill guide holes to line up with holes in bracket.*

Dowel and Dado

Dowel joints (pins or pegs of one member fitted into adjacent holes in the other member) and rabbet and dado joints (a groove cut in one member so as to receive the right-angled edge of the other member) are two common methods of joinery. They are used more for indoor than outdoor work, but should be considered where both strength and a finished appearance are important as, for example, in making patio furniture. These joints can be made stronger by first gluing, then nailing pieces together.

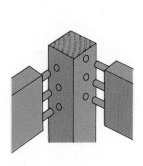
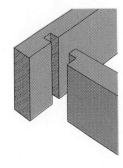

Dowel holes *for faces at right angles should be staggered. Apply waterproof glue and clamp in place. Use maple or birch dowels (diameters from 1/4- to 3/4-inch). Bevel ends and drill holes longer than dowel length.*

Rabbet, *or right-angle cut, is made with a backsaw. Dado, or groove, is cut with backsaw, then cleaned out with a chisel. On a power saw, use a dado head. Fit should be snug, with outside corner flush. Glue, then nail joint.*

Splicing

Where stress is light (a vertical slat in a fence, for example), the splices below are useful and easy to make. To splice a member under stress (as a joist), nail plywood plates to both sides of the joint.

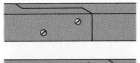

Shiplap, *left, is strongest. Nail or screw both sides on opposite diagonals.*

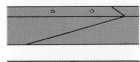

Plain scarf joint *is nailed or screwed (staggered) through top and bottom.*

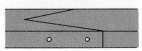

V-splice *makes a stronger joint but calls for careful cutting for snug fit.*

Joining Plywood

To make four plywood sides of a simple gravel sieve, for example, a lap joint is all that is required. In using plywood to build an outdoor storage unit, or drawers for a potting bench, you'll need a firmer joint, such as the dowel or rabbet. These call for plywood ½ inch thick or more. While hand tools are easy enough to use on a 2-x-4, power tools are better for plywood. A table saw, shaper, joiner or router can cut plywood quickly and accurately.

Plywood can also be stiffened at right angles with a cross-lap joint, similar to the dividers in an egg crate. To cross two pieces of ¼-inch plywood 1 foot deep and 3 feet long, first cut a ¼-inch-wide slice 6 inches into each panel; then slide the cut in one panel into the cut in the other.

To fasten plywood, nails are satisfactory for rough work, but screws are better, and adhesives make the cleanest joints. Apply a a waterproof resorcinol or marine type of epoxy glue. Hold the members firmly in place with finishing nails or clamps while the adhesive cures.

Joining Hardboard

For home use, hardboard, which is only ¼-inch thick, must be joined on wood framing, corner blocks or other wood members. Use nails, screws or glue.

Making Lap Joints

The **plain lap** (below left) is the joint used most in outdoor carpentry. It is the easiest to make and, when firmly fastened, long-lasting. A more stable and more attractive method is the **end** or **half-lap,** which is made by cutting away half the thickness of each member so that each overlaps the other at their ends. Other applications are the **notched lap** (below right) and the **center**

half-lap, in which a crossing joint is made flush by notching out half the thickness of each piece. One more useful variation, the **half-lap dovetail,** is good to use when stresses in the object tend to pull the members apart. For the dovetail, walls of the cut are flared, narrow at the edge where the members butt, wide at the outside edge. These joints can be cut with a backsaw and chisel, using the technique shown under "How to Make a Good Fit," but a table saw with a dado blade will make the work go faster and the job will be more accurate.

How to Use Nails

To avoid rust stains and gain long-term holding power, use galvanized, aluminum or stainless steel nails for outdoor projects. An alternative is to protect wire nails by countersinking and then filling the holes with **putty.** Standard nail sizes are shown on the next page.

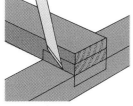

Lap joint *is quick and easy. Use 2 nails or screws or 4 at most. Stagger as shown. Glue, then nail.*

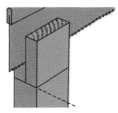

Notched lap *makes a rigid joint. Never cut notch to more than half board depth. Cut for snug fit.*

Nail length *should be at least twice the thickness of thinner piece.*

To prevent splitting, *do not drive nails along the same grain line.*

How to Make a Good Fit

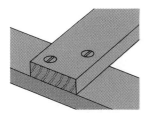

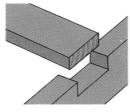

Measure twice *and cut once. Mark so that lapped board is flush with bottom member.*

Cut parallel, *then at right angles, to length, using backsaw. Best to clamp member in vise.*

To increase grip *of nails at a lap joint, drive them in at an angle, as shown.*

As a precaution *against splitting, extend the top member, nail and trim.*

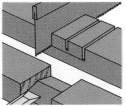

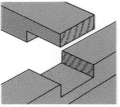

Cut on inner edges *of marked lines to make snug fit. Be exact. Then chisel out scrap.*

Sand cut faces, *if needed, for a tight lap; then nail, drill for screws, or glue and nail.*

To blind-nail *a tongue-and-groove joint, angle nail through the tongue.*

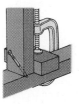

Use clamp and block *to hold member firmly in place for toenailing.*

313

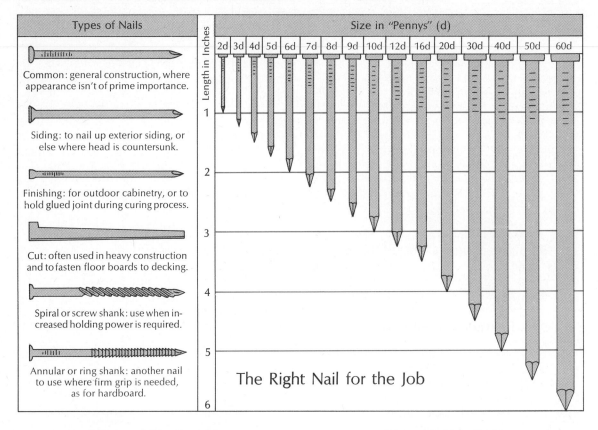

Types of Nails	Length in Inches	Size in "Pennys" (d)															
		2d	3d	4d	5d	6d	7d	8d	9d	10d	12d	16d	20d	30d	40d	50d	60d

Common: general construction, where appearance isn't of prime importance.

Siding: to nail up exterior siding, or else where head is countersunk.

Finishing: for outdoor cabinetry, or to hold glued joint during curing process.

Cut: often used in heavy construction and to fasten floor boards to decking.

Spiral or screw shank: use when increased holding power is required.

Annular or ring shank: another nail to use where firm grip is needed, as for hardboard.

The Right Nail for the Job

How to Use Screws

Joints that are subject to unusual stress and strain require screws instead of nails. For example, screws should be used on all joints of outdoor furniture. Use hot-dipped galvanized, aluminum, stainless steel or brass screws to avoid rust. Screws come in lengths of ¼ inch to 6 inches.

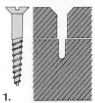

1.

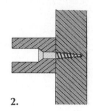

2.

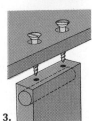

3.

1. To guide screw, *drill two holes, one same diameter as shank, other smaller.* **2. To attach a member wider than screw is long, counterbore and screw, as shown.* **3. For extra grip in end grain, insert and glue dowel across grain; drive screws in dowel.*

How to Use Bolts

Bolts are the heavy-duty performers on outdoor projects. If you're building the frame for an overhead sun screen, fasten the main rafters to supporting posts (side grain to side grain) with at least two carriage bolts. To increase the holding power and protect the wood, use washers beneath the nut on a carriage bolt, beneath the head on a lag screw, and beneath head and nut on a machine bolt. Lag screws are wrench-turned bolts with a pointed screw end for use on a heavy-duty joint that can't take a nut.

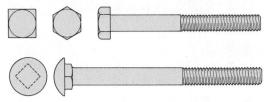

Fasten metal to metal *or metal to wood with machine bolt, top, (3/4 to 39 inches long), carriage bolt (3/4 to 20 inches long), bottom, is best for wood to wood. Drill bolt holes 1/16 inch smaller than bolt diameter.*

314

Finishes for Wood

Weathering

Most early settlers never put a finish on wood siding or fencing. They simply allowed it to weather naturally. You can do this too, of course, because those woods best suited for outdoor use don't really need a finish. Within a year or so their color turns to attractive shades of gray. (See notes on species, page 309). Neither does wood lose strength by weathering.

Certain kinds of wood, such as spruce or hemlock, tend to splinter and should therefore be finished with a sealer (see below) when used for outdoor decks or benches. Other species, like redwood and cypress, hold up much better in the sun and rain.

Sealers and Finishes

Exterior sealers are usually labeled "water repellent." A clear liquid, repellents are applied with a brush or roller. They prevent rain and moisture from soaking into the pores of the wood, and consequently help check warping and cracking. They do not, however, eliminate these problems completely. Repellents are effective in reducing the bleaching action of the sun. Once treated, wood will remain close to its original color for many years. If the wood begins to darken, it is time for another coat. Other clear finishes are seldom satisfactory outdoors. Shellac, for example, hazes and discolors in time. Varnishes, even marine types, need constant renewing, and may yellow. Most successful are the aliphatic, urethane varnishes, but they must be removed before applying a new coat.

Bleaches

To speed up the weathering of wood, use a bleach and, after a season or two, the bleach, together with the action of sun and moisture, will turn the wood an interesting and natural-looking shade of gray. Moreover, it does so uniformly, whereas weathering without benefit of stain sometimes leaves streaks on the surface during the early stages of change. Buy a bleach that contains a mildewcide and apply with a brush or roller.

Normally one coat will do, but some woods call for two—follow the manufacturer's directions.

Paints

A good coat of paint will eliminate splintering on the surface of woods like larch or Douglas fir; paint helps protect the wood from the two principal weathering agents: rain and sun. But paint is essentially a decorative finish and nowhere can it be used more imaginatively than in outdoor design and ornamentation. Always buy a paint labeled for outside use. You have a choice of oil-base or alkyd paints, sold in flat, semigloss and gloss finishes. Or buy the easier-to-use water-emulsion paints, available as a flat finish and recently offered in semigloss. Apply one prime and two top coats, and follow the directions.

Stains

Semitransparent stains will tint wood, but permit the grain to show through. So-called heavy-bodied stains mask the grain, much as paint does. But stains penetrate the wood and are cooler underfoot in the sun. Stains are produced today in a wide range of colors. Ordinarily you should apply two coats over a clean, dry surface. Restain when needed with the same color.

Refinishing

Finished wood eventually needs refinishing. If you apply the same material, it's likely you won't have to do anything but clean the surface, unless the old coat is cracked. In that case, wire-brush those portions before refinishing. You can apply the same or a darker shade of paint without removing the old paint. But if you want to put white over brown, you'll have to take off the brown. Do it with sandpaper, wire brush, or paint-and-varnish remover.

19
Working With Concrete

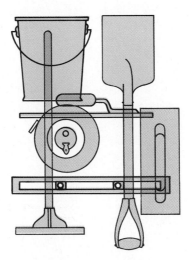

Basic tools, *clockwise: water pail, spade, wood float, level, tamper, tape measure, steel trowel.*

Like water, concrete assumes the shape of whatever form encloses it. Therefore, with no great difficulty, you can create in concrete a number of gracefully shaped outdoor projects, as walks, driveways, walls, benches, patios and pools. In addition, concrete can be beautiful. Its form can be light and graceful or massive and heavy; its texture can be glistening and smooth, primitive and rough, or selected stones can be embedded to enrich the surface. It is durable, strong, fireproof, and it is economical.

What You Should Know About the Material

As the drawing (above right on opposite page) illustrates, concrete is a mixture of Portland cement, water and aggregates (sand mixed with either gravel or crushed stone). Portland cement, which is not a brand name but the generic name for all manufactured cements, is a complex, finely ground material that when mixed with water undergoes a chemical reaction, becoming a kind of glue or paste that binds the aggregates together. It is these latter particles that give concrete its strength, durability and hardness. As the water evaporates slowly, the mix begins to harden. Then follows the process of "curing," during which time (at least three days) the new concrete is kept wet to prevent its drying out too fast. Curing, which will be discussed later in this chapter, must be done with particular care, as the final strength of the concrete can be increased as much as 50 percent if this process is done properly.

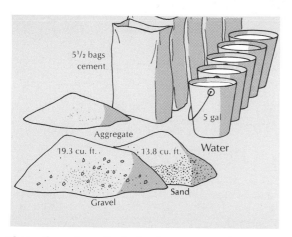

These three ingredients *in the amounts shown are enough to make 100 sq. ft. of concrete 3" thick.*

Choosing the Right Mix

The chart below gives the formula for a 6-gallon "paste," a good, all-purpose mix. The term "6-gallon" is derived from the ap-

Proper Ratios for Concrete Mixes

The less water used in the mix the stronger it will be. The mixture in the trade is called a "paste." A "5-gallon paste" makes a very hard dense concrete. A 7-gallon paste is used for footing and foundations not subjected to wear, weather or water. The "standard" mix today is a 6-gallon paste. It makes a watertight bond and wears well. Note how the moisture in the sand affects the amount of water used.

To Mix a 6-Gallon Paste					
Cement	Aggregate		Water in Gallons		
	Sand	Coarse to 1½"	If Sand is Damp	Wet Sand (Average)	Very Wet Sand
1 sack, 80 lbs.	2½ cu. ft.	3½ cu. ft.	5½	5	4½

proximate amount of water used in the mix. This amount is governed, as the chart shows, by the wetness of the sand. To determine the degree of wetness, squeeze some sand in your hand. Damp sand does not form a ball but falls apart. Wet sand forms a ball, and very wet sand forms a ball with sand sticking to your hand, leaving it moist and muddy.

Concrete for Cold Climates

In climates where concrete will be subject to considerable freezing and thawing, it is best to use Type 1-A Portland cement. This contains a chemical called an air-entraining agent. As the concrete hardens, the agent forms billions of microscopic bubbles which act as cushions against stresses resulting from the freeze-thaw cycle. This action helps to prevent "scaling," often a problem when sodium chloride is used on pavements to melt ice or snow. In some cases, usually with a lean mix (a 5-gallon paste), the air-entraining agent tends to strengthen the concrete. In a rich mix (a 7-gallon paste) air-entrained concrete is not as strong as plain.

Reinforcement

In climates where the ground freezes solid, concrete needs reinforcement. After two winters, a driveway reinforced with wire mesh looks as sound as the day it was cured. One that is not reinforced will be badly cracked and chipped after the same time. Concrete is very strong in compression, but weak under longitudinal stresses. That is why buckling or heaving caused by winter frost or heavy stress from above (as an oil delivery truck on the drive) can crack unreinforced concrete. If wire-mesh reinforcing is needed for your project, buy 6-inch-square meshing (6/6 gauge) for driveways and steps. Lighter gauges, as 8/8 or 10/10, are suitable for a patio or walk. Sandwich the mesh in the slab.

Three Ways to Buy Concrete

Concrete may be purchased in bulk, as ready-mix or as transit-mix, each of which has certain advantages.

Bulk: This means buying cement and aggregate separately. Usually, Portland cement is sold in 80-pound sacks. Many dealers sell concrete aggregate already mixed. Otherwise you must buy stone and sand separately. One advantage in buying concrete in the bulk is that you can mix exactly the amount you need. But it is often inconvenient to do this and you may find that it costs less to buy transit-mix.

Ready-mix: For small jobs, such as casting stepping stones or molding a birdbath, ready-mix concrete is ideal. Cement, sand

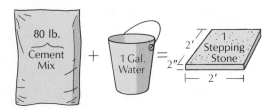

A standard bag of ready-mix (cement and sand-and-gravel aggregate) will make one steppingstone, as shown.

and aggregate are premixed by the manufacturer. You simply add water and stir. In addition, ready-mix is sold in small bags, as light as 25 pounds, enough to make a downspout splashblock, for example. But ready-mix is usually more expensive than either bulk or transit-mix.

Transit-mix: Oddly enough, concrete delivered in a truck is often the least expensive. Usually, however, it is not sold in quantities of less than a yard (one cubic yard) which is enough to make a patio 9 feet square and 4 inches thick. One advantage of transit-mix is that you can get the best formulation (the "paste") for the project at hand. But there must be a firm road or driveway so the truck can get to the job, and everything must be ready for the pour. The ground must be leveled, gravel or sand in place for drainage if needed, and forms ready and braced.

How to Estimate the Amount

A yard of concrete is the amount that will fill one cubic yard of space. In practice, it fills slightly less, since some of the wet concrete settles into earth or gravel crevices. Simple arithmetic will give you the amount to order from the transit-mix company. Here is the formula: width (in feet) x length (in feet) x thickness (in feet, *not* inches), divided by 27. For example, a patio 10 by 14 feet and 4 inches thick equals 1.73 cubic yards (10 x 14 x ⅓ divided by 27). In this case, you ought to order 2 yards. It is inconvenient and can be expensive to run short of concrete a foot from the end of your forms. The chart below tells you how to estimate ingredients when you buy in bulk.

Materials Required	Thickness of Concrete	Amount in Cubic Yards	Sacks of Cement	Aggregate	
				Fine Cu. Ft.	Coarse Cu. Ft.
The following amounts are required for 100 square feet of concrete (an area 10' x 10') of various thicknesses using the "6-gallon paste." This mixture requires 1 sack of concrete, 2½ cu. ft. of fine aggregate and 3½ cu. ft. of coarse aggregate.	3"	.92	5.5	13.8	19.3
	4"	1.24	7.4	18.6	26.0
	5"	1.56	9.4	23.4	32.8
	6"	1.85	11.1	27.8	38.9
	8"	2.46	14.8	36.9	51.7
	10"	3.08	18.5	46.2	64.7

How to Mix, Form and Finish

First, use only potable water and clean aggregates. If you need a yard or more of concrete, it will save time and energy to rent a power-driven mixer like the one on the opposite page. For smaller jobs, a steel wheelbarrow is good for mixing because you can wheel the wet concrete directly to the job. Otherwise, spread ingredients out on a wood or concrete platform. Mix the sand and aggregates first, making sure you measure accurately. Add some of the water so as to form a pool, and fold in the dry materials, as shown below, right. Repeat this until you have used up all of the water. The mix is about right when you can slice it with a spade and make ridges that don't collapse.

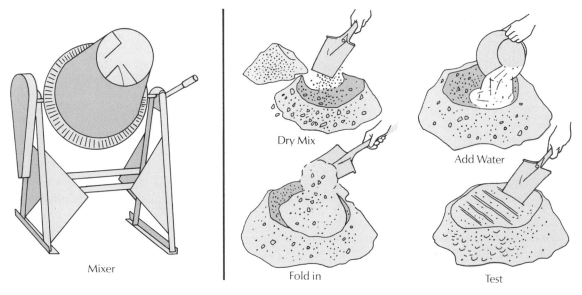

Mixer

Dry Mix

Add Water

Fold in

Test

To mix concrete *by power-driven mixer, turn for about three minutes. In working by hand, first thoroughly mix all dry ingredients, make a hollow in the pile, add water slowly, mix well until ridges made with a shovel stand alone.*

Preparing the Base

Before pouring a concrete slab of any kind, remove all sod, twigs and debris. If the soil drains well, you probably need only

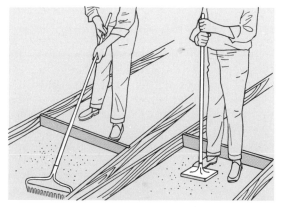

The base *for concrete paving must be well drained, raked smooth and clean and tamped down flat and firm.*

tamp it, put up your forms and pour. But if the soil drains poorly, you must remove 2 to 6 inches of earth, fill the space with gravel or sand and tamp it. How much soil to remove depends on the drainage.

Casting a Slab in Place

Wet concrete is heavy and spreads when poured. Build strong, firm forms. It is very messy and almost impossible to shore up weak forms filled with wet concrete.

A Simple Form

For a simple slab, use 2-x-4 lumber and nail at the corners with two-headed nails (easier to remove later). Brace the edges every few feet with wood stakes driven at least half their length into the soil, and well below the top of the form to make screeding easier. If you use wood forms and

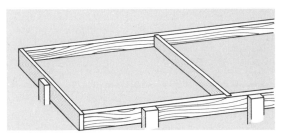

Fasten corner *with double-headed form nails. Paint the inside of forms with light engine oil before the pour.*

319

intend to leave them as a part of the design of the slab, protect the top edge of the boards with masking tape during the pour.

A Curved Form

To lay out a curve, drive three or more 1-x-2-inch stakes as shown below to make the desired curve. Cut two strips of ¼-inch plywood or hardboard and bend between the

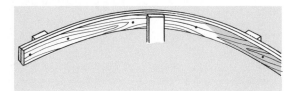

If curve is gentle, *the form will be less rigid. For added strength use three strips and some extra stakes.*

stakes. Nail through the strips at several points along the curve and into the stakes opposite the side on which concrete will be poured. Then move stakes on "concrete side" to outside before pouring. Coat inside of forms with a light motor oil. This makes it easier to pry them away from concrete.

Lap Joint for a Multiple Form

Here is an easy way to fit together wood dividers for a patio or walk. Use redwood, cypress or wood pressure-treated with preservative. Grid is attractive and takes up contraction and expansion that may occur.

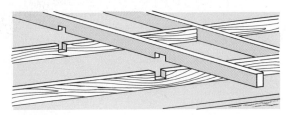

Crosspieces *are held securely in place by nailing into the ends through the piece at the outside edge.*

Expansion Joints

When concrete is laid to adjoin an existing masonry structure, such as a house, public sidewalk, steps or the like, an expansion strip between the old and new work is required. A resilient asphalt-impregnated, fibrous material is used. It allows for expansion from heat and prevents cracking. In a concrete walk or driveway, a contraction joint should be struck at intervals of 10 feet. This is simply a ³⁄₁₆- or ¼-inch gap or crack cut with a steel blade across the wet concrete. Its purpose is to allow for expansion or contraction due to temperature changes.

Establishing a Slope for Drainage

Rain water collects on a dead-level slab of concrete. In cold climates it freezes and cracks the surface. In any climate the puddles are a nuisance. To avoid such problems on a patio, for example, slope the surfaces about ¼ inch to the foot. This will establish good drainage. Walks and driveways should slope the same amount, but from the center outward to the edges. To set forms, use a board and a level.

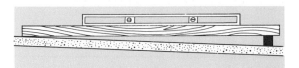

A leveling block, *about one inch high, under the 4-foot board makes the required slope of 1/4 inch per foot.*

Pouring and Leveling

It's a good idea to have some help for these operations and, even so, don't expect to handle more than three yards at one time. Therefore, order accordingly. Before pouring, wet down the tamped bed. This improves

In screeding, *advance board about an inch per stroke. Excess concrete fills low spots; remainder is removed.*

curing. Pour when there is no chance of rain, and ideally at a temperature of 70° F. Dump the new concrete into the form. Spread it around evenly with a shovel, to fill corners and edges. Then, using the tops of the forms as a guide, level the concrete by using a 2-x-4 or 2-x-6 across the surface. Move the board in a sawing motion. This is called *screeding* and must be done as soon as possible after pouring and spreading.

How to Finish Concrete

Now that the heaviest work is done, everything from this point on is easier and more satisfying. In fact, for rough work, such as piers, nothing is required beyond the screeding. Otherwise, floating is next.

Floating

Floating is done with a flat wood trowel when surface water vanishes. Purpose is to bring fine particles to top. Work trowel in sweeping arcs, with the leading edge a

Choice of trowel *determines surface. Metal, at left, makes it smooth. Wood, at right, is for rougher finish.*

fraction above the surface. For *very* smooth concrete, wait until the mix begins to stiffen and all surface water is gone, then do it again, using a steel trowel. Use only a steel trowel for air-entrained concrete.

Brushed Finish

After you have completed the floating operation, if you pull a soft-bristled push broom across the concrete, you can produce a subtle, attractive texture that cuts down considerably on sun glare and makes for safer footing for wet weather. A stiff-bristled brush gives pronounced texture.

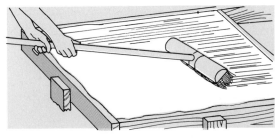

In creating texture with a broom, *tiny balls may form as you are working. If so, let the surface harden more.*

Exposed Aggregate

This is a good-looking finish and not hard to do. For the aggregate in the mix, use gravel that is relatively smooth and uniform

The trick *in exposing aggregate is to remove the surface film of concrete without displacing the stones on top.*

in size. Pour and float concrete in the usual way. When it begins to firm up, gently hose and brush away the surface, exposing stones. Since timing is all-important (stones must hold fast as the surface film is washed away), try a small test area first.

Pebble Mosaic

This makes an attractive surface and offers great flexibility in design. Mix and pour concrete in the usual way. After screed-

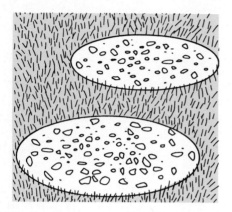

Pebbled concrete *can have a random pattern as shown, or the pebbles of uniform size can be set in patterns.*

ing, spread pebbles, chosen for color and size, over the wet concrete. Press them below the surface with the flat side of a board. Use a wood trowel to smooth the concrete over the pebbles. When top is firm, but not set, carefully brush and hose away the surface to reveal the pattern of pebbles.

Patterns in Concrete

Drawing designs in fresh concrete is one of those urges few people seem able to resist. But resist it you should unless you are

Leaf patterns *are always attractive. Trowel smooth, embed leaves in concrete and remove when concrete has set.*

talented artistically and are quite convinced you can live happily with the results. If you'd like to try, however, here are a few hints: Keep designs simple and preferably abstract. Square cookie tins, when pressed into the concrete, form interesting overlapping grids, and the edges of cans of different sizes can make attractive patterns of random circles. Avoid line drawings. Few of us can create designs, as does an artist, that will continue to hold our interest over the years. Keep in mind that paintings in the house can be removed from the wall, but it takes a jackhammer or a new surface to obliterate concrete drawings and designs.

Adding Color to Concrete

Add pigment during the mixing operation. Use only mineral oxide pigment specifically prepared for concrete. Normally, add 7 pounds of pigment for each 80-pound sack of cement. Or experiment to get the shade you prefer. Use white cement for bright colors; standard gray for darker colors.

Making Precast Blocks

Using the standard, 6-gallon paste, you can cast small items like steppingstones at your leisure (during winter months in your garage or basement, for example) and have them ready for later use. Be sure to build the forms sturdily with an eye to their easy, nondestructive removal after the concrete has set. This can be done with screws at the corners, or hinges, or protruding nails —all of which allow for easy dismantling of the forms. Also, as long as you have time, let the concrete cure fully.

Multiple Form

Using a multiple form, you can pour many blocks or steppingstones at once to save time and effort. Molds are usually made of wood and designed to be easily removed from the hardened concrete and then reconstructed for future use. To further facilitate removal of any kind of wooden form, coat the inside surface with engine oil just before the concrete is poured. The smoother the surface the less chance of sticking.

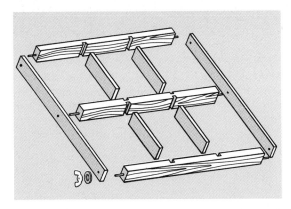

This multiple form is designed so that it can be easily detached from the hardened concrete by removing the six wing nuts. It is then reassembled for new pour.

Individual Forms

Unusual shapes call for special forms that can be made or bought. Circular or curved forms are sometimes made from existing containers or as shown below. In some places metal forms (usually made of aluminum) are available for casting anything from lawn deer to elaborate birdbaths.

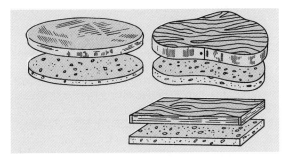

Forms can be made for paving stones, tiles or foundation blocks. Fill, screed and invert to remove when hard.

Curing Concrete

High-quality concrete depends first on a good mix and (only slightly less important) on proper curing, a process which if done correctly can increase the strength of your concrete by as much as 50 percent. The secret is to keep water in the slab, because water is the agent that helps harden concrete. Here is the technique: after you are satisfied with the surface, spray the fresh concrete with water and cover it with polyethylene film. Weight or stake down the film so it doesn't blow away. Leave it for an absolute minimum of three to six days; fourteen days is better, twenty-eight days best.

Casting a Wall in Place

In casting a wall, first build a vertical form strong enough to resist the spread of wet concrete. Plywood, at least ½ or ¾ inch thick, is good for this work because it is not only strong but produces a smooth surface

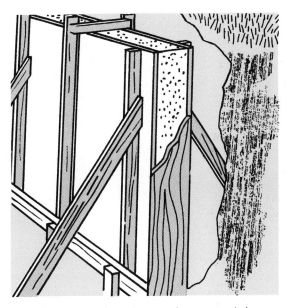

Brace forms to withstand outward pressure of the vertical pour. Leave in place until curing is finished.

on the side of the wall. To keep the sides from bulging, support the outside with 2-x-4s braced on the diagonal and united at the top. Oil the inside of the form before pouring. Do not pour entire wall at once, but rather in layers about 12 to 18 inches deep, tamping down one layer before pouring the next on top of it. Float top of wall with trowel as if it were a slab.

Pouring Concrete in Cold Weather

Leave this to the professionals. They can pour concrete in below-freezing weather by relying upon special chemical additives in the concrete and plenty of experience. You will get best results by pouring when the temperature is about 70° F, and steady.

323

20

Working With Brick

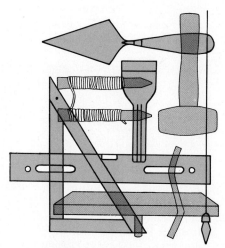

Tools of the trade. *Top, left to right: trowel, hammer, chalk line, chisel, level, right angle, mortar board, pointing tool, plumb bob.*

Brick, in use for at least ninety centuries, has by now proven its value, and for good reasons. Tough, hard-burned brick is highly resistant to weathering. Hot sun, icy winds, sleet and rain have little effect on its surface. And its rich, earthy colors are, for most people, very attractive. Finally, brick is quite simple to produce, which fact keeps the cost relatively low for such a durable and popular building product.

Basic Sizes and Kinds

When you pick up and precisely match two building bricks, you may notice some small dimensional differences. This is normal; it happens during the firing process. But better manufacturing methods, especially the use of sophisticated, electronically controlled kilns, have reduced the differences considerably. In 1946, sizes varied as much as ¾ inch; now they rarely vary more than $\frac{1}{32}$ of an inch, a gap easily made up by using a little bit more or less of mortar.

Listed below are the most popular styles of brick for outdoor projects. They represent perhaps half the sizes and styles available. Those not listed are seldom needed or used in building the comparatively simple structures shown on the following pages.

Building Brick

This brick, also called "standard" brick, is 2¼ inches high, 3¾ inches wide and 8 inches long. Its color is

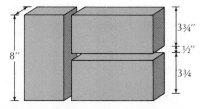

The width *of two bricks is somewhat less than the length of one.*

a pinkish red or sometimes buff. In harsh winter climates, use SW (severe weathering) grade. MW (moderate weathering) is good for warm winter zones or indoors, as a floor or inside wall. Do not use NW (no weathering) grade for any outdoor projects.

Face Brick

Face brick, meant for outdoor exposure, is tougher, more uniform in size and more expensive than building brick. Its sand-finished, handsomely glazed face comes in many colors and it is ideal for garden walks, fences, swimming pools and barbecues. It is usually the same size as building brick.

Used Brick

Used brick is most often new brick made to look old. Sometimes called "antique brick," it is popular, attractive and usually the same size as building brick. Old salvaged brick, especially if pink or salmon-colored, is generally too soft for outdoor work.

Fire Brick

Fire brick, made of high heat-resistant clays pressed to great density, can withstand direct flames, even in a steel mill blast furnace. These bricks are made to use as a firebox wall or floor, in a fireplace or barbecue pit. Their relatively smooth surface is a medium red or buff and the size is $2\frac{1}{2}$ x $4\frac{1}{2}$ x 9 inches.

Roman Brick

To emphasize horizontal lines in a structure, architects often use Roman brick, which is thinner ($1\frac{1}{2}$ inches) and longer (12 inches) than building brick, but has the same width. It has the structural qualities of face brick but the choice of colors and textures is sometimes limited. Many yards stock Norman brick, also 12 inches long but thicker ($2\frac{3}{4}$ inches) than Roman brick.

Split Brick

Split brick, really a paver, is used for patios, walks and flooring. The word "split" refers to its height, often $1\frac{1}{2}$ inches, which is noticeably thinner than building or face brick, which is usually $2\frac{1}{4}$ inches high. Unlike most bricks, which have three large or ten small holes running through the center, split brick is a solid unit.

Paving Brick or Pavers

Pavers are also solid bricks made to use underfoot, as for walks, driveways and flooring. They are made in many sizes and shapes. For example, in rectangles that are 4 x 8, 4 x 9 and 4 x 12; also in 6- or 8-inch squares; in a hexagon that is $7\frac{1}{4}$ inches tip to tip; often they come shaped as shields or Spanish tiles. Thicknesses range from $1\frac{5}{8}$ to about 2 inches, and colors go from light rose to reddish brown.

Laying Brick

On the Ground

Where soil drains well and winters are mild, you can probably lay brick directly on the ground. Strip away sod, level the area and tamp down soil. If leveling is a chore, fill in with an inch or so of sand, then put down the bricks, laying them as closely together as possible.

On Sand

First strip the sod, remove stones and roots, then level soil. If ground drains well, spread 1 to $1\frac{1}{2}$ inches of sand over the soil. Over slow-draining soil, 1 to 2 inches of crushed stone, followed by 2 inches of sand. For bad drainage, add more stone. Smooth out sand, lay bricks tightly together, sweep more sand into the joints to fill in between the bricks.

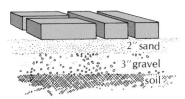

Recommended amounts of sand and gravel to use for the base.

With Dry Mortar

Lay brick in a two-inch bed of sand, leaving a $\frac{3}{8}$- to $\frac{1}{2}$-inch joint between bricks. Mix one part Portland cement to $\frac{1}{4}$ part lime to three parts dry sand. Fill joints with this mixture, tamping it down with a thin board. Turn nozzle of garden hose to the finest spray and open hose bib to a trickle.

Dampen entire brick surface, cleaning loose mortar from the bricks as you spray. To cure properly, spray surface intermittently for the next three days. For a firmer base, substitute for the sand bed a 1 to ½ to 4½ mixture of dry cement, lime and sand.

In Mortar

Over clean, tamped and well-drained soil, pour a concrete slab (see page 319 for details). Cure slab, then mix mortar paste in a ratio of one cement, ¼ lime and

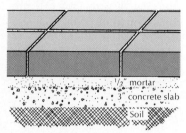

Relative depth of mortar and gravel as a base for a terrace or walkway. Any less would be too little.

three sand. Add water until paste is plastic, not stiff or sloppy. Begin at one corner. Spread ½-inch mortar bed over slab, enough to lay four or five bricks. Wet the bricks. "Butter" inside edges of corner brick to make a mortar joint of about ⅜ inch with next two bricks. Slope surface about ⅙ inch per foot (see page 320). Cure the project as described under "With Dry Mortar."

Brick over Asphalt Paving or Old Concrete

If an extra 2½ to 4 inches of paving will look and function well, brick can be laid (not too successfully) over asphalt paving or (more successfully) over old concrete. **Over blacktop or macadam:** Because of oils in the asphalt, brick in mortar, or in dry mortar, over blacktop or macadam eventually will fail. Best method is to spread sand over the old paving, then lay brick with sand in the joints or with dry mortar joints. **Over old concrete:** With a stiff brush, remove all crumbling concrete. Wet entire surface. Mix mortar, then rewet old surface before laying brick in the mortar, as above, or lay brick in sand spread on concrete.

Establishing the Edge

Under the pressure of normal traffic and weather, brick paving will eventually spread at the edges. An edging not only keeps the bricks in place, but helps guide the measurement of a drainage slope. Below are three common methods for building an edge.

Soldier Course

Bricks on end, called a soldier course, provide a firm border for a walk or patio. To edge brick paving laid in sand, set bricks in a trench with edges butting. All the joints between the bricks are then filled with sand or dry mortar. A

The bricks on end, set in the ground, are "soldiers" to hold edge.

soldier course set in mortar or concrete is even more stable and is required when paving is in mortar or if winters are cold.

Wood and Brick

The combination of wood and brick is attractive and more than sturdy enough to hold brick paving in place. Select 2 x 4 boards and set them on edge in a trench

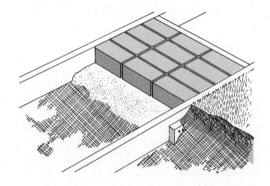

Outside edge made of 2-x-4s can be held in place with stake driven as shown here.

around paving laid in sand; if the paving is laid in concrete, the edging must be set in mortar. Wood ought to be of a durable species, as heartwood of redwood or bald cypress, or lumber that has been pressure-treated with a preservative.

Steel Edging

Flat steel edging can be used as an inconspicuous edge for brick paving. It is made in ¼ x 5 inch or ³⁄₁₆ x 4 inch strips, both of which come in various lengths and are usually painted green.

You can also use a galvanized steel edging that is corrugated. If you do, fill the curved spaces facing the brick with the same material, sand or mortar, as was used in the paving bed. Corrugated sheet metal is easy to install, but brick or durable wood edging lasts longer and most people would agree that it looks better.

Paving Patterns

In building brick walks or terraces, there are hundreds of patterns you can use. The easiest to lay, of course, are the patterns that require no cutting of bricks to fit the space. Paving bricks (4 x 8 inches) work particularly well in such patterns. The fact that, when flat, the width of two bricks equals the length of one brick allows for the use of a variety of patterns, all of which can be laid successfully in a bed of sand with more sand worked into the cracks between the bricks. For firmness, decorative patterns using standard building bricks (3¾ x 8 inches) are best laid in mortar because of the irregular spacing created by the 3¾-

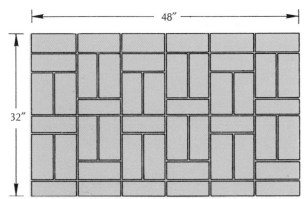

Here's a pattern for a walkway that requires no cuttting of brick. Edges could also be soldier courses.

inch width. Any bricks, however, can be set tightly together with even spacing if a running (lengthwise) bond is used instead of designs that have bricks laid both length-

wise and crosswise adjacent to one another.

A good way to build a brick terrace is to divide the area into a grid of 2-x-4s set on edge. To do this, put down long 2-x-4s running the length of the terrace. Space them four feet apart, then cut four-foot crosspieces of 2-x-4s and nail them between the long pieces at intervals of four feet. This provides the basic four-foot square module inside of which 4 x 8 bricks will fit end to end or side by side or in any combination of the two—without cutting. The grid keeps the bricks firmly in place, even when laid on a bed of sand.

How to Cut a Brick

With the chisel-pointed edge of a brick hammer, tap out a line along the circumference of the cut you want to make. Then hit the center of this line with one sharp blow.

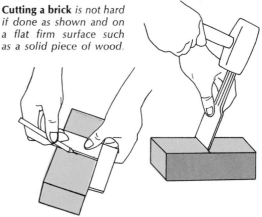

Cutting a brick is not hard if done as shown and on a flat firm surface such as a solid piece of wood.

The brick should split along the line. Clean rough spots with the curved blade on the back end of the hammer. Or cut the brick with a set or brick chisel, as shown above. Practice first, however, on scrap brick.

Laying Up a Brick Wall

Although building a brick wall is not too difficult, especially for those with some experience in setting pavers in mortar, it is not as easy as it looks and is not recommended for beginners. Even for the seasoned amateur, projects like large retaining walls, or garden walls six feet high, are best left to professionals. However, low garden walls, bench piers, tree wells and outdoor fireplaces are good beginning projects. First, however, some definitions of terms.

Headers, Stretchers and Bats

A header is the name given a brick laid so that its long side is at right angles to the outer surface or "face" of the wall. Stretchers are those bricks laid so the long side of the brick is parallel to the face of the wall. A bat refers to a brick that has been cut to fit into a gap that is smaller in size than a whole brick. A bat is also called a closure. The terms are standard with all who use and sell brick.

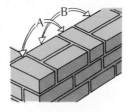

"Headers" (A) are set crosswise. "Stretchers" (B) are set the long way.

Start with a Firm Foundation

All garden walls need to be built on a firm foundation made of concrete or of brick and mortar. Without it, a brick wall only five courses high will settle unevenly and probably crack during the winter freeze-thaw cycle. Such a foundation should be half again as wide at the base as the brick wall and should rest below the frost line.

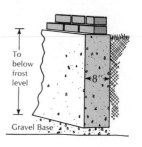

How to Order Brick

Here are some estimates of how many bricks to order if you wish to cover an area measuring 100 square feet, with an allowance of about five percent for waste. If you are using standard building bricks with a ½-inch mortar joint between each brick, order 473. Laying building bricks in sand, with joints butted, order 525. If you are using 4 x 8 paving bricks in sand, order 500, but if paving bricks are in mortar, order 450.

Patterns in Bond

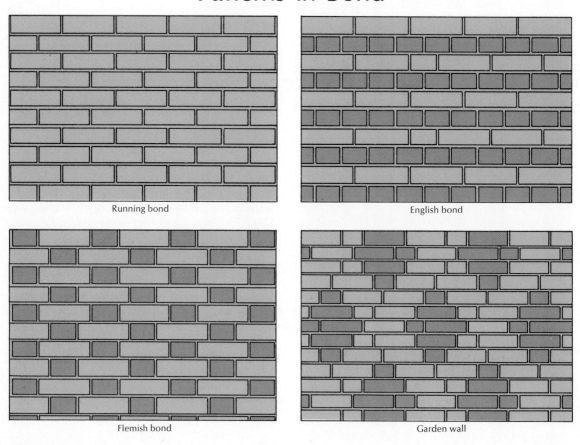

Running bond

English bond

Flemish bond

Garden wall

How to Build a Brick Wall

After choosing the bond for your garden wall, lay up several brick courses dry, to become familiar with the way the bond works. Thoroughly wet the brick while it is in the pile, but allow surface to dry before laying. Dry brick soaks up too much water from mortar, making a poor bond. Recommended mortar mix for a brick wall is one part Portland cement, ½ part hydrated lime, and 4½ parts clean, sharp, screened sand.

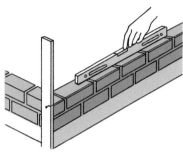

Establish *a level foundation. Drive stakes at ends and make them vertical in both directions. Draw taut level line to mark the first course.*

Cut away *a chunk of mortar from the basic mixture with the trowel and work it on the board into a long, fat, cigar-shaped mound.*

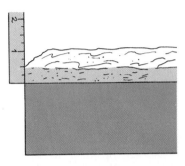

Make mortar bed *3/4 to 1 inch thick and as wide as the brick. Form a shallow furrow in the bed with the tip of the trowel as shown here.*

Trowel up *a portion of the mortar intact. Lay a bed no longer than four bricks in length. Distribute it evenly about a half inch thick.*

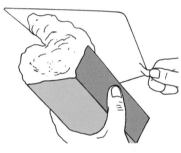

Butter inside *end of the first brick with mortar; press it against the adjacent brick to make a 1/2-inch joint. Fill the joints completely.*

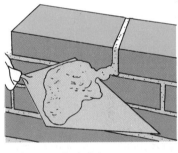

With a 1/2-inch joint, *some mortar will squeeze out between the bricks. Trim off the excess. Check for plumb and for level.*

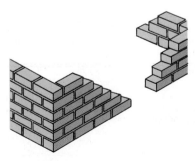

By building up *the corners first, you can use them as a guide to lay the bricks between and keep them level and aligned. Use string for guide.*

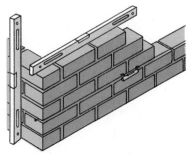

Continue to check *for both plumb and level as you build wall. Move line up to mark each course. Use a nail in the mortar to hold line.*

Before mortar hardens, *rake the joints with a pointing tool. The shape of a "V" or an arc is best. This makes an attractive shadow line.*

21

Working With Concrete Block

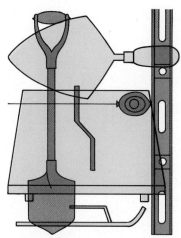

Tools, *from top, left to right: mason's trowel, level, chalk line, shovel, jointing tool, mortar board, horizontal jointing tool.*

In recent years, concrete block, always a strong, durable if somewhat drab building material, has become a glamorous product used in scores of decorative projects. It now comes in many colors, sizes and styles with a wide selection of textured surfaces resembling everything from rough stone to glazed tile. Still comparatively low in cost, block is fast becoming one of the most versatile materials to use for outdoor construction.

Basic Types and Sizes

The basic types, sizes and styles of concrete block are defined and illustrated below. Other varieties are also available since many yards make their own particular designs. Sizes (in inches) are usually rounded off: a $7\frac{5}{8}$ x $7\frac{5}{8}$ x $15\frac{5}{8}$ is called 8 x 8 x 16.

Standard

Heavyweight block is made with sand and gravel or crushed stone. Lightweight block is formed of aggregates such as shale or expanded slag. If its appearance suits the needs of the project, lightweight block is structurally sound for outdoor work. Basic

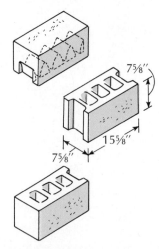

units (left) are the solid top or capping block (top); stretcher (middle); and a corner block (at bottom). Also available are the double corner, rounded corner, and jamb blocks which have a notch in one corner to accommodate framing for doors or windows.

330

Textured

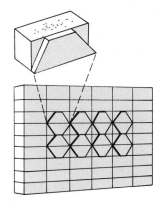

Textured concrete block is made with a three-dimensional bas-relief design on its surface, as the truncated triangle at left. There are hundreds of these designs which can be used alone or with plain block to make handsome patterned dividers. Size is 8 x 8 x 16.

Truncated triangle *forms at least 24 different designs.*

Screen Block

Screen blocks are made in a variety of openwork patterns that form interesting geometric designs when used alone or in combination with solid block. Most screen block is non-loadbearing and the common size is 4 x 12 x 12 but others are available.

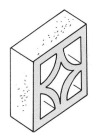

This handy pattern *is only one of hundreds that can be made into lacy walls giving privacy and ventilation.*

Split Block

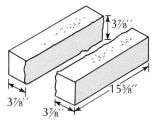

In a wall, *split block is hard to detect from real stone.*

A solid block (4 x 8 x 16) is split lengthwise, making two 4 x 4 x 16 split blocks with surfaces that resemble rough stone. These blocks, often sold in color, make fine walls.

Slump Block

Removed early from its form, a slump block sags slightly and bulges irregularly on its face, thereby resembling an adobe brick. Height averages 4 inches, width about 8 inches and length from 16 to 24 inches.

Patio Block

The patio block comes in a wide range of sizes. The most common are a solid 2 x 8 x 16, and a hollow-core 4 x 8 x 16. Shapes, such as circles and diamonds, are also available.

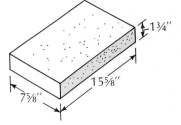

Patio block *comes either in neutral or in pastel shades.*

Laying Patio Block

Because patio block is rectangular, it can be laid in patterns similar to those used for brick. See pages 327 and 328.

In Sand

Border the patio with a row of blocks set on edge, or use an edging of decay-resistant wood. Remove topsoil and add two inches of sand, but if soil drains poorly, dig deeper and lay two to four inches of gravel covered with two inches of sand. Place blocks in sand, butting the joints. Then brush loose sand into cracks and hose down surface. See also "Laying Brick on Sand," page 325.

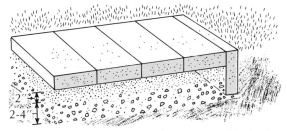

To keep weeds from growing *between the blocks, lay down a sheet of polyethylene on top layer of sand.*

In Mortar

For permanence and solidity, lay block in mortar. Begin with a three-inch concrete slab made with a 1/2½/3½ mix (see page 319). When slab cures, mix one part masonry cement to three parts sand. Add water until it is plastic. Spread a one-inch layer over slab. Butter edges of block with mortar and lay only four or five blocks at a time. Joints are ⅜-inch thick and you should allow a slope of ⅛ inch per foot for drainage on the surface.

Building a Block Wall

If you are unfamiliar with masonry construction, it is best to begin with something small—say, a low garden wall of not more than two or three courses.

Estimating

To estimate the number of blocks (8 x 8 x 16) necessary for your wall, use this formula. (A) Height of wall x $1\frac{1}{2}$ = number of courses. (B) Length of wall x $\frac{3}{4}$ = number of blocks in each course. Thus, A x B = total number of blocks. Buy $2\frac{1}{2}$ sacks of masonry cement and 667 pounds sand per 100 blocks.

Cutting Block

Cutting block is seldom necessary. Ready-made sizes fill nearly all needs. But if a cut is required, either take it back to the yard for cutting, or buy an abrasive blade for your circular saw, or tap along cutting line with a cold chisel and hammer. Concrete block breaks in much the same way as brick.

Construction Steps

Below are six basic steps necessary for building a wall of concrete block.

1. Foundation (below): First, lay a base of 2 to 4 inches of crushed stone. On this, pour a base of concrete 16 inches wide and 8 inches deep. If frost is a problem, make foundation at least 18 inches deep and use reinforcing rod as shown. To build up the foundation to ground level, use either concrete block or more poured concrete.

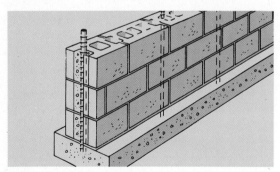

2. First Course: Establish position of corner block. Note that the second course corner block overlaps first, to permit staggered joints. When your wall ends at a corner, use only half-size blocks on every other course

so that joints can be staggered. Accuracy here is of first importance.

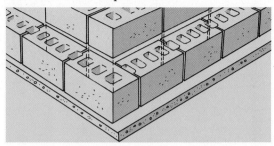

3. Mortar Bed: Once position of corner block is marked, lay a solid bed of mortar, furrowed down the center so that mortar will spread toward the edges of each block. Lay a bed of mortar for only four or five blocks at a time. Then repeat the process.

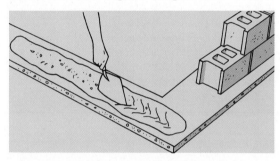

4. Setting Block: First, do *not* soak or wet the blocks. Unlike brick, block should be laid dry into the mortar. Begin by pressing in corner block. Then butter vertical face shells of next block. Work block into the bed and against corner block. Allow a $\frac{3}{8}$-inch joint. Trowel away excess mortar.

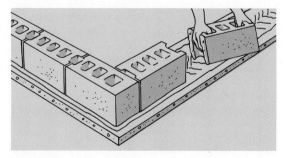

5. Check Level: After laying in the first four or five blocks, check your work with a mason's level—horizontally, then vertically. Make corrections now by tapping block with trowel handle. Any attempt to shift the block's position after mortar begins to stiffen could break the mortar bond.

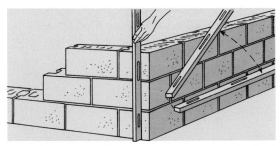

6. Subsequent Courses: Once a neat first course is down, the following courses are less difficult. For example, mortar is needed

on the outer face shells only. Continue to check the level and plumb of the wall. Top off the last course with some form of solid or capping block. While mortar is still slightly malleable, tool the joints. The best two shapes are concave and "V."

Reinforcing Block

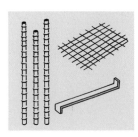

Block walls over four feet high need reinforcing with vertical steel rods, horizontal rods, or a combination. Joint ties may be a part of horizontal reinforcement. Examples: tie footing and wall with ½-inch rods grouted in block cells at four feet on center. Use wire mesh at intersecting non-bearing walls and use tiebars (shown at lower right) for bearing walls.

Painting Block

With a roller or heavy-duty brush, use the water-based vinyl and acrylic paints that are made especially for masonry.

Patterns in Bond

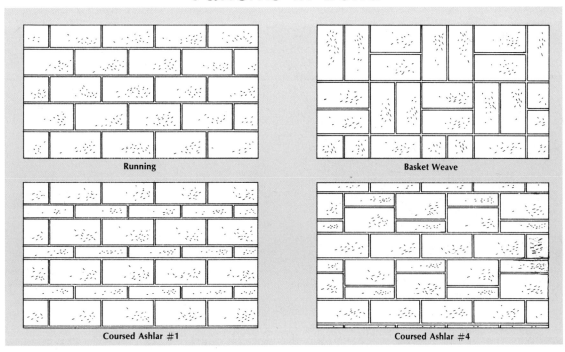

Running

Basket Weave

Coursed Ashlar #1

Coursed Ashlar #4

22

Working With Stone

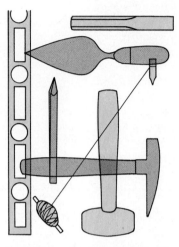

Tools, *from top left to right: Mason's level, cold chisel, trowel, point, club hammer, mason's hammer and a chalk line.*

Earliest man shaped stone for tools, weapons and crude fortifications in Africa. Babylonians built temples and Egyptians built pyramids of amazingly well-cut stone laid without mortar. Then the Romans discovered mortar and raised stonework to the splendid craft it has continued to be throughout history. Stone, which is incredibly rugged and durable, is nevertheless more expensive and somewhat more difficult to handle than either brick or concrete.

Kinds of Stone

The following terms do not describe specific stones (as their names might suggest) but general categories into which many different kinds of stones can be grouped. *Field-stone,* for example, is any undressed, irregularly-shaped, unquarried stone found on or in the ground. *Rubblestone* is the broken residue from a stone-sawing operation. *Flag-*stone is any stone so evenly stratified that it splits into flat pieces suitable for paving. *Cut stone* is stone shaped and made smooth by dressing it with a saw or chisel.

Granite: Very hard and extremely long-lasting, granite is sold in all four categories mentioned above. Ledge rock, in the granite family, is quarried flat. Otherwise, granite comes in many sizes and shapes. Pure granite is gray, but most is mixed with brown, black, white, specks of glassy quartz, pink and occasional iron slivers.

Quartzite: Almost as rugged as granite, quartzite is usually mixed with other minerals. Thus its light gray color and glittering surface of glasslike fragments is toned down with brown and black. Used judiciously, in a garden pool for example, this sun-reflecting stone is handsome.

Limestone: Although only half as hard as granite, limestone is more than strong enough for landscape work. (The weakest strain sustains 60 tons per square foot.) Like sandstone, limestone is porous, which means it absorbs water and is good to use in rock gardens. It is usually machine-sawn and easily shaped. Most limestone ranges from a dark gray to a grayish white.

Sandstone. Similar to limestone in strength, sandstone is made up of a sandy material consisting usually of quartz held together by a natural cement, as silica or iron oxide. Its color varies from buff, tan or brown to yellow, gray and white.

Slate. Excellent for paving, patios and steps, slate (always laid flat, not on edge) is also good for garden walls. It is found primarily in parts of Eastern Canada and British Columbia. The common shades are gray and black, but it also comes in dark reds, blues (some nearly iridescent), greens and mottled combinations of these colors.

How to Cut Stone

If you are totally inexperienced, perhaps it is best not to cut stone but to fit it instead. Match stone to stone in a patio or wall and the resulting irregular pattern will have its own beauty. Or, if some stones must be cut, pay the supplier to do it. It is fun, however, to learn to use stonecutting tools by practicing on scrap. You can split stone with a hammer and cold chisel (see illustration below left), or you can drive a "point"—the sharply pointed tool shown on opposite page

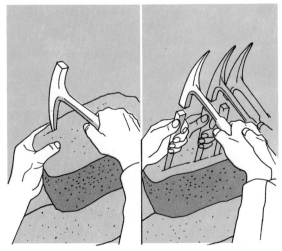

Use cutting edge of mason's hammer to chip off edges. For heavier cuts, use point to scribe line, then break.

—into a natural crevice on the stone's surface and thus split the stone.

Ready-cut stone: Most stone can be bought already cut into various sizes and shapes. Slate is available in flat squares, circles and rectangles, and sandstone and limestone come in blocklike cuts resembling brick. Even granite and quartzite can be sawn to fit a particular pattern or need.

Three Ways to Lay a Stone Patio

First, find or make a level area. Excavate the earth to depth mentioned below, then wet down and tamp the exposed soil.

In sand: Begin by placing an edging of flagstone or one-inch boards (supported by stakes) around the perimeter of the excavation. If the soil drains slowly, make a base of two to three inches of gravel. Fill the area with four to six inches of sand and begin laying stone. Large, heavy stones will stay in place better than smaller ones. Fill the space between the joints with more sand or decorative gravel.

In sand and mortar: Lay flagstones in the

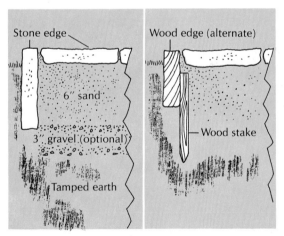

Two ways to edge a stone walk or terrace. Wood, although less expensive, will eventually deteriorate.

sandbed, as described above, leaving ½-inch joints open. Mix one part Portland cement with three parts sand. Sweep this mix into the joints. Using the finest nozzle setting, hose down the joints. Repeat two more times in the next 48 hours.

In mortar and concrete: Excavate earth to

a depth of at least nine inches. Around perimeter of patio, dig a trench the width of a shovel to the depth of frost line. Edge top of the trench with form boards that come to the top of the finished patio. Spread four inches of gravel over excavation, laying 6 x 6"-⅜ reinforcing wire on gravel. Then pour concrete (a mixture of one part cement, two parts sand and four parts gravel), sloping the surface of slab ¼ inch per foot for drainage. (See Chapter 19, "Working with Concrete.")

After pouring, use a rake to pull the reinforcing wire up into the mix so that it rests in the center of the concrete. Leave slab surface rough to make a better bond with grout. Allow to dry for 24 hours. Make a grout mixture of one part cement to three parts sand and enough water to form a ball in the hand. Lay a bed of grout one inch

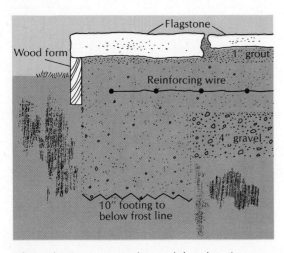

When a footing *is required around the edge of a terrace, it relates to the slab as illustrated here.*

thick and covering only enough space for two or three stones, tamping stone in place and leaving joints open until all stones are laid. After about 12 stones are in place, pick up each stone and pour a concrete "butter" (cement and water mixed to a pea-soup consistency) over the grout and then replace the stone on the butter.

Level stones. When patio is finished and allowed to set overnight, fill in joints with a mix of one part cement to two parts sand and enough water so mix is somewhat wetter than for the concrete base. Pack mixture

tightly into joints with a pointing tool. Sponge away spilled grout from surface.

How to Build Stone Walls

First, some definitions. A *wet wall* is built with mortar, and a *dry wall* without. *Free-standing* walls stand alone and *retaining walls* hold earth in place vertically.

Building a solid wet wall: First, use either flagstones or fieldstones, but flagstones, being flat, stack more easily. Begin with a stone or poured-concrete base built below the frost line, as shown. If you use concrete, make a 1-2-4 mix (the identical mix that was used for the concrete base of the stone patio opposite). Mortar for setting stones should be one part cement to two parts sand and just wet enough to be workable.

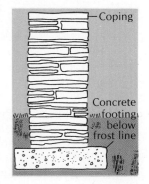

Stone is quite heavy and will squeeze out mortar that is too soupy. When wall is completed, cap it with a solid capping stone that has a tight mortar joint. This cap prevents water from seeping into the wall.

Building a wet veneer wall: Since concrete block is inexpensive, the wall you see below costs somewhat less than a solid stone wall. Yet the mortar and concrete mixes are the same, as are the footings below the frost line and the solid capping. Split stone (cut on five sides, left rough on the exposed side) is well suited to veneering. Small flagstones look well on the vertical, and even granite is cut to use as veneer. To strengthen the wall and lengthen its life, insert metal ties between the interior

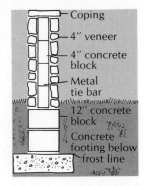

block joints and the veneer joints. Check level frequently as the wall goes up.

Building a Dry Wall

A dry wall is dependent for its stability on two things—the force of gravity and the friction of stones set one upon another.

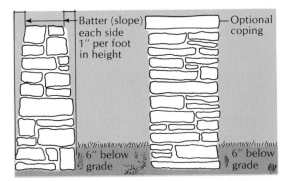

Slope sides *evenly. Use heaviest stones at base. Tilt stone slightly inward.*

A perpendicular wall *must be built with flat, square-edged stones as shown.*

Note in the drawings above that the base stones are the largest, that the wall begins about six inches below grade (not necessary to start below the frost line) and that the fieldstone wall is a slight pyramid having a two-inch setback—called a "batter" by masons—for every two feet of height. The stones are canted slightly inwards so they will lean together and hold firmly in place. Lay all stones flat as you would find them lying naturally on the ground. Don't turn any on end. You can top a dry wall with coping if you want, but it isn't necessary as water will drain out of the crevices.

Building a Retaining Wall

Begin construction just as you would for a freestanding wall, then add these changes. First, build the base below the frost line and begin laying the stones, tilting them slightly toward the earth bank. Batter back a dry retaining wall two to three inches for every foot in height; a wet retaining wall should have a batter of only one to two inches per foot. The top of the wall should be at least 18 inches wide and capped. Install a drain at the back of the wall, as shown. Also install weep holes through the wall, placing them 10 to 12 inches apart, so that water does not back up behind the wall. A non-corrosive pipe, such as tile or copper tubing, is best to use for this through-wall drainage.

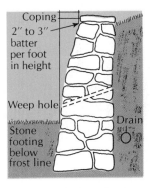

Use weep holes *of tubing to relieve pressure where ground water is a problem.*

Three Different Faces of Stone

A dry wall, *made without mortar, shows off the shape and character of each stone to the best advantage.*

Joints are of mortar *but deeply raked to give the effect of a dry wall and the stability of mortar.*

Mortar wall *with stone. Joints are as obvious as the strength of the wall. Takes less stone than others.*

23
Working With Canvas

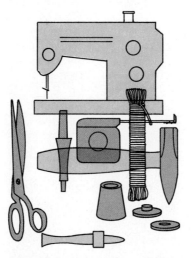

Tools, *from top. Sewing machine, punch, tape measure, lacing cord, hammer, scissors, metal die block, grommet, washer, setting tool.*

Canvas, produced by the Egyptians more than 2000 years ago and now available in handsome colors and modern finishes, is one of the most versatile of all materials in solving unusual shade or shelter problems around the house. The new plastic-treated canvas is strong, durable, flexible and colorfast—in other words, tough enough to meet the most demanding seasonal or year-long requirements. If properly cared for, it will last up to 10 years or longer and can be replaced at a relatively low cost.

Types of Canvas

Most canvas today is still made of cotton, but some contemporary outdoor fabrics are woven of acrylic yarns. Cotton canvas is produced in two ways, as *Army duck* (a heavy-duty material adaptable to any outdoor use) and as *drill* (a lightweight fabric used for sandbox covers or children's furniture).

Usually canvas is ordered by weight per yard, the yard having a standard width of 36 inches. Drill weighs about 7 to 8 ounces per yard and duck about 10 ounces, although a heavier duck is sold that weighs up to 18 ounces. Quality cotton canvas is now treated to resist mildew and repel water. Below are listed five different kinds of colored canvas.

Vat-dyed canvas: This type of canvas is immersed wholly in a dye bath and emerges with a single color. Such a method, used mostly on the lightweight drill, produces a fabric that is not as colorfast as the other four, but it is the least expensive.

Painted canvas: As the name indicates,

338

paint is specially coated onto vat-dyed canvas. These are usually the water-repellent, weather-resistant acrylic paints. Only the topside is painted and striped, although often a stipple print or floral design is applied to the underside. Reasonably durable, painted canvas is usually more costly than vat-dyed canvas.

Yarn-dyed canvas: Before this canvas is woven, the yarns with which it is made are dyed. Yarns of varied color can be blended on the loom to create an infinite number of patterns as colorful and rich on the underside as on the topside.

Vinyl-coated canvas: A thick film of vinyl is permanently fused to the canvas topside, a technique that produces a very durable and colorfast surface. It is also easier to clean and resists soiling better than the materials above. Its finish is bright, and the stability of the vinyl permits a range of colors from pastels to deeper shades, as well as white. This is the most expensive of cotton canvas fabrics.

Acrylic fiber canvas: Not canvas at all, this fabric made of dyed acrylic fibers is, nevertheless, often called canvas by dealers. It is very similar to vinyl-coated canvas although somewhat more durable in areas plagued with noxious air pollution. It is usually the most expensive of all the five fabrics described here because it holds up well and is relatively easy to clean.

Preparing Canvas for Framing

The easiest way, of course, is to have your awnings or patio coverings made professionally. It is cheaper, however, to do your own work and, if you know something about sewing, it is not difficult.

Cutting: You can cut all the fabrics mentioned here. Use a quality pair of fabric shears and mark your cutting lines with chalk which can easily be wiped away.

Hemming and Binding: Canvas, like all fabrics, needs a finished edge. This can be done either by hemming the edge or sewing on an edging tape or binding. Remember when you hem to allow for the loss of an inch on all four sides of the fabric.

Tapes and bindings are somewhat easier to attach, especially at the corners where

bindings butt, whereas hems have to be doubled. Tapes and bindings, in colors or with tassels, are also more decorative.

A home sewing machine can handle just

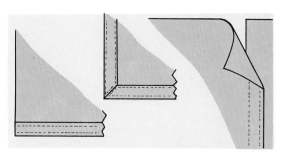

Hem the edges, *using a 45° fold at the corners. Join pieces of canvas with two rows of stitching, as shown.*

about any canvas material up to and including a weight of 10 ounces per yard, although at the corners where the fabric is doubled and then redoubled stitching can be difficult. For heavier fabrics, it is best to have the job done professionally on a commercial machine. In sewing canvas, use your strongest needle and the heaviest Dacron thread your machine will take.

Seaming: Canvas is usually sold in 36-inch widths. If your project calls for a wider section, overlap the fabric by about ¾ inch at the joint and stitch both edges. It is not necessary to hem these edges.

Attaching grommets: Brass grommets (fasteners similar to metal-lined eyelets) relieve the strain on the fabric when canvas is lashed to pipe railing or fastened to wood. You can buy or rent grommet tools at a hardware store or canvas dealer. To attach

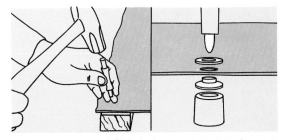

To set grommets, *cut hole in canvas. Set canvas between grommet and washer. Clinch with setting tool.*

grommets, first mark the spots where you want the grommets to go. They should be placed exactly in the center of the hem or binding. Space the grommets according to the demands put on the fabric. For example, a windbreak should have grommets set closely together; for a sunshade, less closely. Always attach a grommet to each corner.

To make the hole, place a block of wood beneath the mark and sharply strike the metal punch. Next, push the tube eyelet through the hole, tube up. Then fit canvas and eyelet over the hole in the metal die block. Place washer over eyelet and drop the narrow point of the setting tool through the eyelet into the hole of the die block below. Strike setting tool sharply with hammer. The washer grommet is now permanently cleated to the canvas.

Fasteners, from left: *Permanent washer and grommet. Spur grommet to use on canvas heavier than 10 ounces per yard. Snap fasteners to use in joining canvas panels that you may want to detach later. Turn fastener has pivoted piece that goes through a hole and turns crosswise to attach canvas to a fixed base.*

Other framing methods: A staple gun is the fastest means of attaching canvas to wood. Or you can use broad-headed tacks. Although quick, these methods are also the

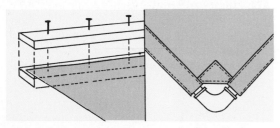

Battens *(left) hold canvas without undue strain. Fold corners (right) to make space for pipe joint.*

least durable. Tacks and staples tend to strain the fibers when the canvas is pulled taut by wind or rainwater. A better solution is to sandwich the canvas between laminated boards, as shown. Still another method is to form sleeves at the edges of canvas to receive pipe framing. This is an excellent way to fit canvas to a metal frame.

Lacing canvas to piping: Lacing canvas to piping with cord is good for seasonal instal-

lation. Use a strong cotton cord, or one of the newer plastic-wrapped cords. Both will weather well. Note especially the lacing detail at the piping corners. No special lacing

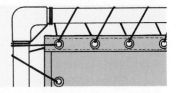

is required at a T-joint in the pipe framing. Depending on the look you want, you can draw the canvas tightly to the piping or you can leave a gap.

The Basic Patio Canopy

To build an attractive, taut canopy over a patio, include these framing elements: a perimeter frame on all four sides of the canopy, supported by posts on centers between six and nine feet, and reinforced by

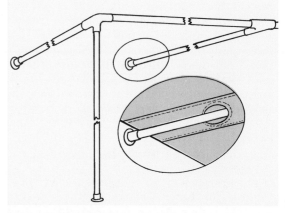

Standard pipe fittings *can be used for the framework. Make the sleeves to fit over the pipe as shown.*

rafters between the outer canopy frame and a framing member at the house eaves. This is true for either wood or metal framing. Fasten canvas to metal rafters as shown. Best canopy pitch for drainage is four inches per foot. Insert grommets for drainage on low pitches.

Maintenance: Hose down canvas periodically and let the sun dry it. If you store canvas in the winter, pack it away dry in a cool and dry place. Repair small rips before they grow larger. Don't let piping get rusty.

24

Working With Plastic

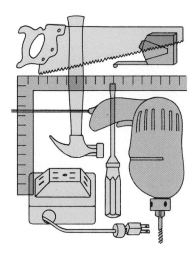

Tools, *from top: Hand saw, hammer, tape measure, framing square, screw driver, electric drill, extension cord (multiple outlet).*

Polyester reinforced with glass fiber is the first and remains the best-known plastic material used outdoors. Produced in rigid or flexible panels, fiberglass (as it is called informally) can be used in many outdoor projects, such as fences, patio covers, awnings, greenhouses, windbreaks, carports and many more. Today's panels come in a wide range of stable colors, resist rot and corrosion and therefore weather well. They are shatterproof and need little more than an occasional hosing to keep them sparkling.

Three Basic Forms

Rigid corrugated: Far and away the most popular style, these panels gain rigidity from the corrugations and are ideally suited to any outdoor project. Panels are produced in lengths of 8, 10 or 12 feet with widths

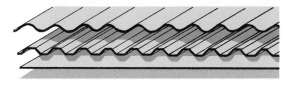

from 26 to 34 inches (and up to 54 inches in some configurations). Typical corrugations are shown at left. Weights run from 4 to 6 ounces per square foot, or, if necessary, up to 8 ounces per square foot.

Flat: Recommended for any vertical use (as fencing, windbreaks, pool enclosures and doors), flat panels are sold in 8, 10 and 12 foot lengths with widths running from 24 to 36 inches and weights from 4 to 6 ounces per square foot. For extra strength, an 8-

ounce panel is also available in the standard lengths and up to 48 inches wide.

Rolled: Corrugated and flat reinforced polyester are both available in flexible rolls for such projects as a curved fence or a barrel roof over an arbor. Corrugated rolls are sold in 50-foot lengths. They are 26, 34 or 40 inches wide and weigh 5 ounces per square foot. Flat rolls are the same, most often 36 inches wide.

Colors and Finishes

Fiberglass panels now come in a wider range of brighter colors than ever, including stripes in bright blues, sharp yellows, oranges and deep grass greens. Remember that sunlight shining through the translucent panels reduces the intensity of the color, making it seem paler outdoors than it is in the dealer's showroom. (On special order, you can buy opaque panels.)

Because the chemistry of plastics has vastly improved, almost no panels today are made only of fiberglass and polyesters. Nearly all are now treated with acrylic, a chemical agent that prolongs the life of the panels up to 15 years or longer and makes the colors more resistant to fading. Also remember that if you are using panels overhead, select colors that transmit less than 35 percent of the sun's heat. The dealer will know what percentage each color transmits.

Building with Plastic Panels

Cutting: It is easiest, of course, to design a project that takes whole panels. But if you must cut, use a fine-tooth, crosscut hand saw or, even better, use one of the new circular abrasive discs fitted to a power saw.

Drilling: Always pre-drill holes before nailing, bolting or screwing panels to a frame. This prevents the appearance of shock marks around the hole. Use a power drill with a bit just a fraction smaller than the diameter of the nail, bolt or screw.

Fastening: Use aluminum-threaded nails and a neoprene (synthetic rubber) washer to fix panels to wood. Aluminum nails won't rust and won't discolor the plastic. The washers prevent leaks through the predrilled holes. If the panels will undergo

strain, as in a windy location, use a larger metal nail (and the washers) or, for the strongest joint, use aluminum, stainless

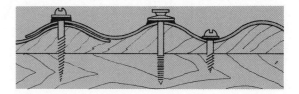

steel or brass screws and the washers. It is important to lap the long panel edges so all edges face down, away from the weather, as shown below. If you must join panels end to

end, overlap them about four to six inches from the joint. Before securing any edge, apply a clear, waterproof sealant along the entire joint, as shown below. Proper sealants are sold by the panel manufacturer. Don't use a substitute. Now take another look at the top drawing in this column. Note the

wood nailing strip beneath the plastic panels. This is redwood and is sold by the manufacturer to match the configuration. When panels are installed on the horizontal or when sloped, fasten through the panel "ridge" to the nailing strip. On vertical applications, fasten through the "valley" as shown at the right in the top illustration. One exception: if you do not install a vertical filler strip on the outside rafter of a patio cover, nail through the valley.

Spans: On any overhead structure, the spacing of the rafters, center to center, should match the panel width, taking into account the overlap as shown in the column at left. When using rigid corrugated panels, the span between the purlins (crosspieces between the rafters) should be 2'6" for 4-ounce panels; 3' for 5-ounce panels; 3'6" for 6-ounce panels and 4' for 8-ounce panels. If you are using panels vertically, follow the same measurements that are specified above.

Flashing: If, in certain places, overhead panels abut the house, you can flash the joint with aluminum or plastic flashing that fits the panel configuration. This makes a

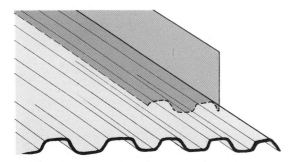

watertight seal between panels and siding. It is better to do this during new construction, but with care, you can work flashing underneath existing house siding.

Ventilation: To maintain a comfortable temperature beneath a panel roof that abuts the house, you must provide for a ventilation system that permits air to circulate but keeps the rain out. The back edge of the

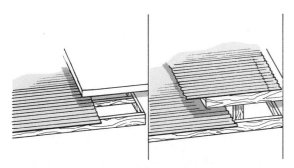

Leave protected space for ventilation as shown under overhang (left) and against a wall (right).

panels should be eight inches away from the house wall and the roof overhang should extend beyond this opening, as at left above. If there is no overhang, a protective cover can be built as at right.

Fundamentals of Building A Plastic Panel Roof

In designing the roof, plan for a pitch of at least one inch to the foot, so the panels will shed rain. If snow loads are heavy, increase the pitch to three inches per foot. Build with 4 x 4 posts that are 6 to 9 feet on center. Attach these posts to an existing patio with angle irons, or if the posts are set over soil, attach them to "U" braces set in concrete footings (as shown below). Top the posts with a 4 x 4 front header posi-

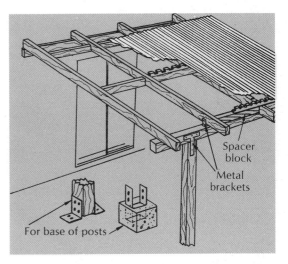

A wooden framework with these basic parts will support a plastic patio cover for a terrace. It is not hard to build. Read the text for sizes of members.

tioned at least 7½ feet from the patio floor. Attach a 2 x 6 back header to house. Use ½ x 5-inch lag screws through non-masonry siding into studs, or use 5-inch expansion bolts into masonry.

Build rafters of 2 x 4 lumber for spans up to 8 feet; 2 x 6 lumber for spans from 8 to 14 feet, and 2 x 8s for spans from 14 to 20 feet. Add cross bracing (purlins) that are the same size as rafters. Then nail configurated wood strips over purlins and half-round moldings down rafters. Finally, apply panels as indicated above, following manufacturer's directions for nailing along strips. Along the rafters, nail at 15-inch intervals. Allow space for ventilation and add flashing where the roof attaches to a wall and a waterproof joint is needed.

How to Use Gravel in the Garden

Gravel, long considered appropriate only for walks and drives, is at last finding its place as a decorative material in Canadian gardens. This is undoubtedly due to the influence of the Japanese, who have used it superbly in their gardens for centuries and are well acquainted with its virtues. It has a neat, clean quality and is particularly at home in gardens that are simple in design. It has also a look of dryness and is an appropriate background for certain desertlike plants, such as succulents.

It is effective in keeping down weeds, holds moisture in the soil, dries quickly after rain, never disintegrates (although you must add to it from time to time). It is clean under foot but can be hard on the high heels of ladies' shoes. Also, it is probably the least expensive of all permanent ground covers. Gravel, of course, will never replace the beauty of a fine expanse of velvety lawn, and in some gardens it would obviously be out of character. But its subdued coloration, attractive texture and easy upkeep make it useful for many garden situations.

There's more variety to gravel than you may realize. In this low-maintenance garden, two colors are tastefully combined. The brown gravel relates to the house, the contrasting light gray material to the concrete planting bed. Gravel is a good topping for a raised bed. The edges keep it from scattering, it cuts down on weed growth and reduces evaporation. The succulents here are in keeping with the dry look of the gravel.

A gravel-topped terrace *bordered with old railroad ties is appropriate for this informal house and garden setting. Containers of flowers edge the terrace as a colorful accent. They can be changed as needed.*

Instead of lawn *this front yard is covered with gravel. For contrast and color interest, junipers and other low-growing plants are used. Where glare is a problem, the shade of a large tree is the best solution.*

Outcroppings of rock *would make this a difficult corner to maintain if it were planted as a lawn. Gravel eliminates the need for trimming and helps to dramatize the interesting shapes and subtle color of the rocks.*

Low-maintenance ground cover *of rounded river-washed stones provides an attractive background for this garden of rocks and sparse plantings. The house and garden are related in character as well as color.*

Wood timbers and low plants *form a handsome pattern on a broad sloping expanse of gravel. Timbers such as railroad ties or 8-x-8s are large enough to be buried firmly in the ground. Shrubs are evergreens.*

345

Gravel is a good substitute *for grass in areas where grass does not grow easily, such as in heavy shade, where the surface drainage is poor or where tree roots are near the surface and exhaust the soil. A patch of gravel can also be used to reduce the size of a lawn where maintenance has become too burdensome. The rectangular bed of gravel, as the one at right, can be brightened with plants, like the small pine here or a bed of ivy. Gravel is also an excellent surface for garden sculpture, raised planting beds, birdbaths and similar objects since the tedious job of trimming grass around their bases is eliminated and gravel is a neutral background.*

▼ **Gravel works well** *in this garden with an Oriental look. It helps unify the design by making a pleasant transition from the weedy slope, with its outcropping of rocks, to the paved areas beyond. If grass were used in place of the gravel, the contrast between the natural and man-made elements of the garden would not be nearly so effective. The edge of the slope is retained and effectively accentuated, and the plantings are held in check by driving small tree rounds into the ground at various heights to follow the curve of the slope. Any kind of saplings can be used but they should, of course, be treated with a wood preservative.*

346

Square panels of herbs and gravel make an unusually effective pattern in this rear garden bordered with shrubs. The neutral color and consistent texture of the gravel enhance the color of the foliage and flowers. Gravel also provides easy access for planting and picking. The gravel helps to give a neat, orderly appearance to this kind of garden that tends, as the season progresses, to become somewhat ragged. The pattern of squares is particularly effective viewed from above, and an herb garden has the added bonus of being a pleasant, fragrant place in which to spend a sunny afternoon. The benches were added as a further invitation.

▶**For relief** in an expanse of paving, this small rectangular bed of gravel provides just the right change of color and texture. Any number of things could be planted here, but the dwarf spruce and blue fescue (Festuca glauca) require little maintenance. A ceramic tray of water is the third element in this simple triangular composition. Note the refinement of placing a handful of stones within the tray in order to relate it to the gravel outside. The overall texture is enriched by using gravel of different sizes, shapes and colors. The light fixture continues the effect into the night.

347

25

Working With Earth

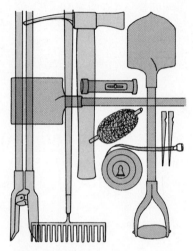

Tools, *from left: Spade, post-hole digger, level-head rake, mattock, hand level, line (with pegs), 100-foot tape measure, D-handle shovel.*

Reshaping the earth to fit a projected landscape design means either filling the downhill side of a slope, or cutting into the uphill side or, as shown below, a combination of the two. This is the most efficient method because no waste has to be carried away (as in cutting) and no new material has to be brought in (as in filling).

To repair an unsightly depression, begin by removing and setting aside the topsoil. (Always save the topsoil, replacing it when you complete the job.) Then build up the

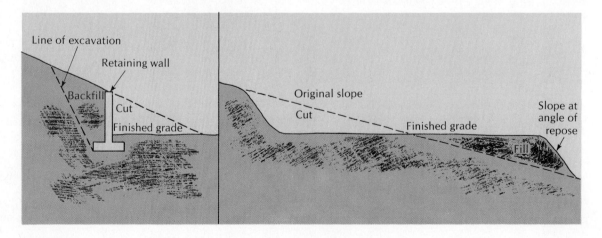

Sturdy wheelbarrow *and a good shovel can serve 90 percent of your earth-moving needs. Mattock, left, with one pointed, one flat blade is a baked-earth breaker, rock-pryer, narrow-trencher. Flat spade keeps garden* *beds and trench edges straight. To dig post holes efficiently use a post-hole digger, or auger, right. A crowbar lifts stubborn rocks; metal rake collects loose materials, smoothes surface. Tamper packs backfill.*

depression about six inches at a time with clean fill, sprinkling and tamping down each six-inch layer. If you plan to finish off with lawn or ground cover, the top layer should be topsoil. Flower or vegetable gardens need 24 inches of good soil.

There are two ways to retain the change of grade created when a sloping area is leveled. The easiest way is to let the soil hold itself in its own angle of repose. This is the angle at which earth naturally remains in place. It is steeper (and requires less space) for clay soil than for sandy soil. Determining the angle is largely by trial and error.

Sometimes a retaining wall is required to hold the change of grade. If it is on the uphill side, soil will have to be excavated from behind the position of the wall and backfilled when the wall is completed. Sprinkle and tamp the earth about every 12 inches so the ground will not sag behind the wall. A wall on the downhill side can be built before the fill is put in.

When topsoil is replaced, resod or seed any sloping areas to stabilize the soil. Cover with burlap or straw until roots take hold. Do the same when you shape mounds or hollows, as at left. And be sure to allow for drainage in every land-shaping plan (see pages 168–169 for more about this).

On the average lot, most cutting, trenching or filling can be done with the hand tools shown on these pages. For larger jobs, a scraper attached to a garden tractor is of value. Or, if you feel you can handle them, and they are available, rent a bulldozer, backhoe or a front-end loader.

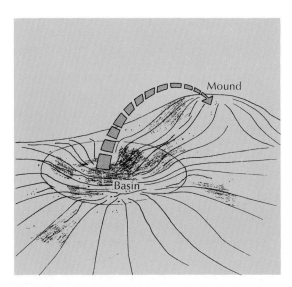

When you move earth *for sculptural effects, conserve and replace topsoil; design basin and mound sides no steeper than angle of repose; plan drainage for basin (or make it a reflecting pool); reseed or resod earth.*

100 PROJECTS YOU

In this section are projects to build for every part of the garden. The scope of the ideas presented here is illustrated below. Some of the projects are so easy to construct that a novice handyman can complete them in a day. Others are more difficult and require knowledge of materials, experience in building and the use of power tools. If you find a project that would be good in your garden but seems too complicated to complete on your own, consider having a professional build it for you. If lack of precision tools stands in the way of taking on a desired project, make arrangements for a local cabinet shop or yard where mill work is done to cut the pieces according to specifications so you can put them together. Remember: "measure twice and cut once."

On the Pages That Follow Are Complete Instructions For Projects To Improve Your Garden. Large and Small, Easy and Complex and Of Varied Cost, They Include…

OUTDOOR LIVING

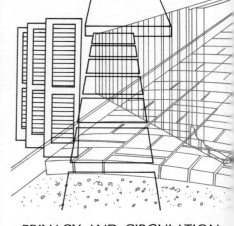

PRIVACY AND CIRCULATION

CAN DO YOURSELF

Each project is explained by means of drawings (cutaways, extended and exploded views) to help you assess the work involved, understand how it's put together and see what it will look like when completed. Dimensions are included for most projects but they can be altered to fit your needs. This is easy once you know exactly how the pieces all go together. It pays to visualize all the steps you will take in construction before you begin.

The principles involved in working with the materials used in these projects are explained in the previous section. Whenever a term used here, such as lap-joint, mortar bed or dado, is not fully understood, check the working information before starting the project.

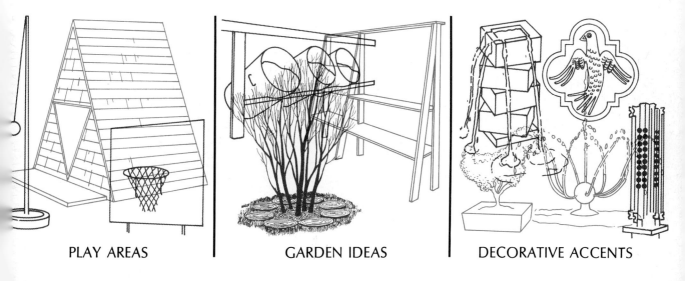

PLAY AREAS   GARDEN IDEAS   DECORATIVE ACCENTS

351

26

Walkways, Paths and Steps

Brick Walk Without Mortar

One of the easiest walks to lay is with brick, using sand rather than mortar as a base and in the cracks. Brick on sand has a pleasant, informal quality and is good to use anyplace except where a smoother surface is required or if there is a fear that the surface will not remain level. In climates where the ground swells and heaves because of frost, some bricks may have to be reset in the spring. But in warm climates they will stay firmly in place for years.

A feature of the walk shown here is the way it is dropped below the surface of the grass. Paving stones are laid on end to hold the sides in place. By setting it below grade, the visual impact is increased and the encroaching grass is restrained.

Dig trench *eight to ten inches deep, removing sod and roots. Level soil. Spread one or two inches of crushed stone topped by one to two inches of sand. Paving stones at side are set four to six inches below surface.*

Pour sand *on top of bricks for filling in between cracks. In this basket-weave pattern, bricks can be laid without cutting. Walk is approximately three feet wide. Note how walk is curved with a crown in center for drainage.*

Work sand *thoroughly into cracks with a level-head rake. Water sand to settle it down and when surface is dry add more to fill. The more firmly the sand is packed into the cracks, the tighter it will hold the bricks.*

352

Paving Patterns

1 Basket weave on edge *Bricks set on edge in this pattern give a more stable walk. It is also more expensive, as it takes three bricks, not two, to equal one length.*
2 Herringbone *A good pattern to use where a subdued effect is required. However, a considerable amount of cutting is necessary to make edges flush. Begin design by first laying the two bricks at lower right-hand corner.*
3 Seven on seven *A variation of the basket-weave pattern, consisting of double rows of seven bricks laid on edge in alternate directions. The pattern is modified here on the left side in order to fit the four-foot frame.*
4 Flemish bond *An interesting but unobtrusive pattern made up of a running bond (bricks laid end to end, flat or on edge) with the addition of a bat (one-half of a brick or less) laid on edge between each brick.*
5 Divided basket weave *An unusual pattern in which panels of basket weave (bricks are laid flat) are divided by vertical and horizontal strips of bricks laid on edge.*

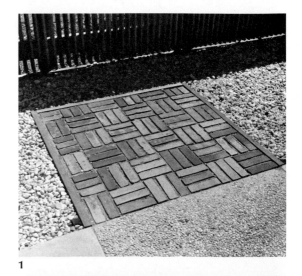

1

2

3

4

5

353

Stone Walk Set in Sand

The original walk of random-patterned stone, below, was set directly on the ground, with mortar between joints. As the ground heaved, because of moisture and frost, the stones moved, the mortar crumbled and the walk became rough and unstable. The improvement, as shown, was to use larger stones laid together on a base of sand.

Original walk *developed wide cracks—inevitable with stone paving laid on bare ground in cold climates. Mortar between stones also broke away, and tedious hand-weeding was required. Use pry bar to displace old stone.*

After removing stones, *use level to align the edge and to check the slope for drainage—about ¼ inch per foot. Crosswise drainage slopes outward from center of walk. Lengthwise drainage can go in either direction.*

Trench is dug deep enough *to allow for a 2- to 4-inch bed of sand upon which stone will rest. After digging, rake soil smooth and of an equal depth throughout. Maintain clean, straight edge where grass joins paving.*

Fill trench with sand *and tamp or roll firmly into place. Smooth sand with back of level-head rake. Sand should be deep enough to allow for adjustment of the stone, the top of which ought to be perfectly flush with string.*

Set stone smooth side up. *For ease in fitting, it is best to have all stone cut to a fixed pattern before laying it. Cutting is hard and, unless one has experience, it should be done by professional stonemasons.*

Check carefully *for proper level and slope. To get good alignment and firmness, work slab back and forth in the sand, or add or remove sand, until it fills the irregularities on the rough underside of the pieces.*

Sweep in sand *to fill cracks between stones. Water sprayed onto the walk will wash sand down deeper into the cracks. More sand should be added. This helps to prevent stones from moving and inhibits weed growth.*

The finished walk *is smooth, solid and, if properly sloped, will dry quickly after a rain. Ground cover of gravel between walk and house eliminates need to grow grass in an area too small for proper maintenance.*

Cast Concrete on the Ground

Ready-made paving or stepping-stones of concrete are used on these pages in three different styles. These stones or blocks can be bought or they can be made at home. (For instructions, see Chapter 19, "Working with Concrete.") If the blocks are to be set directly on the ground, as here, use relatively large units for stability, but not so large that they are hard to handle.

Stepping-Stones in a Lawn

When worn places appear in your lawn, signalling the beginnings of a footpath, it is a fair sign that a hard surface may be required to protect the grass. One of the most attractive solutions is to build a path of rectangular or circular stepping-stones.

A **pattern** of wood the same size and shape as the stepping-stone is made. Then, with a spade, cut a hole in the ground. The hole should be deep enough for both stone and a layer of sand. Use string to line up edges and space stones equally apart.

In the finished walk, spaces between stones are wide enough for grass to grow which can be mowed in conjunction with the lawn. These spaces and the edges must be clearly defined if the walk is to be attractive.

Stepping-Stones in Gravel

The stepping-stones below have had the outer concrete washed away before it was fully set, thereby exposing the smooth stone aggregate on top. This decorative surface makes a handsome pathway, but take care that the blocks are in perfect alignment. Nothing is more unattractive in such walks than ragged edges. In frosty climates, the steps should be laid on sand and gravel.

Stepping-stones are made level and carefully aligned before gravel is placed around them. To prevent growth of weeds, or make those that do come up easier to pull out, put down a layer of sand underneath the gravel.

Paving with Cast Flagstone

The wide, attractive walk below is made of flagstones cast into related dimensions (modules) which can be fitted together in any of several interesting patterns. Because of the interlocking of the parts, this is a more solid, stable walk than one made of separate stones. For greater stability, however, lay the slabs on a bed of sand and gravel. Green grass between the flagstones nicely accentuates the pattern but takes time to trim. Moss can also be used or the stones can be fitted flush together.

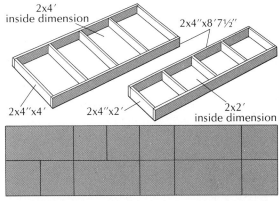

Planning ahead *is necessary if you want the design to come out evenly at its ends and edges. Choose a standard rectangle as the basic flagstone unit. Then make forms for other related units, such as halves, quarters or thirds, depending on the length and width of the walk. Whole and half-size flagstones were used above.*

Walkway Set in Mortar

The most stable walkway of all is one like this, with concrete slabs set in mortar. It is smooth and firm underfoot, long-lasting, and has the added interest of pattern and texture. Also, since nothing grows in the cracks, it requires little if any maintenance.

It is, in effect, a sidewalk of concrete in which the precast slabs are set, then adjusted and leveled before the concrete has hardened. This is a difficult undertaking and, if one is unsure about concrete, it may be a job best left to professionals.

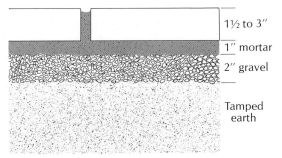

Soil, sand and concrete *are required as a foundation for a permanent walk such as this. Although initially expensive, the walk will retain its attractiveness and hold firm for decades if properly installed.*

27

Fences, Walls, Gates and Screens

How to Build Fences and Gates

Setting a Fence Post

Fence posts, usually 4 x 4's, must be set at least 3 feet deep in the ground and, depending on the style and construction of the fence, placed 5 to 8 feet apart. Align the posts with a stretched cord or, if you have a good eye, by sighting visually. Make certain the posts are vertical and are held in position by supports (right) until firmly set. Redwood, cedar and cypress best resist underground rot, but any wood should be treated with a preservative.

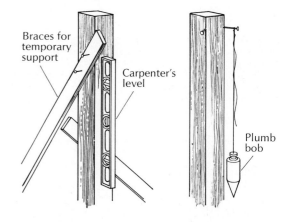

Braces for temporary support

Carpenter's level

Plumb bob

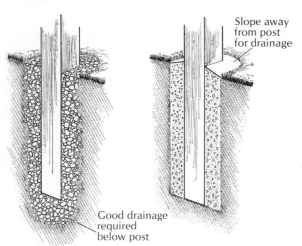

Slope away from post for drainage

Good drainage required below post

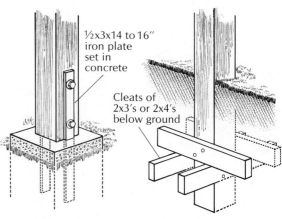

½x3x14 to 16" iron plate set in concrete

Cleats of 2x3's or 2x4's below ground

If set in gravel (left), the post must first be made plumb and held firmly in place while crushed gravel is shoveled around it and thoroughly tamped with a tamper. **In concrete,** do not put concrete under post. This makes a cup that catches water which, in turn, rots the wood.

Brackets of strap iron set in precast concrete piers can be used to attach posts. Or the brackets can be set in concrete poured directly into a hole in the ground. **Posts in the ground** can be given greater stability by digging a hole big enough for wooden bracing.

Hanging a Gate

A gate that hangs askew and won't close properly is hardly an asset to the garden. To keep it from sagging it is essential that the post to which the gate is attached be strong and firmly set in gravel or concrete to a depth of at least 4 feet. Two hinges are usually sufficient to hang most gates, but if the gate is heavy three are better. Use hot-dipped galvanized hardware and screws to forestall rust.

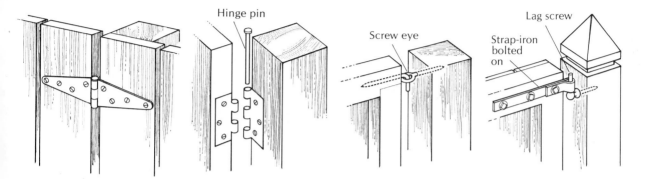

Strap hinge (left) is not the most attractive but it has good leverage and gives strong support.
Butt hinge is not as strong as the strap but it has the advantage of being out of sight when the gate is closed. If you want a flush surface between the post and gate, recess hinges into the wood.

Hook-and-eye hinge is easy to install. To avoid slack and keep gate hanging parallel with post, the screw eye should fit as snugly as possible around lag screw.
A stronger version of the hook-and-eye is at the right. Note that installation of hinge on back of gate puts the front of the gate flush with the post.

Good Latches to Use

There are many types of attractive latches for garden gates. Shown below are four standard models, three of which are available in hardware stores. The one at the left, however, is the classic handmade wooden bolt—a handsome piece of Americana that is a pleasant ornament for any gate. Self-closing hinges and gates are also available and these can be most useful if children or pets must be confined. On page 56 there is the ingenious Williamsburg ball-and-chain weight that closes the gate by gravity.

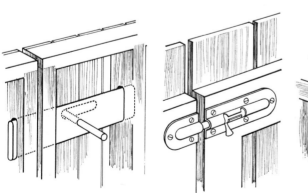 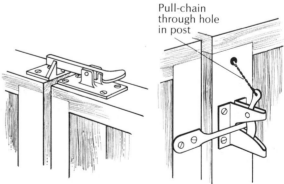

Sliding wooden panel extends from gate into the fence post. Latch can be operated from both sides of the fence by the wooden handle riding through the open slot.
Standard sliding bolt works on the same principle, but can be operated from only one side of the fence.

Lever latch on gate pushes down to release from catch on post. Although out of reach of small children, the lever can catch clothing when gate is open.
Self-latching gate has fixture on post to engage pin as the gate swings shut. Chain releases catch.

Good for Vines

When some kind of divider is needed (especially a large one), an open fence is often the best answer. A solid fence may appear too heavy and forbidding and offend the neighbors, or it may reduce the summer breezes or obscure a pleasant view. The structure shown here avoids these common problems. More a trellis than a fence, its sturdy construction is excellent for vines such as clematis, honeysuckle, climbing roses or even the heavy and vigorous wisteria. If the foliage becomes too thick, the vines can be pruned to preserve the necessary openness.

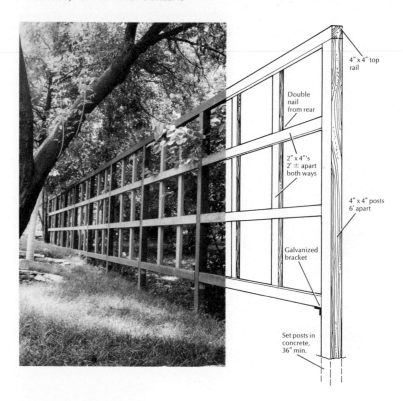

4" x 4" top rail

Double nail from rear

2" x 4"'s 2' ± apart both ways

4" x 4" posts 6' apart

Galvanized bracket

Set posts in concrete, 36" min.

Notch 4" x 4" top & bottom rails

Bevel top of post

2" x 4" nailer set against post with galvanized brackets

4" x 4" posts. 6' apart

1" x 4" vertical, ¼" space

1" x 2" continuous batt

Set posts min. 36" in concrete

Letting Air Through

Austere and simple, this design combines the qualities of both open and solid fencing. The vertical slats, set ¼ inch apart, let the air through as well as occasional glimpses of color and movement, and give a feeling of openness without sacrificing all privacy. This is an advantage if the fence is used, as here, to separate adjoining properties where the complete separation of a solid wall might seem somewhat unneighborly.

The severity of the vertical lines is relieved by the 1-x-2-inch continuous batts running horizontally to the rails. Use plantings at the base to reduce the apparent height of the fence, or add pattern with a tracery of vine such as winter jasmine or one of the colorful clematis. The stems can be easily attached to the batts with pieces of raffia or plastic-covered wire.

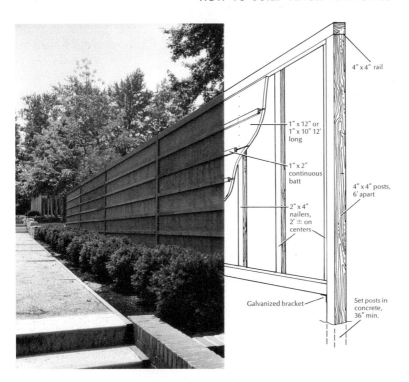

4" x 4" rail

1" x 12" or
1" x 10" 12'
long

1" x 2"
continuous
batt

4" x 4" posts,
6' apart

2" x 4"
nailers,
2' ± on
centers

Galvanized bracket

Set posts in
concrete,
36" min.

Horizontal Accent

A solid fence is an excellent solution where privacy is required or an unsightly view is to be hidden. This handsome fence, with its strong horizontal lines, can be made of any locally available, inexpensive wood. The wood, however, ought to be of a good grade and free of knots or other surface imperfections. Solid fences also give protection from strong winds and they create comfortable warm places on the sunny side. The best finish for a fence with such a dominant façade as this one is a stain of soft brown or green rather than paint.

Good on Both Sides

This is a fine example of the "good neighbor" fence, so-called because it looks equally well on both sides. The vertical slats (which give an illusion of height) are set three and one-half inches apart on each "face" of the fence, but staggered slightly so that there is a one-inch overlap. This ingenious arrangement almost completely screens the view but does not stop the flow of air. The staggered uprights also create pleasing effects of light and shadow between faces as the sun moves through the day. Among truly "good neighbors" this style of fence, which is somewhat expensive to build, could be a joint venture.

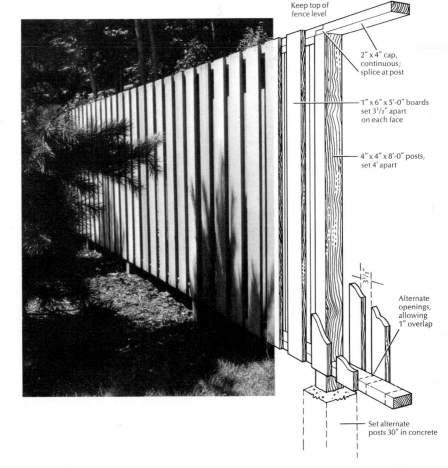

Keep top of
fence level

2" x 4" cap,
continuous;
splice at post

1" x 6" x 5'-0" boards
set 3½" apart
on each face

4" x 4" x 8'-0" posts,
set 4' apart

3½"

Alternate
openings,
allowing
1" overlap

Set alternate
posts 30" in concrete

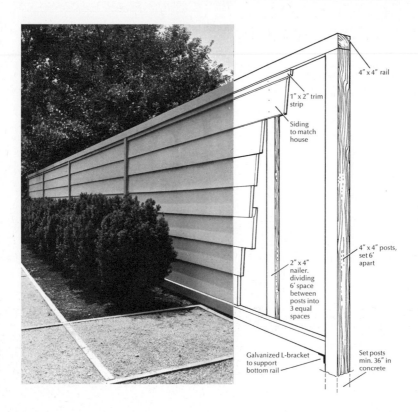

4" x 4" rail

1" x 2" trim strip

Siding to match house

4" x 4" posts, set 6' apart

2" x 4" nailer. dividing 6' space between posts into 3 equal spaces

Galvanized L-bracket to support bottom rail

Set posts min. 36" in concrete

To Match a Clapboard House

If a fence adjoins the house or is constructed nearby, it makes good decorative sense to build the fence out of the same material as the house. Even if the fence is located at the far side of the garden, the use of similar materials has a unifying effect. Paint the fence the same color as the house. The fence sections with shrubs in front seem lower than those sections left bare. This softens the severe long line of the clapboards. Note also the use of 2-x-4 nailers placed two feet apart along the fence behind the siding making vertical accents.

Vertical Panels

The rhythmic design of the panels in this fence is good to consider in a situation where a long run is required. The strong vertical accent of the design is saved from monotony by interrupting the line of stakes with 4-x-4 posts set six feet apart. To increase the paneled look further, the top and bottom rails and vertical posts could be stained a dark color and the stakes left natural. A good way to get more elevation, if the height of the fence is legally restricted, is to put the fence on top of a low wall. Plantings at the base tend to reduce any feeling of excess height.

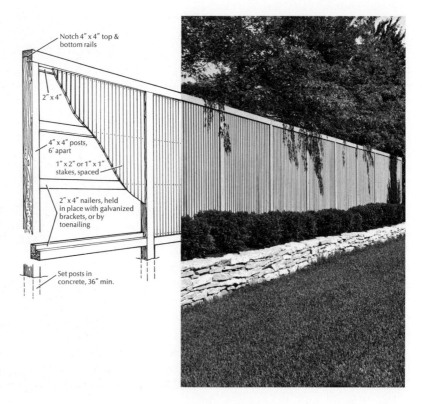

Notch 4" x 4" top & bottom rails

2" x 4"

4" x 4" posts, 6' apart

1" x 2" or 1" x 1" stakes, spaced

2" x 4" nailers, held in place with galvanized brackets, or by toenailing

Set posts in concrete, 36" min.

Screening for Privacy

Unless your home is built in the middle of a forest or surrounded by acres of private land, some kind of screening is required to provide privacy for outdoor living. Such screening may be anything from a seven-foot privet hedge to a row of translucent plastic panels. It may enclose your entire property, your garden, a terrace, or simply a favorite corner where you enjoy retreating from time to time. Whether your screening be elaborate or simple is not nearly so important as that it give you shelter from prying eyes and the unpleasant extremes of sun and wind. Screening can also hide an unsightly view. Presented below are some suggestions for achieving such privacy.

Folding Wall for a Porch

A porch or terrace such as the one at the right may require privacy for such disparate activities as sunbathing and luncheons alfresco. This unique "folding wall" permits all possibilities. Attractive, inexpensive and extremely practical, it is constructed of standard panels that can be bought at any lumberyard and are then hinged together for folding. It rests on casters which give support when it is extended and make for ease in handling.

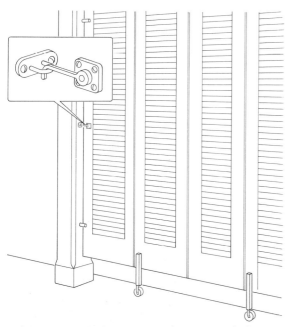

Casters are required to support the screen which is attached at only one end. When a heavy-duty, brass latch is locked, the screen is pulled tightly against the post and against the wooden dowels at top and bottom to keep it from moving from side to side. If the panels are wide enough, the casters can be set directly in the bottom instead of on blocks as shown.

Freestanding Arbor and Seat

This tall, freestanding arbor can be a support for plants and makes a charming screen that can be used imaginatively in various ways. In a corner, for instance, near the property line—especially if the corner is some distance from the house—such a place becomes a somewhat remote, quiet, private and inviting destination.

It can also be used near the house to define and screen a corner of a terrace or patio for privacy and, at certain times of the day, shade. When clothed heavily with vines, the arbor also serves as a windbreak. The wooden seat and low back of bricks provide a solid physical foundation for the screen, and give visual weight to the design by anchoring it firmly to the ground.

To cover the screen, climbing roses are shown here, but such vines as clematis, akebia and, in warm climates, bougainvillea would also be appropriate. For year-round screening, an evergreen vine such as *Euonymus fortunei* or one of the climbing honeysuckles works well. The vines are rooted behind the arbor and, when necessary, tied. Uprights should be stained.

Translucent Windscreen

Surprisingly heavy gusts and crosscurrents can develop around an L-shaped entryway, making it less than a pleasure to pass through on a windy day. The screen above serves the double function of calming the winds around the front door and at the same time serving as an unusual and decorative entrance to the house. Note the house number on the freestanding wall. The screen is constructed of flat sheets of translucent plastic fixed firmly to the wooden frame, as shown. Unlike glass, plastic is easy to cut

with a power or hand saw, it does not shatter, and holes can be drilled to accommodate screws or nails.

Decoratively, the screen presents dramatic visual effects as the shapes and colors of plants are revealed through its milky, translucent surface. For this reason, white plastic seems the most appropriate. It provides clear, soft light and better transmits form and color. For contrast, mount the sheets on a dark-stained wooden frame. Take full advantage of the interesting translucence of the screen by using vividly colored and dramatic shrubs and flowers against it.

Hinges

High Wall and Louvered Gate

The plain gray façade of a concrete block wall cries out for a touch of color or for some kind of decorative accent. In this example the need has been nicely met by introducing a change of texture with the handsome louvered gate, by the warm red of the capping of Roman bricks and by the horizontal and vertical plantings growing in front of the wall. For instructions on how to build a block wall, see pages 332–333. The inset drawing here shows how the louvered gate is set into a wooden frame. The frame can be attached to the concrete blocks with lag screws turned into lead sleeves or into expanding cement placed in pre-drilled holes. Such a high and solid wall conveys a feeling of privacy and, because the gate can be locked with a key, it offers security as well.

Decorative Panel of Brick

This handsome panel set in a low concrete wall has courses of brick running alternately lengthwise and crosswise. Each course is separated by rather thick pads of mortar. The openwork of this design creates a rich yet airy textural surface that is decorative and, at the same time, provides good ventilation at ground level which is often beneficial to plants located in a corner.

Low Wall of Chimney Blocks

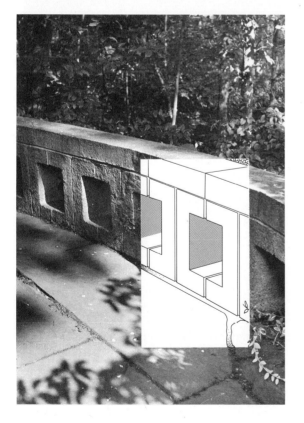

These chimney blocks are made to be stacked one on top of another to form a chimney opening. Here, however, they are set on edge and topped with capping blocks, to make a neat, low wall that is quick and easy to construct. The wall, with its neat square openings is about 24 inches high, and set in mortar on the edge of an existing terrace. As shown here, it is slightly curved, which is accomplished by using narrow mortar joints on the inside of the curve and wider joints on the outside. This is about as much curve as can be recommended.

367

28

Protection from
The Sun and Rain

An overhead sunshade can be built quickly and easily. It may be made of materials such as lath, lattice or vines which provide shade and allow some light through. Solid sheets of plastic are also used. The corrugated kind is more rigid, but flat sheets are generally more attractive. A plastic sunshade blocks out the sun's glare and creates a lovely warm glow of light.

A problem with plastic overheads is that they tend to hold in heat unless there is good ventilation on all sides. This can be created by setting the roof a foot or so away from the wall or by extending it above the vertical surface.

Plastic can also be used for a rainproof overhead, but a built-up roof of builder's felt and tar paper is sturdier. It can be constructed so as to slope or lie almost flat, but there must be enough pitch for water to drain off. Extending the sloping side of a roof is still another way to make a rainproof overhead. The design and construction of most solid roofs require the help of a professional, but lightweight sunshades can be built by any home craftsman.

A Long Narrow Overhead

While the band of shade cast by this dramatic overhead shelter provides a cool place to sit, the structure itself helps to unify the landscape. It links the house to the low wall and turns the adjoining pavement into an open-air living area.

The detailing of the structure relates all of its parts and is particularly attractive in itself. At one end the uprights form a frame for the entryway to the house and at the other end they are extensions of the wall. Because there are no central supporting posts, the overhead has a light and airy feeling and does not dominate the landscape despite its length. In another setting an overhead with a shorter span or a wider spread might be more appropriate. The dimensions of this design, given on the opposite page, can be altered.

The materials used are a further unifying element. They are all in character: the wicker and leather of the lightweight Mexican furniture, the adobe bricks of the wall and the grape stakes used for the overhead. Such a structure could, of course, be made of other materials, as split cedar, lath or 2-x-2s.

This method of overhead construction *can be used in a variety of situations when attached to an existing structure. It is lightweight and relatively inexpensive and easy to build. The secret of its strength is the 2-x-4 stiffeners nailed to both sides of the 2-x-10s. These are, in effect, sturdy, built-up beams, as seen in the inset sketch. The 2-x-10s go through the 3-x-4 upright posts and are bolted to them. Note 2-x-4 blocking is used between posts at the bottom. For added rigidity a 2-x-10 spacer is notched to the stiffeners in the middle of the overhead. This is an attractive method of framing and plastic panels, bamboo or reed screen could also be used for the cover.*

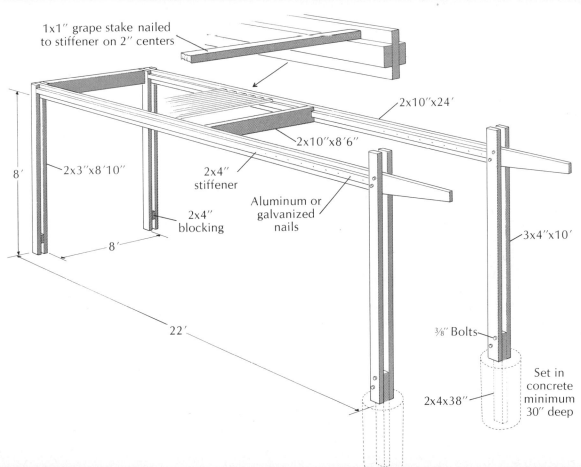

1x1″ grape stake nailed to stiffener on 2″ centers

2x10″x24′

2x10″x8′6″

2x4″ stiffener

2x3″x8′10″

Aluminum or galvanized nails

2x4″ blocking

3x4″x10′

8′

8′

⅜″ Bolts

22′

2x4x38″

Set in concrete minimum 30″ deep

A Straightforward Trellis and Screen

This handsome trellis unifies the house and back garden and creates an out-of-doors living room. Originally, the sliding door of the house opened onto a plain concrete patio, as seen in the plan below. It was too small and the terrace was extended with brick both to the edge of the property and the overhead structure which was built above the entire area. The framework creates a sense of shelter without blocking the sun, and where shade is necessary, reed screening can be tacked onto the top. The height of the trellis adds the needed vertical interest in this flat garden, as do the three planted mounds of earth (one is seen at the far end of the color picture). Baskets of flowers hanging overhead emphasize the vertical dimension and add color.

Seen in the bottom picture is the screen, which gives privacy from the house next door. It is designed as an integral part of the trellis and is, in effect, more a textured wall of the outdoor room than a high fence. It is also attractive on the back side.

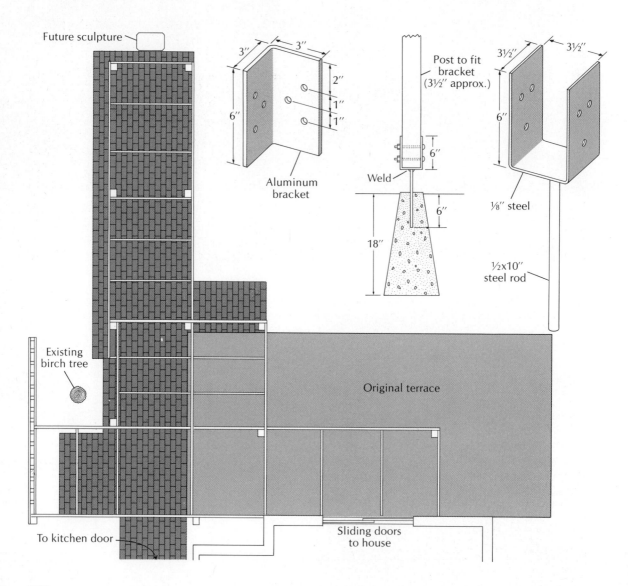

Future sculpture

3" 3" 2" 1" 1" 6"

Aluminum bracket

Post to fit bracket (3½" approx.)

6" Weld 18" 6" 6"

3½" 3½" 6" ⅛" steel

½x10" steel rod

Existing birch tree

Original terrace

To kitchen door

Sliding doors to house

Method of construction *is relatively inexpensive. The trellis posts were set on top of the existing concrete patio with metal post supports. Where brick patio was added, the metal supports are set in concrete poured below grade. Stringers are notched into the posts and bolted. Cross pieces are attached to stringers with right-angle aluminum brackets bolted in place. (A bracket is seen in middle of picture.) Screen at left has 4 x 4-inch posts at each end. 2-x-2s horizontally spaced two inches apart are nailed to posts. 2-x-4s vertically on edge and spaced about eight inches apart are nailed to the horizontals. Galvanized nails and bolts are used throughout.*

29

Pleasures
And Practicalities

For Comfort Under a Tree

There is something singularly pleasant and inviting about a shade tree standing alone in a lawn or garden. People tend to gather beneath its sheltering branches for a quiet talk, for reading, cocktails, a picnic or a nap. The thoughtful gardener should, therefore, provide some kind of seating arrangement, either a cheerful lounging chair or two, or perhaps one of the structures shown on these pages. The seat-planter, below, is both elegant and charming; the seat-and-deck, opposite page, is large and wonderfully comfortable for lounging. Neither is too difficult to make. Before building around a tree be sure that the soil has good drainage and that the tree is free of pests. Both of these structures can be built on hard surfaces, such as a brick or concrete patio. On hard surfaces, the planter can be filled with shallow-rooted plants.

Hexagonal Seat/Planter

This handsome hexagonal garden seat can be built around a tree in the garden, or the middle planting section can be filled with flowers and shrubs. If it sits on a hard surface, such as a terrace, nothing larger than shallow-rooted shrubs can be used in the center.

Dimensions shown here can be altered as needed. In building the planter first make the outer and inner hexagons. Note that the ends of all these boards are cut at a 60° angle. Attach the hexagons to one another with the six radiating boards. Then lay 2 x 4s on top and cut flush to the outer and inner edges of the hexagons. 2 x 2 capping strips nailed to the edges are optional but they make a shadow line and give a finished look to the design.

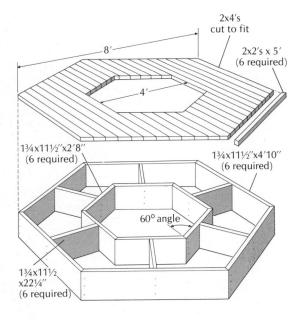

2x4's cut to fit

8'

2x2's x 5' (6 required)

4'

1¾x11½''x2'8'' (6 required)

1¾x11½''x4'10'' (6 required)

60° angle

1¾x11½ x22¼'' (6 required)

Combination Seat-and-Deck

This combination seat-and-deck is just the spot to spend a lazy summer afternoon. The corner posts are set in holes in the bottom of which is a layer of tamped gravel for drainage. The holes are then filled with more gravel or with concrete to prevent decay.

A removable cover of canvas or linen, made with tailored corners, protects clothing and cushions from gummy drippings and other debris. Oversize cushions can also be used in combination with slabs of foam rubber covered in some bright, preferably waterproof fabric.

Make sure there is good drainage so that water doesn't collect underneath the seat, which should properly be built of redwood, or other wood treated with preservative. Soil under the deck is topped with gravel.

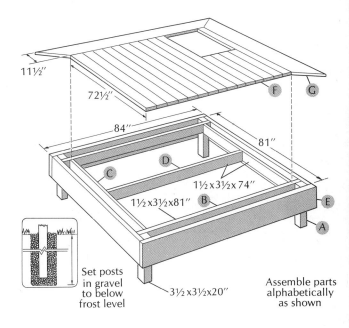

11½"

72½"

84"

81"

D

C

1½ x 3½ x 74"

1½ x 3½ x 81"

B

E

A

F

G

Set posts in gravel to below frost level

3½ x 3½ x 20"

Assemble parts alphabetically as shown

What to Do at the Base of a Tree

One of the most difficult of all mowing problems occurs when a lawn runs right up to and surrounds a tree. Although it is virtually impossible to mow close to a tree with a mower, homeowners sometimes attempt the impossible and succeed only in hitting the trunk, injuring the bark and even exposing the delicate cambium layer which lies just beneath. An occasional exposure of the cambium will not endanger the life of the tree if the wound is treated promptly with a tree sealer. But if this sensitive layer is damaged all around the circumference, the tree will die.

The most obvious solution to this problem is to trim the grass around the tree by hand. But this is a tedious chore if there are many trees on your lawn, and if your trees grow in clumps, it is even worse.

A better solution is to use something other than grass at the foot of a tree. Any inorganic material (as stone, gravel, brick or wood chips), if it is extended outward and contained within an attractive border, makes an ideal base, particularly if the border is set flush with the lawn so that it can double as a mowing strip.

The seven examples below create not only a decorative perimeter in which to accent a tree, but they eliminate the necessity of hand trimming, prevent mowing injuries, and actually aid in the tree's growth by conserving moisture around the roots and reducing the growth of weeds.

Railroad ties *set flush with lawn establish a good mowing edge. For larger trees, use 1-1/2 or 2 ties on each side. Wood chips are the mulch in the center of the bed.*

A mulch of heavy stones *has the value of providing a cool, moist, weed-free root area, but grass around the corrugated aluminum border requires hand trimming.*

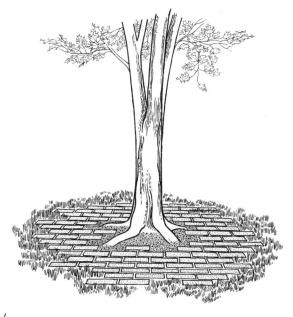

A covering of bricks *set in sand and fitted tightly together is attractive especially if bricks are used in other parts of the garden or if the house is brick.*

For a formal effect, *here is a square of concrete pavers arranged in a module so that no cutting is required. 2-x-4s, inside and out, keep the edges straight.*

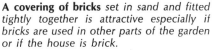

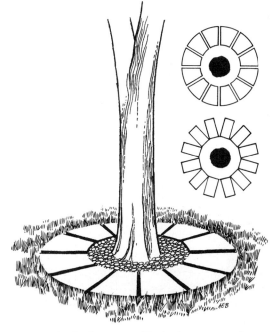

To build a low, raised bed *for plantings, drive 2-x-4 stakes into the ground, as shown, and surround bed with brick or concrete pavers to form a mowing edge.*

◄**For an informal look,** *use log rounds (6 to 8 inches long) set flush into ground. They will rot in a few years but can be replaced. Mulch is river-washed stone.*

A wheel of concrete blocks *is set around the tree and encloses a gravel mulch. The small diagram above suggests special blocks; the one below uses standard block.*

375

Raised Beds

The most obvious characteristic of a raised bed is the sharp, clean edge that borders the plants in much the same way a frame borders a picture. Such a frame, raised as it is above the ground, gives an importance and definition to the plantings that otherwise they might not have. It is a good way to achieve maximum effectiveness with fewer plants. Other advantages are that the soil inside the bed can easily be conditioned to meet the plant's requirements; water does not run off but soaks down into the root area; and the job of weeding, spraying and picking flowers is made easier. A variation of a raised bed is a low retaining wall with planting behind.

A Bed of Masonry Blocks

The clean, creamy effect of the wall above can be had by applying a white mortar finish to concrete blocks. This "parging" requires know-how in both the mixing of the mortar and its application to the wall. Different colors may be had by adding mineral oxides. This overall plastered look gives the bed a unified color and surface texture that helps to reduce the harsh, unfinished appearance of plain concrete block walls. The inset drawing shows how to lay the foundation and corners. When freezing and thawing are problems, the foundation of concrete should go below the frost line, which may be as deep as five feet. In warmer zones the foundation need only be firm, level ground that will solidly support the weight of the wall.

376

A Good Use for Cement Board

One of the many building materials useful in the garden is a mineral paneling sold commercially as asbestos-cement board. The heavy, highly compressed material comes in flat or corrugated panels, is practically indestructible and therefore excellent for outdoor use. It can be set directly on the ground and will not rot. It need not be painted, and the panels are heavy and rigid enough to retain their shape against pressure from the soil with minimum bracing. The bed below is easy to construct since each corner overlaps in such a way that only simple bolting is necessary. Flat panels, which some might prefer to corrugated, would require metal or wooden corner joints, which can rust or rot. Raised beds are a good device, as illustrated here, for displaying art objects or sculpture too small to be properly seen at ground level.

Mowing Strips

One of the important principles of low maintenance is that the edges of a lawn should always be clearly defined and neatly trimmed. When, for example, the lawn abuts a wall or an open bed of flowers, it requires tedious trimming with shears, or digging with a spade or shovel, to maintain a clean edge. Most of this labor can be eliminated by taking the initial step of creating a mow-ing strip along the edges of a lawn where it is not already bordered by a sidewalk or drive. Mowing strips of brick, concrete block, or even railroad ties, must be flush with the lawn so one wheel of the mower can run on the hard surface. They must also be wide and firm enough to accommodate the wheels of the mower without becoming dislodged. Drawings below and at right show details.

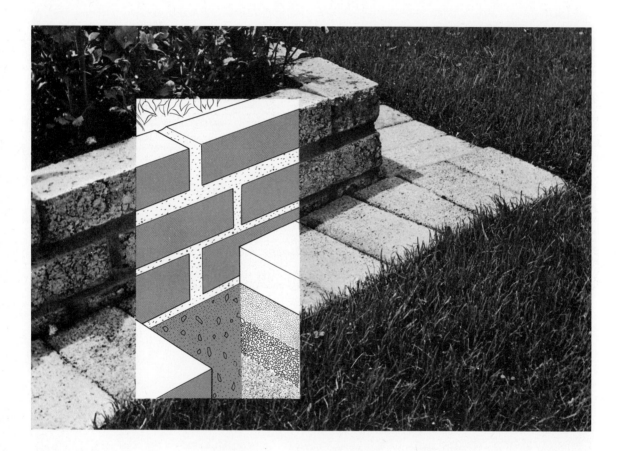

Concrete Brick and Pavers

The unity of this design was achieved by making the mowing strip of paving blocks of the same material as the concrete bricks in the raised bed. The blocks or "pavers" here are laid in sand, but they would be more dependably firm and level if set in mortar. In climates where alternate freezing and thawing is a problem, they should properly have a concrete foundation that goes below the frost line. However, if this requires more labor and money than you want to spend, lay the pavers on a good bed of gravel and sand and accept the chore of occasional resetting and releveling after the spring thaw. Concrete bricks and paving blocks can be bought or made at home.

378

Clay Brick and Wood Ties

In the garden below, bricks are used for the mowing strip because an adjacent terrace is paved with the same material. Railroad ties that establish the raised bed of yews are also used in another area as a retaining wall. This repeated use of similar materials is a good way to help establish a unity of design all through the garden. In many informal settings old railroad ties look perfectly at home. They have a rustic, weathered texture and color that blends easily with plantings of all kinds, they are durable, and heavy enough to stay in place as edges and low retainers.

By allowing the foliage of nearby plantings to grow over the edge of the ties, as in the picture below, their somewhat harsh, unadorned look can be softened.

Unfortunately, railroad ties are not always easily available, but your local landscape nursery can tell you whether or not they are.

379

Establishing the Edge

Edges that are "hard," such as wood, stone, brick or concrete (as shown here), are an effective way to achieve a neat, precise appearance in the garden. They eliminate the ragged look that so often results when plants overlap—such as grass growing up to the edge of a planting bed. They also reduce the constant, exacting trimming necessary to keep such edges tidy and separate. And if your garden is built on a slope, the edges can be extremely useful as retainers to help keep the soil from washing away.

Raised Edge of Brick

A welcome splash of color in any very dry zone is provided by the varied plantings in this panel of brick. Not only is it attractive but there are practical values, too. Weeding is made much easier because of the easy access to the flowers on all sides of the bed. Also, and especially in dry climates, plants tend to do better in enclosed beds because the enclosure holds the water in the root area. The surrounding plot of pebbled concrete on grade with the lawn serves as a mowing strip. This establishes a clean, neat edge that is relatively easy to maintain. The well-defined edge gives particular importance to the planting, as a frame does for a picture, and is itself decorative.

Seat Wall at Edge of Terrace

This wall, constructed at a comfortable height for seating (about 18 inches), is made of railroad ties laid horizontally, then faced with vertical boards and capped with 2-x-8 planks for a more finished look. The wood surface is stained. Stain weathers well and is easier to refinish than painted wood.

To create level space for a terrace, it was necessary here to dig back into an adjoining slope. This created a definite change in grade and the wall was designed to retain the bank and provide an attractive edge separating the bricked living area from the wooded section beyond.

An interesting feature here is the use of strawberries as a ground cover between the seat wall and the trees and shrubs beyond. The everbearing variety of trailing strawberry has handsome foliage, covers the ground thoroughly and offers the occasional bonus of colorful and flavorful berries, thereby enhancing the terrace in several ways.

Edges for an Informal Setting

In the woodland setting at the right, there was good reason for some kind of "edge" to maintain a neat, clean appearance and at the same time reduce what could prove to be difficult maintenance problems. The use of a low flagstone wall at the base of the tree plus a gravel covering for the ground practically assures that little if any work will be necessary to keep the pathway neatly separated from the saturation planting of ferns, columbine and rock plants.

The flagstones also function as a retainer to maintain the level of soil above the roots of the tree. Another kind of edge is established where the pathway curves. Here, too, the use of gravel and strategically placed plants and stones not only avoids the problem of mowing in awkward places but serves as a subtle transition from the clean path to the rocky wooded area beyond. Slate could be used for informal edges.

Containers for Plants

Flower-filled window boxes are a time-tested way to add color to the outside of a house and to the inside, as seen through the glass. They are also easy to build and maintain. The boxes must be sturdy and well attached, and the choice of plants must fit the pattern of sun and shade they will receive.

Flowers with a long season of bloom may be planted directly in a box, but it's better to plant others in pots first so they may be easily exchanged when out of bloom. The pots may then be set in peat moss, which holds moisture and is almost as good as planting in the ground.

An Easy Box to Build

The classic window box is simply five pieces of wood nailed together; 1 x 8s or 1 x 10s are the common sizes of lumber used for the ends, sides and bottom. To make sure the box is strong enough to hold the heavy soil and the pots placed inside, all joints should be glued with waterproof epoxy and the wood finished inside with a preservative.

Other ways to waterproof a window box are to paint the entire inside with roofing asphalt or place a metal tray on the inside. For protection and appearance, the outside of a window box is usually stained or painted to match the trim of the house. The begonias planted in the container shown here do well in shaded areas.

A Box to Match the House

For a built-in look a window box can be faced with a material that relates to the outside of the house. Vertical or horizontal siding or shingles might be used. Facing the box to blend with the house has the advantage of making it attractive even when empty, especially if it is then neatly filled with peat moss in the off-season.

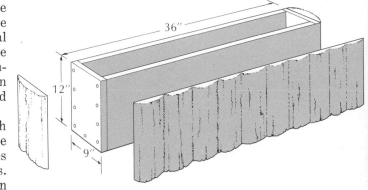

The boxes shown here are faced with slabs of bark to match the log cabin. The planting of flowers under the boxes creates a striking display of massed color in tiers. Both the wallflowers on the ground and in the boxes require full sun. For color during the winter an attractive way to fill any window box is with an arrangement of evergreen boughs and pine cones, holly branches or a composition of driftwood.

A Long, Low Planter Box

A long, low box can act as a kind of substitute hedge, add a decorative line of color beneath a series of windows or, at the edge of a porch or deck, it can serve as a colorful low railing. The one below is built in a shiplap effect and is particularly effective against a wall or fence having horizontal siding. Red-

wood is an ideal material for outdoor planters, but pressure-treated fir or other wood works equally well. The inside of the box can be waterproofed by using a heavy coating of asphalt roofing tar which, when thoroughly dry, is not harmful to plants. Although the proportions given here are excellent, they can be changed to fit a particular preference or space.

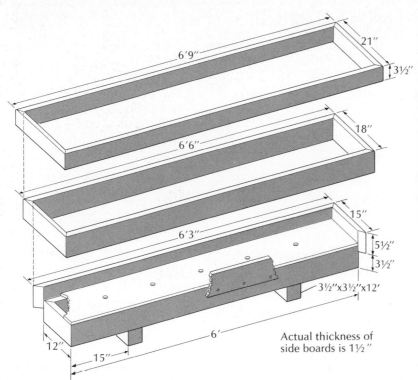

6′9″ — 21″ — 3½″
6′6″ — 18″
6′3″ — 15″ — 5½″ / 3½″
12″ — 15″ — 6′ — 3½″x3½″x12′

Actual thickness of side boards is 1½″

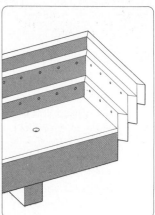

First make basic box *before nailing the bottom course of sideboards to box from the outside. Using a wall or other solid surface as a support, nail remaining sideboards from the inside for best appearance. Cut all miter joints with a table saw. Also note holes cut in the base for drainage.*

384

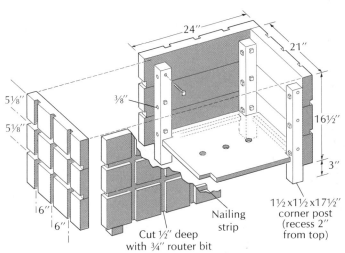

A Cube of Squares

This box looks good against a background of squares or rectangles, as a wall or walk of bricks or concrete blocks. The motif of squares is made with a power router. Recess the corner posts so that they can be hidden by the soil and construct the box with stock that is a full 1½ inches thick. Note the holes for drainage in the base.

A Cube of Linear Design

The handsome linear pattern on this box is also cut with a power router. It is tricky work and must be done precisely. Attach the recessed corner posts from the inside with 2¼-inch lag screws in pre-drilled ⅜-inch holes. As in the box above, use full 1½-inch stock and do not forget to drill drainage holes in the base.

385

Large Enough for a Tree

Almost any tree can be grown in a container. (There is an oak bonsai over 400 years old and only two feet tall.) The mature height of the plant is determined by the size of the area in which the roots grow. The box at the left, although useful for many varieties of shrubs and plantings, is nevertheless larger and deeper than most plant containers and will provide plenty of root area for a good-sized tree—even larger than that shown on the opposite page.

The side panels and the bottom of the box are made of marine plywood, but a mineral paneling known as asbestos-cement board could also be used here. It has the advantage of being impervious to weather. The basic box is built first, then the 2 x 2″ trim is attached to the panels from the inside, using screws through pre-drilled and countersunk holes. The bottom is attached to the corner posts with lag screws, again through pre-drilled holes. Seal this seam all the way around with epoxy glue. Base is optional.

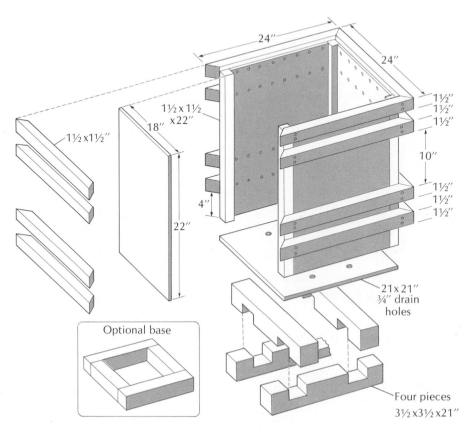

Optional base

24″

24″

1½ x 1½
x 22″

18″

1½ x 1½″

22″

4″

1½″
1½″
1½″

10″

1½″
1½″
1½″

21 x 21″
¾″ drain holes

Four pieces
3½ x 3½ x 21″

Easy to Build

Although simple in construction, this box is interesting to build. It is made by nailing together nine courses of wooden blocks, all of the same dimensions, with ends alternating as shown in the drawing. The first course of blocks can be nailed directly to the bottom and the box built up from there, or the courses can be nailed together first and the bottom added later. At the corners, when adding a new course of blocks, position the top nails so that they are on alternate diagonals from the nails below.

For its size, this box is heavy and is good to use for tall plants that might blow over in a lighter container. If the wood used is other than redwood, apply a preservative to all the pieces before construction begins. The base can be made of marine plywood (as here) or of any dimension lumber cut to fit. A handsome finish for this container would be a wood stain of soft green or driftwood gray. Be sure to give the end grain at least two coats to help prevent checking.

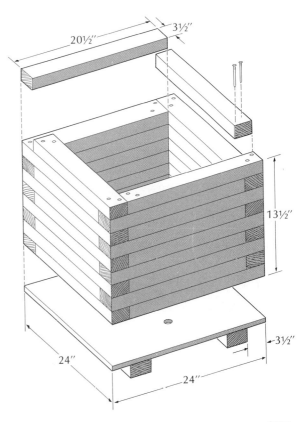

387

30

Ideas for Outdoor Living

Add on to a Small Terrace

The picture below illustrates an all-too-familiar problem—the terrace that doesn't work. The house was obviously designed with a terrace in mind and the builder provided it, but the result—a tiny, cramped bit of brick paving—adds little to the appearance of the house and less to the pleasure of outdoor living.

The area is too small to accommodate graciously the four straight-backed chairs shown, not to mention such added necessities as a table for dining, a sunning chaise or two and some room to move around in. It is plain and bare with nothing about it to suggest the spacious, easy comfort that is the proper purpose of a terrace. All of these shortcomings can be surmounted by enlarging the terrace and adding an overhead structure which can either be blanketed with a cool, green vine; covered with bright, adjustable canvas awnings; or paneled with translucent plastic that filters the light.

The problem *of a too small and unattractive terrace could be solved as shown on facing page. While the dimensions may not fit your own specific needs, the principles of making a terrace larger and more attractive are sound and the size can be adjusted to fit. Just be sure that the span between posts is not increased for beams of the dimensions shown here. For the sake of safety, a longer span would require heavier beams.*

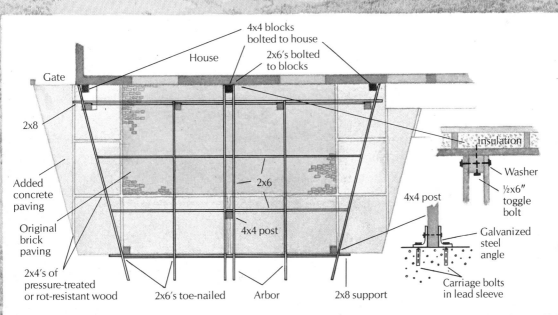

4x4 blocks
bolted to house

House

2x6's bolted
to blocks

Gate

2x8

Added
concrete
paving

2x6

Original
brick
paving

4x4 post

2x4's of
pressure-treated
or rot-resistant wood

2x6's toe-nailed

Arbor

2x8 support

insulation

Washer

½x6″
toggle
bolt

4x4 post

Galvanized
steel
angle

Carriage bolts
in lead sleeve

From the roof of a wing of the house one looks down on the deck and street beyond. To the left is carport roof and driveway. Entry walk parallels the drive. The fence not only reduces wind, acts as a backdrop for flowering tree, but provides privacy by screening off street. Bench, stained to match trim of house, is also a safety rail.

Before the deck was built *this area off the living room had limited use. The soil was too sandy to support a lawn, and going in and out of the house was made awkward and unpleasant by a deep step leading down to ground level.*

Adding a Deck for Outdoor Living

A deck can be an excellent solution, and is often the only solution, to the problem of creating extra space for outdoor living. On a hillside, for example, where the slope is too steep to be leveled off, a deck extended out from the house can provide an attractive surface for any number of open-air activities. In beach country, where houses are built on sand, a deck is the most logical way to make a smooth, solid place for furniture and outdoor meals.

Here, in this west-coast garden, the living area could have been extended by means of a wood deck or a paved terrace at ground level. The deck was chosen to avoid the work of trimming around the edge of a solid terrace or weeding between the paving stones. It was also relatively easy and economical to build and was raised to floor level to provide easy access in and out of the house rather

After the deck was built, *this pleasant, sunny spot became literally and figuratively an extension of the living room. Saturation planting of junipers in the foreground is used to hide irregular slope of the land.*

391

than requiring that a person step down to the ground. Double doors in the south wall of the living room established the perfect location for an entryway to the deck. It should not be forgotten, however, that a deck can be a welcome addition to a bedroom or kitchen as well as to a living room.

The simple 4-foot grid construction shown in the photos below uses 2-x-6 joists and 2-x-4 decking all resting on precast concrete piers to raise the deck to floor level. Wood posts on top of the piers could raise the deck

higher. For a deck over three feet high, however, consult a qualified carpenter.

In cold climates, the piers should extend at least three feet below ground level in order to avoid movement of the foundation, caused by alternate freezing and thawing of the ground, and possible cracking or warping of the deck floor. Redwood was used here, but fir, pine or any durable construction lumber can be used. No matter which wood you choose, however, treat it with a wood preservative, such as pentachlorophenol.

Building a Deck Step-by-Step

1. Drill holes in house foundation, fit lead expansion plugs into the holes and use bolts to attach 2-x-6 planks to concrete at the proper level for decking.

2. Nail galvanized joist hangers every four feet to the 2-x-6s, using a carpenter's square in order to make certain that each joist is at right angles to the planks.

3. Rest far end of joist on concrete pier. Bring it to the correct level with wood shims set on pier. Additional piers are then placed under joist every four feet.

4. Dig holes for piers. Fill holes with ready-mixed concrete to bring pier to correct height. Place pier on its base under joist. Level the joist with wood shims.

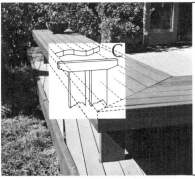

How to Add a Seat Rail

Decks more than a step above ground should have a safety rail. Here it doubles as a seat. Before decking, bolt bench supports to joists, as at A. At the corner, attach supports with hangers, as at B. Fit decking around supports. Nail crosspieces to supports and add seat top, as at C.

5. Nail hangers to each side of long joists at juncture of pier and joist. Fit cross joists into hangers, forming 4-x-4-foot grid. Nail decking to the grid.

6. Complete construction of entire grid. Level it by driving, where necessary, cedar shims between piers and joists. The shims are then nailed into place.

7. Nail 2-x-8 fascias to ends of joists in order to give a neat edge to the completed grid. To outline deck effectively, you may plant juniper or other greenery.

8. Add decking of 2-x-4s to cross joists, with a 3/16-inch space between boards. Decking has been here aligned with living-room floor rather than with joists.

393

A-Frame for Shade

This easy-to-build A-frame shelter combines the cozy feeling of a tent with the light, airy quality of a gazebo. The shape is handsome in the garden, and there's a pleasant pattern of light and shade (which varies with the size and spacing of the wood strips used). This is a quiet place for reading, enjoying a cup of tea or lounging. It could also be an elegant display case for a collection of shade plants—ferns and fuchsias, for example—and an ideal backdrop for a garden-party buffet table.

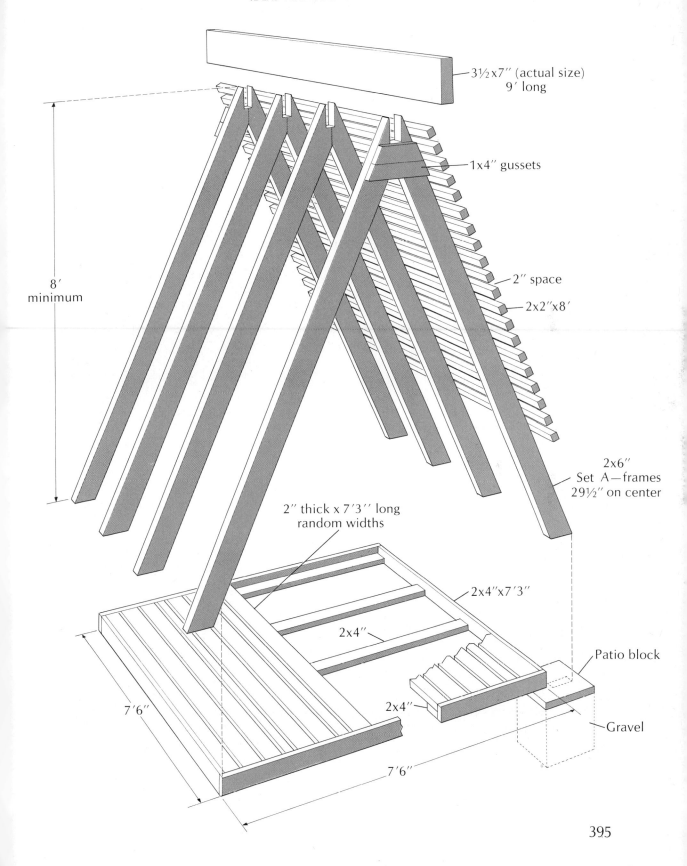

3½ x 7'' (actual size)
9' long

1x4'' gussets

2'' space

2x2''x8'

8'
minimum

2x6''
Set A—frames
29½'' on center

2'' thick x 7'3'' long
random widths

2x4''x7'3''

2x4''

Patio block

2x4''

Gravel

7'6''

7'6''

The Inner Workings of an Outdoor Room

Although the fence, overhead trellis and exposed aggregate paving are attractively combined here to make an intimate enclosed terrace, each of the parts is adaptable to different situations and could be handled as a separate project.

The material used for the fence and overhead is redwood, but cedar, pine, fir or other locally available dimension lumber could serve just as well. A wood stain should be applied. It is easiest to put this on before the pieces are fastened in place. Use galvanized nails, screws and bolts to prevent rust stains. For details on making the pebbled surface used on the paving here, see Chapter 19 on "Working with Concrete."

2x12 support

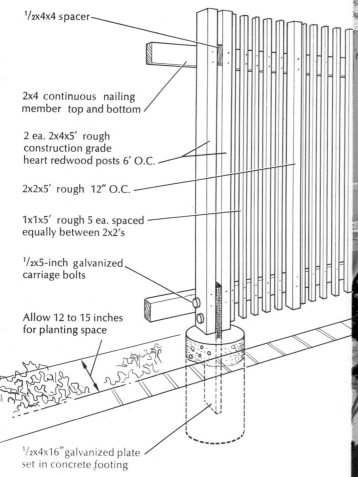

½x4x4 spacer

2x4 continuous nailing member top and bottom

2 ea. 2x4x5' rough construction grade heart redwood posts 6' O.C.

2x2x5' rough 12" O.C.

1x1x5' rough 5 ea. spaced equally between 2x2's

½x5-inch galvanized carriage bolts

Allow 12 to 15 inches for planting space

½x4x16" galvanized plate set in concrete footing

396

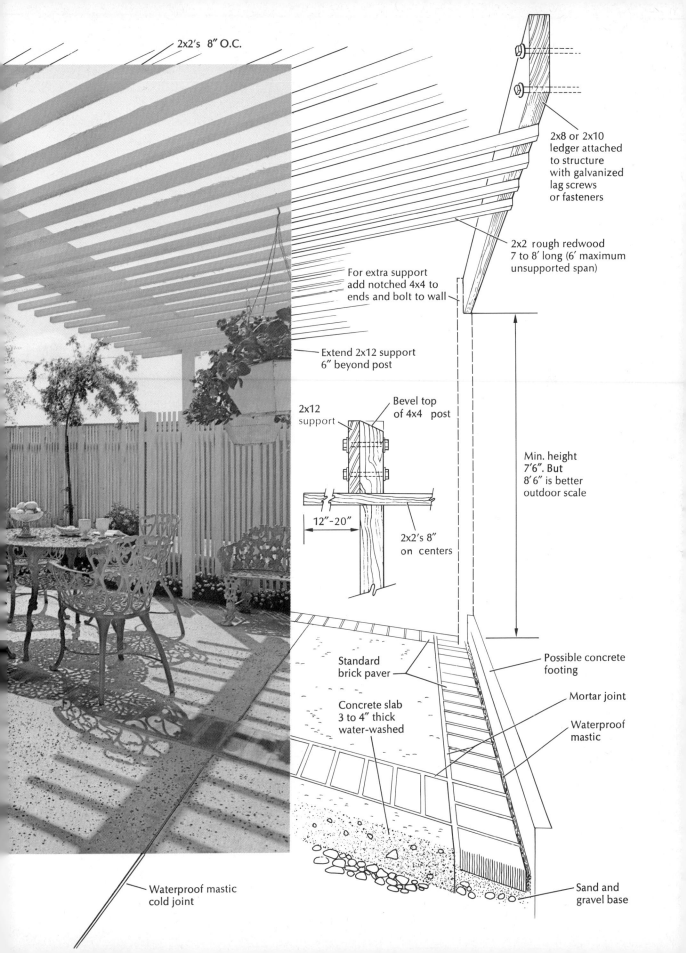

2x2's 8" O.C.

2x8 or 2x10 ledger attached to structure with galvanized lag screws or fasteners

2x2 rough redwood 7 to 8' long (6' maximum unsupported span)

For extra support add notched 4x4 to ends and bolt to wall

Extend 2x12 support 6" beyond post

Bevel top of 4x4 post

2x12 support

12"-20"

2x2's 8" on centers

Min. height 7'6". But 8'6" is better outdoor scale

Standard brick paver

Concrete slab 3 to 4" thick water-washed

Possible concrete footing

Mortar joint

Waterproof mastic

Waterproof mastic cold joint

Sand and gravel base

All-Weather Table and Bench

The handsome table and bench below are solid, weatherproof and practically indestructible. The redwood slats of the table top are spaced for quick drying and to allow for expansion and contraction. The top of the bench is a slab of cast concrete. Decorative concrete blocks bought at a masonry yard are used as supports for both the table and bench. Each support is made of two half blocks joined with mortar.

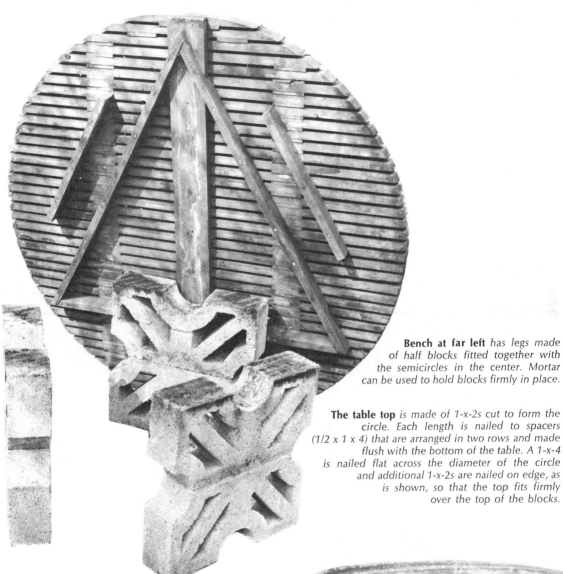

Bench at far left has legs made of half blocks fitted together with the semicircles in the center. Mortar can be used to hold blocks firmly in place.

The table top is made of 1-x-2s cut to form the circle. Each length is nailed to spacers (1/2 x 1 x 4) that are arranged in two rows and made flush with the bottom of the table. A 1-x-4 is nailed flat across the diameter of the circle and additional 1-x-2s are nailed on edge, as is shown, so that the top fits firmly over the top of the blocks.

The Same Block Used For a Birdbath

In another part of the garden two sets of blocks are placed side by side to support a Chinese cooking wok which is used as a birdbath. The blocks are bonded with mortar to a stone at the base and strips of fresh mortar are placed on top of each block. When the wok is pressed briefly into the mortar, the imprint conforms to the shape of the bowl and provides a base on which it can rest.

399

31

Ideas for Children's Play

Equipping an outdoor play area brings extra advantages. It's a joy for the children, parents know they are happy and safe, and the rest of the garden has a better chance to grow and serve for quiet relaxation.

A playground for toddlers who need close supervision is best near the house. Older children appreciate the independence of playing as far from the house as possible (and parents appreciate the comparative peace and quiet). For more privacy the area can be screened off in a season with quick-growing vines on a wire fence. Portable equipment—slide, playhouse, swing—has the advantage of being easily moved as children grow, or it can be passed on to another family. Patchy ground left behind can be restored as a lawn in a season or two.

Here and on the following pages are some child-tested ideas for play areas. See the Planning section, page 180, for the required dimensions of lawn and court games.

A Stable Base that is Easy to Move

Ordinarily, tires are not at home in a garden. But when a tire is filled with concrete it makes an excellent base that is heavy enough to support a tall pole for games such as tetherball. Two tires and poles will hold a net for volleyball. The rubber protects surfaces, grips well, prevents chipping around the edges and makes it easy to move the base by tilting it on edge and rolling. As indicated by the picture, an adjustable rope for tetherball allows setting for short or tall players.

Pour in enough concrete to fill the inside of the casing and then fill the center opening of the tire until the concrete is level with the inner edge at top . To do this dig a tire-sized ditch in the ground by scribing lines around the inner and outer circles of the tire and scooping out the earth between the two. Place the tire in the ditch and pour in concrete to fill, as described above. For information on concrete see chapter 18.

To secure the pole in base put a metal spike through a hole drilled in the pole and set in place before concrete hardens.

A-Frame for Play

This A-frame playhouse has the appealing look of a tent pitched at a campsite in the woods and the advantages of a permanent shelter. Set on posts, it is warm, dry and has good drainage underneath to prevent rot and mildew in rainy weather. Surrounding trees shade the roof and keep the heat from building up inside during the summer.

Unlike the typical "miniature home" playhouse design, which often looks incongruous in a backyard, the handsome shape and woodsy quality of the A-frame sit well in the garden. As shown here, plywood is used for sheathing. The 4 x 6 foot sheets are more economical to use than the standard 4 x 8 foot pieces. All the triangular parts for the front and back can be cut from one 4 x 6 and one 4 x 8 foot sheet.

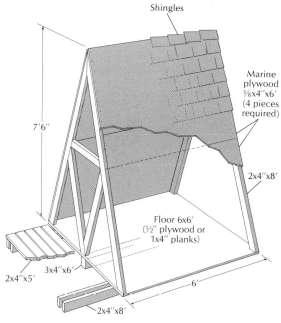

Shingles

Marine plywood ⅜″x4′x6′ (4 pieces required)

7′6″

2x4″x8′

Floor 6x6′ (½″ plywood or 1x4″ planks)

2x4″x5′

3x4″x6′

6′

2x4″x8′

Children's Climbing Frame

This climbing frame is a decorative source of amusement for children. The parts can be arranged for varied uses—to make a hut at one end, for instance.

Construction

Cut 1⅜-inch-wide x 1³⁄₁₆-inch-deep notches in side rails 1½ inches from each end and notch upper pair ¹¹⁄₁₆ inch on each side of the center of the piece.

Cut same-sized notch in top corner of notched blocks (2) and counterbore blocks for screwing. A detail of the block is shown in figure A.

Glue and screw notched blocks to edges of end posts (3), make the undersides flush with the bottom and 4⅜ inches down from top. Use 3-inch screws.

Bolt side rails to end posts with 3-inch carriage bolts and timber connectors. Set upper rails 2 inches from top; lower rails flush at bottom. Inner edge of notch in rail is flush with outer edge of post. Fix middle posts to side rails, between notches in upper rails, with 3-inch lag screws.

Set end crossrails in notches in side rails and screw to posts with 3-inch countersunk screws, ends projecting 2⅞ inches beyond posts. Set upper middle crossrails in notches and bolt to posts with 5-inch carriage bolts. Bolt lower middle crossrails to posts at same height as central end crossrails.

Bolt short post (5) between middle cross-rails at center.

Screw decking slats (6) to battens (7) with 2-inch countersunk screws. Set battens 2 inches from ends of slats. Space slats ⅝ inch apart, with end slats overlapping battens by 1¾ inches.

Screw battens (8) to deck boards (9), 1¾ inches from edges.

Cut two 2-inch-long x ½-x-½ inch rabbets on each short side of wall panels (10 and 11), 4 inches from corners. Finish panels with weatherproof paint.

Screw 1½-inch single-ended turn buttons to panels at center ⅜ inch above top edge of rabbet. See detail at figure B.

Drill ½-inch-diameter holes for dowel pegs (12) ¾ inch deep in posts, ¾ inch from outside faces and edges. Space holes to match rabbets in wall panels, when bottom edge of panel is level with top of rail below it. Fit pegs into holes, but do not glue.

Drill 1¼-inch-diameter holes ¾ inch deep in ladder rails (13) at centers 5½ inches from bottom end and spaced 5½ inches apart. Glue rungs (14) into rails.

Drill clearance holes for No. 10 countersunk screws ½ inch and 2 inches from end of mild steel strips. Bend strips to make ladder hooks (figure C).

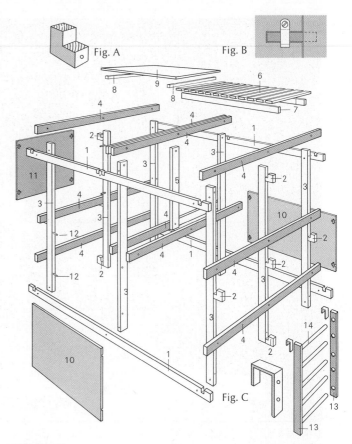

Fig. A Fig. B

Fig. C

PARTS LIST

No.	Name	Quantity	Long	Wide	Thick	Material
1	Side rails	4	96"	2-3/8"	1-3/8"	softwood
2	Notched blocks	10	2-3/8"	2-7/8"	1-3/8"	softwood
3	Posts	8	60"	2-7/8"	1-3/8"	softwood
4	Cross-rails	10	60"	2-3/8"	1-3/8"	softwood
5	Short post	1	28-9/16"	2-7/8"	1-3/8"	softwood
6	Decking slats	13	25"	2-7/8"	7/8"	softwood
7	Battens	2	42-1/2"	1-7/8"	7/8"	softwood
8	Battens	6	25"	7/8"	7/8"	softwood
9	Deck boards	3	46"	25"	3/4"	marine plywood
10	Long wall panels	3	41-1/2"	25"	3/4"	marine plywood
11	Short wall panels	2	25"	25"	3/4"	marine plywood
12	Dowel pegs	20	2-3/4"	1/2" dia.		dowel
13	Ladder rails	4	30"	2-7/8"	1-3/8"	softwood
14	Rungs	10	16"	1-1/4" dia.		dowel

Hardware: eight 3" carriage bolts; six 5" carriage bolts; 22 3" lag screws; ten 3" countersunk screws; 2" countersunk screws; 1-1/2" countersunk screws; eight timber connectors; four 7 x 1 x 1/8" mild steel strips; 20 1-1/2" single-ended turn-buttons

Note: dimensions are finished sizes; when ordering lumber, allow extra for waste

Part of the fun *of this climbing frame is the fact that the panels can be removed, thereby allowing the children to rebuild the frame to suit their fancy. It is good to construct the frame on soft ground in case of tumbles.*

How to Put Up a Basketball Backboard

When there are boys around the house, requests for a basketball backboard are bound to occur. The hoops and boards are available in sporting goods stores but the installation is usually up to father. Some methods of installing a backboard (official height: ten feet from the ground) are relatively easy, others are more difficult. Poles, for instance, require a sturdy underground concrete base and are not easy to set up. Several methods are shown here so that you can choose the one that will best suit your situation.

Ultimate in home backboards *is this one set about four feet away from posts to avoid running into them. Use of two poles (2-1/4″ and 3-1/2″ in diameter) with welded iron spacers makes a rigid vertical support. The two poles give width enough for the two-point suspension necessary for the cantilevered backboard.*

Easiest solution *for a freestanding support is a single pole. This one is 3-1/2 inches in diameter and 16 feet overall. It is in two parts joined with a metal sleeve bolted in place. This system makes it easy to set pole straight and avoids using guy ropes to hold it while cement base (3 feet deep) is setting. Two 94-pound bags of readymix cement are used for the foundation. Metal cross-piece clamped in place below ground (in cement) adds to rigidity. Backboard is attached to pole with standard fittings. Use deeper footings in sandy soil.*

Most popular place for a backboard is a wall of the garage. Flat side of the wall acts as a rebound surface for missed baskets. The backboard should be firmly attached to the structural members of the wall (the 2 x 4 framing) with bolts or lag screws.

On this pitched roof a support of angle iron is used to go around the gutter. On a flat fascia wood could be substituted. Top supports are attached to rafters under roof with lag screws. The roof provides self return for stray balls, but this is not the best thing for the shingles.

Base of backboard is attached directly to the fascia with 90 degree angle iron brackets. The top is supported by lengths of angle iron attached to the roof in the same manner as the one at left. While this backboard is less than the official height of ten feet, most of its users are still less than their full height. As they get taller another kind of installation will be required. An adjustable backboard is a good idea.

405

32

Good Ideas
For Garden Storage

The best places to store garden equipment are those hidden from view. When this is not possible, the thing to do is make storage areas as attractive as you can. The efficient work-storage shelter seen below is a good example, as is the closed storage space (op-posite) built as part of an existing fence. You'll see another idea on the following page, a storage building. It's the kind of place needed for large power equipment—garden tractor, snow thrower, power mower —as well as other storage.

Shaded Working Center

A sheltered workbench for potting indoor and outdoor plants is easy to build. Brightening it up with hanging flowers still leaves space to work. Large tools (rake, hoe, pruning shears) hang on the rear of back panel.

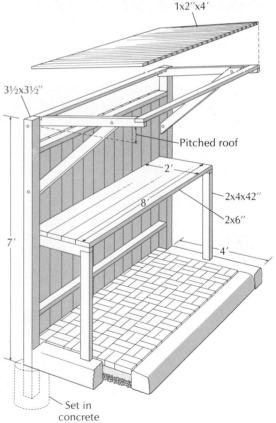

406

The Stow-It-All Fence

Any sturdy fence can be used as the back wall for a closed storage space. (See plan below.) If the three added sides are faced with the same fencing material, the storage unit becomes a subtle sculptural extension of the fence. An outdoor mural could be made by decorating the front with a painting, collage or arrangement of hanging flower pots. If more storage space is needed, the unit can be extended. A hinged folding ramp by the doorway would be good for the easier handling of wheeled equipment.

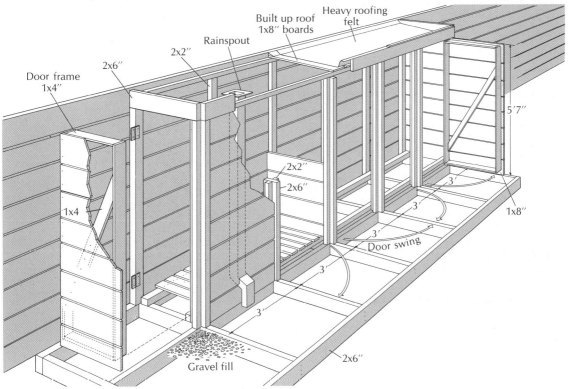

Door frame 1x4″

2x6″

2x2″

Rainspout

Built up roof 1x8″ boards

Heavy roofing felt

5′7″

1x4

2x2″

2x6″

3′

3′

3′

Door swing

3′

3′

1x8″

Gravel fill

2x6″

Outdoor Storage
One Plan; Two Options

Here's a storage shed for families whose basement and garage are overflowing with garden and sports equipment and assorted clutter. It has the advantage over most storages areas of being large enough for the power equipment (power mower, small garden tractor and attachments for snow-blowing and leaf-sweeping) that seems to be a necessity for most gardens.

Storage shed *is divided into open and closed compartments. On the plan one open area is for wood and the space to its right with the shelf is for refuse. These two sections could be built as one unit to be used for wood or refuse. A gardener might want to set up a work area here with running water and space for pots and tools. The three doors opening to the outside can be built in other positions and a pitched roof can be substituted for the flat one shown here. If the whole building is too big, only part could be built, as shown bottom left on the plan. An existing fence or wall could serve as the back. The dimensions given here are those of the shed in the photographs, but they could be altered as necessary. The floor is a concrete slab with a deeper foundation around the perimeter, as shown in the plan sketch bottom right. Note here how the 2-x-4 plates are attached to bolts set in the concrete. In frost-free climates a flat slab is sufficient foundation.*

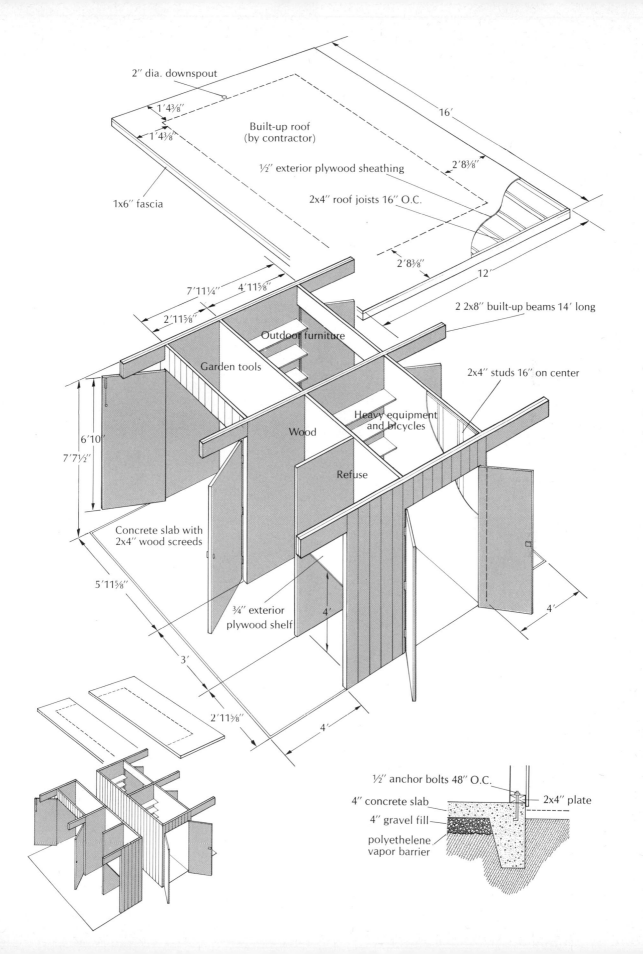

2″ dia. downspout

1′4⅜″

1′4⅜″

Built-up roof
(by contractor)

½″ exterior plywood sheathing

2x4″ roof joists 16″ O.C.

16′

2′8⅜″

1x6″ fascia

2′8⅜″

12′

7′11¼″   4′11⅝″

2′11⅝″

Outdoor furniture

Garden tools

2 2x8″ built-up beams 14′ long

2x4″ studs 16″ on center

Heavy equipment
and bicycles

Wood

Refuse

6′10″

7′7½″

Concrete slab with
2x4″ wood screeds

5′11⅝″

¾″ exterior
plywood shelf

4′

4′

3′

2′11⅜″

4′

½″ anchor bolts 48″ O.C.

4″ concrete slab

4″ gravel fill

polyethelene
vapor barrier

2x4″ plate

Storage in Small Places

Gardeners and handymen are forever trying to squeeze more storage space out of a garage, basement or closets when they're already packed full. Here are some good ways to do just this. To state the obvious first, make more space by throwing out things never used and unworthy of being saved. Look for unused space between studs on the wall, in back corners and below overhead rafters. In fixing up such small areas it's helpful to make special places for each thing stored and then paint a matching shape on the wall. This is a great aid to neatness and lets you know right away when something is missing.

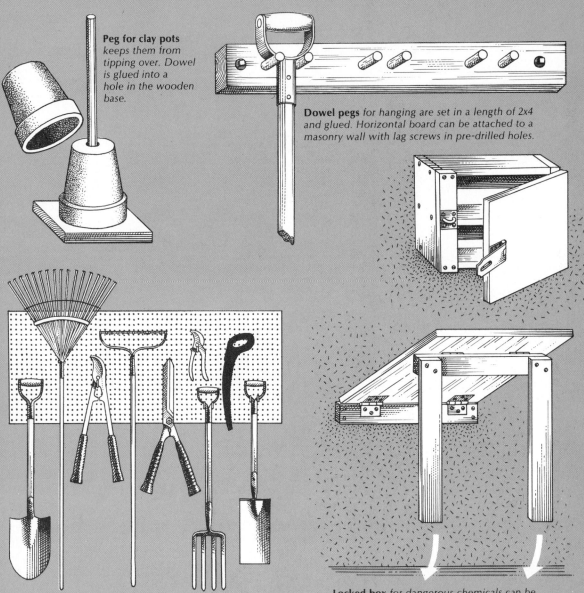

Peg for clay pots *keeps them from tipping over. Dowel is glued into a hole in the wooden base.*

Dowel pegs *for hanging are set in a length of 2x4 and glued. Horizontal board can be attached to a masonry wall with lag screws in pre-drilled holes.*

Panels of peg board *with standard hangers set into holes make a handy portable wall storage unit. Note painted pattern.*

Locked box *for dangerous chemicals can be nailed to a wall between studs. Folding table (below) has hinged legs that fold flat against the wall and open as table is lowered.*

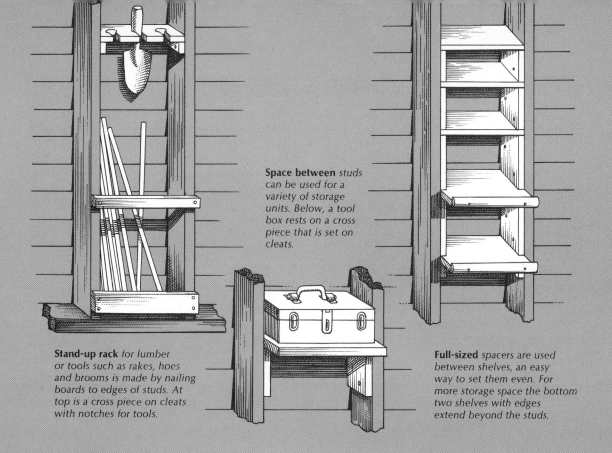

Space between studs can be used for a variety of storage units. Below, a tool box rests on a cross piece that is set on cleats.

Stand-up rack for lumber or tools such as rakes, hoes and brooms is made by nailing boards to edges of studs. At top is a cross piece on cleats with notches for tools.

Full-sized spacers are used between shelves, an easy way to set them even. For more storage space the bottom two shelves with edges extend beyond the studs.

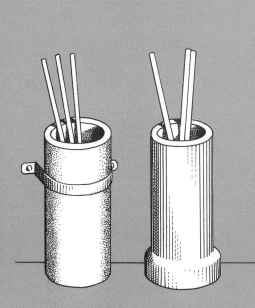

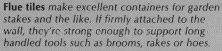

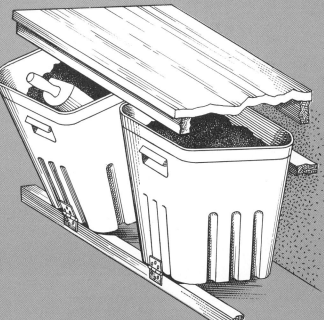

Flue tiles make excellent containers for garden stakes and the like. If firmly attached to the wall, they're strong enough to support long handled tools such as brooms, rakes or hoes.

Tilt-out storage for peat moss, potting soil or fertilizer is made with garbage cans hinged at the bottom. Front cleat under table keeps cans from falling forward.

Large-scale Bulk Storage

For anyone who does considerable gardening in large pots, containers and raised beds where fertilizing and conditioning of the soil are a regular part of the operation, it is a great help to have the soil conditioners and fertilizers readily at hand. This arrangement of standard galvanized garbage cans makes it easy and convenient to reach in with a shovel, take out whatever is needed and place it in a nearby wheelbarrow.

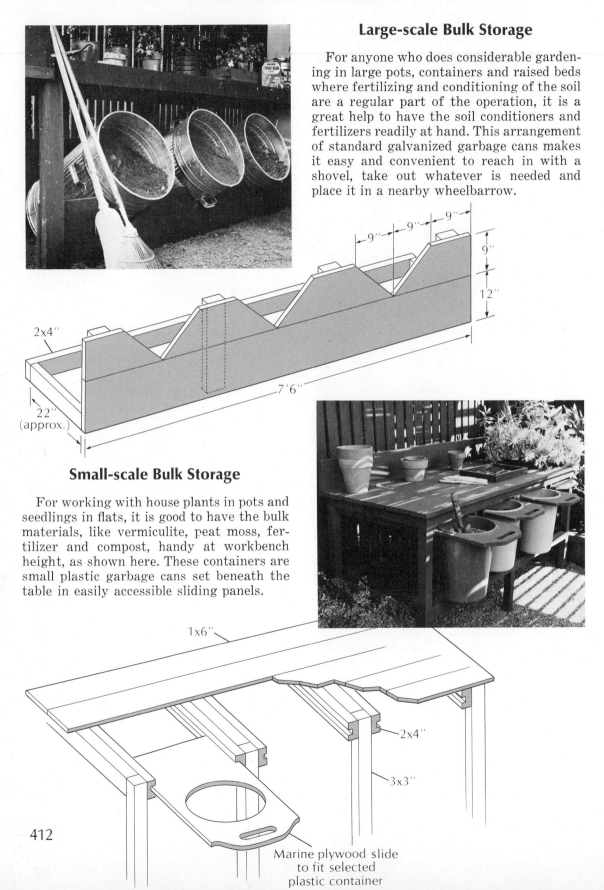

Small-scale Bulk Storage

For working with house plants in pots and seedlings in flats, it is good to have the bulk materials, like vermiculite, peat moss, fertilizer and compost, handy at workbench height, as shown here. These containers are small plastic garbage cans set beneath the table in easily accessible sliding panels.

Marine plywood slide
to fit selected
plastic container

412

Outdoor Stand for Work, Storage and Display

This useful addition to a garden work area is easy to build and can be placed against any fence or outside wall. If properly located, where there is good air circulation and sun for at least part of the day, it's the perfect place to rejuvenate house plants that are on the wane and to store seedlings in flats or pots. When stocked with colorful plants, it's an attractive and decorative accent in its own right.

An optional extra is the storage compartment for small tools and supplies. It has a fold-down door that can double as a work space for repotting. The insert drawing shows how chains are used to support the surface. Screw the cleats on from the inside and countersink the heads.

Shelves are 1-inch dimension lumber set on 2 x 4 cleats nailed or screwed to the uprights. Dimensions, of course, can be varied to suit individual needs and available space, but the proportions shown are attractive.

Inserts at the right show angles of cuts required to make the base parallel to the ground. Use bricks to keep wood from the soil and treat base of each leg with a wood preservative to prevent decay.

33

Working with Water And Light in the Garden

Water for Pleasure and Function

The pleasure of living near a large body of water is obvious. Less recognized is the joy of even a few gallons of water in the garden. By means of a recirculating pump, an inexpensive piece of equipment that is easy to install, the homeowner can create a waterfall, fountain or small stream. (The fol-lowing pages have information on pumps.) Even the water used for the lawn can bring pleasure. When buying a sprinkler, choose one that throws the water in a lovely pattern of spray. And in rainy climates, the runoff from the roof can be a refreshing sight, as seen on the facing page.

Chimney blocks *of cast concrete can be stacked to any height in a pool of water. Holes, or, as here, notches can be cut with a masonry saw to make water spouts. The result, with the use of a submersible recirculating pump is a homemade fountain. For stability, the concrete blocks are mortared together.*

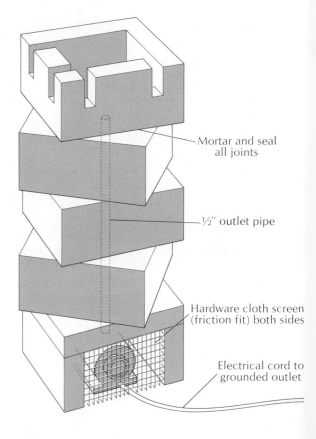

Mortar and seal all joints

½" outlet pipe

Hardware cloth screen (friction fit) both sides

Electrical cord to grounded outlet

Handsome concrete basin *catches water from a down-spout extended beyond the roof line. When it rains, a glistening strip of water falls from the spout, splashing into the basin. Overflow drains into gravel surface below. In cold climates the basin should be reinforced with metal mesh to prevent cracks.*

How to Make a Splash Basin

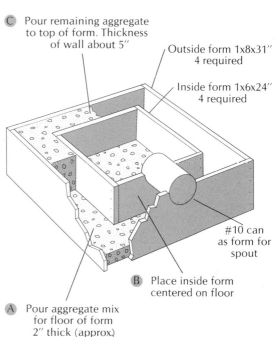

C Pour remaining aggregate to top of form. Thickness of wall about 5″

Outside form 1x8x31″ 4 required

Inside form 1x6x24″ 4 required

#10 can as form for spout

B Place inside form centered on floor

A Pour aggregate mix for floor of form 2″ thick (approx.)

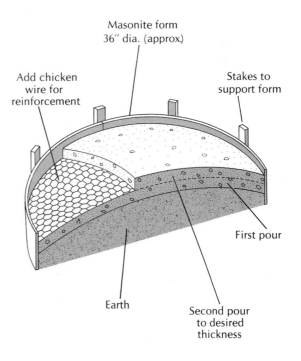

A shallow saucer *filled with water makes a reflecting pool. It could also be planted with shallow-rooted succulents, provided a drain hole is made in the bottom. There is no need to worry about professional precision when molding the saucer. Rough surfaces only add to the charm of the finished product.*

Making a Saucer of Cast Concrete

Masonite form 36″ dia. (approx.)

Add chicken wire for reinforcement

Stakes to support form

First pour

Earth

Second pour to desired thickness

415

Exposed aggregate top and edges

Plastic pipe

Submersible pump

Hardware cloth screen (friction fit) both sides

Electrical cord to grounded outlet

Block up to proper height

The Magic of the Submersible Pump

A fountain or waterfall can be a part of any garden with the help of an electrically driven submersible pump that simply recirculates some of the water in which it sits. For a fountain, water from the pump is forced up through a pipe and into the air. The spray shown here is one of many kinds available at garden centers where pumps and accessories are sold. For a waterfall, a plastic hose (hidden by plants or buried underground) carries water from the pump in the pool at the base of the falls to the top, and the force of gravity does the rest.

A submersible pump runs on regular 110 voltage and comes equipped with a three-pronged plug which should always be con-nected to a grounded outlet to prevent shock. Once installed (an electrician should put in the outdoor outlet), submersible pumps require little attention. They're waterproof, self-lubricating and have a screen to keep out dirt; they can work indefinitely.

How high the water must flow for a particular fountain or waterfall determines the pump size that is needed. Most fountain sprays, including the one above, can be operated with a pump that provides 145 gallons an hour. This size pump shoots water up from one to seven feet high depending upon the water pressure and the setting of the control valve. A 15-foot waterfall with approximately the same rate of flow as the one seen on the opposite page requires a $\frac{1}{3}$-horsepower pump that will deliver 2400 gallons an hour to the top of the falls.

416

½" plastic hose

Grounded line to outlet

Submersible pump

2" cement

Screen

Earth

Earth

Underground Sprinkler With Plastic Pipe

An underground sprinkler system was once considered a luxury only a few could afford. But now, with the advent of durable plastic pipe, the cost is within reach of most homeowners. The system comes as a complete unit and the installation requires no special tools or skill. The entire assemblage of pipes, nozzles and valves is laid out and put together on the lawn and then buried in V-shaped trenches six to eight inches deep so that nozzle heads are flush with the turf. If this is done properly, it in no way interferes with mowing the grass or other maintenance chores. The "pop-up heads" are below the surface when not in use.

The best time to install such a system in a new lawn is before it is seeded. But the pipe can also be installed in an existing lawn by inserting it into slits cut carefully into the turf.

In climates where freezing is a problem, special valves are available to drain all water from the pipes and protect them from damage. Also make certain that the plastic pipe is rodentproof. On the following page are step-by-step directions for installation.

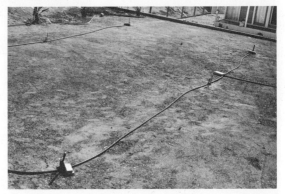

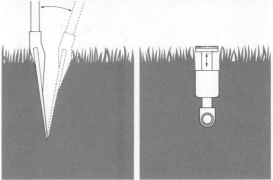

Best method of installing sprinkler system is first to lay it out, then connect it up and test the spray pattern for coverage before covering with soil. The system is completely adjustable so that any area can be watered.

To connect *two ends of pipe, place slip nut onto pipe in reverse. Back edge serves as guide for squaring the cut at the end of the pipe.*

Remove slip nut *and replace on the pipe in the correct way. Next slide O-ring (between thumb and forefinger) onto pipe one inch from the end.*

Insert *brass expansion ring into end of pipe. By expanding the plastic pipe, ring prevents pipe from moving and slipping out of the fitting.*

Drive *brass expansion ring flush with end of pipe, using end of knife, wooden mallet, or a soft-faced hammer.*

For a tee assembly, *prepare all three ends of pipe as illustrated above. Screw the tee into pipe and then tighten with the hands to bring it up good and snug.*

Completely assembled *tee connection is leakproof and is able to be swiveled onto the pipe, thereby forming the equivalent of a union joint.*

Insert riser *into "L" fitting at end of pipe. If riser provided is not long enough, use a length of galvanized pipe, as is shown here.*

Screw sprinkler head *on riser. Insert nozzle unit into head fitting. Nozzle pops up whenever the water is turned on and then falls back when the water is turned off.*

Tighten nozzle *unit with specially supplied wrench. Nozzles are available that project water in circles, squares or rectangles for more effective coverage.*

419

Lighting the Garden

Lighting is a necessary part of the landscape to illuminate pathways, steps and entryways. But because it is usually considered primarily as a safety measure, the opportunity to enhance the garden with an imaginative use of light and fixtures is all too often overlooked. The drawings on page 422, "Using Light for Dramatic Effect," will help you in experimenting with lighting in your own garden. Another deterrent to the decorative use of outdoor lighting is the high cost of installation. This expense cannot be avoided, however; the work must be done by an electrician. A low-voltage system is described on page 424.

The two pictures opposite show that lighting fixtures in the garden can be attractive during the day as well as at night. The examples shown here diffuse the light through openings covered with transparent plastic to create a glow of stripes and circles. By day the rectangular frame of the fixtures themselves gives them a different kind of character and interest.

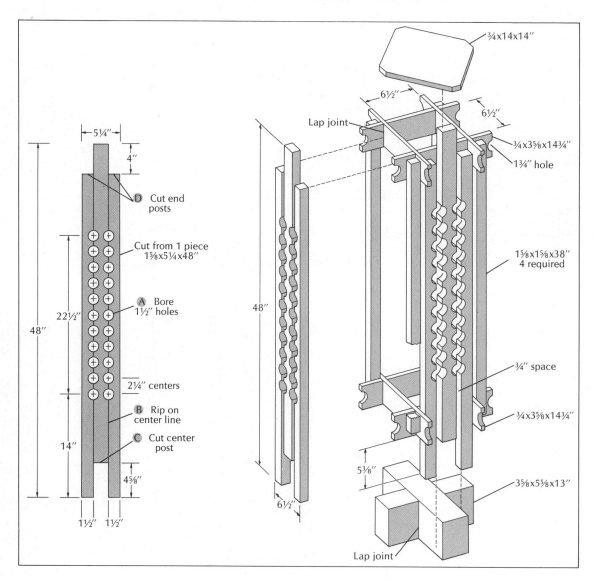

Sculptural Forms for Garden Lights

By night and by day these tall light fixtures are in harmony with the character of the contemporary house. Pedestals of cast concrete set the fixtures above the ground cover of juniper, displaying them as the sculptural objects they are, and the junipers help to conceal the electrical wiring on the ground below. In another setting, by an entryway, for example, the dimensions might be inappropriate. The fixtures can vary in size and be made of any kind of wood suitable for outdoor use. The openings could be triangular or square as well as round. This principle of making a structural framework with openings for light can be applied in many interesting ways.

Using Light for Dramatic Effect

Outdoor lighting is used mainly for safety —to illuminate front steps or a driveway, for instance. But the many opportunities to use light in the garden for decorative and dramatic effect are all too often not considered.

These pictures show the six basic ways to use light in the garden and illustrate how satisfying the results can be.

The basics, of course, can be combined in many ways.

The first two drawings are examples of lighting a tree.

When light shines up from the ground (1) a design of leaves and branches glows against the dark.

Light shining down from a branch (2) also creates an interesting pool of brightness at the base.

Plants are gracefully silhouetted (3) when a fence or walk is washed with light from below.

In turn, the shapes of light and texture of material are featured on a fence (4) by means of down-lighting.

And when fixtures below eye level (5) are evenly spaced beside a walk (or on grass or pavement) they create "stepping stones" of light along the way.

Finally, the source itself becomes a decorative accent when the light fixture is an attractive shape of translucent material well placed in the garden.

1. A tree *is "sculpted" by a light on the ground.*

3. A fence or wall *lit from below becomes a back-*

5. Low-level lighting *along a path illuminate.*

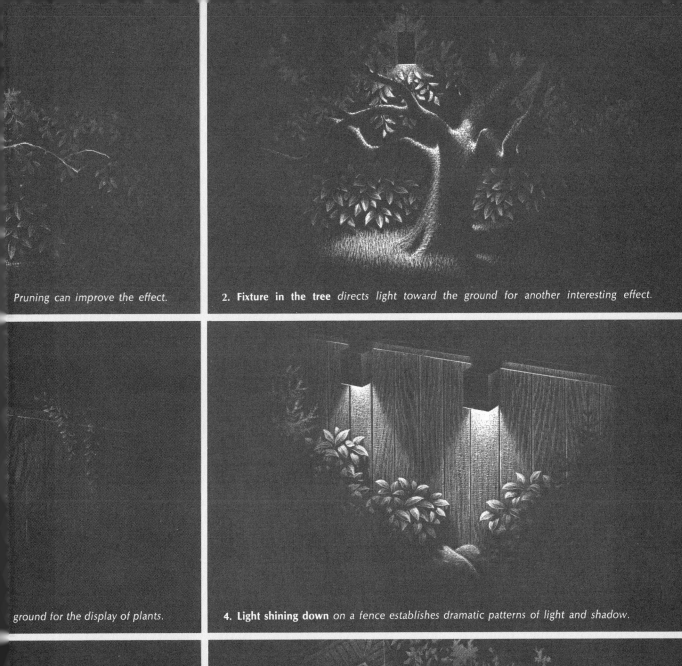

Pruning can improve the effect.

2. Fixture in the tree *directs light toward the ground for another interesting effect.*

ground for the display of plants.

4. Light shining down *on a fence establishes dramatic patterns of light and shadow.*

borders and is easy on the eyes.

6. An attractive light *source—lantern, candle or glowing shape—is itself a dramatic accent.*

How a Low-Voltage System Is Installed

The heart of a low-voltage system is a transformer, which reduces dangerous 120-volt house current to a safe 12 volts. Some transformers are plugged into existing outdoor outlets. Others are attached directly to house wiring and require an electrical

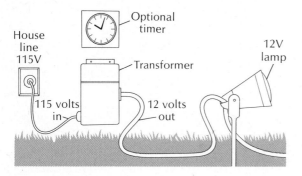

inspection. The transformer is installed as close as possible to the 120-volt source. If the lights are to be some distance from the house, it is best to have a 120-volt outlet installed near the fixtures.

Extension cords must never be used. Nor should more wiring be run out (normally about 100 feet) or more fixtures attached (usually a limit of six) than recommended for the transformer that is used.

Too much wire running from a transformer results in dimmer lights at the end of the line (more line means more resistance to current). Too many fixtures cause dimming and can also overload the transformer, which might then burn out. Many transformers have an on-off switch safely mounted on the housing. A unit without a switch is installed on the 120-volt side so that electricity *to* the unit is safely cut off. Timers for turning the lights on and off are available options.

Two Ways to Light Garden Paths

Low-voltage lighting fixtures are generally smaller than the 120-volt kinds and much easier to camouflage behind a planting of junipers or azaleas. This, in turn, makes it easier to fulfill the basic rule of outdoor lighting: Design to see the effect of light but

never the source. The range of fixture stylings allows you to throw a small patch of light here and there for direction along a garden path, as at left below, or spread large pools of light, as at right, when safe footing is important.

Low-voltage wiring need not be buried. It may be more convenient to snake the wire along the ground behind plants.

Two Ways to Light Garden Steps

Low-voltage garden fixtures, as at right (top), are usually equipped with "quick connect" pronged clamps that are easily attached by hand to the wire. Some fixtures still demand individual wiring connections, but even that job is made simpler with the special twist-on wiring nuts. When wiring for such free-standing fixtures is laid out (or buried), it is wise to allow about 12 inches of slack wire around each one, in case you want it moved later. The plant under which the fixture is put, for example, may need more room for growth. Plastic-insulated wire leading to built-in louvered fixtures, right, can be cast directly into the concrete or laid through a mortar joint in the masonry.

Specialty suppliers have wire and fittings for interesting fixtures. Be sure that only stranded cable with heavy plastic insulation is used. Wire should be no smaller than #12 and no larger than #8. Bulbs are rated from 7 to 75 watts.

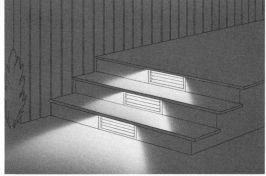

Patterns of Light For Use and Beauty

Both beauty and function are served with low-voltage lights hanging freely from the branches of trees, as at right, above. When an evening breeze ripples the leaves, soft wavering patches of light move over the ground. These lights are attractive in themselves and can also illuminate a path, steps or garden furniture, as shown. To minimize the appearance of the wire, select wire colored to match the bark, and run it up the least-seen side of the trunk. Fasten wire to the trunk with a minimum of insulated staples, and allow the wire to hang loosely through the staples to accommodate the movement of the tree. These same lights won't perform as well if hung in an evergreen. Its shape and density make soft lighting ineffective and functional light nearly useless. To effectively floodlight a large tree from below, it is better to use the standard 120-volt system with its brighter outdoor bulbs. It is, however, more expensive.

425

34

Creating
Decorative Accents

Ideas for All Around the Garden

The great advantage of decorative accents is their dramatic return on an investment of relatively little time. They can be used for color, line and form in a landscape still in the planting stage or can add to a mature garden the same finished look that wall decorations and window coverings contribute indoors. Outdoor accents go anywhere: near an entryway, in a narrow side yard or by a terrace. The accents on the four following pages are among the easiest to create but, nonetheless, effective.

For Movement and Color

This handsome mobile is quick and easy to make with flower pots and rope. Simply thread rope through the hole in the pot, tie it around a short stick on the inside, and hang from a beam or the limb of a tree. Groups of five or seven make the most attractive arrangements. The display emphasizes the rich, warm color of terra cotta and the interesting shape of the pots, which are often obscured by planting. Here they relate well to the entry and the brick wall.

For Dramatic Display

A dead tree with sound wood need not be a total loss. As alternatives to cutting it right to the ground, it can be carved into a setting for sculpture or a display of flowers in pots, or it can be made into a garden seat. Carving a tree trunk is not easy, but it can be done with a handsaw (or power saw), patience and determination. The carved tree shown here was sealed and treated to hold its color and forestall decay.

Decorative Castings
with Concrete and Sand

Outdoor living areas can be made more attractive with art and ornamentation. Sculpture, of course, is perfect for gardens, but expensive. These attractive three-dimensional hangings made in sand with ready-mix concrete will provide the same charm and decorative accent for a garden fence or patio wall as do paintings and pictures indoors. They are weatherproof, surprisingly easy to make and visually interesting, the sand mold giving a rough, primitive texture to the concrete. There is no end to the design possibilities, and the materials used are inexpensive enough to allow for trial and error. You may first want to try your hand with a simple "free-form" shape. The technique is the same: carve design in wet sand, fill design with concrete and allow to harden.

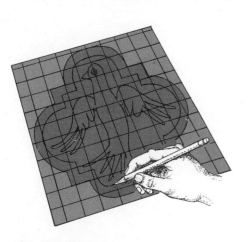

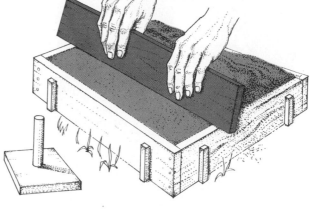

1 **The design** *should be at least 12 to 14 inches high for ease of sculpting and in proportion for outdoor use. To enlarge a design, superimpose grid of squares on the original. Construct, on heavy paper, an identical grid with larger squares. Draw design, square by square, on larger grid.*

2 **Firmly pack** *wet sand at least four inches deep in solidly anchored box or frame. Use fine-grained "builder's" sand. Smooth top surface with edge of straight board. Lay design on sand in the opposite direction in which you want the final casting to face.*

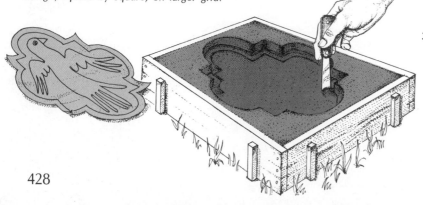

3 **Trace edge** *of outline in sand. Remove sand from within the outline to depth of about an inch; then level surface. This will be the background. Then make channel around edge (as shown) to form outer molding. Be aware that everything nearest you in the sand mold will finally be farthest from you.*

428

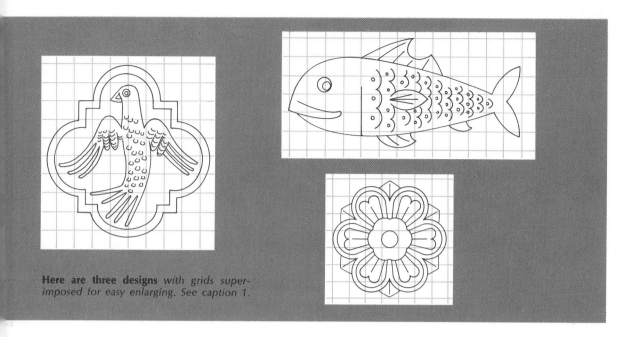

Here are three designs *with grids super-imposed for easy enlarging. See caption 1.*

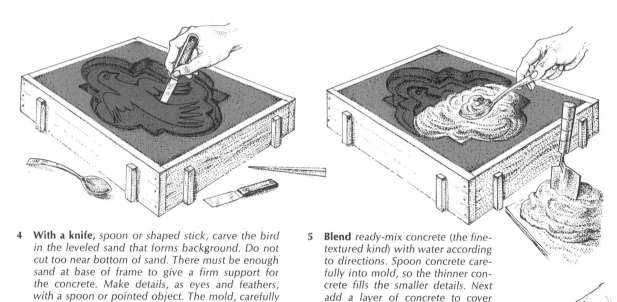

4 **With a knife,** *spoon or shaped stick, carve the bird in the leveled sand that forms background. Do not cut too near bottom of sand. There must be enough sand at base of frame to give a firm support for the concrete. Make details, as eyes and feathers, with a spoon or pointed object. The mold, carefully cleaned out, is ready for the mix of fine concrete.*

5 **Blend** *ready-mix concrete (the fine-textured kind) with water according to directions. Spoon concrete carefully into mold, so the thinner concrete fills the smaller details. Next add a layer of concrete to cover entire face of design. Level gently.*

6 **Add hardware cloth.** *Set hook for hanging at top end of casting. Cover with remaining concrete. Level concrete with top of sand; clean edges. Let set for 48 hours. Then lift out.*

7 **Wrap casting** *in damp burlap to cure for several more days. Unwrap and gently wash away sand. Repair mistakes. Finish off with water-seal.*

Good Uses for Railroad Ties

Old railroad ties are an ideal building material in the garden. They have modular dimensions (usually 7 x 9 x 86 inches), which makes them easy to work with and helps relate the various parts of the garden where they are used. The pictures here of ties in various combinations of steps, retaining walls, borders and raised planting beds illustrate this unifying effect. Railroad ties are less expensive than new timber, they are sturdy (each weighs about 175 pounds) and need no preservative (they are already treated with creosote). They also have a rustic look that blends well with informal garden settings. A decade or two of wear and tear on the track creates surfaces worn smooth in places, rock-scarred in others and sun-bleached to warm shades of brown. The ties are usually available in most parts of the country through landscape architects, contractors and garden centers and sometimes are free for the carting away at railroad yards.

Beware: Haphazard workmanship can ruin the natural look of railroad ties. (They shouldn't be used at all where elegance is required.) Corners must be neat, lines straight, levels even. Illustrations showing ways to join ties are on the following pages.

Excellent camouflage for sloping ground is a stepped-down retaining wall. Slope is further hidden by the junipers on top of the wall and the flowers at the base. The ties overlap at the corners log-cabin style.

To make space for a pool this slope was cut back and retained. Terracing strengthens the wall and lowers its apparent height. The shrubs and vines relieve the strong horizontal character of the wall.

Half ties on the vertical are used for the retaining walls, in contrast to the horizontal ties of the steps. Extending the right wall beyond the steps leaves room for a useful planting bed on the upper level.

These trim corners are made with mitered joints. There is a square nailing block holding the ties together on the inside of each corner. To do this neatly requires good tools and excellent workmanship.

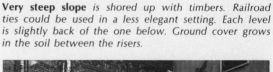

Very steep slope is shored up with timbers. Railroad ties could be used in a less elegant setting. Each level is slightly back of the one below. Ground cover grows in the soil between the risers.

Steps from the curb to the front entry walk are made of bricks laid in sand. Railroad ties are used here as risers, but they have the additional function of holding the brick edges of the steps firmly in place.

Railroad-tie steps are partially extended at the side to form terraced beds filled with choice plants, vines and trees. This unified setting is part of a city garden often looked down upon from bedroom windows and was designed with the overhead view in mind. The flagstone paving inset halfway up relates to the walkway (barely seen) at the top of the steps. Above is a detail of the steps showing how, for added interest, the level of the beds is alternated between the upper and lower steps of each pair instead of simply matching each step.

Decades of use give railroad ties a weathered look. The underside of the ties has a nubby texture from resting so long on the rocky roadbed. Here, an underside is used for each riser, its rough surface emphasized by the textural quality of the ferns planted alongside the steps. On this gentle slope, steps with risers one tie high and treads four ties wide look good and are easy to walk on. The edges of the steps are uneven to make planting pockets alongside. Where a more tailored or formal design is in order, as in the setting shown above and on the facing page, use ties that are less weathered than those shown here.

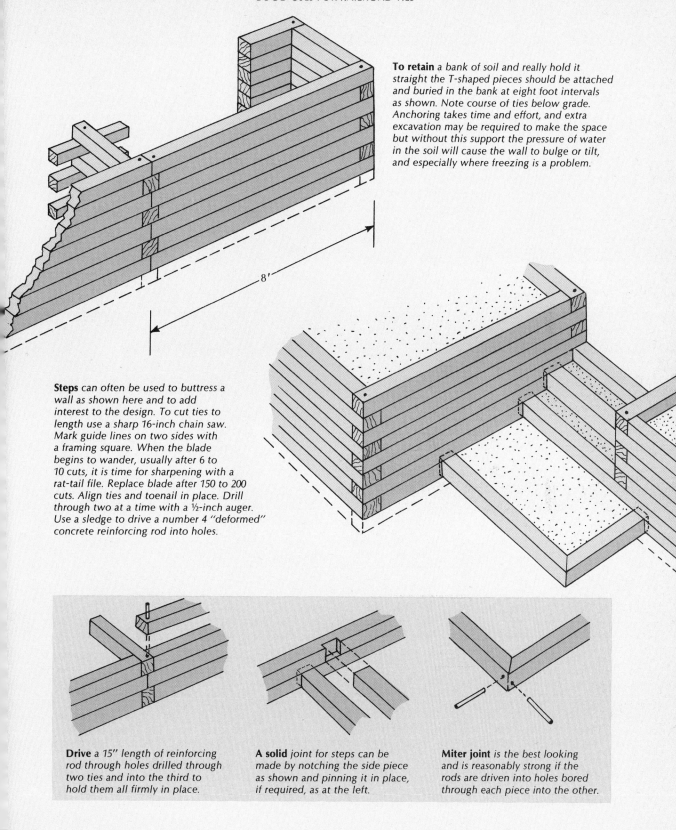

To retain a bank of soil and really hold it straight the T-shaped pieces should be attached and buried in the bank at eight foot intervals as shown. Note course of ties below grade. Anchoring takes time and effort, and extra excavation may be required to make the space but without this support the pressure of water in the soil will cause the wall to bulge or tilt, and especially where freezing is a problem.

8'

Steps can often be used to buttress a wall as shown here and to add interest to the design. To cut ties to length use a sharp 16-inch chain saw. Mark guide lines on two sides with a framing square. When the blade begins to wander, usually after 6 to 10 cuts, it is time for sharpening with a rat-tail file. Replace blade after 150 to 200 cuts. Align ties and toenail in place. Drill through two at a time with a ½-inch auger. Use a sledge to drive a number 4 "deformed" concrete reinforcing rod into holes.

Drive a 15" length of reinforcing rod through holes drilled through two ties and into the third to hold them all firmly in place.

A solid joint for steps can be made by notching the side piece as shown and pinning it in place, if required, as at the left.

Miter joint is the best looking and is reasonably strong if the rods are driven into holes bored through each piece into the other.

Patterns on the Vertical

The classic device for growing plants on a vertical surface is a framework of wire or wood to which the plants are attached and trained in various patterns. Both the framework and plants are called "espalier." Certain plants, such as dwarf fruits and other trees, will after a time retain the shape of the original patterns even though the framework is removed. Other plants, with a less rigid structure, as clematis or ivy, must always be tied or tacked to the frame if they are to maintain the intended design.

Training Vines on Wire

To achieve the decorative effect of English ivy, as on the wall above, first fix the pattern of wire firmly to the support. Ivy, or any climbing vine, is planted at the base and, as it grows, is tied to the wire frame, then trimmed to maintain the design. For the luxuriant growth of vine necessary to such a project, a heavy schedule of feeding and watering is required to produce this much top growth from such a limited root area. The wall is further adorned with staghorn ferns in pots suspended from hooks.

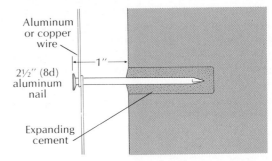

Aluminum or copper wire

2½″ (8d) aluminum nail

1″

Expanding cement

Use a star drill to make hole in masonry. Expanding cement (as shown) holds any fastener when it dries. Or tap a lead plug into masonry. A lag screw turned into the plug expands the lead to make a tight fit.

This unusual espalier *is almost like an abstract painting done in rich green on an expanse of blank wall. The design is based on and retains much of the natural form of the weeping spruce and is carefully controlled by stapling the branches to the wall and by judicious pruning. Gravel area in front does not detract from design.*

Informal Espalier

An informal espalier is not symmetrical. If you draw an imaginary vertical line through the center of the design, the left side will not be an exact mirror image of the right side, as it must be in a strictly formal arrangement. Practically speaking, this means that an informal espalier can take almost any shape. It is adaptable to a variety of outdoor areas, especially in casual, relaxing places in the garden where a rigorously symmetrical plant design would look too severe and out of place. The classic, formal espalier also demands careful, precise pruning. This job is made considerably easier by using the informal style. However, some trimming is always required in order to maintain the flat, two-dimensional effect that is characteristic of espaliers.

Mountain ash and its frame are set out from the wall to increase the air circulation around the tree and to prevent mildew. Once the branches have matured and become set in the design, the frame is removed.

Both color and form *are involved in working with pyracantha, a fast-growing shrub that if left alone will blanket an entire wall with its thorny foliage and colorful fruit. Judicious pruning, above, has resulted in this handsome espalier which, after an initial training period, is sturdy enough to stand without support against the white wall.*

An unusual *but effective handling of a rosebush, the canes of which are stapled to a high wooden fence. The bush is pruned more for shape and pattern on the wall than for flowers, but the latter are a nice bonus. Part of the pleasure of this technique is constantly refining the design, and mistakes can be amended when the bush puts forth new growth in the spring.*

Formal Espalier

The classic espalier is formal—that is, symmetrical—in design. Such designs require that the plants be trained with precision on a framework of wood, wire or metal pipe. When the branches are young and flexible, they are tied firmly to this frame and allowed to mature in the desired shape. As new growth appears, it in turn is fastened to the frame. Once the design is complete and the branches have become rigid, the framework can be removed. Dwarf apple and pear trees are commonly used.

Pear trees *are trained on this lattice framework of 1-x-2s attached at bottom to tree fork and at top to iron pipe, then lashed together for added firmness.*

Mature and well established, *this pear tree is rigid and strong enough to stand alone and will continue to grow in this traditional design.*

437

The Ancient Art of Topiary

Topiary, the art of training and cutting shrubs into ornamental figures, first flourished in the royal gardens of France and Italy. It became popular on the great estates in England, too, where there are still many fine examples.

The art can be effectively used in contemporary gardens not in the traditional way, as elements of a formal design, but to create important individual decorative accents. One or two shrubs whether cut in geometric, natural or animal shapes can be a pleasure to see, provided they are well cared for. Untrimmed topiary is not worthwhile.

Cutting, trimming and the gradual development of a shrub into a finished topiary requires careful work and patience. It can take 10 years or so to establish the basic form. For many gardeners this involvement is the main satisfaction of the art. Hedge shears and loppers are needed for the original heavy work of cutting the shape. After that, minimal but regular trimming with pruning shears will maintain crisp outlines.

The privet *is a shrub often used in topiary. Here it is cut and trimmed in a swirling pattern.*

Boxwood (Buxus sempervirens) *has two smaller elements on top to balance the larger base.*

Shrubs in Geometric Forms

Large examples—around six feet high—are more dramatic as geometric shapes than small ones. But whatever the size, the finished shape should be in scale with the general surroundings.

The aim of the initial cutting with hedge shears is to make the geometric shape symmetrical and of proper proportion. It's mainly the eye that guides the cutting, though stakes and string can be used as guides. Walking around and around the shrub while cutting and trimming helps establish the symmetry. Creation of animal shapes requires the wiring of branches to hold them in place. Don't worry if all that's left after cutting are stems and twigs. Shrubs used for topiary, such as privet, boxwood and yew, can take the cutting and grow new foliage.

Portable duck *fashioned of the tender plant* Eugenia myrtifolia *is displayed outdoors in mild weather.*

Privet *is trained and cut into shape of a dog. A similar shape could be obtained with an evergreen yew.*

Animal Forms

Topiary animals are abstracted forms but nonetheless recognizable. Their simplicity, in fact, is what makes them so appealing. Like any sculpture, a topiary animal adds interest to a terrace, garden or lawn.

The form of an animal topiary can be dictated by the shape of the plant itself, like the duck above left. The dog in the right-hand picture was made by another method: a few branches were bent, restrained with wire and tied down with rope. Though the result is not a true topiary, there is still another method of creating an animal form from plant material that only takes a year or so to develop fully. Moss-filled chicken wire is shaped into an animal form and set in a dirt-filled box. Small leafed ivy is then planted and trained to cover the form.

Informal Shapes

The shape of a shrub often indicates a way of cutting that will accentuate its natural form. Sometimes a bit of trimming that is hardly noticeable will make the shape of a plant more interesting. Needled evergreens, such as hemlocks, junipers and yews, lend themselves to this subtle kind of clipping.

The Japanese yew shown here has not been allowed to grow anywhere near its full height. All branches, except the main upright stem and two horizontal branches, were removed. The foliage at the end of the remaining branches was shaped and is trimmed regularly. Even a slight bulge would destroy the balance and be disturbing to the eye. Slow-growing plants, like the yew, require less maintenance but of course they also take longer to become established.

439

Creating a Bonsai

A true bonsai is a plant in miniature, carefully trained and potted according to rules of design developed by the Japanese over the centuries. To keep a bonsai small, it is grown in little soil; roots and branches are drastically pruned and foliage frequently trimmed. Obviously, the art of bonsai cannot be explained in a page, but some of the

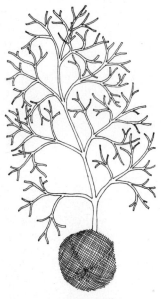

1. Choose tree, *deciduous or evergreen, with good shape.*

2. Expose *roots to see if widely spread and of good size.*

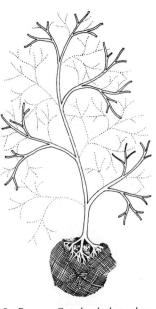

3. Prune. *Cut back branches to the desired shape.*

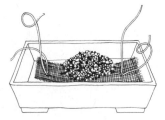

1. True bonsai *pot is shallow. Put screen over holes.*

2. Fasten *roots with wires through drain holes.*

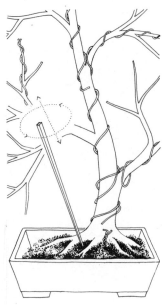

3. Press *sifted soil down to eliminate the air spaces.*

aesthetic principles can be seen in the two photographs on the right: spareness of line, careful shaping, exposed trunk and surface roots.

The top row of drawings shows how to develop a balled and burlapped plant from a nursery into a container plant like the top picture. Although not a true bonsai, it has the characteristics and because it is grown in a good amount of soil and is not drastically pruned it does not require the constant care of a bonsai. The bottom row of drawings shows how to develop a true bonsai, such as the evergreen shown.

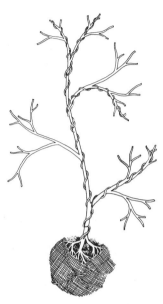

4. Wind copper wire around branches to "set" shape.

5. Prune large roots to encourage fine, fibrous growth.

6. Plant in good-sized, attractive container for a potted plant in the tradition of bonsai.

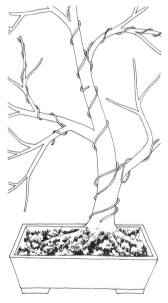

4. Grow moss on topsoil to give plant aged, natural look.

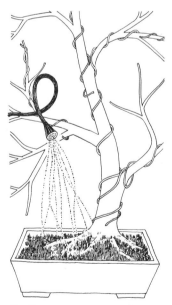

5. To water, spray with syringe until soil is saturated.

6. True bonsai, if kept trim, watered daily and attended with care can last for centuries.

Patterns on the Ground

When planning a garden, a major decision is how to cover the ground. The usual alternatives are grass, other low-growing ground covers, a terrace or a combination of the three. Another interesting possibility is bold patterns on the ground. These might be planting beds, rocks, stones or gravel in contrasting textures and sizes, or a combi-nation of plant material as shown in the knot garden on the opposite page. Ground patterns are particularly effective in small areas with little opportunity for vertical decoration or in an area that is looked down upon from a window or is on sloping ground. Such patterns must, of course, be in scale with the surroundings.

Masonry and Imagination

When concrete tiles are stacked on a construction site or in a masonry yard they look cold and uninteresting. Lay these same tiles on the ground in patterns and the effect is quite different. A multitude of designs is possible by combining tiles laid flat and on edge. Shown here are tiles arranged for a walkway, terrace and a narrow decorative bed filled with railroad spikes, gravel and moss. (Low, slow-growing succulents such as sedums can also be used.)

The detail below the picture shows how concrete tiles are put into a bed of gravel and sand. Before setting the tiles, it is a good idea to place them on top of the bed in the desired pattern to make sure the surface is flat and all lines are even. Concrete tiles are cast in uniform sizes; if a pattern calls for sections of tile, use a masonry-cutting diamond-tooth saw or have the masonry yard cut them to size.

Knot Garden in the Classic Style

Almost any linear design that you draw on paper can be re-created on the ground with plants. Small, slow-growing plants that hold their shape like those shown opposite must be used, and, of course, regular trimming and weeding are required. Creating and maintaining a pattern of plants is worth the effort, especially if located where it can be looked down upon so the design and the variations in color and texture can be fully appreciated.

Once a suitable design has been developed —the classic knot garden is always sym-metrical—it is translated into furrows on the ground. Use stakes and string to insure that the straight furrows really are straight. For the curved lines, use a garden hose to establish the exact shape, and dig the furrow between lines etched on both sides of it with a stick. The furrows and the setting of plants and seeds must be done precisely so the design will grow as planned. The plants used here are lemon thyme, chives, rosemary and lavender, as well as primula and *Ajuga reptans*. This is a welcome accent here in an informal landscape.

Panel of Raked Sand

A bed of sand offers a variety of decorative possibilities and is easy to make. Shown here is a large rectangular bed with a potted tree for vertical accent and a border of gray concrete blocks to complement the buff-colored sand. The border is inlaid with four red-clay flue tiles (as shown in the diagram) set in a bed of moss.

Patterns in the sand were drawn with a 30-inch sawtoothed rake cut from Masonite. They can be changed with a pull of the rake. If in scale, a sand bed can be any size or shape, and instead of a tree, the accent can be a rock, cluster of shrubs or sculpture. Maintenance is easy. All that's needed is occasional light weeding and a raking after rain.

Free-Form Pachysandra

The pachysandra-and-gravel pattern shown here covers a large area of the garden, but these materials are equally effective when designed for a small space. During the two or three years it takes pachysandra to carpet the ground, weeding is necessary. Afterward maintenance consists mainly of hand-trimming the edges. This is not too hard when, as here, plants are prevented from spreading and a clean line is established with a steel edging strip. Pachysandra grows best in a temperate climate. In places where it does not thrive, other ground covers such as ivy can be used.

Reward for Rock Hounds

There are two kinds of rock hounds, those interested in the mineral content and those who can't resist a rock with a pleasing shape and texture. The latter ends up with a pile of rocks at home and wonders what to do with them. The rock enthusiast who lives in this west-coast house used part of his collection for a walkway and has carefully arranged others around the base of a tree.

The walkway was laid out in a bed of mud and the surface made level. Then each rock was lifted and set back in place with concrete mortar. The borders, made when the walkway dried, are of concrete poured over chicken wire and topped with a surface of exposed aggregate. For information on exposed aggregate, see chapter 19.

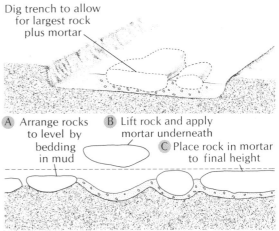

Dig trench to allow for largest rock plus mortar

A Arrange rocks to level by bedding in mud
B Lift rock and apply mortar underneath
C Place rock in mortar to final height

For the first step of bedding the rocks in mud to establish the arrangement and level the surface, the grade will be lower than when finished. Lift a few stones, put down mortar, reset stone to finished grade.

445

Index

447

(hydrangea, *cont.*)
  Chinese 'Blaauw' *(J. chinensis*
        'Blaauw')*, 241
  climbing *(H. petiolaris)*, 277
  oakleaf *(H. quercifolia)*, 55

I

Ilex convexa, 41, 148
  See also holly
impatiens, 158, 264, 271-72
Indian currant, coral-berry
    (Symphoricarpos
    orbiculatus), 55
indigobush, common *(Amorpha*
    fruticosa), 246
insects
  protection against, 86-87, 259
iris, 52, 264-66, 270
  bearded, 263
  cristata, 270
ivy, 20, 25, 47, 51, 148, 250
  English *(Hedera helix)*, 55, 240,
    260-61
  as ground cover, 53, 55, 82-84, 155
  planted near fence, 71, 73
  to prevent erosion, 168
  training, 434
  upright *(H. h. carborescens)*, 240

J

Japanese pavilion, 79
jasmine *(Jasminum)*
  common *(J. officinale)*, 55
  Confederate
    (Trachleospermum), 240
  winter *(J. nudiflorum)*, 274, 277
jessamine, Carolina *(Gelsemium*
    sempervirens), 55
joinery
  corner joints, 311
  dowel and dado, 312
  expansion joints, 320
  lap joints, 313, 320
  mailing, 313-14, 342
  metal brackets, 311-12, 343
  screws and bolts, 314, 342
  splicing, 312
jointing tool, 330

joists, in deck construction, 392-93
juniper(s), 49, 168, 345, 391, 421
  espaliered, 73
  as ground cover, 37, 41
  mass plantings of, 142-43
  topiary designs for, 439
  varieties
    common *(Juniperus*
      communis), 239
    compact *(J. pfitzeriana*
      compacta), 232
    golden flecked *(J. communis*
      depressa aurea-spica), 240
    gold-tipped *(J. chinensis*
      pfitzeriana aurea), 241
    pfitzer *(J. chinensis*
      pfitzeriana), 190, 244
    pfitzer, compact *(J. chinensis*
      pfitzeriana compacta), 242
    Sargent *(J. chinensis*
      sargentii), 235
    scaly-leafed Nepal
      (J. squamata meyeri), 244
    upright *(J. virginiana)*, 95
      226, 227, 247
      'Burkii,' 247
      'Canaertii,' 247
      'Glauca,' 247
      'Skyrocket,' 247
    Waukegan *(J. horizontalis*
      douglasii), 239
    Wilton, 239, 261

K

Kalm's Saint-John's-wort
    (Hypericum kalmianum), 239
katsura tree *(Cercidiphyllum*
    japonicum), 219
kerosene lanterns, 99
kerria *(K. japonica*
    pleniflora), 190, 244
kitchen, built-in, 67

L

lacing cord, 338
lamps, parasol, 153
landing strip, brick, 42, 49
landscape architect, 164-65, 204-05

landscape design, 164-71
  costs and contracts, 204-05
  diagramming, 194-95
  Japanese principles of, 126-33
lantana, 104, 283
lantern(s)
  stone, 132
lap joints, 313, 320, 420
larch
  European *(Larix decidua)*, 211
  western, 309
latches, 359
lath house, 14-15, 18, 125
lattice, 62, 69
laurel *(Laurus nobilis)*, 249
  California *(Umbellularia*
    californica), 220
  cherry *(Prunus laurocerasus)*, 246
    'Schipkaensis,' 246
    'Zabeliana,' 246
  mountain *(Kalmia latifolia)*, 190,
    227, 244, 283
  Portugal- *(P. lusitanica)*, 249
  sheep-laurel *(K. angustifolia)*, 239
lavender, 50-51, 442-43
  cotton *(Santolina*
    chamaecyperissus), 57
  dwarf, 286
lawn
  aerifying, 259
  basic needs, 252
  care, 258-59
  fertilizing, 257-59
  grass for, selecting, 253-55
  liming, 259
  mowing, 257, 258
  pests, 259
  planning, 250, 252
  sodding, 258
  stepping-stones in, 356
  steps in making, 256-58
  underground sprinkler system,
    418-19
  watering, 257, 258-59
  "weed and feed," 259
  weeding, 259
  See also grass; mowing
lemon tree, dwarf, 283
lettuce bed, minimum sizes, 193
leucothoe
  fontanesiana, 190
  pruning, 300-01
level, 316, 324, 330, 358
  hand, 196
  mason's, 334
lever, 237
lever latch, 359
liatris, 264, 270

Credits

ASLA indicates members of the American Society of Landscape Architects. FASLA indicates Fellows of the ASLA.

Location of pictures on the page is indicated by the letters *a, b, c, d,* etc. First picture on top row is *a.* Others follow in sequence left to right, top to bottom.

Landscape Architects and Designers

Fred Akers: p. 356*b.*
Armstrong/Sharfman, ASLA: pp. 116, 285*b.*
Douglas Baylis, FASLA: pp. 360*ab*, 361*ab*, 362*ab*, 374, 375.
Beardsley and Brauner, ASLA: pp. 98, 416.
Arthur and Marie Berger: pp. 42*a*, 106*ab*, 107*c*, 123*c.*
Brad Bowman: p. 117*c.*
Theodore Brickman: p. 29.
John Broughton: p. 119*b.*
Everett Brown: p. 89*a.*
Jack Chandler: pp. 431*b*, 134.
William Childester: p. 93*a.*
Robert W. Chittock: p. 421*ab.*
Catherine Cole Church, ASLA: p. 70.
Thomas D. Church: pp. 24, 26, 61*a*, 67*b*, 73*b*, 104*b*, 107*b*, 113*bd*, 118*ab*, 123*a*, 150, 152, 153, 154, 155, 366, 385*b*, 432*abc.*
Agnes S. Clark, FASLA: p. 101.
Darling and Webel, ASLA: p. 90*a.*
Russell Day: pp. 442, 444*a.*
Edouard Dreier: p. 77*d.*
Alice L. Dustan: p. 260*b.*
Constance Fiorentino, ASLA: pp. 82*ab*, 83*ab*, 84*ab*, 85*abcd.*
Herbert Frost: p. 43*c.*
Goldberg and Rodler: pp. 38*b*, 39*b*, 42*b*, 59*b*, 117*ab*, 120*a*, 137*a*, 138*b*, 379, 381*a*, 430*b*, 431*c.*
Lawrence Halprin, FASLA: pp. 67*cd*, 279*e*, 431*d.*
Joan Hamilton: p. 396.
George Hinkicke: p. 285*a.*
James Hostetter: p. 380.
Glen Hunt: p. 81*a.*
Huntington and Roth, ASLA: p. 73*a.*
Alice Ireys, ASLA: pp. 120*b*, 430*a.*
Casey A. Kawamoto, ASLA: pp. 156, 157.
Klonsky Landscape Associates: pp. 108, 115*a*, 119*c*, 139*b*, 140*b*, 141, 146, 431*a.*
Gertrude Kuh, ASLA: p. 59*a.*
Linesch and Reynolds, ASLA: p. 73*c.*
Robert Malkin, ASLA: pp. 16*ab*, 17, 18*ab*, 19, 20*ab* and 21*abc*, 43*a*, 159*ab*, 203*c*, 370, 371*ab.*
Charles Middeleer, ASLA: p. 367*b.*
Al Miller: p. 87*b.*
Theodore Osmundson and Associates, FASLA: pp. 390, 391*ab*, 392*abcd*, 393*abcde.*
Ray Rahn: pp. 144*ab*, 145*ab.*
Paul and Katy Steinmetz: p. 125*b.*
William Teufel: pp. 40*c*, 61*c.*

Lawrence D. Underhill: p. 63*a.*
Stanley Underhill, ASLA: p. 149*a.*
Zion, Breen and Associates, ASLA: p. 444*b.*

Architects

Welton Becket and Associates: p. 114.
Alvin Dreyer: p. 421*ab.*
Stanley Gettle: p. 88.
Kenneth and Robert Gordon: p. 74*d.*
Kruger/Bensen/Ziemer: p. 345*c.*
Burr Richards: pp. 40*c*, 61*c.*
Donald T. Ross: p. 60*c.*
Tucker, Sadler and Bennett: p. 65.
Evans Woollen and Associates: p. 107*a.*

Designers

Benjamin Baldwin: pp. 62*c*, 99*c.*
John Brookes: p. 373.
Joan Neville: p. 38*a.*
Allen Vance Salisbury: pp. 40*c*, 61*c.*
Superior Swimming Pool Company: p. 119*a.*

Photographers and Special Permissions

Molly Adams: pp. 41, 104*a*, 120*b*, 281*a* Duke Gardens, 291*acd*, 347*a*, 352*abc*, 430*a.*
Duane C. Alan from Woodward Radcliffe: pp. 96*b*, 120*c.*
American Plywood Association: p. 408*ab.*
Morley Baer: pp. 61*a*; 67*cd* for *House and Garden* magazine; 117*c*, 118*ab*, 153, 154, 155; 150, 152, 156 and 157 for *House Beautiful* magazine; 279*b*, 347*b*, 431*d.*
Ralph Bailey: pp. 71*b*, 77*c*, 89*b*, 270, 272.
Ernest Braun: pp. 24, 25, 27, 369, 432*abc*, 437*a.*
James Brett: pp. 87*a*, 108, 112*ab*, 115*a*, 119*ac*, 139*b*, 140*b*, 141.
Guy Burgess: pp. 36, 75, 97, 103*a*, 228*c*, 273*ab*, 363, 426, 428.
Lorraine Burgess: pp. 95*c*, 346*b.*
Barney Burstein: pp. 148, 149*abc*, 158*ab*, 283*b*, 427*a.*
California Redwood Association: p. 81*b.*
Carroll C. Calkins: pp. 28*ab*, 30*ab*, 31*ab*, 32*abc*, 33, 34*abc*, 35*abc*, 37*c*, 42*b*, 43*a*, 52*b*, 53, 54*abc*, 56*abce*, 57*bcef*, 66*b*, 82*ab*, 83*ab*, 84*ab*, 85*abcd*, 92*ab*, 94*bc*, 96*ac*, 115*c*, 137*b*, 203*abc*, 261*bed*, 281*d*, 289*a*, 337*abc*, 346*a*; 353*abcde* for *Home Garden* magazine; 367*c*, 379, 381*a*, 386, 406, 412*b*, 438*b*, 439*ac.*